Designed for
DEVOTION

Designed for DEVOTION

A 365-DAY JOURNEY from GENESIS to REVELATION

DIANNE NEAL MATTHEWS

BakerBooks
a division of Baker Publishing Group
Grand Rapids, Michigan

Published by Baker Books
a division of Baker Publishing Group
P.O. Box 6287, Grand Rapids, MI 49516-6287
www.bakerbooks.com

Printed in the United States of America

Library of Congress Cataloging-in-Publication Data
Matthews, Dianne Neal.
    Designed for devotion : a 365-day journey from Genesis to Revelation / Dianne Neal
Matthews.
        p.   cm.
    ISBN 978-0-8010-7273-4 (pbk.)
    1. Devotional calendars. 2. Bible—Meditations. I. Title.
BV4811.M3389 2012
242'.2—dc23   2012015838

Published in association with MacGregor Literary Agency.

12   13   14   15   16   17   18   7   6   5   4   3   2   1

Introduction

When the team at Baker suggested *Designed for Devotion* as the title for this book, it took a day or so to grow on me. But the more I thought about it, the more I appreciated its threefold meaning. First, as human beings, we are designed to be devoted to our Creator. We are wired to worship—if not God, then something or someone else. Secondly, our Creator designed his Word to reveal himself and to help us enter into that intimate relationship with him we naturally long for. And finally, this book in your hands is designed to be your companion as you take a journey that will hopefully increase your devotion to God and his Word.

On this journey, we'll stop at each book of the Bible to review its purpose, author, and historical background. We'll revisit highlights of Old Testament stories and meet some fascinating characters, both heroes and villains. Along the way, we'll keep an eye out for passages that portray Jesus. As we move into the New Testament, we'll get a close-up look at him through the Gospels. Traveling through the rest of the New Testament books, we'll witness the birth of the church and review the major teachings of Paul and the other letter writers. Our journey will wrap up with a look at our ultimate destination as we study John's visions of heaven and end-time events in Revelation.

If reading the Bible makes you feel like a stranger in a strange land, I hope you discover new things you haven't seen before. If the Scriptures are familiar terrain for you, I pray that this trip renews your passion for the Bible and its relevance to your life. But wherever you are in your faith journey, may God's Holy Spirit guide you every step of the way.

> *Glory belongs to God, whose power is at work in us.*
> *By this power he can do infinitely more than we can*
> *ask or imagine. Glory belongs to God in the church*
> *and in Christ Jesus for all time and eternity! Amen.*
>
> Ephesians 3:20–21

The Bible

God's Masterpiece

God's word is living and active.
Hebrews 4:12

How could the writings of at least forty people from different walks of life, writing over a span of twenty centuries, flow together to tell one continuous story? Second Timothy 3:16 gives us the answer: "Every Scripture passage is inspired by God." The Greek word usually translated as *inspired* literally means "God-breathed." Although God allowed each author to write from his unique perspective and in his own personal style, God's Spirit controlled the outcome.

Just as God breathed life into Adam and Eve, he breathed life into his Book, giving it power to transform lives. The Scriptures help us understand our sinful condition and God's offer of forgiveness and eternal life. Our Creator shows us how to enter into a personal relationship with him. We receive practical instruction in how to live life to the fullest. By studying and applying God's Word, we allow his Spirit to control us so that we can reflect his character to the world.

No book has ever been more loved—or more hated. Through the ages, many people have risked imprisonment or death to share God's Word; others have dedicated their lives to destroying it. At one time, church leaders tortured or killed anyone who translated the Bible into a language that allowed people to read it for themselves. Through all these vicious attacks, God protected his Word, and today we have many choices of translations and languages.

How could we ever take such a treasure for granted? To think that the Creator of the universe went to such great lengths to make himself known to us is mind-boggling. Many people search for spiritual experiences involving miracles or emotional highs while ignoring the primary way God reveals himself. We can't grow in our relationship with God without studying what he wrote to us. Why would we let a day go by without taking the time to see what he has to say?

Genesis

The Beginning

In the beginning God created heaven and earth.

Genesis 1:1

Most scholars agree that Moses authored the first five books of the Bible, referred to collectively as the Law, the Torah, or the Pentateuch (derived from the Greek words for *five* and *scroll* or *book*). Moses certainly possessed the necessary literary skills since he had been "educated in all the wisdom of the Egyptians" (Acts 7:22). But it was his close communion with God that qualified him to write this sweeping work, which covers a longer time period than the other sixty-five books of the Bible put together. Numerous Scriptures throughout the Bible refer to Moses as the author of the Law, including Joshua 1:7, Ezra 6:18, Mark 12:26, and Luke 16:29.

Genesis is a book of beginnings, introducing God as the Creator and tracing the origins of the universe, the human race, marriage, sin, family, civilization, and government. It also unveils God's plan to save people from the disastrous effects of sin and restore them to a personal relationship with him. The second part of Genesis relates the history of Abraham and his descendants as God developed them into the nation of Israel, a people who would be set apart to reveal God's glory to the world and through whom the promised Savior would come.

Packed with dramatic stories of people who were flawed yet used by God, Genesis lays the foundation for the rest of the Bible and for our understanding of who God is. We see God's love in his acts of creation, his holiness in the necessity for judging evil, his mercy in providing a sacrifice to cover sin, and his sovereignty in shaping history to fulfill his plan of redemption.

Genesis shatters the image of God as an uninvolved supreme being or force. We see him walking in the garden with Adam and Eve, making an everlasting covenant with Abram and his descendants, and speaking to Moses face-to-face. As you read Genesis, remember that the same Creator who shaped the universe in the beginning wants to be involved in shaping your life today.

Handcrafted by God

Genesis 1–2

The first few chapters of Genesis have sparked countless debates over the "how" and "how long" of creation. Believers may hold differing views on the interpretation of certain verses, but hopefully we agree on the main point: our all-powerful God created the universe and everything in it, with the exception of the first man and woman, through just his spoken word. If we get tripped up by trying to explain details that we'll never fully understand, we can miss the beauty and majesty of the creation account—and the wonder that God wanted to share it with us.

At God's command, light burst forth from the darkness, waters gathered together, and dry ground produced plants and trees. The sun, moon, and stars appeared in the sky. The waters, sky, and land teemed with a dizzying array of animals. For the final step, God used a more personal approach than a verbal command. God lovingly shaped the first man from the ground and breathed life into him. To make a perfect companion for Adam, God put him to sleep and formed Eve from one of Adam's ribs. This first couple represented the pinnacle of God's created world, set apart from other living creatures by their origins, their instruction to govern the earth, and their relationship with the Creator.

During the creation process, God pronounced each day's completed work as "good," but only after forming Adam and Eve did he affirm his created world as "very good." Of God's vast and varied creation, only human beings were made in his image and designed to reflect his character. This fact represents the only solid foundation for our self-worth.

Without a biblical worldview, life becomes cheapened and even disposable. Our world often defines the value of a human life by physical attractiveness, intellectual abilities, material assets, or achievements. Psalm 139:13 tells us that God knit us together inside our mother's womb. Every life has dignity and worth simply because we have been handcrafted by God, and that is a "very good" thing.

> *And God saw everything that he had*
> *made and that it was very good.*
>
> Genesis 1:31

The Worst Decision Ever Made

Genesis 3

From Eve's point of view, the serpent made a convincing case. She could see that the tree in the middle of the garden bore fruit that looked pretty and seemed good to eat. And what could be wrong with wanting to gain more wisdom? Satan-in-disguise contradicted God's warning that eating this particular fruit would bring death. He even questioned God's motives, implying that God selfishly kept the fruit from Adam and Eve because he didn't want them to become like him.

Satan's smooth talk awakened Eve's natural desires and she chose to ignore God's command. She and Adam ate fruit from the one tree that God had withheld from them. It didn't take them long to realize they'd made a terrible decision that brought deadly consequences. After that first sinful act, nothing would ever be the same.

The world and everything in it became distorted by sin. Adam and Eve lost their intimacy with each other and with their Creator. Because of their disobedience, God had to expel them from their perfect garden home into a hostile environment filled with hard work, conflict, suffering, and death.

As much as Adam and Eve's mistake cost them, it cost God far more. In order to restore what had been broken, he would one day become a man and "bruise Satan's heel" as he died to pay the penalty for our sin (see v. 15).

Satan still works to get people to disobey God, and his tactics haven't changed. He encourages us to follow our desires rather than God's commands. He plants thoughts in our mind that prompt us to question God's character. But it's always a mistake to evaluate choices based on human reasoning when it contradicts God's Word. If we're not careful, what looks like a no-brainer at first glance may just turn out to be one of the worst decisions we ever make.

There is a way that seems right to a person,
but eventually it ends in death.
Proverbs 14:12

The First Murder

Genesis 4:1—16

It didn't take much to instigate the first murder in the world—just a disgruntled brother who burned with anger and jealousy. Abel brought an offering to God in a way that pleased him, but apparently his older brother Cain gave his offering with improper motives. Cain became incensed when God rejected it. Even when God tried to encourage him, Cain refused to admit his mistake or change his attitude. He ignored God's warning that if he didn't master his sinful urges, then they would control him.

Out in the fields, Cain attacked his brother and killed him. When God asked about Abel's whereabouts, Cain tried to lie his way out of the crime. Instead of repenting after God exposed his guilt, he complained that God's punishment was more than he could bear. God showed mercy by putting a sign on Cain to prevent anyone from killing him in order to avenge Abel's murder. In response to this kindness, Cain demonstrated defiance by settling in a city rather than wander the earth as God had sentenced him to do.

Cain's descendants formed a society opposed to God, in contrast to the line of Seth, his younger brother. The life story of the first baby born in the world paints a chilling picture of how far sin can drag us if we don't respond to correction. God gave Cain ample opportunity to repent and seek forgiveness, yet Cain never admitted to any wrongdoing.

Disappointment, anger, and jealousy may not seem like such a big deal. These emotions are natural and will come to us all at some point. But how we handle them determines the course of our life. If we don't resist sinful urges, admit our mistakes, and yield to God's discipline, then we can expect trouble ahead. We may not murder someone, but something in our life will die.

> [The LORD said] *"If you do what is right, will you not be accepted? But if you do not do what is right, sin is crouching at your door; it desires to have you, but you must master it."*
>
> Genesis 4:7 NIV

A Strange Building Project

Genesis 6

As people multiplied on the earth, the human race grew so corrupt that people thought about evil "all day long" (v. 5). Seeing their wickedness, God was heartbroken and decided to wipe the earth clean. Since Noah loved and obeyed him, God determined to preserve Noah's family to give the human race a fresh start.

God revealed his plans to Noah and gave detailed instructions for building a huge ark that would hold his family plus two of every kind of animal, along with provisions. God vowed to delay his judgment for 120 years, giving Noah's family plenty of time to complete such an enormous project.

Noah immediately set to work, carefully following God's instructions. His strange building project must have made him a curiosity to the people around him. Here was a man who dedicated himself to building a ship on dry land—an ark 450 feet long, 75 feet wide, and 45 feet high. For more than a hundred years, he warned about a coming flood at a time when it had never rained on the earth. Perhaps people traveled far to see such a sight for themselves. They most likely laughed and called Noah a fool.

Following God can make us look foolish in the world's eyes. Unbelievers can't understand why we would give money back to God when we're struggling financially. It doesn't make sense to them when we forgive someone who has hurt us terribly, or when we put aside our own desires in order to hold our family together.

God may call us to leave a lucrative career for mission work, take in a homeless person, or do something else that seems illogical from a human standpoint. People may even question our sanity. But even when our actions seem strange to those around us, it's always wise to follow God's instructions in our most important building project—a life that brings glory to him.

Again I say that no one should think that I'm a fool.

2 Corinthians 11:16

A Cleansing Flood

Genesis 7–8

God's love and mercy make him patient with people, but his holiness requires him to judge sin eventually. While building the ark, Noah preached and urged onlookers to repent and turn to God (see 2 Pet. 2:5). More than a hundred years passed and not a single person responded to the message. Finally, God put a stop to their wickedness. He sent a parade of animals to board the ark, and once Noah's family stepped inside, God shut the door himself.

Seven days later, the springs of the earth "burst open" and the skies poured down rain for forty days and nights, wiping all life from the face of the earth (Gen. 7:11). By the time the waters receded and the earth dried, Noah's family had spent more than a year on the ark. At last, God called them to come out. These eight people stepped onto a land that was like a new creation, cleansed of all evil and ready for a fresh start.

The New Testament teaches that the moment we accept Christ, we become a new creation. We don't automatically change into the image of Christ, but God begins a gradual process of transformation. As we deal with one problem area in our life, he nudges us toward the next one. At times, he has to take away something in our life that causes us to stumble or that interferes with his will for us.

There are times when God takes a more radical approach. We may have gone so far astray that he has to purge our life of whatever keeps our eyes off him, or he may strip away things we hold dear in order to prepare us for some special work. It may seem frightening when God's hand moves through our life like a sweeping flood, but we can be sure that his purpose is to cleanse us and make us more like the new creation he wants us to be.

Whoever is a believer in Christ is a new creation.

2 Corinthians 5:17

A Tower of Pride

Genesis 11:1—9

God had commanded Noah's descendants to fill up the whole earth, but the people who settled on a plain in Shinar were more interested in making a name for themselves than in obeying God. They agreed to work together to build a city featuring a great tower that would reach to the sky (probably a Babylonian ziggurat, which looked like a pyramid with steps leading up the sides). The whole world would see their achievement and recognize their greatness.

Since God knew that people uniting in rebellion opened the way for great evil, he acted swiftly. One moment the whole world spoke a common language; the next minute, mass confusion erupted. Suddenly, friends and co-workers couldn't understand each other; everyone seemed to be babbling. The great building project halted. People eventually divided themselves into groups according to their new languages and scattered across the earth, as God had intended for them to do. The unfinished tower—the intended monument to their greatness—became evidence of their arrogance and foolishness instead.

The human race has been blessed with great capacity for inventing, creating, and problem-solving, especially when we work together. Evidence of these God-given abilities especially abounds in the fields of technology, medicine, and space exploration. But when we forget that all we have comes from our Creator, we become arrogant instead of thankful. We start to think that our achievements stem from our own greatness rather than from God's goodness and wisdom.

Letting our focus drift away from God can be a very dangerous thing. We may end up using our resources and talents to build little "towers" that call attention to ourselves. Even good things like church attendance and Bible study can become a source of pride if we're not careful. When other people look at our life, we want them to see only one monument—our testimony of God's goodness that points them toward our Lord and Savior.

Pride precedes a disaster,
and an arrogant attitude precedes a fall.

Proverbs 16:18

Answering the Call

Genesis 12–13

When God got ready to form a new nation of people to call his own, he started with a seventy-five-year-old childless man from a pagan culture. God called Abram to leave behind the security of his home to go to a location that would be revealed to him later. God also made amazing promises to Abram: he would make him into a great nation and bless the whole world through him. Later, God promised to give Abram the land of Canaan, as far as he could see, and descendants as numerous as the dust of the earth.

Abram's response to God's call shows why the Bible often points to him as a picture of faith. He walked away from his prosperous, settled lifestyle and the gods of his past to follow Yahweh. Not that Abram was perfect; on two different occasions he deceived people into thinking that beautiful Sarai was not his wife, motivated by fear that he might be killed by someone who wanted her.

As a result, two powerful rulers took Sarai into their palace until God intervened. But despite his lapses in judgment, Abram followed God to the best of his imperfect ability. And he held on to God's promises even as years dragged by with no tangible fulfillment.

God probably doesn't want to make us into a new nation, but he does want to do new, exciting things in our life. Sometimes God calls us to leave behind old habits, addictions, and behaviors that weigh us down. Or he may call us to make a dramatic change in our lifestyle or move into a new area of service for him.

It's always tempting to hover inside our comfort zone where we feel safe and at home. But God often challenges us to demonstrate our faith by following him even when the destination seems unclear. It may seem frightening, but when God calls, it's best to start walking wherever he sends us.

So Abram left, as the Lord had told him.

Genesis 12:4

God Cuts a Covenant

Genesis 15

Although many years passed while Abram and Sarai remained childless, Abram still clung to God's promise that he would have a son, and eventually descendants as innumerable as the stars in the sky. Then God declared that Abram's descendants would possess the surrounding land. This time Abram asked for some confirmation that would let him know these things would indeed happen. God instructed Abram to gather and prepare animals for a sacrifice and the formal "cutting" of a covenant.

When birds of prey swooped down on the carcasses, Abram drove them away. God explained the symbolism: Abram's descendants would be enslaved for approximately four hundred years, then return to possess the land after the current inhabitants' sins had reached the limits of God's patience. After the sun went down, God took on the physical form of a smoking oven and a flaming torch. God passed between the pieces of the sacrificed animals, demonstrating to Abram that he had bound himself to the unbreakable covenant.

Although Abram would not see the ultimate fulfillment of the promises, he knew that nothing could undo the covenant God had cut. Despite disobedience and mistakes on the part of his descendants, generations of them living in slavery, and numerous attacks from their enemies, the great nation of Israel would return to possess the land God had promised them.

As believers today, we live under the new covenant that God cut for us through the death and resurrection of Jesus. Once we accept the sacrifice made for us, we have his guarantee of forgiveness of sin, acceptance as his child, and an eternal heavenly home. In spite of mistakes and failures on our part, the hatred of the world, and attacks from the enemy of our soul, God's promises concerning us will come to pass. No matter what happens in our life, we have the assurance of God's unbreakable word.

I'm convinced that God, who began this good work in you,
will carry it through to completion on the day of Christ Jesus.

Philippians 1:6

Sarai's Mistake

Genesis 16:1—6

Just like the rest of us, Sarai found it hard to wait. God had promised to give Abram descendants as numerous as the stars in the sky, but years had passed with no sign of the promised son. Elderly and frustrated, Sarai suggested that Abram sleep with her slave Hagar. After all, many barren women took advantage of this custom to get children for themselves and heirs for their husbands. What could be more convenient and logical? And God could begin forming the "great nation" he planned to bring about through Abram's descendants.

Sarai soon regretted her decision. Hagar's pregnancy made her arrogant and caused friction within the household. Later, the conflict would worsen when Sarai gave birth to a son, the heir originally intended by God all along. Hostilities between the sons of the two women would last well past their lifetimes, developing into two rival nations. Sarai's idea to help God's plan move forward turned out to be a terrible mistake affecting much more than just her own family. She had to learn the hard way that God doesn't need our help to accomplish his purposes.

It's never easy to wait, especially when we're longing for something with all our heart. If we look around and see no sign of God acting to resolve a situation, we may be tempted to come up with our own ideas to hurry the solution along. Our impatience may lead us to make choices that don't line up with God's will. We can find ourselves regretting the long-range consequences of an idea that seemed convenient and logical at the time.

God asks us to prove our trust in him by surrendering to his plan and waiting for him to work in ways that he considers best. We may find it hard to wait patiently when nothing seems to be happening, but taking matters into our own hands apart from God's leading is always a terrible mistake.

Surrender yourself to the LORD, and wait patiently for him.

Psalm 37:7

Close Encounters of the Divine Kind

Genesis 16:7—15

In retaliation for Hagar's arrogant behavior, Sarai mistreated her so badly that she ran away. As she journeyed through the desert, the Egyptian slave had an encounter with a heavenly being who transformed her attitude. The angel, or messenger of the Lord, confronted Hagar and instructed her to return and submit to Sarai. He also promised that Hagar would have numerous descendants, beginning with her son Ishmael. Hagar obeyed God's message and acknowledged him as "the God Who Watches Over Me."

This passage marks the first Old Testament reference to the angel of the Lord. Later incidents include the angel of the Lord telling Abram his plans to destroy Sodom and Gomorrah (Gen. 18) and directing Abram to sacrifice a ram instead of his son Isaac (Gen. 22). In Judges 6, the angel of the Lord appoints Gideon to deliver Israel from enemy oppression and encourages him for his task ahead.

The Scriptures identify this divine being with Yahweh, yet often show him as distinct from the Lord (see Judg. 6:22). For this reason, many scholars believe that the angel of the Lord represents a *theophany* (Greek for "appearance of God"), in this case a physical appearance of Jesus Christ before his human birth. Others contend that this divine being is an angel appointed to speak on God's behalf.

Being face-to-face with the angel of the Lord must have been an awe-inspiring experience, but believers today are privileged to communicate with God in a much more personal way. With the combination of God's written Word and his Spirit living within us, we can hear from him on a daily basis. We can receive encouragement, comfort, and guidance. God may appoint us for some special task or reveal his will in a specific area. We don't have to wait for the angel of the Lord to make an appearance; we can have a close encounter of the divine kind at any given moment.

We know that we live in him and he lives in
us because he has given us his Spirit.

1 John 4:13

Just One Look

Genesis 18:16—19:29

The time had come to put a stop to Sodom and Gomorrah's ever-increasing wickedness. God had agreed to spare the city if ten righteous people could be found there, but the godlessness was so pervasive that even Abram's relative Lot had been tainted by it. When men surrounded his house and demanded sex with his two guests, Lot offered the crowd his virgin daughters instead. Lot's guests, who were actually angels, saved him from the crazed mob that threatened to kill him. They explained that they had come to destroy the city.

As soon as dawn broke, the angels urged Lot to flee with his wife and daughters so they wouldn't be swept away when disaster struck the city. Still, Lot hesitated to leave. The angels grabbed the family members' hands and literally pulled them out of Sodom. When Lot asked to be sheltered in a nearby small city rather than flee to the mountains, the angels granted his request. But they warned the family to run for their lives, without stopping or looking back.

As Lot's family neared safety, God rained down burning sulfur on Sodom and Gomorrah. Whether out of curiosity about what was happening or from a sense of longing for what she had left behind, Lot's wife disobeyed the angels' instructions. She turned around and looked back. Her punishment came swiftly; she turned into a column of salt.

Sometimes looking back can be helpful. Reflecting on how God has worked in our life strengthens our faith. Examining past behavior can help us learn from our mistakes. But a tendency to dwell constantly on past failures and regrets hinders our spiritual growth. If we allow ourselves to think with longing about what we left behind to serve Christ, our commitment may falter. Following Christ means being focused on him and the future he has planned for us. Compared with that, nothing from our past is worth a second glance.

> *This is what I do: I don't look back, I lengthen my*
> *stride, and I run straight toward the goal to win the*
> *prize that God's heavenly call offers in Christ Jesus.*
>
> Philippians 3:13–14

A Miraculous Birth

Genesis 18:1—15; 21:1—7

A ninety-year-old woman giving birth to a son fathered by a hundred-year-old man? Impossible—but that's what Sarah heard the Lord telling Abraham as she eavesdropped at the tent entrance. Sarah couldn't resist laughing to herself at the idea. "Why did Sarah laugh?" God asked Abraham. "Is anything too hard for the LORD?" (18:13–14). God restated his promise that Sarah would have a son within a year. Frightened at the exposure of her thoughts, Sarah tried to deny her laughter.

A year later, Sarah laughed openly and unabashedly with joy, inviting others to join her. At the predicted time, Sarah gave birth to the promised son and heir whose name had already been chosen by God in Genesis 17:19. The miraculous birth of Isaac ("He Laughs") testified to God's faithfulness and his power to accomplish what is impossible from a human standpoint. At last Abraham and Sarah understood why God had waited so long to send their son. With Sarah well beyond the normal childbearing years, no one could deny God's miraculous intervention in a situation so obviously contrary to the laws of nature.

God often reveals his power by doing something that looks impossible. In the Old Testament, he enabled small bands of Israelites to conquer powerful armies. God parted bodies of water to provide a dry crossing path, made water gush from a rock, and even made time stand still. In the New Testament, Jesus turned water into wine, multiplied tiny amounts of food to feed thousands, healed incurable diseases, made blind eyes see, and raised the dead back to life.

God has already done the impossible in our lives by taking on our sins, dying in our place, implanting his Spirit within us, and giving us eternal life. Why should we have trouble accepting any of his promises, even when they sound too good to be true? When God asks us to believe the unbelievable, it's no laughing matter.

> *The things that are impossible for people
> to do are possible for God to do.*
>
> Luke 18:27

Abraham's Greatest Test

Genesis 22:1—19

Surely God's words must have shocked and horrified Abraham. After Abraham had waited so many years for the promised son and heir, now God wanted him to sacrifice this precious boy as a burnt offering? The pagan culture around him practiced child sacrifice, but how could this possibly be a part of God's plan? Hadn't God said that his descendants would come through Isaac? But Abraham had learned the importance of trusting and obeying God regardless of his feelings or his circumstances. Early the next morning, he set out on the fifty-mile journey to Mount Moriah with wood, a knife, and his beloved son.

On top of the mountain, Abraham arranged the wood and tied up his son. Just as he raised his hand to plunge the knife into Isaac's chest, a voice from heaven stopped him. The test was over; Abraham had passed. He would withhold nothing from the God he worshiped and served, obeying him no matter what it cost. Turning around, Abraham discovered that God had provided a ram for the burnt offering in place of Isaac.

This ordeal strengthened Abraham's character and faith, and it set the stage for God to one day provide a sacrifice that would affect the entire human race. Yet even though we see the purpose from our vantage point, it's hard to imagine the emotions that Abraham must have struggled with when God made such a strange request. His example of unquestioning obedience and implicit trust in God's goodness serves as an example of the kind of commitment that God wants from us.

If God calls us to give up something we dearly love, can we make the sacrifice and trust that he has a reason for it? Whenever our obedience is tested, we can remember that God did not withhold his only Son, but gave him up as an offering for our sins. How could we refuse to trust and obey a God who loves us so much?

> *Trust the LORD with all your heart,*
> *and do not rely on your own understanding.*
>
> Proverbs 3:5

Playing Favorites

Genesis 25:19—34; 27

Esau and Jacob may have been twins, but their personalities couldn't have been more different. The rugged Esau grew up to be an outdoorsman who loved to hunt, making him the favorite of his father Isaac. But quiet Jacob preferred hanging around the tents and cooking, so his mother Rebekah preferred him. Such partiality created a family rift and fueled conflict and hostility between the brothers that lasted far beyond their lifetimes.

Before the birth of the twins, God had told Rebekah that the normal roles would be reversed, with the older son serving the younger. After the boys grew up, one day a famished Esau impulsively traded his birthright to Jacob for a meal. Later, when Rebekah heard that Isaac was about to pronounce the special blessing reserved for the firstborn son, she sprang into action to help Jacob get it instead.

Using goatskins to mimic Esau's hairy arms, Rebekah coached Jacob on how to trick his father. Their deception succeeded; Isaac gave the blessing of the firstborn to Jacob. But painful consequences soon followed. Rebekah had to send Jacob away to escape the murderous rage of his brother. She would never see her favorite son again. By the time Jacob returned home twenty years later, Rebekah would be dead.

Many people have felt the effects of favoritism on the part of parents, teachers, employers, or in other contexts. This is one thing we never need to worry about with our heavenly Father. God loves each one of his children equally. He doesn't dispense either his favor or his discipline on a whim. If we see another believer who seems to be especially favored, perhaps they've positioned themselves to receive more of God's blessings by obeying his guidelines for living. If someone seems to have a closer relationship with God than we do, it's probably because they're more committed to the disciplines that foster spiritual growth. In any case, God never shows partiality; we're all his favorite children.

God does not play favorites.

Romans 2:11

A Taste of His Own Medicine

Genesis 29:1—30

Jacob began a four-hundred-mile journey to Paddan Aram to escape his brother's rage and to find a wife among his mother's relatives. On the way, he had a personal encounter with God and received the same covenant promises that God had given first to Abraham and then to Isaac. Jacob arrived at his destination a changed man, but he still had a long way to go to become the man God wanted him to be. Jacob needed some character-shaping.

Uncle Laban welcomed Jacob into his family. He agreed to let him marry his younger daughter in return for seven years of work tending Laban's herds. Jacob's love for Rachel made the years seem to fly by, and at last the wedding feast took place. The next morning, however, Jacob discovered that Laban had substituted his older daughter Leah for the beautiful Rachel.

Jacob now knew something of the anger that Esau must have felt, but surely the irony of the situation wasn't lost on him. The deceiver had become the deceived. Jacob had tricked his father by pretending to be his older brother; Laban had tricked Jacob by pretending that his older daughter was the younger one. Jacob accepted the arrangement and a week later he also married Rachel, committing to give Laban another seven years of free labor.

Sometimes God allows us to experience injustice or mistreatment from others in order to discipline us for similar behavior. He may be trying to point out character flaws or harmful patterns that we need to acknowledge and change. If we evaluate a difficult relationship honestly and prayerfully, we may learn that what annoys us most about another person is something we're guilty of ourselves. When God lets us have a taste of our own medicine, it's usually a bitter experience. But at least we know that he prescribes it for our own good.

> *Make no mistake about this: You can never make a fool*
> *out of God. Whatever you plant is what you'll harvest.*
>
> Galatians 6:7

Trying to Earn Love

Genesis 29:31–35; 30:1–24

Jacob's dysfunctional relationship with his twin brother Esau foreshadowed his own household, which was filled with conflict, jealousy, and sibling rivalry. Unloved Leah hoped to gain her husband's affection by giving him sons, which her culture considered the ultimate fulfillment of a woman's role. Although Rachel already possessed Jacob's love and devotion, her inability to have children fueled her envy of Leah. The two sisters engaged in an intense childbearing competition, each trying to win recognition and attention from their shared husband.

God saw Leah's misery and allowed her to have four sons in quick succession. Rachel became jealous and decided to give Jacob children through her servant Bilhah, who bore two sons. Leah had stopped conceiving but she determined not to be outdone. She insisted that Jacob also take her servant as a wife, and Zilpah added two more sons to the family. Then Leah gave birth to two additional sons and a daughter, still hoping to win Jacob's love by the children she provided for him. Finally, God answered Rachel's prayer and she had a son. The family would be completed later, as Rachel died while giving birth to Jacob's twelfth and final son (see Gen. 35:16–20).

Like Leah, we sometimes try desperately to win another person's affections; like Rachel, we sometimes feel the need to earn love rather than accept it as a freely given gift. These patterns of thinking can keep us from enjoying healthy relationships with other people. They can also creep into our attitudes toward God, causing us to forget that he loves us unconditionally.

If we believe in Jesus Christ as our Savior, then we already have God's approval. There is nothing we can do to make him love us more. Such a mindset is out of place in our relationship with a Father who has proved his love by shedding his blood for us. God has already lavished on us what we could never have earned in the first place.

> *[The LORD said] "I love you with an everlasting love.*
> *So I will continue to show you my kindness."*
>
> Jeremiah 31:3

A Thirst for Revenge

Genesis 34

After twenty years of self-imposed exile, Jacob finally set out for home to reconcile with Esau. When the two brothers met up, Jacob pretended he planned to follow Esau to Seir, but he didn't. Eventually he set up camp outside the city of Shechem, where disaster struck his family. One day Jacob's only daughter Dinah ventured out to visit some of the Canaanite women, and the son of the local leader, a young man also named Shechem, raped her.

Jacob seemed to react passively, but the news incensed his sons. When Shechem's father tried to negotiate a marriage between his son and Dinah, the brothers pretended to agree—on the condition that every male in the town be circumcised. Shechem and his father convinced the men to agree to this proposal, with a view to getting their hands on Jacob's possessions. Before the men healed from circumcision, Simeon and Levi slaughtered every one of them. Then Jacob's sons looted the town.

We can understand the brothers' outrage at the heinous crime committed against Dinah. But their bloodthirsty revenge far exceeded the demands of justice. They lied, stole, and murdered, putting Jacob's entire household in danger. They used circumcision, the sign of God's covenant blessings, as a means of manipulation and death. Their impulsive actions would have far-reaching consequences, especially for two of the brothers.

It's only natural to want to pay someone back for the hurt they cause us or our loved ones. God does want us to do everything in our power to see that justice prevails, but he doesn't want us to harbor a desire for revenge. There will be occasions when we won't see justice done in this lifetime, but God promises to ultimately avenge all wrongdoing. We should not try to make things right by doing more wrong; rather, the Judge of the earth asks us to leave such matters in his capable hands.

> *Don't take revenge, dear friends. Instead, let God's anger
> take care of it. After all, Scripture says, "I alone have the
> right to take revenge. I will pay back, says the Lord."*
>
> Romans 12:19

The Green-Eyed Monster

Genesis 37

Jacob's personal experience should have taught him how easily blatant favoritism can tear a family apart, but he failed to learn the lesson. Since Joseph was the first son of his beloved Rachel and born in his old age, Jacob loved him most out of his twelve sons. The special robe Jacob provided for Joseph served as a daily reminder of this partiality. Joseph's half-brothers already resented him for telling their father the bad things they did. When Joseph described his dreams, which seemed to portray his brothers bowing down to him, it intensified their hatred for him even more.

One day when Jacob sent Joseph to check on his brothers as they tended the flocks, the jealous siblings decided to get rid of him. At first they plotted to kill Joseph, but Reuben persuaded them to put him in a pit instead. Reuben planned to rescue Joseph later, but without his knowledge the others came up with a different plan.

As a caravan of traders passed by on their way to Egypt, Judah suggested selling Joseph to them. After the transaction, the brothers dipped Joseph's special robe in goat's blood to show Jacob. The distraught father could not be comforted over the apparent death of his favorite child; he vowed to mourn for Joseph until the day he died.

The actions of Joseph's brothers show how jealousy can drive someone to do unspeakable things. We may find ourselves in a situation where jealousy seems to be a justified response, but if left unchecked such negative emotions will grow until they take over our thought life. Several Bible passages include jealousy or envy in a list of sins that believers need to guard against (see Gal. 5:20–21). We can't afford to take our feelings of jealousy lightly; we need to confess these thought patterns to God and ask for his help. That way we won't be in danger of doing something we never dreamed we'd do.

> *Wherever there is jealousy and rivalry, there*
> *is disorder and every kind of evil.*
>
> James 3:16

Double Standards

Genesis 38

The levirate law explained in Deuteronomy 25:5–10 seems strange to us today, but as always, God had a purpose for giving it. This custom required a man to marry his brother's widow and provide offspring if the union had been childless. This arrangement ensured that widows would have sons to care and provide for them; it also preserved the family name and line of the deceased man.

When Judah's first son died, he sent his second son Onan to marry Tamar according to the custom. But Onan wanted to take advantage of the physical relationship while avoiding the responsibilities involved, so God put him to death. Fearing for his third son's life, Judah deceived his daughter-in-law by urging her to return to her father's house, supposedly until his son Shelah got old enough to marry her.

Tamar eventually grew tired of waiting. When Judah's wife died, Tamar disguised herself and sat beside the road. Mistaking her for a prostitute, Judah slept with her. When he heard that his daughter-in-law was pregnant, Judah demanded she be executed. Tamar showed him the personal articles he had left with her as promise of payment. Judah recognized his own hypocrisy. He had been ready to condemn Tamar while ignoring his own guilt.

We often judge other people by a stricter standard than we use for our own actions. Sometimes we rush to condemn another person but make excuses when we exhibit the same behavior. We may try to impose double standards, but God never does. His standard is the same for all of us—perfection. Since we've all sinned, none of us can measure up, no matter how good we think we are. Fortunately, God offers us a way to meet his requirement by accepting the sacrifice of his perfect Son. Since God uses the same measuring stick for everyone, it makes no sense for us to impose double standards on people.

> *There is no difference between people. Because all people*
> *have sinned, they have fallen short of God's glory.*
>
> Romans 3:22–23

A False Accusation

Genesis 39

Joseph's life changed forever the instant his brothers betrayed him. The favored son from a prosperous family in Canaan suddenly became a slave for sale in a foreign land. But God was with the frightened teenager and blessed him throughout his ordeal. The high-ranking official who purchased Joseph soon recognized the young man's integrity that made him a valued addition to his household. Potiphar trusted Joseph so much that he put him in charge of everything he owned.

Trouble began brewing when Potiphar's wife decided to seduce the good-looking servant. Joseph refused her persistent advances, declaring that such behavior would be a betrayal of his master's trust and a grievous sin against God. One day she arranged for them to be alone, grabbed his clothes, and commanded him to go to bed with her. Joseph raced out of the house, leaving his robe behind. Potiphar's wife later used his garment to accuse Joseph of trying to force himself on her.

Joseph had done everything in his power to handle the situation in a way that would honor God, but he still ended up in prison falsely accused of a crime. While he must have struggled with periods of discouragement, Joseph clung to his faith. Once again God granted Joseph favor and the warden put him in charge of all the prisoners. And once again Joseph made the best of the situation where God had placed him.

When we suffer from false accusations or unjust treatment, it's tempting to think that God has abandoned us or perhaps is punishing us for some wrongdoing we're not aware of. If our conscience is clear that our circumstances aren't the result of sinful behavior, we can trust that God has a definite purpose in mind. Perhaps he's helping us grow more dependent on him or preparing us for an important role, as in Joseph's case. Even when other people believe false accusations against us, the most important thing is that God knows our innocence.

The one who pronounces me innocent is near.

Isaiah 50:8

A Major Promotion

Genesis 40—41

At last Joseph saw a glimmer of hope that he would escape the drudgery of prison life. In a fit of anger, Pharaoh had imprisoned his cupbearer. After Joseph interpreted the cupbearer's dream, he asked the king's servant to mention his name to Pharaoh and help get him out of prison. But when the cupbearer regained Pharaoh's favor, the promise slipped his mind. Two more years dragged by. Joseph had now spent thirteen years in Egypt, first as a slave and then as a prisoner.

Then one day Joseph's world again turned upside down. Pharaoh had troubling dreams that his wise men couldn't interpret. This jogged the cupbearer's memory and he told Pharaoh about the prisoner who had explained his own dream. Officials hurried Joseph from the dungeon to the palace. After first giving God the credit, Joseph explained that Pharaoh's dreams warned of seven years of famine that would follow seven years of abundance. Joseph boldly outlined a survival plan to prepare for the disaster.

Pharaoh sensed a divine presence in the young man before him. He gave Joseph control over his palace and the nation of Egypt, making the former slave second-in-command only to himself. Joseph's training in Potiphar's house and in prison had prepared him to step into his new role. As before, he worked diligently. Joseph stored up food that would feed not only Egypt but also the surrounding areas, including one particular family dear to his heart.

Sometimes other people fail to give us the recognition we deserve; sometimes they completely overlook us. When we feel stuck in a life of drudgery, we can be confident that our difficulties and suffering won't last forever. If we submit to God and trust him to control the events in our life, he will honor us at the right time. It might be during our earthly life or when we stand before him in heaven, but either way believers are in for a major promotion.

> *Be humbled by God's power so that when the*
> *right time comes he will honor you.*
>
> 1 Peter 5:6

Family Reunion

Genesis 42—47

When ten of Joseph's brothers showed up to buy grain in Egypt, he recognized them immediately. Twenty years had passed since the day they ignored Joseph's cries for mercy and sold him into slavery. Now he held their lives in his hands. Joseph set out to test his brothers' character and to see if they had changed. He accused them of being spies and imprisoned them for three days. Retaining Simeon, Joseph then ordered the other nine to bring their youngest brother to Egypt.

After the supply of grain ran out, Jacob reluctantly allowed Benjamin to go to Egypt with his brothers. Joseph invited them to dine at his house, where he showered extra attention on Benjamin, his full brother and the only one not involved in his betrayal. As the brothers left for home, Joseph arranged to have Benjamin framed for theft so he could claim him as his slave.

Judah's impassioned plea revealed how his heart had changed. The brother who had suggested selling Joseph so long ago now offered himself in place of Benjamin as a way to spare their aged father grief that would surely kill him. Unable to control his emotions, Joseph finally revealed his identity. He also tried to ease his brothers' burden of guilt by emphasizing that God had used their actions to bring him to Egypt in order to save lives. Years of grief washed away as the brothers embraced and cried. Then Joseph sent them to bring Jacob and his entire family to Egypt, where they would be protected from the remaining five years of famine.

Many people suffer from the effects of dysfunctional relationships or past wounds inflicted by people they once trusted. Joseph's story demonstrates that God can restore any relationship when there is a spirit of forgiveness. We can let go of our hurts more easily when we remember how much Jesus has forgiven us. With his help, we can forgive and embrace others in spite of painful memories.

*Put up with each other, and forgive each other if anyone
has a complaint. Forgive as the Lord forgave you.*

Colossians 3:13

The Days to Come

Genesis 48—49

Seventeen years had passed since Jacob joined Joseph in Egypt; at age 147, Jacob knew the end of his life was near. During a private visit with Joseph and his two sons, Jacob gave Ephraim and Manasseh the status of full sons rather than grandsons. Once again God displayed his sovereignty by choosing the younger brother over the older one. Prompted by God, Jacob gave the blessing of the firstborn son to Ephraim, whose descendants would eventually become a leading tribe in Israel's northern kingdom.

Later, Jacob gathered all twelve sons to offer blessings and predictions concerning their "days to come." These prophecies often reflected the individual's past actions. Reuben forfeited his special status as the oldest son because he had slept with one of his father's concubines. Because of Simeon and Levi's violent dispositions and their slaughter of the men of Shechem (see Gen. 34), their tribes would be scattered.

About half of Jacob's speech details special blessings given to Joseph and Judah. Despite Judah's immoral behavior in his dealings with his daughter-in-law (see Gen. 38), and the fact that he initiated the selling of Joseph, the tribe of Judah would take the lead in the nation of Israel. Judah had shown a heart ready to repent of sin. God had chosen him to be the ancestor of the kingly line through which the Messiah would come.

It's clear that while God holds our future in his hands, our life will be affected by the consequences of today's choices and actions, whether good or bad. These chapters in Genesis give us two keys to living a life open to God's continued blessings. Joseph's life encourages us to hold on to our integrity and belief in God's goodness even in the worst of times. Judah reminds us to have a teachable spirit, learning from our past mistakes, acknowledging our sins, and letting God transform our heart. If we let these examples guide our attitudes and behavior today, we'll reap the benefits in our own days to come.

My future is in your hands.

Psalm 31:15

Jesus in Genesis

The first chapter of John explains that Jesus existed with God "in the beginning" and participated in the creation process. It's appropriate that in the beginning of the Bible, we already see clues to the role Jesus would later fulfill in God's plan to bring salvation to a fallen world. In Genesis 3:15, God promises that a descendant of Eve will crush the serpent's head, while the serpent will bruise that descendant's heel. Most scholars accept this as a foreshadowing of Jesus's defeat of Satan through submitting to crucifixion and then being resurrected.

Jesus is also pictured in Genesis through the use of "types," historical facts that illustrate spiritual truths. It's hard to ignore how significant events in Joseph's life mirror aspects of Jesus's life centuries later. Both Joseph and Jesus were hated, plotted against, and sold for silver. Both were falsely accused and condemned, but later exalted by God after their humiliation and suffering. Both men were thirty years old when they came to the public's attention.

Another striking similarity is their willingness to forgive their enemies. Joseph freely forgave the brothers who had treated him so cruelly. He reminded them that although their actions had been evil, God used them for good, to save the lives of many people. Jesus prayed for God to forgive his executioners even as he hung on the cross. He lived his life on earth with full awareness that his suffering and death would be the means of reconciling the human race to God.

Today, God still uses people's evil intentions and actions to accomplish his own purposes. As God's children, we have his promise that everything that happens to us will somehow work for our ultimate good. Even when people want to harm us, we can trust God to turn it around to fit into his plans for our life and to bring him glory.

> *Even though you planned evil against me,*
> *God planned good to come out of it.*
>
> Genesis 50:20

Exodus

The Birth of a Nation

> Then I will make you my people, and I will be your God. You will know that I am the LORD your God, who brought you out from under the forced labor of the Egyptians.
>
> Exodus 6:7

Moses wrote the book of Exodus to record events surrounding the development of Israel as a nation. God began to fulfill his promises to Abraham, Isaac, and Jacob to make their descendants into a great nation that would bless the earth. His plan unfolded despite powerful opposition from other nations, and often in spite of the Israelites' disobedience and stubborn unbelief.

The first half of Exodus focuses on the Israelites' miraculous delivery after spending four hundred years in slavery in Egypt. (Exodus describes more miracles than any other book in the Bible.) The original seventy members of Jacob's family had grown to more than two million people, fulfilling God's promise of numerous descendants. This part of the book also shows God's establishment of Moses as Israel's leader and mediator of God's covenant with them.

The second half of Exodus relates how God prepared Israel to be a people set apart from the nations around them. God revealed his guiding presence to the Israelites in tangible ways. He gave them the law so they could understand his character and how he expected them to live. God also gave them detailed plans for constructing a tabernacle where they could worship him.

Despite God's miraculous delivery, protection, and provision, the Israelites sometimes rebelled against him and refused to trust him. Still, the book of Exodus ends on a high note with God's glory filling the newly constructed tent of meeting. Yahweh had come down to dwell among his chosen people.

As believers, we are delivered from the slavery of sin's control. God wants us to be set apart from the people around us as a testimony to his character. As we read Exodus and compare our responses to God with the Israelites', a good question to ponder is: Am I living like one of God's chosen people?

A Change in Policy

Exodus 1

Because of Joseph's high-ranking position, Pharaoh welcomed his family and invited them to live in the best part of Egypt. He even entrusted them with the care of his own livestock. Jacob and his family settled in the fertile region of Goshen, where they thrived. When Jacob died seventeen years later, the Egyptians honored him by observing a seventy-day mourning period. All of the royal officials and national leaders accompanied Joseph as he carried his father's body to Canaan for burial.

After many years, Joseph, his brothers, and that entire generation died. Then a new ruler came into power, one who had never heard of Joseph or his service to Egypt. Joseph had not only saved the nation, but had allowed Egypt to prosper and gain power during the seven-year famine. Now Joseph's deeds had passed from memory, and the Egyptians no longer viewed the Hebrews as welcome guests; they viewed them as a national threat because of their sheer numbers.

The new pharaoh appointed slave drivers over the Hebrews and forced them to do backbreaking work. But the more brutally oppressed they were, the more the Hebrews multiplied. Finally, the pharaoh tried to control the population by ordering the Hebrew midwives to kill all newborn baby boys. The midwives feared God more than Pharaoh, and disobeyed the command. The Egyptians couldn't stop the Hebrew people from growing in numbers, but they made their lives miserable by harsh treatment.

We may not aspire to being second-in-command over a nation as Joseph was, but most of us occasionally dream about some reward or honor—something that would make us feel like we had reached the pinnacle of success. We can save ourselves grief by remembering how fickle public opinion is. Any earthly recognition will be short-lived at best. A better goal would be to please God and be honored by him. Any rewards or honor he gives will last throughout eternity.

We don't try to please people but God, who tests our motives.

1 Thessalonians 2:4

A Basket Case

Exodus 2

In a desperate attempt to control the Hebrew population in Egypt, Pharaoh issued a cruel edict. He commanded his people to throw every Hebrew newborn boy into the Nile River. One Hebrew baby was put into the Nile by his own mother—and ended up being raised in Pharaoh's palace. God had seen the plight of his chosen people, and he set a plan in motion for their rescue.

Moses's parents hid him from the Egyptians for three months; when that was no longer feasible, his mother waterproofed a basket, placed her son in it, and set it among the reeds near the riverbank. The pharaoh's daughter found the basket and the baby's cries melted her heart. Thanks to a quick-thinking big sister, Moses's own mother nursed and cared for him the first few years of his life. Then Pharaoh's daughter adopted him as her son.

Moses enjoyed a privileged life as a prince in Egypt, but as an adult he felt drawn to his own people. After he killed an Egyptian for beating a Hebrew, Moses had to flee the country. At age forty, he began working as a shepherd in the desert of Midian. His former life in Pharaoh's palace was gone, and he was separated from the people he wanted to help. Moses had no idea that God was preparing him for a very special role.

We all experience times when we feel oppressed and beaten down. During difficult times, we may remember the cliché that "God helps those who help themselves." But the truth is that God wants us to be dependent on him. He urges us to demonstrate our faith by calling out to him in times of trouble. Even if we don't see immediate relief, we can be sure that God has already set a plan in motion. There's no reason for our circumstances to make us a basket case when we have God's promise to rescue us.

> *Call on me in times of trouble.*
> *I will rescue you, and you will honor me.*
>
> Psalm 50:15

Who, Me?

Exodus 3–4

As Moses tended sheep on the far side of the desert one day, God got his attention. Moses saw a bush that was on fire but not burning up. When Moses's curiosity drew him close to the burning bush, God introduced himself as the God of Moses's ancestors. Frightened, Moses covered his face to avoid looking at God. When God announced the assignment he had in mind for the eighty-year-old shepherd, Moses tried to convince God that he had the wrong man.

God told Moses he would send him to confront Pharaoh and lead the Israelites out of Egypt. "Who am I that I should go to Pharaoh?" Moses asked (3:11). God promised Moses that he would be with him; he gave a detailed message for Moses to deliver to the Israelites. "They'll never believe me or listen to me!" Moses protested (4:1). Then God demonstrated how he would enable Moses to accomplish miracles that would prove he spoke for God. God temporarily turned Moses's staff into a snake, and inflicted his hand with a skin disease for a moment.

Still unconvinced, Moses argued that he wasn't a good speaker and often got tongue-tied. The Lord countered that just as he was the one who gave humans their mouths, he would give Moses the ability to speak and the right words to say. This time Moses angered God by asking him to send someone else to do the job. God graciously proposed a compromise: Moses's older brother Aaron would go with him and serve as his spokesman.

God often calls us to do something that falls way outside our comfort zone. Like Moses, we may even feel shocked by what he expects of us. But if God gives us an assignment, he will provide whatever we need to carry it out. Instead of focusing on our feelings of inadequacy, we can concentrate on God's power and his promise to provide the resources we require. Then we'll remember that it's not a question of our ability, but of his will.

I can do everything through Christ who strengthens me.

Philippians 4:13

God Plagues Pharaoh

Exodus 5—10

After Moses and Aaron explained their mission to the Hebrew leaders, they delivered a message to Pharaoh: the God of Israel commanded him to allow the Israelites to go into the desert to celebrate a festival. Pharaoh responded defiantly, "Who is the LORD? Why should I obey him?" (5:2). That same day, he added unreasonable demands to the slaves' workload, requiring them to gather their own straw while making the same number of bricks as before. Pharaoh's main concern was the possible loss of slave labor; he had no idea how much he would lose by opposing Yahweh.

Pharaoh refused a second chance to obey God's command, ignoring Moses's warning that God would turn the Nile River into blood. A week after this sign, God made all the bodies of water teem with frogs, which infested every home. This time Pharaoh agreed to let the Israelites go if God would remove the frogs. But the next day he reneged on his promise. So God turned the dust into biting gnats. For the first time, the Egyptian magicians couldn't duplicate the miracles.

Pharaoh clung to his stubbornness when God sent swarming flies to cover the Egyptians and fill their houses, when he killed their livestock, and when boils covered the people and animals. These signs were followed by violent hailstorms, an infestation of locusts, and darkness that covered the land. Throughout these plagues, Pharaoh sometimes relented but then changed his mind; other times he tried to strike a compromise. But he never surrendered to God's will—so the worst was yet to come.

Rebelling against God is always a dangerous choice. Even believers suffer from resisting his will. If we ignore his promptings or refuse to obey a direct command, we'll be plagued by uneasiness and a lack of peace. The longer we refuse to yield, the more we risk a hardened heart. When it comes to God's authority, the price of stubbornness is too high.

> *As the Holy Spirit says, "If you hear God*
> *speak today, don't be stubborn."*
>
> Hebrews 3:7

Passed Over

Exodus 11–12

God displayed his mercy by warning Pharaoh before several of the plagues struck Egypt, and by removing the plague whenever Pharaoh agreed to release the Israelites. When Pharaoh continued to harden his heart, God used the opportunity to reveal his power, giving the Egyptians a chance to turn from their many deities to the one true God. At last the time came for the final plague that would break Pharaoh's grip on Israel. Moses made a chilling announcement: at midnight, every firstborn son in Egypt would die.

Just as he had done before, God shielded the Israelites from the effects of this plague. But this time, God required them to follow specific instructions to ensure their protection. Each family was to kill an unblemished lamb and brush some of the blood on their doorframes. God promised that when he carried out his judgment on Egypt that night, he would pass over the homes that had blood on the doorframes.

God also commanded Israel to observe an annual celebration so they would always remember the day. He designed the Passover meal and Feast of Unleavened Bread to remind the people of their bitter years of slavery, their protection when God destroyed the Egyptian firstborn, and their hurried departure when God delivered them. The symbolism also pointed to the time when Christ, the Lamb of God, would be sacrificed at Passover to protect believers from the death penalty of sin.

Observing holidays and traditions helps us remember and reflect on spiritual truths. We can also celebrate milestones in our personal history. We might want to remember a decision that changed the course of our life. Or a time when God answered the deepest prayer of our heart or freed us from the grip of bondage. Since even our most precious memories fade with time, it helps to have something tangible to remind us of all that God has done in our life, and to point us toward the Lamb of God.

> *I remember the days long ago.*
> *I reflect on all that you have done.*
>
> Psalm 143:5

No Way Out

Exodus 13:17—14:31

After the tenth plague, Pharaoh finally urged Moses to take his people and leave Egypt at once. Later, he thought about the slave labor he had lost and changed his mind. Pharaoh set out with his army and hundreds of chariots in hot pursuit of the Israelites. The Egyptians were surprised to see Israel setting up camp by the Red Sea. *Aha!* they must have thought. *Now we've got you just where we want you.* In reality, God had the Israelites—and the Egyptians—just where *he* wanted them.

The Israelites' jubilant mood plunged into despair when they saw Pharaoh's immense army rushing toward them. In their eyes, they had been led into a trap. With the Red Sea in front and a powerful enemy behind, there seemed to be no way out. The terrified people railed against Moses for bringing them out of Egypt. Moses told Israel to stand still and see what God would do to rescue them.

The messenger of God, who had taken the form of a column of smoke, moved from the front of the Israelite camp to the back to prevent the Egyptians from drawing near. During that night, God sent a powerful wind to divide the water of the Red Sea. The astonished Israelites walked across on dry ground. When the Egyptian army tried to follow, the two walls of water crashed down and drowned them.

We're all familiar with that nauseating feeling of being trapped by our problems with no way out. Sometimes God puts us in difficult circumstances that help us learn to trust his power rather than our own. We can be sure that God is fighting for us as he did for Israel. His presence will lead and guide us and also cover our back. When there's nothing we can do to help ourselves, it's time to calm our fears, stand firm, and see what God will do to save us.

> Moses answered the people, "Don't be afraid! Stand still,
> and see what the LORD will do to save you today."
>
> Exodus 14:13

Manna on the Menu

Exodus 16

As the Israelites journeyed on into the desert, their food supplies soon ran out. This food shortage gave God an opportunity to test the people's trust and obedience, and to prove his faithfulness in providing for them. It also revealed the true condition of their hearts. The hungry Israelites reminisced about the good food they'd enjoyed in Egypt and accused Moses of dragging them into the desert to starve to death. Moses warned the Israelites that they were really grumbling against God. He also relayed God's promise to provide all the food they could eat.

That evening, God sent quail into the camp to satisfy the people's craving for meat. The next morning, after the dew dried, the Israelites found the ground covered with white flakes that tasted like wafers made with honey. God instructed them to gather only enough of this manna to feed their family for that day. When some people disobeyed and tried to hoard extra manna, it stunk and had worms by the next morning. To introduce the concept of a day of rest, God instructed the Israelites to gather and prepare twice as much manna on the sixth day. This extra portion did not spoil, providing food for the Sabbath.

God promises to meet his children's needs, but he doesn't promise to supply whatever we want. He also doesn't bestow everything we need all at once. God wants us to trust him to provide for us day by day, moment by moment. Once we learn to rely on him and accept whatever comes from his hand, we can experience freedom from worry.

We may not always like what's on the menu, but an attitude of complaining and continual dissatisfaction is a sin against our Provider. We'll find contentment when we grasp the truth that God promises to sustain us through any shortage. When we leave the providing up to God, we have more time to focus on obeying him and enjoying his daily blessings.

Give us our bread day by day.

Luke 11:3

Moses's Support Staff

Exodus 17:8—16

At Rephidim the Israelites faced their first battle; as always, God used the event to teach them more about their relationship with him. The Amalekites were a cruel, warlike nation descended from one of Esau's sons. When they started attacking the weary stragglers at the rear of the Israelite column, Moses called for his assistant Joshua to lead the battle against the Amalekites. In time, Joshua would prove himself to be a capable commander, but God planned for this military victory to be won in a most unusual way.

While the fighting raged, Moses stood on a nearby hill holding up his staff. As long as Moses held his hands up, Israel was winning the battle; when Moses lowered his hands, the Amalekites gained control. Eventually, Moses's hands felt so heavy he could no longer keep them raised. Aaron and Hur came to his aid. Seating Moses on a rock, the two men stood on either side of their leader and held up his arms. They maintained this position until sunset, when Israel defeated the Amalekites. The Israelites experienced their first military victory; in the process God reminded them of their dependence on his power and reiterated his choice of Moses as the nation's leader.

This Old Testament battle illustrates a valuable lesson for us today. All of us grow spiritually weary at times, especially when we're under attack from Satan, the enemy of our souls. Our leaders within the church are also vulnerable to battle fatigue. That's why God calls us to uphold those serving in the ministry as well as one another. Believers can strengthen each other by sharing the responsibilities of serving God, offering verbal encouragement, and being dedicated to intercessory prayer. It's important for us to be sensitive to the needs of others so that when a fellow believer grows weary, we can stand by them and help hold them up.

Encourage each other and strengthen
one another as you are doing.
1 Thessalonians 5:11

Ten Commandments

Exodus 19:1—20:21

A couple of months after Israel escaped from Egypt, they came to the desert at Sinai, where they camped for almost a year. The place where God spoke with Moses from a burning bush also served as the location for one of the most important events in Israel's history. Here God gave Israel the terms of the covenant he was making with his chosen people. If they faithfully obeyed his laws, they would be his own special possession out of all the nations, a kingdom of priests and a holy people.

On top of Mount Sinai, God gave Moses the ten basic commandments that formed the core of the covenant stipulations. The first four commandments dealt with the Israelites' relationship with God, forbidding them to have any other god or to make an idol to worship, and admonishing them to treat God's name with reverence and observe a day of rest and worship. The remaining six described proper relationships between members of the community. Israelites were expected to honor their parents and to refrain from murder, adultery, stealing, lying, and desiring to have what belonged to someone else.

Israel discovered that they could not keep God's standards by their own power; the Mosaic law showed them their sinful condition and their need for a Savior. The Bible makes it clear that "people don't receive God's approval because of their own efforts to live according to a set of standards, but only by believing in Jesus Christ" (Gal. 2:16). Believers today live not under the old Law, but in the grace that Jesus died to make available.

The Ten Commandments still provide good instructions for living in proper relationship with God and others. As God's chosen people, we are called to be set apart by our morally pure lifestyle and to act as mediators between God and those around us. The ten steps found in Exodus 20 are a good beginning point.

You are chosen people, a royal priesthood,
a holy nation, people who belong to God.

1 Peter 2:9

The Ultimate Treasure Chest

Exodus 25:10—22

God gave Moses directions for constructing the furnishings of the tabernacle before he described the tent itself. He began with the most important and sacred article, the ark of the covenant, which was a wooden chest overlaid with gold. The chest had a solid gold lid, often called the mercy seat or atonement cover. On top of the lid, carved from the same piece of gold, sat two cherubim with their wings outstretched and their faces looking downward. The mercy seat, or throne of mercy, represented God's throne where he would meet and speak with Moses.

According to Hebrews 9:4, the ark contained the stone tablets that God engraved with the Ten Commandments, a jar of manna, and Aaron's staff that budded, blossomed, and produced almonds (see Num. 17:1–11). The ark was the only object in the most holy place, hidden at all times by the curtain that separated this forbidden inner section from the rest of the tabernacle. Since the ark was never to be touched by human hands, the Israelites carried it with poles that stayed in place at all times. Once a year the high priest entered the most holy place and sprinkled blood on the mercy seat to atone for the sins of the people.

The arrangement of the ark in the tabernacle emphasized the fact that our sin separates us from a holy God. After Jesus died to pay for the sins of the world, that separation was no longer necessary. God took on human form and sacrificed himself so that we can come near to him. If we've accepted God's gift of salvation, we've been cleansed of our sins and have free access to God's throne room. Through Jesus Christ, God did all that was necessary to remove the barrier between us and him. The natural response to such a great love is to walk right into his presence.

> *Brothers and sisters, because of the blood of Jesus*
> *we can now confidently go into the holy place.*
>
> Hebrews 10:19

A House for God

Exodus 25—30

Most of the second half of Exodus focuses on God's instructions for building a tabernacle and relates how those directions were carried out. During the forty days that Moses spent on Mount Sinai, God described a blueprint for a sanctuary, or holy place, where he would live among the Israelites. The plans covered every detail of the tent and its furnishings, including the dimensions, materials, colors, and exact placement of objects. God made it clear that he expected his people to worship him according to his directions, not on the basis of their own ideas or those of surrounding nations.

God's plans called for costly materials to be used, with objects inside the tent being overlaid or constructed with gold to illustrate God's greatness and majesty. Other requirements included silver, bronze, fine linen, and precious stones. When God requested voluntary donations of these supplies, the Israelites could easily see how God had planned ahead for their future. As they had left their life of slavery, God had instructed them to ask the Egyptians for gold and silver jewelry and clothing. God prompted the Egyptians to be extra generous, so that the Israelites left with much of Egypt's wealth (see Exod. 12:35–36).

God also arranged the tent and its equipment to be portable, illustrating his desire to be with the Israelites as they traveled. Today, believers are God's dwelling place on earth, but sometimes we act as though he only lives in a church building. God never intended for his people to attend services on Sunday and then forget about him the remaining six days of the week. Since our heavenly Father lives in us, we can go to him at any time for worship, prayer, and communion. God desires to be with us on every step of our life's journey. How could we try to relegate him to a building and ignore his standing invitation to seek his face?

When you said,
"Seek my face,"
my heart said to you,
"O Lord, I will seek your face."

Psalm 27:8

A Day of Rest

Exodus 31:12—17

The fourth commandment acted as a sign of the covenant between God and Israel. Observing a special day of rest and worship each week helped the people remember what God had done for them when he delivered them out of slavery in Egypt. The break from work restored their bodies and refreshed their spirits. The Sabbath also served as a test of their commitment to God and their willingness to obey him. Failure to observe the Sabbath day of rest brought separation from the community that resulted in death.

God reminded Israel that he had set the example himself by creating the heavens and earth in six days, then stopping work on the seventh day. The concept of the Sabbath identified Israel with their Creator and marked the nation as a unique community of people that belonged to him.

By Jesus's day, the religious leaders had made the complicated rules and regulations surrounding the Sabbath more important than the original intent of the command. When Pharisees criticized Jesus for healing on the Sabbath, he challenged their distorted view (see Mark 2:23–27). Jesus declared that the Sabbath was made for the benefit of people, not the other way around.

While believers today are not required to observe the Sabbath as a law, the principle still holds value for us. Setting aside a special day to focus on communion with God refreshes our spirit and reenergizes us for further service. Taking a rest from work restores our body and mind. It's easy to convince ourselves that we're too busy to take a day off. But if we choose to honor God in this way, we'll understand that God gave the fourth commandment to benefit people, not to burden them. If we follow God's example, we'll discover that taking a Sabbath rest—on any day of the week—is a valuable gift that God has given us.

The day of worship was made for people,
not people for the day of worship.

Mark 2:27

The Gold Calf

Exodus 32

The Israelites grew nervous while waiting for Moses to come down from Mount Sinai; they feared he would never return. So they went to Aaron and asked him to make gods for them to follow. Although they had seen mighty displays of Yahweh's power, they wanted something tangible to represent this invisible God. Aaron collected their gold earrings and crafted a statue of a calf. The familiarity of the image may have comforted the Israelites since the Egyptians used a bull and heifer to represent two of their gods. The Canaanites around them worshiped Baal, who was portrayed as a bull.

Aaron also made an altar, and the next day the people sacrificed the same offerings as when they had committed to follow God's covenant (see Exod. 24:5). Soon their "festival in the LORD's honor" dissolved into drunkenness and immorality. The people had now broken at least two of the commandments they had promised to obey. God's anger burned so hot that he threatened to destroy them all, but Moses pleaded on Israel's behalf. Still, such a serious breach of the covenant and blatant rebellion against God demanded judgment. Several thousand people who had participated in the idolatry were put to death.

We may scoff at the Israelites' ridiculous behavior in this incident, but sometimes we're not so different from them. We've all been tempted to try to reshape God according to our desires, personal needs, or our present circumstances. Sometimes we allow our idea of God to be determined by how those around us portray him.

The Israelites had no excuse for breaking the commandments they had received directly from God. We have no excuse for not having an accurate view of God since he's revealed himself and his character through his written Word and through Jesus. The New Testament teaches that Christ is God in the flesh; the Son is the exact likeness of the Father. We may worship an invisible God, but all we have to do to see him is look at Jesus.

He is the image of the invisible God.

Colossians 1:15

Jesus in Exodus

The book of Exodus doesn't contain any specific prophecies related to the Messiah, but Jesus is pictured in it from beginning to end. We see him in the Passover lamb, in the seven feasts and festivals that God commands, in the role of the high priest, and in numerous aspects of Moses's life. The New Testament compares Jesus with the manna that fed the Israelites in the desert (see John 6:48–58) and with the life-giving water from the rock (see 1 Cor. 10:3–4). The tabernacle, its furnishings, and their arrangements all mesh together to paint a vivid portrait of Christ and his future work of redemption.

Upon entering the tabernacle courtyard, the Israelites first encountered the altar of burnt offering, pointing to Jesus's sacrifice of himself. After a person's animal had been sacrificed, the priest stopped at the bronze basin to wash himself, picturing the blood of Christ that cleanses us from sin. Then the priest passed through a curtain into the holy place, which contained three objects.

The golden lampstand burned at all times, symbolizing Christ as the light of the world. The table that always held bread represented Christ, the bread that came down from heaven. The altar of incense spoke of Christ's role of intercessory prayer on our behalf. Beyond the next curtain stood the ark with its atonement cover, a testimony to the atonement that Jesus would achieve once and for all.

The New Testament explains that the observances under the old covenant foreshadowed a future reality centered on Jesus Christ. Through his ministry, death, burial, and resurrection, Jesus fulfilled everything that the tabernacle, Mosaic laws, sacrifices, festivals, and special holy days represented. Even so, we can still get caught up in rituals, regulations, and external shows of faith. We want to make sure that we're not focusing on mere shadows; after all, we are privileged to know Christ, who is the real thing.

> *These are a shadow of the things to come, but the*
> *body that casts the shadow belongs to Christ.*
>
> Colossians 2:17

Leviticus

How to Worship and Walk in Holiness

> Live holy lives. Be holy because I am the LORD your God. Obey my laws, and live by them. I am the LORD who sets you apart as holy.
>
> Leviticus 20:7–8

At the end of Exodus, God has delivered Israel from slavery in Egypt, the tabernacle has been completed, and God's glory has filled the tabernacle. But how can a holy God live among a people prone to sin? How are they to approach him? The book of Leviticus picks up the story as God teaches his people how he desires to be worshiped and how he expects their lives to reflect his holiness. Still camped at the base of Mount Sinai, the Israelites will receive training in how to be a people set apart from the nations around them.

Because sin must be dealt with before true worship takes place, the opening chapters lay out a system of sacrifices and offerings, explaining the work of the priests as mediators between God and the people. Next, God gives purity laws and instructions for living a holy life, covering family and social responsibilities, sexual behavior, and all levels of relationships. Leviticus closes with God announcing special observances and celebrations to help the Israelites remember his goodness and rededicate themselves to his service.

Jewish children studied the book of Leviticus, yet many Christians today ignore it. A grasp of Leviticus is necessary for understanding many New Testament passages, including the book of Hebrews. The New Testament writers refer to Leviticus dozens of times to explain what Jesus did on the cross and to encourage believers to live for Christ.

The Old Testament system of sacrifices ended when Jesus paid for our sins; ancient rituals have been replaced by contemporary worship practices. But Leviticus serves as a reminder that sin disrupts our fellowship with God. It offers spiritual truths to help us live a life pleasing to God. Since God repeated his command to "be holy" in the New Testament (see 1 Pet. 1:16), we can be sure that the message of Leviticus is relevant to our lives today.

Living Sacrifices

Leviticus 1–7

The idea of animal sacrifices may seem repulsive today, but the Israelites were familiar with the concept. At the time, many cultures and religions sacrificed animals to try to please or appease their gods. In contrast, the sacrificial system designed by God held benefits for Israel. The animal's death reminded the people that there had to be payment for sin. Their obedience to the regulations represented a way for them to seek forgiveness and reconciliation. Most importantly, each element of the ritual pictured the perfect Sacrifice who would one day make the final payment for sin.

The first seven chapters of Leviticus describe the five different types of offerings that were sacrificed. The burnt offering atoned for sins in general, while the sin offering covered unintentional sins. A guilt offering paid for a specific sin and included restitution when appropriate. In these offerings involving cattle, sheep, or goats, the person laid his hand on the animal's head to symbolize his identification with the animal as his substitute. The grain offering acknowledged respect for God and the peace offering expressed gratitude for God's fellowship.

God demanded that the Israelites obey the rules surrounding the system of sacrifices, but he was more interested in their attitudes. Periodically throughout Israel's history, God complained that their sacrifices had become nothing more than empty rituals. They made an outward show of devotion but had no heart for living a life of obedience.

God is still displeased when his people go through the motions of worship while lacking a repentant attitude or a desire to serve him. Instead of dead animals, today God calls us to offer him ourselves—body, mind, and soul. Belonging to God means that we continually set aside our personal desires and put all that we have and all that we are at his disposal. Because of Jesus, we don't need to offer a sacrifice for sin, but out of gratitude we can offer our life back to God.

> *I encourage you to offer your bodies as living*
> *sacrifices, dedicated to God and pleasing to him.*
>
> Romans 12:1

Unauthorized Fire

Leviticus 8:1–10

Through Moses, God prepared Aaron and his sons to serve as priests and mediators between himself and the Israelites. After a seven-day ordination service, the historic moment arrived for daily sacrifices at the tabernacle to begin. After Aaron offered the sacrifices, God revealed his glory to all the people. To express his approval of the offerings, he sent out supernatural fire to consume the partially burned sacrifices on the altar. Filled with awe, the people shouted and bowed in worship.

Then disaster struck.

God had given a precise explanation of how he wanted to be served and worshiped, but Aaron's two oldest sons decided to try a variation. Nadab and Abihu used their censers to offer "unauthorized fire" in the Lord's presence. Perhaps they took the coals from another source instead of the altar, as God had commanded. In any case, the day's sacrificial ritual had already ended. Leviticus 16:1–2 indicates that the two men tried to enter the most holy place; 10:8–11 hints that they were drunk. Regardless of their motivation, God could not allow this violation of his holiness. The brothers' presumption and willful disobedience brought instant death by fire.

The sobering story of Nadab and Abihu reminds us that no one can approach God in his own way. This goes against the teaching of a culture that worships diversity and claims that one belief system is as good as any other. The Bible teaches that the only way to come to God and have a relationship with him is through Jesus Christ.

While believers are free to approach God at any time, we would be wise to do an attitude check. Do we treat him with the reverence he deserves, or have we become flippant and presumptuous? To have the right perspective, we need to remember what a high price God paid so that we can freely enter his presence. There is one way to God and one right way to approach him.

Jesus answered him, "I am the way, the truth, and the life. No one goes to the Father except through me."

John 14:6

The Day of Atonement

Leviticus 16

After the drunken intrusion into the most holy place by two of Aaron's sons, God explained that even the high priest could not enter his presence whenever he wanted to. The high priest would be allowed to approach God one day each year, following the preparations and rituals described by God. The Day of Atonement, or Yom Kippur, became the most important date in the Jewish calendar. On this day, the high priest made peace with God and atoned for the sins of Israel from the previous year.

After preparing himself, Aaron sacrificed a bull for the sins of his own household and sprinkled blood on the throne of mercy. Next, he drew lots for two goats that had been brought before him. The first goat was sacrificed to pay for the sins of the people. Aaron used its blood to purify all the areas of the tabernacle so that God could continue to live among his people.

Aaron then laid his hands on the second goat and confessed the people's sins before sending it out into the desert. The releasing of the second goat signified that Israel's guilt had been removed for another year. The ceremony ended with rams being sacrificed for the high priest's and the people's sins.

If we are believers, Christ has permanently atoned for and removed our sins. Even so, we will struggle with our sinful nature for the rest of our earthly life. It's important to daily examine our thoughts and behavior for sins that we need to address. If we don't, these sins will become an impediment to our fellowship with God and will hinder our spiritual growth. God wants us to enjoy an intimate relationship with him and a life free from a guilty conscience. He no longer requires animal sacrifices but still looks for what he wanted all along: honest repentance and confession of sin.

> *God is faithful and reliable. If we confess our sins, he forgives them and cleanses us from everything we've done wrong.*
>
> 1 John 1:9

The Jubilee Year

Leviticus 25

Leviticus 23 describes the national feasts and festivals that God planned for Israel. These celebrations helped the people remember what God had done for them, encouraged appropriate worship, and set aside special times of rest, rejoicing, and fellowship. Chapter 25 adds two additional observances that God designed to shape Israel into a holy people and to set them apart from the surrounding nations whose celebrations were often based on immorality.

God commanded Israel to allow the land to have a Sabbath rest every seventh year after they entered Canaan. During these years there would be no planting or harvesting of produce to sell, yet God promised that the land would yield enough food for all the people and animals in the nation. This special observance reminded Israel that God was really the one who owned and controlled the land. It also symbolized and proved his faithful provision for their needs.

Every fiftieth year, the people celebrated the Year of Jubilee. The blowing of rams' horns proclaimed liberty throughout the land, as all Hebrew slaves were freed and could return to the property inherited by their family. Land that had been sold, with a few exceptions, reverted to its original owner. The Year of Jubilee kept families and their inherited lands intact, and it prevented permanent poverty since every fifty years all debts were canceled.

The Sabbath and Year of Jubilee principles apply to believers every day of every year. The sacrifice that Jesus made for us gives us rest from working to try to earn God's approval. It also canceled our sin debt, which we could never have repaid. But through that transaction, we incurred another debt. Since we have experienced God's love and mercy through Jesus Christ, we have a lifelong obligation to share that love with everyone we meet. If we're thankful that God has settled our sin debt, we'll be glad to make a payment on our debt of love every day.

> *One debt you can never finish paying is the*
> *debt of love that you owe each other.*
>
> Romans 13:8

Numbers

Wandering in the Wilderness

Since the LORD was angry with the Israelites, he made them wander in the desert for 40 years until the whole generation of those who had done evil in the LORD's presence was gone.

Numbers 32:13

God completed the Israelites' orientation while they were still camped at the base of Mount Sinai. He'd already given them rules for living and worshiping; now he described a plan to organize the camps of the two-million-plus multitude so they could march to the Promised Land in an orderly fashion. Finally, the time came for the people to move out and claim their inheritance—and what should have been an eleven-day trip turned into forty years of wandering.

Numbers contains a great deal of statistical information, but the book is an account of Israel's journey from Sinai to the borders of Canaan and their struggle with unbelief and disobedience on the way. (The itinerary is listed in chapter 33.) Despite God's efforts to prepare them, the people complained, grumbled, and rebelled against Moses and God. When the moment came to enter Canaan, they chose to be controlled by their fear rather than believe God's promises. Their lack of faith doomed them to forty years of wandering in the wilderness until that unbelieving generation died.

Despite the Israelites' many failures, Numbers ends on a hopeful note. A new generation is poised to cross the Jordan River and enter the Promised Land. The Israelites have experienced victory over some formidable enemies, but have they conquered their own tendency toward unbelief? Have they learned to trust God enough to move forward and claim what is rightfully theirs?

First Corinthians 10:11 explains that God recorded Israel's early history to serve as a warning to others of the consequences of disobedience and unbelief. God may lead us through some wilderness experiences of our own. But if we heed the lessons in Numbers, we'll spend less time wandering in circles and more time enjoying the blessings of our spiritual inheritance.

A Bad Report

Numbers 13:1—14:38

When Israel reached the southern edge of Canaan, God had Moses send out twelve leaders to explore the land. These men spent forty days traveling throughout Canaan, a round-trip of five hundred miles. Their report confirmed that the land was rich and fertile; they exhibited a cluster of grapes that required two men to carry it on a pole. Then they shared the bad news: Israel had no hope of conquering such large, well-fortified cities filled with people whose size made the spies feel like grasshoppers.

Joshua and Caleb reminded the people that they had God's protection and he would give them the power to overcome their enemies. Unfortunately, the people chose to listen to the mixture of exaggeration and lies from the other ten spies. They discussed choosing a new leader and returning to Egypt. When they talked about stoning Moses and Aaron, the Lord threatened to destroy them.

Once again, Moses interceded for the Israelites; once again, God forgave them. But he vowed that they would wander in the desert for forty years as punishment for their unbelief. During that time, every Israelite age twenty years or older would die. Out of that generation, only Joshua and Caleb would enter the Promised Land, because they had believed God's promise to give it to his people.

Whenever we face a tough situation or decision, we have the same choice to make as the Israelites did. Will we let ourselves be intimidated by how things look, or will we take God at his word? If we concentrate on the intimidating aspects of our circumstances or listen to others' negative opinions, our faith may falter. God wants us to focus on his character and power, trusting that his promises will be fulfilled even when the obstacles make us feel small. Then we can be like Caleb and Joshua, ready to take possession of all that the Lord intends for us.

Indeed, our lives are guided by faith, not by sight.

2 Corinthians 5:7

The Danger of Dissatisfaction

Numbers 16–17

As a Levite, Korah enjoyed the high privilege of serving God in the tabernacle. After a while, that wasn't enough—he wanted to fill the role of priest, a position granted only to Aaron's sons. Korah spread his discontent to 250 prominent Israelite leaders, and together they confronted Moses. Korah accused Moses and Aaron of setting themselves above the rest of the Israelites and reminded them that God had called the entire nation his holy people. Dathan and Abiram, two of Korah's coconspirators, chastised Moses for pulling them away from the comforts and abundant food of Egypt only to kill them in the desert.

Moses warned Korah and his followers that they were actually rebelling against the Lord. He challenged them to gather at the tabernacle the next morning with incense burners; Aaron would do the same. God would reveal his choice for the priesthood and for Israel's leadership.

The next day brought swift judgment as the ground opened and swallowed up the ringleaders along with their families and possessions. God sent fire to destroy the 250 men offering incense. Instead of learning the obvious lesson, the rest of the Israelites complained that Moses had done the killing and banded together to oppose him and Aaron. As a result, 14,700 people died from a plague.

Korah had enjoyed the status of an influential leader; Exodus 6 mentions him as one of the chief men of Israel. But because of his distorted ambition for more power and prestige, he lost all he had. Korah's life story reminds us of the dangers of wanting more than what we've been given. If left unchecked, a persistent feeling of dissatisfaction can lead us into bitterness, resentment, and jealousy, culminating in open rebellion against God and others. Rather than looking around at what others have, we would be better off learning to be content with what God has given us and where he has placed us. If we don't, we may be swallowed up by our own dissatisfaction.

I've learned to be content in whatever situation I'm in.

Philippians 4:11

Water from a Rock

Numbers 20:1–13

Thirty-seven years of wandering brought the Israelites back to Kadesh, the place where they had let themselves be frightened by the spies' negative reports instead of trusting God. Most of that older generation had died off. Those who were left had already forgotten that their disobedience had caused their problems. When they found the springs at Kadesh dry, they fell into their old familiar routine: they whined, complained, and blamed Moses for their circumstances.

God told Moses to take his staff and, together with Aaron, gather the community. As the people watched, Moses would tell the rock to give up its water. Moses had always been careful to do exactly what God commanded, but this time he slipped up. Instead of speaking to the rock, the exasperated leader addressed the people: "Listen, you rebels, must we bring water out of this rock for you?" Then he hit the rock twice with his staff (vv. 10–11).

Water gushed out of the rock, but Moses and Aaron paid a penalty for not strictly adhering to God's instruction. Besides disobeying a direct command, they had dishonored God by drawing attention to their own authority. Moses's words gave the impression that he and Aaron were providing the water rather than God. As a result, the two brothers lost the privilege of entering the Promised Land.

As leaders and role models for Israel, Moses and Aaron had the responsibility to help people see God and recognize his provision. As believers, we are responsible for pointing people to Jesus Christ. Any gift, resource, or opportunity that comes our way is to be used to shine the spotlight on him. Our human nature often desires to draw attention to our own achievements; we're especially vulnerable if we serve in positions of authority or high visibility. Remembering how much Moses's lapse cost him will remind us to direct people's eyes to Jesus, not to us.

*Our message is not about ourselves. It is
about Jesus Christ as the Lord.*

2 Corinthians 4:5

Balaam and His Talking Donkey

Numbers 22:1–35

The news of Israel's military victories terrified Balak, the king of Moab. Balak decided to hire Balaam, a famous sorcerer, to curse Israel so that he could defeat them. Although he was a pagan prophet, Balaam wanted to try to consult Israel's God. When the Lord warned him not to go with Balak's messengers, Balaam sent them away. Balak then sent a more impressive envoy with a promise that Balaam would be richly rewarded for his services. Although Balaam vowed that no amount of wealth would make him disobey the Lord's command, he offered to consult the Lord again. This time God permitted Balaam to go to Moab, on the condition he would only do as God told him.

Riding his donkey, Balaam set off on the nearly four-hundred-mile trip to Moab. On the way, God intervened to stop the prophet. Although Balaam couldn't see the messenger of the Lord, his donkey could. Three times she turned aside or lay down, and each time Balaam hit her. Finally, God allowed the donkey to ask Balaam why he had beaten her. The enraged prophet vowed that he would kill her if he had a sword. Then God opened Balaam's eyes to see how his donkey had saved his life.

At first glance, it seems that God suddenly changed his mind about allowing Balaam to go to Moab. But according to 2 Peter 2:15 and Jude 11, Balaam loved money and wanted to make a profit. In spite of Balaam's words about obedience, God knew his true intentions.

We're all like Balaam sometimes. When we desire something, we can easily rationalize our willful behavior while ignoring our heart attitude that displeases God. We may convince ourselves we're innocent and even look that way to others, but God sees the motives behind our actions. We need to rely on prayer, the Bible, and God's Holy Spirit to keep us from being self-deceived. We don't all have a donkey to talk sense into us.

> *A person thinks all his ways are pure,*
> *but the LORD weighs motives.*

Proverbs 16:2

Balaam's Response

Numbers 22:36—24:25

When Balaam arrived in Moab, Balak took him to a mountaintop with a view of Israel's camp spread out below. The men offered pagan sacrifices as part of divination rituals, then Balaam went to a solitary place. God gave him a message about Israel's special status in God's eyes. This infuriated Balak; he took Balaam to a different mountaintop, still hoping for a curse against Israel. Once again Balaam blessed Israel, prompting another change in location.

This time Balaam abandoned his attempts at using sorcery, and God's Spirit came upon him. Balaam declared that God had opened his eyes to see how he had redeemed and protected his chosen people. The prophet also alluded to Israel's future powerful monarchy and prosperity. The angry Moabite king dismissed Balaam with no payment. Before Balaam left, he shared a fourth prophecy about Israel's conquest of nations, including Moab, under King David.

God graciously revealed much about himself and his people to Balaam. The pagan prophet could have renounced his old way of life, turned from his false gods to Yahweh, and shared in the blessings; instead he responded by returning to his home and his practice of sorcery. At some point, he advised Balak to send Moabite women to entice Israel into sexual immorality and idolatry (see Num. 31:16; Rev. 2:14). Later, when Israel attacked Midian, Balaam was killed in the battle.

Although Balaam professed obedience to the Lord and even spoke by God's Spirit for a brief time, it didn't change his life. Paul warned believers not to be fooled by people who have an external appearance of godliness but lack the working of the Holy Spirit. It's easy to look spiritual on the outside, even experiencing occasional bursts of excitement for God. But the real test is a life transformed by God's power. If we have truly accepted what God offers us, we will never want to go back to our old life.

> *They will act religious, but they will reject the*
> *power that could make them godly.*
>
> 2 Timothy 3:5 NLT

A Bold Request

Numbers 27:1–11

As Israel looked ahead to the allocation of land in Canaan, five women approached Moses with an unprecedented request. Their father, Zelophehad, had died in the wilderness along with the rest of his unbelieving generation, leaving only daughters behind. Since Hebrew law allowed only sons to inherit land and possessions, Zelophehad's name would die out. Zelophehad's daughters asked to be given the land that would have been assigned to their father. This would ensure the preservation of the family line, something that God obviously valued.

This unique situation stumped Moses and he took the case to the Lord. Agreeing with Zelophehad's daughters, God instructed Moses to give them their father's inheritance in the Promised Land. God also dictated a permanent law that would address any future cases where a father died without having sons. Later, God added the stipulation that women who inherited land had to marry within their own tribe in order to keep it. This would ensure that tribal lands remained intact.

It's hard for us to appreciate the boldness of the request made by Zelophehad's daughters in the light of cultural attitudes that often viewed women as property. But we can relate their example to our prayer life. These women didn't let intimidation or the status quo keep them from asking for what they wanted; if they had, they would have missed out on the blessings of receiving an inheritance of land and preserving their family name. How often do we miss out on material and spiritual blessings simply because we don't ask for them?

Holding back from bringing our requests to God often demonstrates a lack of trust in his goodness. As long as we're seeking God's will and asking with proper motives, God is pleased with boldness in our prayer life. He loves to lavish gifts on his children. If we approach him in faith and humility, we may be surprised at the unprecedented answers we receive.

> *You don't have the things you want,*
> *because you don't pray for them.*
>
> James 4:2

Joining the Fight

Numbers 32

The tribes of Reuben and Gad noticed that the land east of the Jordan River (sometimes called the Transjordan area) would make excellent grazing country for their large numbers of livestock. Since the land had already been cleared of enemies, they asked permission to settle in the area. Their request shocked Moses. He feared that their unwillingness to cross the Jordan would discourage the other tribes from entering the land that God had promised to give Israel. Moses reminded them how the previous generation had lost heart about the conquest after the spies' negative report, bringing God's judgment. He accused the tribes of Gad and Reuben of being just like their ancestors.

The men of Reuben and Gad assured Moses that they had no desire to shirk their responsibility to help conquer the Promised Land. After they built pens for their livestock and cities for their families to live in, their fighting men would head the army invading Canaan. The two tribes would not return to their homes until every Israelite had taken possession of his own land. Moses agreed to this proposal. On condition that they keep their promise, he assigned the Transjordan area to be the inheritance of Reuben, Gad, and half the tribe of Manasseh.

As believers, we all have the responsibility to fight for each other. Unfortunately, it's easy to get so comfortable in our own little pew that we ignore the struggles of the people around us. Our prayers can dissolve into nothing more than self-centered petitions without us noticing it. God grants us the privilege of interceding for others as they battle against sin and our common enemy, Satan. Our efforts may help a fellow believer conquer an enemy or claim their rightful spiritual inheritance. Just as God still fights for his people today, he still expects us to work together. Will we shirk our responsibility, or will we cross the Jordan River and join in the fight?

> *Stay alert and be persistent in your prayers*
> *for all believers everywhere.*
>
> Ephesians 6:18 NLT

Jesus in Numbers

Numbers 21:4–9

Even God's patience has limits—and the Israelites kept testing those limits. Despite the miracles God had performed to rescue them and to provide for their needs, the people still didn't trust him. God heard their complaints about the long journey and their whining about the lack of variety in their diet. They even accused God of intending to let them die in the wilderness. This passage marks the eighth recorded incident of the Israelites complaining and murmuring. And this time they went too far.

The people's refusal to believe God's promises angered him, and he judged their sin by letting poisonous snakes bite many. Soon the Israelites repented. They begged Moses to intercede on their behalf as he had done before. The Lord responded by having Moses make a bronze snake mounted on a pole. When a person was bitten, they could be healed by looking up at the snake. This simple act of obedience to God's instruction demonstrated their belief in him.

Centuries later, Jesus revealed that the bronze snake pictured his role as Savior of the world. Just as Moses lifted up the snake on a pole, Jesus would be lifted up on a cross to cure people of something far deadlier than a snake bite. By "looking up" to Jesus's sacrifice on our behalf, we can receive healing from the disease of sin. Just as God provided a way for the Israelites to escape death as punishment for their disbelief, he has provided a way for us to escape the penalty that sin brings.

Jesus endured a horrible death to take away the punishment for our sin. When we choose to accept God's offer, his healing presence enters our life and we can look forward to a new life cleansed of sin. To think—the ultimate cure begins with the simple act of looking up!

> As Moses lifted up the snake on a pole in the desert,
> so the Son of Man must be lifted up. Then everyone
> who believes in him will have eternal life.
>
> John 3:14–15

Deuteronomy

Choices for a New Generation

> He is a faithful God, who keeps his promise and is merciful to thousands of generations of those who love him and obey his commands.
>
> Deuteronomy 7:9

Moses wrote the fifth book in the Pentateuch near the end of the fifteenth century BC. A new generation is camped on the east side of the Jordan River with Canaan in sight. Their parents have died in the wilderness because of sin and unbelief; the current generation now stands ready to claim the inheritance of land promised to Abraham and his descendants. But first, Moses calls for a renewed commitment to God and the covenant terms.

Deuteronomy follows the structure of a treaty commonly used in Moses's time between a king and his vassal country. The content is a series of messages that Moses delivered in a month-long review session to prepare the Israelites for the monumental step they were about to take. First, Moses summarized Israel's history, emphasizing God's past faithfulness to the nation and warning them not to repeat their ancestors' mistakes. Next, he reviewed the laws, including interpretations for various situations.

Finally, Moses restated the terms of God's covenant with Israel. He urged the Israelites to obey and love the Lord so they could enjoy his promised blessings. After officially handing over the reins of leadership to Joshua, Moses taught the Israelites a new song reminding them of God's kindness, their obligation to obey him, and the consequences of failing to do so. Moses ended by offering each tribe a special blessing from God. The final chapter, probably written by Joshua, tells of Moses's death at age 120.

Believers today face the same choices as this generation of Israelites did. We can learn from the mistakes of others who lived before us, or we can repeat them. We can either enjoy a fulfilling life by obeying God's commands, or suffer the consequences of disobedience. Deuteronomy reminds us that if we want to claim our rightful spiritual inheritance, we need to continually renew our dedication to our faithful, covenant-keeping God.

Battle Plan

Deuteronomy 20

As God prepared the Israelites for their conquest of the Promised Land, he restated his promise to fight for them and listed several reasons for exemption from military duty. Then he laid down general guidelines for warfare, making a distinction between cities outside the borders of Canaan and those within it. Israel would offer cities at a distance a chance to surrender. If they refused and initiated war, every man would be executed and the women and children taken along with the plunder. When the Israelites came to cities that were part of their inheritance, they were to completely wipe out the people and animals.

Many people wonder how a just and merciful God could order the destruction of entire populations. We forget that in order to be just, God has to punish sin. He had already patiently waited for these nations to turn from their sin; instead they plunged deeper into degradation, sexual perversion, and in some cases, human sacrifice. God knew that cohabitation with pagan nations would end in disaster for the Israelites as they would be lured into immorality and idolatry. God's ultimate goal in establishing the nation of Israel was to reveal himself and draw people to him so they could accept his gift of salvation freely offered to the world.

We live under the New Testament principles of grace and mercy toward our enemies, but when it comes to sin, God wants us to be ruthless. The moment we believe in Jesus as our Savior, God initiates the process of making us holy through his Spirit. He expects us to participate in the lifelong process by battling any tendencies to follow our old nature when it fights against our desire to please God. Since there's no such thing as a harmless sin, any compromise is dangerous. God's battle plan is clear: wipe out any sinful desires, attitudes, and habits before they lead us into disaster.

> *Put to death whatever is worldly in you: your sexual sin, perversion, passion, lust, and greed (which is the same thing as worshiping wealth).*

Colossians 3:5

Good News and Bad News

Deuteronomy 28:1–30:14

Before he passed the baton of Israel's leadership to Joshua, Moses led the people in a covenant renewal ceremony. He recounted the blessings they would enjoy if they chose to obey God's commands and resist following other gods. If Israel kept her end of the covenant agreement, God promised to place her high above all other nations on earth and to grant financial prosperity, military strength, and abundance in every aspect of life. Moses also relayed God's warning that unfaithfulness and disobedience would bring every imaginable affliction on the people and the land, culminating in captivity and exile.

In Deuteronomy 28:45 Moses began treating the curses as a reality instead of a possible scenario. What follows is a sad preview of Israel's future. After leading the Israelites for so many years, Moses knew that they would soon rebel against God again, bringing disaster on themselves. But Moses also knew God's character. He told the people that when they returned to God and obeyed him with all their heart and soul, they would find mercy and forgiveness. God would not only restore their fortunes; he would give them a new will to love and obey him.

Soon after we accept the Good News about the salvation that Jesus made possible, we learn some bad news. No matter how much we love God, our human heart still has a tendency to stray. Giving in to that sinful nature can block our communication and fellowship with God.

One of Satan's favorite tricks is to convince us that we've gone too far and messed up so badly that we'll never enjoy God's blessings again. But the Bible clearly teaches that God stands ready to forgive his children when they turn away from their sin and return to a committed, obedient relationship with him. We can never go so far that we're outside the reach of his mercy. And that is truly great news.

> *You, O Lord, are good and forgiving,*
> *full of mercy toward everyone who calls out to you.*
>
> Psalm 86:5

Joshua

Taking Possession of the Promised Land

> Now you and all these people must cross the Jordan River into the land that I am going to give the people of Israel. I will give you every place on which you set foot, as I promised Moses.
>
> Joshua 1:2–3

A new generation has inherited the ancient promises first given to Abraham, Isaac, and Jacob. The disobedient generation who passed up the chance to enter the Promised Land has died, hopefully impressing on their children the sad consequences of rebellion and unbelief. Before Moses died, he led the current generation to renew their commitment to their covenant with God. Now the Israelites are camped on the eastern edge of Canaan, ready to move forward in faith. God has already given them the land, but the actual possession of it will require trust in God, courage, obedience, and some hard fighting.

The Pentateuch showed the gradual fulfillment of God's promises to Israel; now Joshua continues the story. The first half of his book covers the seven-year conquest of Canaan, accomplished by three military campaigns. The second half describes the allocation of the land among the tribes. While the destruction of the Canaanites demonstrates God's judgment of sin, the episode with Achan (see Josh. 7) shows that same judgment applied to his chosen people. On the other hand, Rahab's history (see Josh. 2) proves that God's mercy extended to people outside the covenant community who chose to believe and act on God's revelation of himself.

Ephesians 1:3 says that God has given believers every spiritual blessing in Christ; however, we won't take possession of those riches without encountering a great deal of conflict. The book of Joshua gives us the keys to clearing the enemies out of our own promised land. Like Israel, we must be courageous, obey God, and be prepared for some hard fighting. As we yield to God, he will give us the power to conquer sin in our life. Only then will we enjoy the blessings that are rightfully ours.

A Pep Talk for the New Leader

Joshua 1

Joshua certainly qualified to be Israel's new leader. Born into slavery in Egypt, he had been an eyewitness of Israel's miraculous deliverance and God's supernatural protection. Joshua led the battle against the fierce Amalekites soon after the exodus. He was one of the spies who explored Canaan for forty days, and he spent forty years serving as Moses's aide. Most importantly, God had instructed Moses to commission Joshua as his successor.

With all his credentials, Joshua faced a daunting challenge ahead in leading two million people to settle in a strange land. Joshua knew that walled cities and well-trained armies would have to be conquered. He also knew the Israelites' track record for rebelling against authority. Despite God's many supernatural proofs that he had appointed Moses, Israel had still periodically challenged Moses's leadership.

God personally gave Joshua all the encouragement he needed. He urged Joshua to meditate on and carefully obey the book of the Law so that he would prosper and succeed. Three times God told Joshua to "be strong and courageous," and he gave him a good reason to do so. God promised to always be with Joshua wherever he went, to never leave or abandon him. At those words, the new leader took charge with confidence.

Life is full of difficulties and challenges, some of them so overwhelming that the very thought makes us tremble. During those times, God calls us to live out our faith by not giving in to fear. As in Joshua's case, our best resource is the written Word of God. Saturating our mind with the Scriptures and obeying them will transform a fearful attitude into one of bold trust. Instead of thinking about our reasons to be afraid, we'll remember our reason to be strong and courageous: God has promised to be with us wherever we go.

> *Be strong and courageous! Don't tremble or be terrified,*
> *because the LORD your God is with you wherever you go.*
>
> Joshua 1:9

Rahab and the Spies

Joshua 2

Joshua sent out two spies to gather information about Jericho, the first city the Israelites had to conquer. The men ended up spending the night at a prostitute's house, but not just any prostitute. Rahab had heard reports of how Israel's God parted the Red Sea for his people and gave them victory over two Amorite kings. These stories convinced her that Yahweh was the one true God of heaven and earth, not the pagan gods of her people. Now two men who worshiped Yahweh had shown up at her very door.

Unlike Balaam, who received a direct revelation from God, Rahab chose to act on the little that she understood. She even risked her life on it. Rahab hid the Israelite spies on her roof and sent the king of Jericho on a wild goose chase. Then she requested protection from the Israelite spies for herself and her family when the inevitable attack on the city came.

The spies agreed, as long as Rahab didn't betray them. They instructed her to tie a red cord in her window when Israel invaded Jericho. Rahab wasted no time. As soon as she let the men down through her window in the city wall, she hung the scarlet cord.

Rahab gives us a marvelous picture of trust. So often we get caught up in what we don't know or can't understand. Or we focus on the lack of tangible proof that God is working in our life. God wants us to act on the basis of what he's already revealed to us.

As we obey and demonstrate our trust, our understanding will grow. When we meditate on God's character, we'll see that his greatness more than compensates for our weak faith. Like Rahab, we can trust our safety and well-being into his loving hands, no matter what lies ahead.

> *For I know whom I have believed and I am convinced that He*
> *is able to guard what I have entrusted to Him until that day.*
>
> 2 Timothy 1:12 NASB

Unusual Instructions

Joshua 6

The gates of Jericho stayed bolted and barred shut as the terrified inhabitants watched for the impending attack from Israel. Over in the Israelite camp, God gave Joshua detailed instructions for the invasion. The battle plan didn't include the usual strategies of battering rams or ladders to scale the wall. Israel's marching orders were just that—an order to march around the city once a day for six days. On the seventh day, they would march around seven times while the priests blew trumpets, then the men would shout at the top of their lungs.

God's instructions didn't make sense, especially to someone with any military experience. The plan exposed the Israelites to arrows or whatever else might rain down on them from the top of Jericho's walls. It also left them vulnerable to a sudden attack coming out of the gates. But Israel followed Joshua's lead and obeyed God without question. As the week wore on, they must have been subjected to ridicule by Jericho's inhabitants. In spite of the humiliation and danger, Israel followed God's instructions to the letter. On the seventh day, they shouted, and the thick walls of Jericho collapsed. But Rahab's house stood intact.

Occasionally, God's Spirit may prompt us to approach a problem in a way that seems illogical. Some of his commands in Scripture, like turning the other cheek, sound downright unreasonable from a human standpoint. God's wisdom is so much greater than ours that we can never expect to fully understand his thoughts and plans. We may think of all sorts of reasons why we shouldn't do things God's way. If we truly believe that God knows best, our main concern will be to obey him even when we feel or look foolish. When we do that, we just might see some walls fall down.

> *"My thoughts are not your thoughts,*
> *and my ways are not your ways," declares the* LORD.
> *"Just as the heavens are higher than the earth,*
> *so my ways are higher than your ways,*
> *and my thoughts are higher than your thoughts."*
>
> Isaiah 55:8–9

One Bad Apple

Joshua 7

After the remarkable victory over Jericho, Israel suffered a humiliating defeat—and all because of one man. Spies sent to Ai underestimated the number of forces there; they insisted that two or three thousand men would be enough to take the small city. The attack failed miserably as men from Ai chased the retreating Israelites and killed more than thirty of them. Shocked by this unexpected turn of events, Joshua questioned whether God had withdrawn his favor and help from Israel. God informed Joshua that he needed to look for the cause of Israel's defeat within the camp itself.

The next day Israel gathered and God pinpointed the guilty individual. All through the lengthy process, Achan had kept quiet. When Joshua confronted him, Achan admitted taking an expensive robe along with silver and gold from the plunder at Jericho. God had specifically forbidden the Israelites to keep any spoils from Jericho; the silver and gold were to go into the Lord's treasury. Achan's defiance brought God's anger down on the entire nation, causing him to withhold his blessing until they dealt with the sin. The Israelites stoned Achan and his children, who were presumably accomplices in the crime (see Deut. 24:16), and then burned their bodies.

Achan's story took place at a unique period in history, when God was preparing Israel to show his holiness to the world. But the incident still reminds us that one person's sin can affect many people. Although each person is held responsible for their own actions, consequences of sin often cause innocent bystanders to suffer. Our association with someone who is leading an immoral lifestyle can draw us away from following Christ. While God calls us to share his love with unbelievers, we need to avoid relationships that might weaken our faith. We don't want to risk letting one bad apple spoil our witness for Christ.

> *Don't let anyone deceive you. Associating with*
> *bad people will ruin decent people.*
>
> 1 Corinthians 15:33

Israel Falls for a Scam

Joshua 9

The Israelite leaders eyed the strangers with suspicion. They had to be careful when they entered into peace treaties since God had commanded them to destroy the cities within the borders of the Promised Land. The visitors explained that they came from a distant country, motivated to seek an alliance by the stories about Israel's God. To prove their case, they pointed to their worn-out sandals, tattered clothes, and wineskins that had dried out and split. They showed the Israelites how their bread had dried and crumbled on the long journey.

Since the evidence seemed plain enough, Joshua saw no need to seek guidance from the Lord. Israel enacted a formal peace treaty with the strangers. Three days later, the facts came out. Israel learned that they had been tricked by a people who lived nearby. The deception angered the Israelites, but their leaders had sworn an oath in God's name. The treaty forced them to spare the lives of everyone in Gibeon and its three dependent cities. Joshua reproached the Gibeonites for their dishonesty and made them permanent servants. But this curse could turn out to be a great blessing for these Canaanite people. They would serve as woodcutters and water carriers for the house of God.

Most of us get advice from a trusted source when we face a difficult problem. When the solution seems simple and clear-cut, however, we may feel as though we can handle it on our own. But since people and situations aren't always what they seem, it's dangerous to rely on surface impressions.

Even when the answer looks obvious, we'd be wise to seek God's advice. If we don't, we may find out later that we've fallen for a scam. As believers, we have the privilege of seeking guidance from the Creator of the universe through his written Word, his Spirit within us, and prayer. Why wouldn't we make use of such an amazing opportunity?

With your advice you guide me.

Psalm 73:24

Time Stands Still

Joshua 10:1—15

Reports of Israel's military success alarmed the king of Jerusalem. When he heard that Gibeon had made a treaty with Israel, Adoni Zedek called on four other kings to help him destroy Gibeon. As soon as the attack began, the Gibeonites sent an urgent message begging Joshua to save them. Even though Gibeon had used deception against Israel, Joshua and the Israelite army rushed out to defend the city. Although the peace treaty had not been part of God's original plan, he promised to give Joshua victory over the powerful coalition of kings.

Joshua and his men surprised the Amorite armies after an overnight uphill climb over difficult terrain. After the initial clash, the enemy panicked and tried to flee. God killed many of them with large hailstones. As the Israelites chased their enemies, Joshua knew there wouldn't be enough hours of daylight left to finish the job. This need prompted him to make an unusual request: he asked God to make the sun and moon "stand still." God answered by delaying sunset for almost an entire day. In order to fulfill his promise of victory, God used the forces of nature to give Israel supernatural help.

This passage has sparked much debate as to whether God literally stopped the progression of time, and if so, how he accomplished it. Many people feel uncomfortable with this and other miracles in the Bible, seeing them as conflicting with science. If we accept God as the Creator who designed the laws of nature, why should we have a hard time believing that he can bend those laws to accomplish his purposes?

The One who made the sun certainly has the right and power to use it as he wishes. As long as we have trouble seeing God as a miracle worker, we won't recognize his supernatural hand at work in the world around us, or in our own life.

He does great things that are unsearchable
and miracles that cannot be numbered.

Job 9:10

A Senior Citizen Ready to Fight

Joshua 14:6—15

The time had come for the land to be distributed among the nine and a half tribes who would live within Canaan's borders. As the tribe of Judah assembled to receive their assignments, an old man stepped forward to claim a reward promised long ago. Caleb remembered being one of the spies sent out to explore Canaan. Along with Joshua, he had tried to convince the Israelites to believe God instead of listening to the other spies' frightening report. God promised Caleb a special blessing, because instead of going along with the crowd, "he wholeheartedly followed the LORD" (Deut. 1:36). Moses swore that Caleb would receive the very land he had explored.

Forty-five years later, the mountain region of Hebron was still home to the Anakites, the same people who had terrified the ten spies. They still lived in large, fortified cities. But Caleb chose to believe God rather than be intimidated by obstacles in his way. The eighty-five-year-old declared that he was just as strong and ready to fight as he had been when Moses first sent him to explore Canaan. With the Lord's help, he would drive the enemies from his inherited land, no matter how formidable they were.

Caleb wasn't ready to lay down his sword just because of his advanced age. During the long years of wilderness wandering, he had focused on God's promise; now he stood ready to do his part. We may be tempted to let our age or lack of ability keep us from being active in God's work. Caleb's example shows that God can always use someone who commits to following him wholeheartedly. Even when our body is frail, our spirit can stay strong by focusing on God's promises. Just because we're a senior citizen doesn't mean that God won't assign us important kingdom work—or even send us out to fight enemies that would terrify most people.

They shall still bear fruit in old age;
They shall be fresh and flourishing.

Psalm 92:14 NKJV

A Dangerous Misunderstanding

Joshua 22

The tribes who had claimed land on the east side of the Jordan River had kept their promise. The men from Reuben, Gad, and half the tribe of Manasseh had fought alongside the other Israelites during the seven-year conquest of Canaan. Joshua commended their faithfulness, then sent them home with a blessing and a reminder to serve God with all their heart and soul. Soon afterward, the Israelites heard some disturbing news. The eastern tribes had built a prominent altar beside the Jordan River.

The idea that these tribes would set up their own altar for sacrifices instead of using the place designated by God horrified the Israelites. They prepared to go to war against their countrymen. Fortunately, Joshua decided to first send a delegation to confront the tribes on the other side of the Jordan. When Phinehas and the Israelite leaders accused them of rebelling against God, it was the eastern tribes' turn to be horrified.

The men from Reuben, Gad, and Manasseh explained that they didn't erect the altar as a place to offer sacrifices. They intended the altar to be a witness to all future generations that they belonged to Israel and worshiped Yahweh, even though they lived on the opposite side of the Jordan. The rest of Israel accepted this explanation and praised God.

Misunderstandings can cause arguments, fights, broken relationships, and worse. Instead of jumping to conclusions and rushing to pass judgment, we need to slow down and follow the Bible's advice. When we confront a fellow believer about sin, Galatians 6:1 urges us to do it in a gentle way. If we're the ones being accused, Proverbs 15:1 explains that a gentle answer can deflect the other person's rage, while a harsh answer only stirs up anger. By taking the time to let people explain their actions and not reacting angrily to unjust accusations, our misunderstandings can have a happy ending instead of escalating to all-out war.

A person in a hurry makes mistakes.

Proverbs 19:2

A Daily Choice

Joshua 24

As Joshua drew near the end of his life, he delivered a farewell address to the people he had led so faithfully and courageously. The land of Canaan had been subdued and divided among the tribes, but some original inhabitants remained entrenched in the area. Joshua understood the moral and spiritual threats to Israel as they tried to live side by side with people from a pagan culture. He also knew that some Israelites had already been pulled into idolatry. Just as Moses had done before his death, Joshua used his last message to instruct, warn, and encourage Israel to stay true to their covenant with God.

Joshua reviewed Israel's history, highlighting the many miracles God had performed on their behalf. Then Joshua issued a challenge: "But if you don't want to serve the LORD, then choose today whom you will serve" (Josh. 24:15). If they didn't want to serve Yahweh, then they should choose other gods to worship, whether the gods of their ancestors or those of the people in Canaan.

The Israelites protested that it would be unthinkable to abandon the Lord after all he had done for them. When they vowed to serve only Yahweh, Joshua demanded that they prove it by getting rid of any foreign gods or idols in their possession.

Joshua tried to make the Israelites see that they could not mix worship of the true God with idols. Jesus also stressed that there can be no middle ground—we either follow him or we don't. Many people try to take a neutral stance when it comes to God, but each one of us will worship something.

We may bow down to idols of money, success, popularity, relationships, work, or pleasure. If we want to stay faithful to God, we have to make a deliberate decision moment by moment to obey and follow him. Every day we make the decision to choose whom we will serve.

[Jesus said] "Whoever isn't with me is against me."

Matthew 12:30

Judges

A People with No Standards

In those days Israel didn't have a king. Everyone did whatever he considered right.

Judges 21:25

The book of Judges leads us through a dark period in Israel's history. When Joshua and the elder generation died, the Israelites had no appointed leader to rule over them. Just as Joshua had feared, the people let themselves be influenced by the Canaanites they had allowed to remain in the land. The Israelites intermarried with the pagan people around them and worshiped their gods, breaking the covenant vows they had sworn to uphold. As a result, God allowed the Israelites' enemies to oppress them. Even after their rejection of him, however, God remained faithful to his covenant and delivered Israel whenever they repented.

Judges covers a span of more than three hundred years, encompassing several cycles of rebellion, sin, oppression, and deliverance. Each repetition of the cycle dragged Israel deeper into degradation; yet every time they cried out to God, he forgave them. Because of his mercy and promises, God responded by raising up several military and civil leaders called judges. Many of these were highly flawed and hardly represented godly examples for the Israelites, but God used them to break the grip of Israel's oppressors.

The book of Judges shows what happens when a society rebels against God's authority. As people reject his standards of right and wrong, gross immorality and chaos result. Judges explains much of what we see happening around us in our own culture. It also serves as a personal warning of how our mind can become darkened when we substitute our personal ideas of morality for God's clear-cut instructions in the Bible.

On a positive note, we can find encouragement in the accounts of the judges' exploits. They remind us that in spite of our imperfections and failures, God can still use us. With his help, we can make a difference in our world as long as we submit to his leadership and commit to following his standards.

A Slippery Slope

Judges 1

United as a single army, Israel had fought to subdue and gain control of the Promised Land. But the job wasn't finished yet. Each individual tribe still had to drive out the Canaanites that remained in their assigned territory. Although Judah captured three major Philistine cities (temporarily at least), they didn't force out the people in the plains. The other tribes also failed to completely drive the Canaanites out of their land. Even though the Israelites had God's promise that he would fight for them and give them victory, they did not follow through and finish the conquest of Canaan.

Perhaps the Israelites were tired of fighting, or they gave up when they saw their enemies' strength and, in some cases, more sophisticated weapons. Maybe they were attracted to the possible benefits of making alliances with the Canaanites and felt confident in their ability to withstand the temptations of coexisting with them. Whatever factors were involved, Israel's failure to completely obey God's command represented the first step in their downward spiral. Soon, the people began to worship the Canaanite idols, something they had vowed to Joshua they would never do. As a result, they drifted further and further from God's standards—and plunged deeper and deeper into immorality and depravity.

Incomplete obedience does not satisfy God. We can have the best of intentions to obey God faithfully and still let fear, complacency, or spiritual laziness keep us from following through. Although we may not consider it a big deal at the time, such failures put us in danger of slipping into sin. Incomplete obedience is always a slippery slope that will take us where we never intended to go. We may end up being shocked at how far we've drifted from God. Each time Israel lost their focus on obeying God, their control over the Promised Land weakened. Anytime we fall short of fully obeying what we know to be God's will, we will also lose ground.

Without any hesitation I hurry to obey your commandments.

Psalm 119:60

Deborah: A Well-Rounded Leader

Judges 4–5

Deborah stands out among all the judges, and not just because of her gender. She provided a strong role model at a time when the northern tribes had suffered cruel oppression from the Canaanites for twenty years. As a prophet and judge, Deborah held court under a palm tree in Ephraim to settle disputes. One day she summoned Barak and delivered God's command for him to lead an army against King Jabin. Even though God promised to give Barak the victory, he refused to go unless Deborah went with him. Deborah agreed and rode out to the battlefield with Barak, urging him on at the moment of attack and reminding him of God's promise.

After the battle, Deborah's victory song revealed her lack of interest in garnering any of the credit for herself. She honored the Israelites who fought, listing the individual tribes by name. She applauded Jael for killing the Canaanite army commander. Most of all, she praised God and gave him the glory for the victory. Deborah had determined to focus on God and his power and promises regardless of what was going on around her. This commitment gave her the confidence to step into whatever role God set before her, and the ability to do it well.

Deborah still provides a role model for anyone who desires to influence their culture for God. We may not be in a formal leadership position, but we can still exercise sound judgment. When people bring their problems to us, we can share God's truth and show them how to apply biblical wisdom to their situation. We can act as someone's spiritual cheerleader, spurring them on to obey God. We can honor those we serve with while giving God the glory for any successes in our ministry, work, or personal life. Above all, we can place our confidence in God's power and promises no matter what's happening around us. Then we too will be ready to step into whatever role God assigns us.

> *We have this confidence as a sure and
> strong anchor for our lives.*
>
> Hebrews 6:19

Gideon: A Reluctant Leader

Judges 6–7

Once again Israel turned away from God, and as a result suffered under an enemy. For seven years, the Midianites periodically swarmed across the land and devastated the crops, forcing the Israelites to hide out. One day the angel of the Lord paid a visit to a man secretly threshing his grain in a winepress. The messenger told Gideon he had been chosen to rescue Israel from Midian's oppression. Gideon protested that he was the least important member of the weakest family in Manasseh. When the messenger insisted, Gideon asked for confirmation of God's promise to be with him. The angel complied by consuming Gideon's food offering with fire.

Gideon mustered soldiers from four tribes to march out against Midian, but he still hesitated. God's promise and the previous sign were not enough. Gideon asked God to perform a miracle using a wool fleece and the dew. The next day Gideon requested another miracle, the opposite of what had happened the day before. Finally he had all the reassurance he needed.

Then God trimmed his army of 32,000 down to a mere three hundred men. Understanding Gideon's fear at being so vastly outnumbered, God sent him into the enemy camp to overhear a conversation. The Midianite's dream and his friend's interpretation spurred Gideon into action. That very night God gave Gideon the easy victory he had promised.

Sometimes we tell ourselves we need confirmation of God's will even though we already know what he wants us to do. Our hesitation to act may be due to unbelief, fear, or an unwillingness to obey. God patiently obliged Gideon when he asked for miraculous signs, but we have something that Gideon lacked: the complete written Word of God. We can find all the reassurance and guidance we need by turning to Bible study and prayer. It's much wiser to depend on those resources than on "putting out fleeces."

*Then you will always be able to determine what God
really wants—what is good, pleasing, and perfect.*

Romans 12:2

A Woman and a Millstone

Judges 9

After the victory over the Midianites, Gideon urged the people to let the Lord rule over them. Later, however, he made some poor choices that contributed to Israel's downward spiral into sin. Gideon made a gold ephod and set it up in his hometown. The people worshiped it, and as soon as Gideon died they returned to Baal worship. Gideon also took many wives, plus a concubine. After Gideon died, his concubine's son, Abimelech, set himself up as king over Shechem and the surrounding area. Abimelech hired a gang of hoodlums and murdered all but one of his seventy half-brothers.

After three years, the citizens of Shechem turned against Abimelech. Catching the people off guard, Abimelech destroyed the city and killed all the inhabitants, burning a thousand of them alive after they took shelter in a temple of Baal. As Abimelech moved on to the city of Thebez, all of its citizens locked themselves in the tower. The people looking down from the roof were horrified to see their attackers setting a fire at the base. Then a woman picked up a millstone and dropped it on Abimelech's head, cracking his skull. As Abimelech died, he asked his armor-bearer to finish him off so he could avoid the disgrace of being killed by a woman.

The woman from Thebez used a stone for grinding grain to save her city from a bloodthirsty madman. As believers, we also fight with unconventional weapons. The Word of God and prayer are more powerful than any earthly weapons; together they constitute an effective arsenal for spiritual warfare. No earthly or satanic opposition can withstand God's power made available to us through these resources. When we find ourselves under attack, we need to remember the powerful weapons we hold in our hands—and then fold our hands in prayer.

> *The weapons we use in our fight are not made by humans.*
> *Rather, they are powerful weapons from God.*
>
> 2 Corinthians 10:4

Jephthah: Rash Words

Judges 11

As punishment for worshiping Canaanite idols, several Israelite tribes fell under oppression from the Ammonites. The people of Gilead didn't wait for God to raise up a deliverer; instead, they chose Jephthah, Gilead's illegitimate son, who had been chased out of the area by his half-brothers. The leaders offered to let Jephthah rule over them if he defeated the Ammonites, calling God as a witness to their vow. Jephthah agreed and first tried verbal negotiations with the enemy, skillfully refuting Ammon's claim to the land. The Ammonite king refused to listen.

Even though God had not commissioned Jephthah as a leader, he sent his Spirit to empower Jephthah to gather an army and lead an attack against Ammon. But before the battle, Jephthah made a foolish vow: if God gave him a victory, he promised to sacrifice whatever came out of his house to meet him when he returned home. After the successful battle, Jephthah ripped his clothes in anguish when he saw his only child dancing out to greet him. Although devastated, he and his daughter agreed that he could not break his vow.

God had clearly forbidden human sacrifice, but the Israelites' thinking had been contaminated through their worship of Canaanite gods. Some scholars believe that Jephthah literally offered his daughter as a burnt sacrifice. Others interpret the passage to mean that Jephthah's daughter became a lifelong virgin dedicated to service at the sanctuary. Either way, his vow was unnecessary—and something that later caused him much grief.

Jephthah's example serves as a warning about the dangers of speaking without thinking first. Before making a promise to God or another person, we need to weigh our words carefully to make sure we are willing and able to follow through. And when we're tempted to lash out at someone in anger or bitterness, we need to consider the effect our speech will have. We can avoid a lot of embarrassment, regret, or worse if we learn to think before speaking.

Don't be in a hurry to talk.

Ecclesiastes 5:2

Samson: Rash Behavior

Judges 13—16

The last judge of Israel had a promising beginning. The angel of the Lord predicted Samson's birth and gave instructions for him to be set apart for life through special Nazirite vows. When Samson was an adult, God gave him superhuman strength so he could begin to deliver Israel from the Philistines. But Samson wasted his potential because he let his weaknesses control him and used his gift for selfish purposes. He never raised an army, engaged the enemy in battle, or provided spiritual leadership for Israel. Samson preferred to spend his time following his lusts or pulling childish pranks. The Philistines he did face were killed during acts of personal revenge or outbursts of anger.

Samson broke every one of his Nazirite vows and ignored God's laws. When he told Delilah that his hair was the secret of his strength, the Lord's Spirit left him—and took away his God-given gift. As the Philistines gathered to jeer at their famous prisoner, God allowed Samson to have a victory over them. Samson pulled down the building and killed thousands of Philistines. Yet even Samson's final prayer seemed motivated by his desire for personal revenge and not the deliverance of Israel.

We may not have superhuman strength, but God has given each one of us special gifts and abilities to do his work. If we live a self-centered, undisciplined life, we'll miss the joy of fully using those gifts for God's purposes. Samson let himself be controlled by physical desires such as hunger and sex, and by negative emotions such as anger and petty annoyance.

As believers, we have God's Spirit living in us at all times. When we yield to his control, God will give us the power and strength to resist our natural impulses that would lead us into sin. By following God's leading, we can live a godly life and make sure that our potential is not wasted.

> *If God's Spirit lives in you, you are under the control of your spiritual nature, not your corrupt nature.*
>
> Romans 8:9

Micah and His Mother: Muddled Thinking

Judges 17

Micah's story shows how confused the Israelites' thinking became when they tried to mix the truth with elements of the pagan religions around them. When Micah confessed to stealing his mother's silver, she tried to turn her previous curse on the unknown thief into a blessing. The mother wanted to dedicate the silver to God, but she disobeyed one of God's commandments in her misguided attempt.

She had a silversmith create a couple of idols for her son. Micah kept these, along with the ephod and household idols he made, in a shrine that he set up in his house. He even "ordained" one of his sons to serve as priest even though he was not descended from Aaron.

One day a young Levite passed through Ephraim. Micah offered to provide a home and salary to the man if he agreed to be a priest to Micah's family. God had made it clear that the role of priest was a public service, not a private job, and was to be performed only by Aaron's descendants. And Micah's homemade shrine full of idols was certainly no substitute for the rightful place of worship at Shiloh. Even so, the Levite jumped at the offer, convincing the superstitious Micah that God would be good to him now that he had his very own Levite.

The Israelites had perverted true worship of Yahweh by doing things their own way. Today people still gravitate toward a custom-made spirituality, wanting to pick and choose the elements that appeal to them from different belief systems. We don't have to look far to see examples of the distorted thinking that results from such an approach.

Even within churches, we see people standing for things that God clearly opposes. It's imperative that we saturate our mind with the Bible so that we never mix truth with something else. Trying to do that is a surefire recipe for disaster.

> *Their thoughts were total nonsense, and their*
> *misguided minds were plunged into darkness.*
>
> Romans 1:21

Hitting Rock Bottom

Judges 19–21

It's hard to imagine a more sordid story than the incident related at the end of Judges about a Levite and his concubine. Reconciled after a four-month separation, the pair left her father's house and set off for home. That evening they stopped in the city of Gibeah in Benjamin, where an old man invited them to stay at his house. Later that night, some men pounded on the door and demanded that the Levite be sent out to have sex with them. In his fanaticism for following the hospitality code, the old man offered to let the mob rape his daughter and the concubine instead.

When the men persisted in their original demand, the Levite shoved his concubine out the door in order to protect himself. As he left the next morning, seemingly unconcerned about her fate, he found her lifeless body just outside the door. Once he had brought her home, the Levite cut her body into twelve pieces, which he sent to the twelve tribes. Israel gathered to hear the Levite's account of the heinous crime, which conveniently left out his part in the murder.

When the Benjamites refused to hand over the guilty men, the outraged Israelites attacked and nearly annihilated the tribe. After the battle, Israel felt grieved and wanted to save Benjamin from extinction. They obtained wives for the six hundred survivors through slaughtering the men in a town and kidnapping other young women at a festival.

The last verse of Judges emphasizes the reason for the breakdown of Israelite society and the resulting chaos and rampant perversion. When a nation or an individual rejects God's standards, it opens the door to all kinds of evil. Our ability to distinguish right from wrong becomes weakened. We may not notice how desensitized to immorality we've grown until something happens to shock us out of our complacency. If we sense that we've drifted away from God, honest self-evaluation is in order. Have we been doing what our King says is right, or whatever seems right in our own opinion?

> *In those days Israel didn't have a king. Everyone*
> *did whatever he considered right.*
>
> Judges 21:25

Ruth

A Model of Faithfulness

> But Ruth answered, "Don't force me to leave you. Don't make me turn back from following you. Wherever you go, I will go, and wherever you stay, I will stay. Your people will be my people, and your God will be my God."
>
> Ruth 1:16

The book of Ruth provides a much-needed dose of encouragement after the heartbreaking ending of Judges. Although the author and date of writing are unknown, the events took place during that same dark time of corruption, chaos, and violence. Such a setting makes the godliness of the main characters shine even more. It also highlights God's grace and favor, which he extended even to a Moabite woman who responded to him in faith.

The narrative begins on a tragic note. Years earlier, Naomi's family had moved to Moab to escape a famine. Now she found herself a destitute widow, bereft of her sons as well as her husband. When Naomi decided to return to Judah, one of her Moabite daughters-in-law insisted on going with her. Ruth must have been irresistibly drawn to this Jewish family and their God.

Once in Judah, Ruth worked in the fields to provide food for herself and her mother-in-law. But God had set a plan in motion to provide much more than grain. He would renew Naomi's zest for life and make Ruth one of the most honored women in Israelite history.

The book of Ruth is more than a love story with a happy ending. Ruth's background shows that God will accept anyone who responds to him in faith. Ruth and Naomi's closeness reminds us to appreciate the blessing of a relationship based on love and respect. The integrity of the three main characters encourages us to stay faithful to God regardless of how people around us are living. The ending reminds us that God is always at work even in the most devastating circumstances. Finally, Boaz's redemption of Ruth through the law of levirate marriage paints a picture of Jesus redeeming us from sin—and shows us the heart of our own love story.

Traveling Companions

Ruth 1

Naomi and Elimelech had originally moved their family to Moab to escape a famine. They never intended to stay in a pagan country considered an enemy of Israel. But the years passed and their two sons married Moabite women. Eventually, Naomi's husband and sons died, leaving her with no male relatives for support. When she heard that the famine had lifted in Israel, Naomi started the long journey back to her hometown in Judah. Ruth and Orpah set out with their mother-in-law, who loved them as her own children. On the way, Naomi began to wonder if she was being selfish.

Wouldn't it be in the girls' best interests to return to their parents' homes? That way, they would have a chance of remarrying and having families. Naomi urged Ruth and Orpah to go back and she kissed them good-bye. Through a torrent of tears, the young women insisted on going with Naomi. After more urging and more tears, Orpah turned back.

But Ruth refused to leave Naomi, declaring that she accepted Naomi's people—and her God—as her own. How the destitute widow's heart must have warmed at Ruth's vow that nothing but death would separate them. How glad she must have been to have a traveling companion on the long road ahead.

At times, life can seem like a long, hard road with no end in sight. We may take a detour that makes us feel lost for a while. But at least we know that we are never traveling alone. Before Jesus ascended to heaven after his resurrection, he promised to be with his followers. He didn't say "sometimes" or "during those times you're feeling and acting spiritually mature," but always, "until the end of time." Jesus goes with us every step of the way, offering encouragement, guidance, and his comforting presence. With such a traveling companion, surely we can find the courage to go wherever our road leads us.

> *[Jesus said] "And remember that I am always*
> *with you until the end of time."*
>
> Matthew 28:20

A "Chance" Meeting

Ruth 2

Once Ruth and Naomi arrived in Bethlehem, Ruth took advantage of the Israelite custom that allowed the poor to feed themselves. She picked out a field and began gathering the stalks of grain that had been accidentally dropped by the reapers. When the owner of the field stopped by, he singled Ruth out for special attention. Boaz invited her to work alongside his own servant girls instead of moving from field to field with the other gleaners. That way she would be protected and could use his workers' water supply. Such unexpected favor astonished Ruth and she asked the reason. Boaz expressed admiration for her loyalty and kindness to Naomi and her courage in coming to a foreign land.

At mealtime, Boaz invited Ruth to share the food prepared for his harvesters and himself. After Ruth returned to the field, Boaz ordered his reapers to make her work easy and to even deliberately drop grain in her path. Ruth worked until evening and took home a half-bushel of barley. Her amazed mother-in-law asked in whose field she had worked. When Naomi heard the name Boaz, she immediately recognized God's hand in the situation. As a close relative of the family, Boaz had the responsibility to marry Ruth and raise up a son to carry on Elimelech's family line.

We love stories involving a chance meeting that seems too good to be true, but believers understand there is no such thing as coincidence. God allows us to make choices, but he holds ultimate control over our life. If we're doing our best to follow God's will, we can trust him to order the details of our day-to-day activities. He will direct us toward people and circumstances that help us grow more like Christ. He will lead us to opportunities to share our faith and minister to others, to bless and to be blessed. For God's children, any "chance" meeting is really a divine appointment.

> *The Lord directs the steps of the godly.*
> *He delights in every detail of their lives.*
>
> Psalm 37:23 NLT

Surprise Endings

Ruth 3—4

Naomi didn't expect much when she returned to her hometown in Judah. She faced a bleak future as a widow with no male offspring. Being a Moabite, Ruth never expected to receive such favor and kindness as Boaz showed her. For his part, Boaz had strong feelings for Ruth, but their age difference limited his expectations. He could see that Ruth would make a wonderful wife but assumed she would prefer a younger man.

In the meantime, God was busy unfolding a plan that would surprise them all—and bless the entire human race. The action intensified when Naomi coached Ruth on how to propose marriage to Boaz. The instruction to lie at Boaz's feet and ask him to cover her must have sounded strange to Ruth, but she trusted Naomi implicitly. Ruth's request delighted Boaz but he told her of a complication: Naomi's late husband had another relative closer than himself.

The next morning the other relative declined the role of family redeemer, so Boaz gladly stepped in to fill it. The marriage between Boaz and Ruth restored security and joy to Naomi, especially when they had a son. But Naomi had no idea of the importance of this birth. Little Obed, whose mother was a Moabite and whose father was born to Rahab, a former Canaanite prostitute from Jericho, became King David's grandfather and the ancestor of the Messiah.

We may be tempted to give in to discouragement and bitterness when we face hardships or adversity. But even when our situation looks hopeless, God is working out his plan. It may take a long time to unfold or it may seem to happen suddenly. God loves to reward his children for their faithfulness, and he often works things out in ways we never could have imagined or dreamed. If we hold on to our trust in his goodness and our commitment to obey him during the dark days, we never know when we'll be surprised by one of God's happy endings.

> *By this power he can do infinitely more*
> *than we can ask or imagine.*
>
> Ephesians 3:20

Jesus in Ruth

According to Leviticus 25, if poverty forced an Israelite to sell family property, a close relative had the responsibility to buy it back. The same held true for an Israelite who sold himself into slavery in order to pay his debts. Another law required the brother-in-law of a childless widow to marry her and provide a male heir to preserve the deceased man's family line and inheritance.

All these regulations point to the role of a *ga'al*, translated as "close relative," "family redeemer," or "kinsman-redeemer." Boaz's godly character and his love for Ruth motivated him to take on this role, beautifully illustrating Jesus Christ and his relationship to us.

A redeemer had to be closely related by blood to those he took responsibility for. Hebrews 2:14 explains that Jesus "took on flesh and blood" to become like us so that he could become our Redeemer. The family redeemer also had to be willing to pay the price. When the man most closely related to Naomi's late husband declined to accept the responsibility, Boaz gladly stepped up. In John 10:18, Jesus emphasized that he willingly gave up his life as payment for sin.

Ruth's actions in chapter 3 illustrate our part in the redemption process. By going to the threshing floor and following Naomi's instructions, Ruth demonstrated her trust in Boaz's character. When she asked Boaz to spread his covering over her, she was requesting him to be her family redeemer and provide for her. Once he received this invitation, Boaz sprang into action.

Jesus paid a high price to buy us back out of slavery to sin, but he waits for an invitation to serve as our Redeemer. Once we ask him to cover us, we find joy, security, and a rich inheritance instead of a life of spiritual poverty.

> *For you know that it was not with perishable things*
> *such as silver or gold that you were redeemed from*
> *the empty way of life handed down to you from your*
> *forefathers, but with the precious blood of Christ.*
>
> 1 Peter 1:18–19 NIV

1 Samuel

Heart Conditions

God does not see as humans see. Humans look at outward appearances, but the LORD looks into the heart.

1 Samuel 16:7

The book of 1 Samuel opens near the end of the twelfth century BC. Three hundred years of political, moral, and spiritual turmoil and deterioration have taken their toll on the nation of Israel. Instead of serving as an example to the people, the sons of the high priest Eli are using their office for personal gain and sexual immorality. Meanwhile, a godly woman desperately prays for a son and God gives her the desire of her heart. Her son Samuel grows up to provide strong leadership for Israel, serving as judge, prophet, and priest.

Unfortunately, Samuel's sons have no heart for following God and are unfit as spiritual leaders. When Israel demands to have a king like all the other nations around them, God leads Samuel to anoint Saul, a seemingly obvious choice. The nation's first king starts out strong but grows cold and indifferent about obeying God. Samuel then anoints David, a not-so-obvious choice but a young man with a heart that beats in tune with God's.

Originally, 1 and 2 Samuel formed one book named after the first major character who appears in the narrative. Samuel is considered the author of most of the first book; perhaps other prophets compiled the remainder of the material. In any case, 1 Samuel is a book of transitions. The rulership of Israel moves from judges to a monarchy. The significance of the priests gives way to an emphasis on prophets. Through such major changes, we still see God guiding people who have a heart for following him.

All of us can relate to periods of transition; life often seems to be one change after another. Although God never alters, we can't say the same about our own emotions, attitudes, and behavior. Since the characters in 1 Samuel offer both positive and negative examples of relating to God, reading the book is a good reminder to check our own heart condition.

Hannah's Heartache

1 Samuel 1

Hannah had a bitter life, living in a culture that regarded childlessness as a curse from God. To make matters worse, she had to endure cruel mocking from Elkanah's second wife Peninnah, who had given birth to several children. Peninnah especially tormented Hannah when the family made the annual journey to offer sacrifices at the tabernacle. Although Elkanah loved Hannah dearly, he seemed unable to understand her pain. His clumsy attempts to comfort her probably didn't help as he asked, "Don't I mean more to you than ten sons?" (v. 8). Hannah took her heartache to the only One who could help heal it.

As her family worshiped at the tabernacle in Shiloh, Hannah poured out her anguish to God once again. She promised that if she had a son, she would give him back to the Lord for a lifetime of service. The high priest watched Hannah's emotional but silent prayer and accused her of being drunk.

Hannah defended herself, explaining that she had been praying out of distress and sorrow. Eli accepted her explanation and offered a blessing that God would grant her request. Hannah left with her spirits lifted. Within a year, she gave birth to her long-desired son and named him Samuel, acknowledging that God had heard her prayer.

Each one of us has a deep longing in our heart. We may yearn for a marriage partner, a child, or the restoration of a broken relationship. Our heart's desire might be a change in our present circumstances or the fulfillment of an old dream. We're often reluctant to share those deep longings with other people for fear of being misunderstood or ridiculed. But there is Someone we can trust with all our disappointments, heartaches, and sorrows. God wants us to feel free to pour out our heart to him. He may grant our desires or he may change them to reflect his will, but we can be sure that he will always understand.

Trust him at all times, you people.
Pour out your hearts in his presence.

Psalm 62:8

A Voice in the Night

1 Samuel 2:22—3:21

Eli's sons had no interest in the Lord and no respect for the priesthood. They used their position to indulge their greed and sexual lusts. When Hophni and Phinehas ignored their father's warning to stop sinning against God, Eli failed to take proper action as high priest. Eventually, God decided to put a stop to the sons' evil behavior that dishonored his name and sanctuary and corrupted the people. In the meantime, a boy in a linen ephod quietly served the Lord, gaining favor with God and with people (2:26).

One night as Samuel slept in the tabernacle, a voice called his name. Samuel ran to the aging priest's bedside and asked what he wanted. Eli insisted that he hadn't called Samuel. This happened two more times before Eli understood that the voice Samuel heard must be God's. He instructed Samuel to respond the next time by saying, "Speak, Lord. I'm listening" (1 Sam. 3:8–9). That night Samuel received his first direct revelation as God shared his plan to judge Eli's family.

Both the Old and New Testaments include instances of God speaking in an audible voice. Most often, he speaks in quiet, gentle ways. We may sense a nudging from his Spirit within us or he may speak directly to us through his written Word. It's not always easy to recognize God's voice in a world filled with so much noise. It can be hard to differentiate between God's promptings and our own thoughts. That's why it's important to deliberately set aside a time when we can quiet our mind before God and be ready to say, "Speak, Lord. I'm listening."

> As the Lord was passing by, a fierce wind tore mountains
> and shattered rocks ahead of the Lord. But the Lord was
> not in the wind. After the wind came an earthquake. But
> the Lord wasn't in the earthquake. After the earthquake
> there was a fire. But the Lord wasn't in the fire. And
> after the fire there was a quiet, whispering voice.
>
> 1 Kings 19:11–12

The Ark Is Captured

1 Samuel 4

When the Israelite army suffered defeat at the hands of the Philistines, the leaders wondered what went wrong. Instead of asking God about it, they came up with their own idea: Why not take the ark into battle? Surely that would guarantee God's presence and a military victory! Hophni and Phinehas brought the ark from Shiloh and were greeted by deafening shouts of joy. At first the news frightened the Philistines, who had heard of miracles done on Israel's behalf. Nevertheless, the Philistine army rallied and easily defeated Israel's army, inflicting heavy casualties and capturing the ark.

Eli heard the devastating news of his sons' deaths and the ark's capture from a messenger who ran back to Shiloh. At the mention of the ark, the elderly, overweight high priest fell off his chair and died. Later, Phinehas's pregnant wife heard about the ark's capture and the deaths of her husband and her father-in-law. She went into premature labor and delivered a son. Before she died, she named him Ichabod to reflect her belief that Israel's glory was now gone.

The Israelites' thinking had been influenced by the pagan nations around them. Although they had turned away from God, they treated the ark as their good-luck charm. They considered the gold and wood box itself a source of power. We can fall into similar superstitious thinking, although ours will probably be more subtle. Many people treat symbols of faith like charms or they cling to medals, icons, or other objects. Some people rely on a specific prayer or recitation, a ritual such as baptism, a person, or a specific location.

Such dependence may seem harmless but God views it as idolatry. Symbols of faith mean nothing in themselves; they become dangerous when they take our eyes off what we truly have to glory in. Thankfully, our relationship with him can never be taken away.

> *But you, O LORD, are a shield that surrounds me.*
> *You are my glory.*
> *You hold my head high.*
>
> Psalm 3:3

Israel's First King

1 Samuel 9—11

The prophet Samuel had grown old and his sons had failed to follow his godly example. Israel's leaders demanded that Samuel appoint a king to rule them so they would be "like all the other nations." After warning them of the negative consequences of having a king, God directed Samuel to a young man who was more handsome and a head taller than everyone else. Saul's impressive physical appearance, however, belied his insecurity.

Saul's father was a rich, powerful man, yet he protested that his family was the most insignificant within their tribe. After Samuel privately anointed Saul, God gave signs to confirm his choice. Later, all Israel gathered to learn the new king's identity. When the lots pinpointed Saul, no one could find him. God told the Israelites that their new king was hiding among the baggage.

Saul began his reign admirably, but his subsequent behavior showed that he thought more about his reputation and self-gratification than wholehearted obedience to God. As his power increased, his pride grew and he turned away from God. His initial humility gave way to disobedience, jealousy, and mental instability.

It's important for us to have a realistic assessment of our strengths and weaknesses. Both an inferiority complex and an inflated opinion of ourselves will interfere with our relationship with God and with others. What matters most is what God says about us. Admitting our propensity to sin will instill a proper sense of humility. Remembering that true self-worth comes from being God's dearly loved child will take away any impulse to "hide among the baggage." Then we can be free to concentrate on following and serving God. The more we focus on him, the less we'll think about ourselves—and the more wholeheartedly we can love him.

> *Because of the kindness that God has shown me, I ask you*
> *not to think of yourselves more highly than you should.*
> *Instead, your thoughts should lead you to use good judgment*
> *based on what God has given each of you as believers.*

Romans 12:3

A Man after God's Own Heart

1 Samuel 15:1—16:13

Saul's passion for the Lord that marked the beginning of his reign dissolved into an arrogant, stubborn desire to do things his own way. Instead of waiting for Samuel to offer sacrifices before a battle, Saul grew impatient and performed the ritual himself, breaking God's law (see 1 Sam. 13). Before another battle he uttered a foolish curse that led his soldiers into sin and almost cost his son Jonathan's life (see 1 Sam. 14). When Saul disobeyed God's command by keeping the best plunder from a battle, he first lied to Samuel and then tried to make excuses for what he'd done. Samuel delivered the message from God that because of Saul's disobedience, his kingdom would not last.

Samuel knew that the Lord had "searched for a man after his own heart" to appoint as king (1 Sam. 13:14). Although God led Samuel to Jesse's family, Samuel had some searching to do himself. One by one, Jesse brought out his sons. Their physical appearance impressed Samuel, but God was more interested in their attitudes and motivation. Finally, Samuel insisted that the youngest son be brought in from tending the sheep. As soon as David arrived, God told Samuel, "He is the one."

God knew that David's behavior would be far from perfect, but he saw a young man wholeheartedly committed to following him. When David sinned, he confessed and repented. He freely acknowledged his dependence on God. Unlike Saul, David was more concerned about God's reputation than about what people thought about him personally.

God still searches for men and women who are motivated by a desire to honor and obey him above all else. Our performance doesn't have to be perfect in order for God to use us, but we do need a heart that beats in tune with his. If we choose to make that commitment, he will help us become a person "after his own heart."

> The LORD's eyes scan the whole world to find those whose
> hearts are committed to him and to strengthen them.
>
> 2 Chronicles 16:9

David and the Giant

1 Samuel 17

For forty days the Philistine and Israelite armies were locked in a standoff. Each day Goliath, the Philistine champion, strode out and challenged Israel to send someone to fight him. The match between the two representatives would determine the outcome of the battle. Each day Saul and his fighting men cowered in fear. Goliath stood more than nine feet tall. He wore armor weighing more than a hundred pounds and carried a spear with an iron head that weighed fifteen pounds. When David arrived at the camp to visit his brothers, he wondered why no one had defended God's honor by taking up this Philistine's challenge.

David's offer to fight Goliath amazed Saul. He protested that a boy couldn't stand up to a powerful, seasoned warrior like Goliath. David nonchalantly explained that he had killed lions and bears while protecting his father's sheep. Just as God had given him victory in those situations, he would give David victory over Goliath.

Since David had no experience with armor or a sword, he took only the weapons that were familiar to him. Goliath ridiculed the boy with the shepherd's staff coming out to confront him, but one stone from David's sling knocked the giant down.

David had spent years in the wilderness working as a shepherd for his father. God used that time to prepare David for his future role as he learned to depend on God's power. In a similar way, God uses our everyday challenges to train us for bigger roles to come. We can find courage by remembering how God has helped us in the past.

When Jesus taught about finances, he explained that someone who is faithful with a little can be trusted with a lot. The same principle applies to spiritual life in general. As we learn to trust God in our daily struggles, we'll be ready to face our own giants with the same confidence that David displayed.

> *Whoever can be trusted with very little*
> *can also be trusted with a lot.*
>
> Luke 16:10

A Jealous Heart

1 Samuel 18—19

After David defeated Goliath, Saul made him an army commander. But David's soaring popularity soon troubled the king, especially when he heard women singing David's praises more than his own. Jealousy clouded Saul's mind and he began to view David as an enemy. More than once, Saul tried to kill David by hurling a spear at him in the palace. When Saul ordered his son and officers to kill David, Jonathan was able to bring about a temporary reconciliation between his father and his beloved friend. Even though David married Saul's daughter Michal, Saul eventually sent soldiers to murder David in his bed. Finally, David had to flee from Saul's murderous envy.

For the next ten years, David lived like an outlaw. He moved from place to place in the wilderness and hid in caves with his followers as Saul and his army hunted him. In the face of such unjust persecution, David continued to respect Saul's God-given position. On two occasions, God placed Saul's life in David's hands. Even though David's men urged him to kill his enemy, David refused. Samuel had anointed David as Israel's next king, but David determined to wait for God's timing instead of gaining the throne through assassination. He even promised never to take revenge on Saul's family.

God put Saul at David's mercy, but fortunately for Saul, David had placed himself under God's mercy. David's trust in God kept him free from bitterness, so he didn't take advantage of the chance to pay Saul back for the evil he'd done. We can learn from David's example when we face a similar situation. Sometimes what looks like an opportunity to our advantage is really a temptation we need to resist. God calls us to take the high road and trust our future to him. If we avoid the chance for payback, it just might soften our enemy's jealous heart.

> *Don't pay people back with evil for the evil*
> *they do to you. Focus your thoughts on those*
> *things that are considered noble.*

> Romans 12:17

The Heart of a Friend

1 Samuel 18:1–4; 20

When David first came to stay in the palace, he and Saul's oldest son Jonathan became close friends. Jonathan honored David by giving him his coat, battle tunic, belt, and weapons. Most of all, Jonathan gave David a pledge of loyalty because "he loved David as much as he loved himself" (18:1). Jonathan stood in line to inherit the throne, but at some point he understood that God intended David to be the next king. Since Jonathan honored God above all else, that knowledge didn't change his feelings toward his friend. Jonathan's love for David remained untainted by self-centered interests.

In the early stages of Saul's jealousy, Jonathan braved his father's unpredictable temper to defend David and work toward reconciliation between the two men. Later, David insisted that Saul still intended to kill him. Jonathan found it hard to believe, but he agreed to test his father's attitude. When he learned the awful truth, Jonathan warned David by a prearranged signal. The two young men wept together before David fled for his life. As Saul prepared to attack David at Horesh, Jonathan visited his friend. Jonathan couldn't change his father's mind or alter David's circumstances, but he strengthened David's faith and reminded him of God's promise.

Our friendships usually spring from shared interests or the fact that we simply enjoy someone's company. But deep inside, we all long for something more. As believers, our closest friendships will be based on a shared faith in Jesus Christ and a common goal to please him. When we put God first, all of our other relationships will fall into place. We'll be free to love others unselfishly, through good times and bad, no matter what obstacles crop up between us. We'll be able to enjoy friendship the way God intended it to be—helping each other grow and stay strong in our faith. Then we will know what a treasure a true friend can be.

He strengthened David's faith in the LORD.

1 Samuel 23:16

A Way with Words

1 Samuel 25

This wasn't the first time Nabal's mouth had caused trouble. The man had a reputation for being surly, rude, and downright mean. This time, however, Nabal went too far. David's request for provisions for his men seemed reasonable in light of the protection they had given Nabal's shepherds and flocks. Being such a wealthy man, Nabal could easily have complied with the hospitality code and furnished David's men with food. Instead, he refused and sent back an insulting message. David ordered his men to strap on swords, vowing to kill Nabal and every man in his household.

Nabal's servants knew where to go for help. When they told his wife Abigail what her husband had done, she quickly loaded donkeys with food supplies and sent them ahead. Abigail met David on a mountain path and bowed respectfully. She acknowledged her husband's foolishness and even accepted the blame for what had happened.

Speaking as though David had already changed his mind about killing Nabal, Abigail reminded him that God would make him king one day. Such an act of personal vengeance was beneath him and would only trouble his conscience. David's anger dissolved. He thanked Abigail for her good judgment and for preventing him from committing unnecessary bloodshed.

We have all probably resembled each of these three characters at some time or other. Haven't we all blurted out a rude, mean-spirited comment without thinking of the effect it might have? Don't we sometimes react in anger and make a declaration we wish we could take back? And hopefully, we've all been able to use our words to soothe another person's emotions and keep them from rushing into sinful behavior. Words are powerful and can have either positive or negative effects. That's why the Bible includes many warnings about guarding our speech. When we open our mouth, we want to be more like Abigail and less like the fool named Nabal.

The tongue has the power of life and death.

Proverbs 18:21

Saul and the Psychic

1 Samuel 28

The prospect of battling the Philistine army terrified Saul, especially since Samuel had died. Saul missed the prophet's guidance, and God refused to answer Saul's prayers because of his past rebellion and disobedience. Desperate for help, Saul resorted to a practice that had been strictly forbidden by God. He ordered his officers to find a medium he could consult. Although the land had been purged of psychics and necromancers, the men pointed him to a woman in Endor with a reputation for contacting the dead.

Biblical scholars agree that mediums based their practice on either trickery or satanic power, but they disagree on exactly what happened that night. The woman screamed in fright when Samuel's spirit appeared, indicating that she was taken by surprise. Some people believe that God raised Samuel's spirit to prophesy one last time to Saul. In any case, the spirit restated Samuel's earlier prophecy that God had torn the kingdom from Saul and given it to David. He added that Saul and his sons would die the next day when the Philistines defeated Israel. Saul left dejected; he'd found no help or comfort. Instead he had added one more sin to his list of offenses against God.

When a person is grieving, the idea of contacting their loved one's spirit can seem comforting. That desire can grow into an obsession, fueled by books, movies, and television shows supposedly sharing stories of people who have contacted the spirit world. God warns us to avoid anything related to the occult. Even activities that sound harmless can open us up to demonic deception and influence. Rather than trying to contact the spirit world for comfort or guidance, how much better would it be to seek help from God? After all, he is the only One who truly has authority over the spirits of the living and the dead.

> *People will say to you, "Ask for help from the mediums*
> *and the fortunetellers, who whisper and mutter."*
> *Shouldn't people ask their God for help instead?*
> *Why should they ask the dead to help the living?*
>
> Isaiah 8:19

2 Samuel

The Story of Israel's Greatest King

Your royal house will remain in my presence forever. Your throne will be established forever.

2 Samuel 7:16

Saul and his three oldest sons had been killed in battle. After the Philistines soundly defeated Israel, the people in the surrounding areas fled from their cities. The nation of Israel stood at a crossroads. Would the twelve tribes come together and conquer their enemies? Would they acknowledge the man already chosen by God to be Israel's next king—the man who had been hunted like an outlaw by Saul for the past ten years? Second Samuel records the history of David's forty-year reign, first over Judah and then over all of Israel.

Under David's capable leadership, Israel reached its pinnacle of power, extending its borders and subduing its enemies. The nation achieved prosperity and unity under a strong centralized government. David made Jerusalem his capital and brought the ark back from exile. During his reign, he modeled a life of humility, obedience, and devotion to God, despite occasional serious lapses in judgment.

Second Samuel gives an honest account of David's weaknesses as well as his strengths and successes. He committed adultery and murder, offended God with his pride, and failed to deal with sin among his children. Each time David confessed and repented, he found renewed fellowship with God. But the consequences of his sins brought great suffering on himself, his family, and the entire nation. In spite of his failures, God promised that David's royal line would never end—a promise to be fulfilled when David's descendant, Jesus Christ, begins his future millennial reign.

David's life serves as a powerful reminder of the connection between obedience to God's commands and the enjoyment of his blessings. God's anointed king wasn't immune from the consequences of sin; neither are believers today. Reading 2 Samuel can encourage us to seek a restored relationship with God through needed confession and repentance. It should also make us grateful that we have a King ruling over our life who is untouched by human weakness and sin.

David Finally Takes the Throne

2 Samuel 2:1–5:5

Since Saul had been anointed by God as Israel's king, David believed only God had the right to judge Saul's sins and remove him from office. David respected Saul's authority even during the long years he spent on the run from the mentally unstable king. Even though Saul had treated him like an enemy, David mourned his death and honored his memory as a ruler of Israel. Then David turned to embrace the future God had promised him.

David took nothing for granted; he didn't rush out to seize the throne for himself. When he asked God what his next step should be, God directed him to move back to his home territory. In Hebron the people formally anointed David as king over the tribe of Judah. At last God's promise would be fulfilled—except that the rest of Israel recognized Saul's youngest son Ishbosheth as king. Even when Ishbosheth's men assassinated him two years later, the battle between Saul's royal family and David's followers raged on. Seven and a half years passed from David's anointing over Judah until his acceptance as king over the entire nation of Israel.

What kept David going during the twenty-plus years between his initial anointing by Samuel and the actual fulfillment of his God-given role? David's hope of becoming king was combined with an implicit trust in God's control over his life. Like David, we can learn to find our strength in God even when we grow weary of waiting for something to happen. We can call on God to help us endure and depend on him to uplift us emotionally and spiritually. If we cling to hope in his promises, at the right time God will help us embrace our own future.

> *The strength of those who wait with hope in the LORD*
> *will be renewed.*
> *They will soar on wings like eagles.*
> *They will run and won't become weary.*
> *They will walk and won't grow tired.*
>
> Isaiah 40:31

Michal's Mistake

2 Samuel 6

When David began reigning over Israel, he captured Jerusalem and made it his capital since it was a more centrally located and neutral city than Hebron. He subdued the Philistines, Israel's bitter enemies since the days of Samson. David then turned his attention to another matter. For a hundred years the ark had been separated from its rightful place in the tabernacle. David set out to bring the ark to Jerusalem, which would make that city the religious center for the nation. The first attempt ended in disaster due to improper handling of the sacred object.

Finally, the procession started out again, this time following God's instructions. David removed his kingly robes, donned the simple linen garment worn by priests, and joined the celebration. Filled with joy that God was coming to live among his people in Jerusalem, David danced and shouted. As the parade entered the city, David's wife Michal watched from a palace window.

Like her father Saul, Michal apparently had no real heart for worshiping God. She felt nothing but contempt for David's display of enthusiasm and rebuked him for humiliating himself. Michal paid a price for her sarcastic remarks; she remained childless her entire life. Either David permanently separated from her or God prevented her from having children.

Michal's example warns us to resist the temptation to criticize other believers because of different worship styles or expressions of praise. Our perceptions are colored by our personal tastes, childhood training, and cultural bias. We have no right to judge someone for showing too much or too little enthusiasm. Only God sees a person's motivation; each one of us is accountable to him alone. Christians may worship in different ways, but we would all be wise to follow David's example. He didn't think about how he looked to other people, only about how he looked to God.

Why do you criticize or despise other Christians?
Everyone will stand in front of God to be judged.

Romans 14:10

One Sin Leads to Another

2 Samuel 11

It all started with a single lapse in judgment. Kings usually led their armies to war, but for some reason David decided to stay home that spring. One evening he had trouble sleeping and walked along the palace roof. He saw a beautiful woman bathing and investigated to find out her identity. Even though David already had plenty of wives, he had Bathsheba brought to the palace. Soon afterward, Bathsheba sent word that she was pregnant. The fact that Bathsheba's husband Uriah was away fighting in the war compounded the problem.

Desperate to cover up his adultery, David brought Uriah home so that he would sleep with his wife and assume the child was his. Uriah was a foreigner but deeply devoted to Israel. He refused to enjoy the pleasures of home life while the army remained camped on the battlefield. Even when David got him drunk, Uriah stayed away from his house. David then sent the faithful soldier back to the war carrying a letter that ensured his death. The king instructed Joab to place Uriah on the front lines and then withdraw from him.

Sin is a progression. It starts out with an inappropriate thought or desire that we choose to dwell on. Maybe we allow our eyes to linger where they shouldn't or indulge in a dangerous daydream. Eventually, we give in to the temptation to compromise our behavior "just this once."

After we swallow the bait of sin, we find ourselves being pulled in deeper and deeper. Each time we try to cover up our actions, we commit more sins until it's hard to see any way out. How much pain we could avoid by resisting temptation at the very beginning! God wants us to call on him for help before we make that first lapse in judgment and end up getting reeled in.

> *Everyone is tempted by his own desires as they lure him*
> *away and trap him. Then desire becomes pregnant and gives*
> *birth to sin. When sin grows up, it gives birth to death.*
>
> James 1:14–15

"You Are the Man!"

2 Samuel 12:1–25

David was a sensitive man. He wept easily and he wasn't ashamed to express tender feelings, as evidenced by his poetry in the book of Psalms. The deeper he plunged into sin, however, the more his heart hardened. David had deeply mourned the death of Saul, his enemy, yet he coldly took steps to ensure the death of one of his devoted followers and a member of his elite group of fighting men (see 2 Sam. 23:39). Uriah's death cleared the way for David to marry his wife Bathsheba and cover up their sin of adultery. Or so David thought.

About a year after David began his relationship with Bathsheba, the prophet Nathan told the king a story about a rich man who owned large flocks and a poor man who owned a single lamb. The poor man treated the lamb as part of his family until his rich neighbor stole it to serve as a meal for a visitor. David erupted in anger and demanded the thief's death. Then Nathan identified David as the villain: "You are the man!" (12:7).

The words pierced David's heart and he immediately confessed his sin. God forgave him, but there would be consequences. There would be trouble and bloodshed within David's family. While he had taken Uriah's wife in secret, God would give David's wives to someone else in broad daylight. And the baby conceived from David and Bathsheba's unlawful union would die.

We may think we're doing something in secret, but even when no one on earth knows, God still sees. He promises that every word and every action will be exposed. How would our behavior change if we let that truth guide our decisions every moment of every day? It may seem as though we've been able to cover up a sin. But we need to remember it's only a matter of time before God points a finger at us and declares, "You are the man!" or "You are the woman!"

> *Nothing has been covered that will not be exposed.*
> *Whatever is secret will be made known.*
>
> Luke 12:2

Not the Real Thing

2 Samuel 13

David's oldest son Amnon convinced himself that he was in love with his beautiful half-sister Tamar. Day after day, he obsessed about her until he made himself sick. When he confided in his cousin, Jonadab schemed to help Amnon get alone with Tamar, even involving King David in the ruse. Tamar followed her father's instructions and went to Amnon's house to prepare food for her supposedly ill half-brother. After ordering all the servants to leave, Amnon grabbed Tamar and tried to seduce her. She refused and tried to reason with him, but Amnon ignored her pleas and raped her.

As soon as Amnon had satisfied his physical lust, his infatuation with Tamar turned into intense loathing. Amnon had already committed the crime of rape; then he made matters even worse. He had Tamar thrown out of the house and the door bolted behind her, acting as though she were the one to blame. Tamar left his house devastated, knowing that her culture now considered her unfit for marriage.

Tamar's brother Absalom took her into his house and advised her to keep quiet about the incident. Amnon may have been relieved and thought he'd gotten away with his conquest, but he had no idea what lay ahead. His selfish act led to his murder two years later by Absalom and a bloody rebellion against King David, ending in Absalom's violent death.

People today still confuse infatuation or lust with love. The media bombard us with images that urge us to act on our physical impulses, leading people to use each other to satisfy their desires. As a result, we're surrounded by wounded women and men. Sometimes we're even betrayed by the very ones who should love and protect us. The biblical definition of love is acting in a way that puts the other person's best interests ahead of ours. If we feel like we've been used, then we've probably accepted a cheap substitute for love instead of the real thing.

[Love] doesn't think about itself.

1 Corinthians 13:5

A Rebellious Son

2 Samuel 14—18

David proved to be an effective leader but a weak parent in the area of discipline. Perhaps he neglected to train his children because of his heavy responsibilities as king. Maybe David avoided dealing decisively with his children's sins because of guilt over his own sins in the past. In any case, David failed to punish Amnon's incestuous rape of Tamar. Two years later, Absalom avenged the crime against his sister by having Amnon murdered. Absalom then lived in exile for three years until Joab persuaded the king to allow his return.

Even then, David's indecisiveness kept the matter from being resolved. He didn't discipline Absalom, but he also didn't offer complete forgiveness since he refused to meet his son in person for two more years. By the time David reached out in reconciliation, Absalom had grown bitter and lost all respect for his father. He used his charisma to gain the people's favor and stir up a rebellion against David. The widespread revolt forced David and his loyal followers to flee from Jerusalem. In the bloody struggle that ensued, Absalom met a violent death that left David brokenhearted.

Eli and David were both godly men but indulgent fathers with out-of-control sons. They neglected to effectively discipline their children for their godless actions, causing much grief and heartache. In a similar way, believers can be careful to outwardly live a godly lifestyle while neglecting their inner thought life. Since our thinking affects our behavior, it's important to exercise mental discipline.

When we saturate our mind with the Scriptures, we can evaluate each thought to see if it would be pleasing to God. If it contradicts his Word or will, we can confess and ask him to transform our thinking. We can't afford to be careless about what goes on in our mind. If not checked, improper thoughts can get out of control, and a rebellious mind will end up causing us—and those around us—much grief and heartache.

We take every thought captive so that it is obedient to Christ.

2 Corinthians 10:5

A Senseless Census

2 Samuel 24

Late in David's reign, he angered God by taking an unauthorized census. According to 1 Chronicles 21:1, God allowed Satan to tempt David with the idea. David's desire to count the military men in Israel might have indicated his reliance on the nation's military strength instead of on God for protection. Perhaps such an attitude of pride and self-sufficiency also prevailed among the population at large. When David ordered the census, Joab protested and questioned why David felt it necessary. But the king overruled Joab and the other army commanders.

As soon as Joab reported the numbers to David, the king regretted his decision. He confessed and asked God to forgive his "terrible sin." The next morning Gad the prophet told David he must choose his punishment: famine, being chased by enemies, or plague. David vowed he would rather fall into the hands of his merciful God than be at the mercy of men. Seventy thousand people died from a plague over the next three days. David begged God to let the punishment fall on him and his family alone. Once he had followed God's instructions to build an altar, offer sacrifices, and intercede for the people, the plague stopped.

Whenever David obeyed God, Israel enjoyed God's blessings and peace; when he sinned in his personal life, the entire nation suffered from the consequences. The life of a leader can affect everyone under his or her authority. That is why it's important for us to do all we can to ensure that godly leaders are elected.

We're also responsible to pray consistently for our civil government and for leaders around the world. That can prove distasteful when they stand opposed to our beliefs and convictions. But remembering that we're subject to the consequences of their decisions should be enough to send us to our knees.

> *First of all, I encourage you to make petitions, prayers,*
> *intercessions, and prayers of thanks for all people, for*
> *rulers, and for everyone who has authority over us.*
>
> 1 Timothy 2:1–2

1 Kings

Divided Heart, Divided Kingdom

So Solomon did what the LORD considered evil. He did not wholeheartedly follow the LORD as his father David had done.

1 Kings 11:6

While David lay on his deathbed, his son Adonijah declared himself Israel's next king. David quickly arranged to have Solomon, his son by Bathsheba, crowned as he had promised earlier. Solomon began his reign with fervent love and devotion for God, building a magnificent temple to be God's dwelling place and the center of worship for the nation. God blessed the new king with unprecedented wisdom, riches, and fame. Unfortunately, Solomon also acquired an unprecedented number of foreign wives who eventually influenced him to worship their pagan gods. As a result, God allowed the kingdom to be split. Israel's golden years of peace, prosperity, and glory came to an end.

The first eleven chapters of 1 Kings narrate Solomon's reign; the second half of the book lists the rulers of the northern kingdom of Israel and the southern kingdom of Judah. We get a close-up portrait of Ahab, one of the most evil kings, who plots with his wife Jezebel until they meet a horrendous end. We also see Elijah, one of Israel's greatest prophets, as he courageously stands against government-sponsored Baal worship.

We can learn much about God's character from 1 Kings. He proves his power in the thrilling showdown on Mount Carmel as Elijah challenges hundreds of pagan prophets. God also demonstrates his tender loving care as he provides food for Elijah in a highly unusual way, and reveals himself in a gentle whisper when the prophet is exhausted and discouraged.

Solomon's life also offers valuable spiritual lessons. Even though he enjoyed every blessing imaginable, he ignored God's command about intermarriage with people from pagan nations. As a result, he let his affections be pulled away from God. First Kings prompts us to check our own life. Does our heart still completely belong to our heavenly Father, or are we trying to divide it between God and something or someone else?

Make a Wish

1 Kings 3:1–15

Solomon loved God and tried to follow in his father David's footsteps, but he went along with the prevailing trend of offering sacrifices at locations not specified by God. In the beginning of his reign, Solomon offered a thousand sacrifices to God on the altar at Gibeon. Although God could not condone the sacrifices, he acknowledged Solomon's motivation and humility. That night God appeared to Solomon in a dream and invited him to ask for anything he wished. The new king's response greatly pleased God.

Solomon felt the weight of his immense responsibility as leader of God's chosen people. He was also fully aware of his inexperience and youth (he was probably around age twenty). So he asked for a discerning heart tuned in to God's voice, so that he could distinguish between good and evil and govern Israel effectively. God promised to give Solomon a wise and understanding heart without equal.

And since Solomon put his God-given role and his people's welfare above personal gain, God also granted what he didn't ask for. Solomon would have riches and honor greater than any other king. If he followed God and obeyed his commands, Solomon would also have a long life.

Our culture prizes intelligence and the accumulation of knowledge. While these things are good, we need something more. We need the wisdom to know how God wants us to live. God encourages us to ask him for wisdom, especially when we're going through trials or facing difficulties. God's supernatural wisdom helps us distinguish between right and wrong, understand spiritual principles, and apply biblical truth to our daily life. Since genuine wisdom leads to godly living, Proverbs 3:16 associates it with riches, honor, and long life. If we prize God's wisdom enough to ask for it, then, like Solomon, we'll discover that it's a gift that brings other blessings with it.

If any of you needs wisdom to know what you should do, you should ask God, and he will give it to you.

James 1:5

A Difficult Case

1 Kings 3:16—28

Solomon needed all the wisdom God gave him as he administered justice for the nation of Israel. God recorded an example to show us how Solomon put his discernment into practice when he settled a particularly difficult case. Two prostitutes who lived together both had newborn sons. One of the mothers accidentally killed her baby by rolling on top of him during the night. While the other woman slept, this mother switched babies. The next morning, the second mother woke up and found the dead baby beside her, but recognized that he was not her son.

The two women appeared before Solomon, each one passionately claiming to be the mother of the living child. Since there were no witnesses to offer evidence, Solomon called for a sword. He gave orders for the living baby to be cut in half and divided between the two women. One woman reacted in horror, begging the king to let the other woman have the baby. The second woman agreed with the grisly plan. Solomon then knew the real mother—the woman who was willing to give up the child in order to save his life.

God's wisdom gave Solomon an understanding of human nature. It allowed him to see past the superficial and penetrate to the heart of the matter. We need that kind of wisdom in our everyday life. At times we find ourselves faced with two choices that look equally appealing. Our human reasoning makes a convincing case for both courses of action.

Only God can give us the discernment required for understanding his will. It's not always easy to tell right from wrong; sometimes it seems impossible to distinguish between what's just okay and what is God's best for our life. When the answer isn't obvious, God can give us the understanding we need to resolve our own difficult cases.

Evil people do not understand justice,
but those who seek the LORD understand everything.

Proverbs 28:5

Solomon's Fame

1 Kings 10

As Solomon's fame spread, the Queen of Sheba decided to pay him a visit. She wanted to see if the incredible reports about his wealth and wisdom were true. Traveling more than a thousand miles from Arabia to Jerusalem, the queen arrived with her own impressive envoy. She presented Solomon with more than four tons of gold and huge quantities of precious stones and exotic spices. But her gifts paled in comparison to the wealth she saw displayed in the palace, the temple, and Solomon's other building projects. These riches, along with Solomon's ability to answer every question and riddle she asked, astounded the queen.

When the visit ended, the queen did not return home empty-handed. Solomon had showered her with gifts and then added anything she asked for. More importantly, the queen had been exposed to the one true God. She had seen the temple where his Spirit dwelled and heard Solomon give him the credit for his kingship. The two of them must have shared many conversations about Yahweh. If the Queen of Sheba embraced Israel's God, then she left with riches far greater than what was loaded on her camels' backs—or even what could be found in the entire city of Jerusalem.

Many people seem fascinated with the lifestyles of the rich and famous, but once we become believers, our values change dramatically. We may still desire a solid bank account, material possessions, popularity, or career success, but we know those things don't have eternal value. Knowing God surpasses anything the world has to offer so greatly that everything else seems worthless in comparison. When we find ourselves getting dazzled by worldly ideas of wealth or success, we can remember that our relationship with Christ Jesus is priceless.

> *These things that I once considered valuable, I now consider*
> *worthless for Christ. . . . I consider everything else worthless*
> *because I'm much better off knowing Christ Jesus my*
> *Lord. . . . I threw it all away in order to gain Christ.*
>
> Philippians 3:7–8

Solomon's Folly

1 Kings 11

For the wisest man who had ever lived, Solomon did some very foolish things. Before Israel had even entered the Promised Land, God had looked ahead to the day when the people would demand to have a king like other nations. In Deuteronomy 17:16–20, God commanded that the king should not own a large number of horses because he might become dependent on military strength instead of on God's protection. He should not possess a lot of gold and silver since that could lead to greed for personal gain. God also forbade the king from marrying a lot of wives because then his heart might turn away from God.

Solomon began his reign by humbly seeking God's will and urging the Israelites to keep their hearts committed to the Lord. Yet, one by one Solomon broke God's prohibitions. He accumulated vast amounts of gold, using much of it for his extensive building projects. Even the eating and drinking utensils in his palace were made of gold. Solomon also amassed twelve thousand war horses and a large number of chariots.

But marrying foreign women proved to be Solomon's most dangerous obsession. He ignored God's command against intermarriage with certain nations and ended up with seven hundred royal wives and three hundred concubines. In his old age, Solomon's wives influenced him to worship their gods, just as God had warned would happen.

In the Deuteronomy passage, God instructed the king to keep a copy of the Law and read it throughout his lifetime. God expects something similar from each one of us today. Just knowing what the Bible says is not enough; we are to continually meditate on how to apply its teachings to our life. If we don't, our commitment to God will weaken and our heart can be easily led astray. Solomon's foolishness reminds us that the only safe obsession is wholehearted obedience to God.

> *I thank God that you have become wholeheartedly*
> *obedient to the teachings which you were given.*
>
> Romans 6:17

The Kingdom Splits

1 Kings 11:9—12:33

As Solomon indulged his desires for riches, buildings, and women, his attitude toward God changed. Eventually, Solomon began worshiping other gods even though the Lord had appeared to him twice. God promised to tear the kingdom away from Solomon as punishment, but for David's sake, he would wait until after Solomon died. In the meantime, Solomon had to revise his earlier statement that he was surrounded with peace, having "no rival and no trouble" (1 Kings 5:4). God raised up two men who opposed Solomon in his later years: Hadad in the north and Rezon in the south.

After Solomon's death, his son Rehoboam succeeded him as king. At the coronation, the Israelites promised to serve Rehoboam if he would reduce the oppressive tax and labor requirements that Solomon had instituted. Instead of agreeing, the new king vowed that he would put an even heavier burden on them than his father had. His harsh answer prompted the ten northern tribes to rebel and make Jeroboam their king.

God averted the threat of immediate warfare between the two groups, but the nation had now split. Israel became the northern kingdom under Jeroboam's rule, while Rehoboam ruled the southern kingdom of Judah, which also included the tribe of Benjamin. According to 1 Kings 14:30, there was war between Jeroboam and Rehoboam as long as they lived.

As believers we must deal with our old sinful nature that fights against our devotion to Christ. If we indulge our personal desires that oppose God's will, we lose the peace that comes from being close to him. When we try to divide our loyalties between God and anything else, we can expect trouble just as surely as a divided kingdom means rivalry and war. Every day we're called to settle the question of where our allegiance lies. If we're willing to set aside our selfish interests to follow God, then we can experience the security of being surrounded by his peace.

> *What causes fights and quarrels among you? Aren't they*
> *caused by the selfish desires that fight to control you?*
>
> James 4:1

Catered by God

1 Kings 17

As the first ruler of Israel's northern kingdom, Jeroboam set up two alternative worship centers to prevent his people from traveling to the temple in Jerusalem, which was located in Judah. For the next three hundred years, a succession of wicked kings followed this pattern of leading the people to worship pagan gods. God raised up a line of prophets to urge people to turn back to God. Elijah prophesied during the reign of Ahab, a king who "did more to make the LORD God of Israel furious than all the kings of Israel who came before him" (1 Kings 16:33).

God sent Elijah to Ahab to announce a drought that would last several years. Afterward, God told Elijah to hide out near a stream where he would have drinking water. At God's command, ravens brought Elijah food every morning and evening. When the stream dried up, God sent Elijah to Zarephath. There the prophet met a starving widow who planned to use her last bit of oil and flour to prepare a last meal for herself and her son. When she obeyed Elijah's request to first make a small loaf for him, God rewarded her faith. Until the drought ended, God kept flour in the woman's jar and oil in her jug.

God promises to supply the needs of his children, but sometimes we receive his provision from unexpected sources. In Elijah's case, God used unclean birds and a woman from the evil Queen Jezebel's homeland to feed the prophet. In God's provision for the widow, he required her to demonstrate her faith by an act of obedience.

Sometimes God meets our needs by asking us to do something that goes against our natural impulses. We can miss out on God's blessings if we're looking from the perspective of our narrow expectations. When we struggle with a need, it's best to remember that we may find God's help in a place where we least expect it.

My God will richly fill your every need in a
glorious way through Christ Jesus.

Philippians 4:19

Showdown on Mount Carmel

1 Kings 18:1—40

Just before the drought ended, Elijah paid a surprise visit to Ahab to issue an invitation. Later, all Israel gathered on Mount Carmel to watch what looked like a one-sided contest. Baal was represented by his 450 prophets kept by Jezebel. On the sidelines sat the 400 prophets of Asherah, Baal's consort. Since Mount Carmel was considered Baal's dwelling place, his team enjoyed a home court advantage. On the other side, Elijah stood and challenged the Israelites to make a choice between the Lord and Baal.

Elijah let the prophets of Baal go first. They prepared a bull for the sacrifice and called on Baal to send fire to consume it. They chanted and danced the rest of the morning with no sign of an answer. At noon Elijah began to mock them, suggesting that they needed to shout louder to get Baal's attention. For the next three hours, the prophets ranted, raved, and cut their bodies trying to get a response from their god.

Then Elijah prepared a sacrifice and had someone pour water over it and the wood three times. He prayed a simple prayer, asking God to show his power to the people. Fire immediately consumed not only the sacrifice, but the stones, mud, and water in the trench. The people fell down, shouting, "The LORD is God!"

God calls each one of us to take a stand for his truth. That means we're often pitted against popular opinion, widespread false teaching, or flawed philosophy that has become entrenched in our culture. Sometimes it seems as though we're standing alone. When we feel outnumbered, we can take courage from Elijah's example.

It may look like we're involved in a one-sided contest, but if we're obeying God's directions, we don't have to worry about the outcome. We have aligned ourselves with the living, all-powerful God, and that gives us a heavenly advantage. No matter what happens, we're on the winning side.

If God is for us, who can be against us?

Romans 8:31

Breakdown in Beersheba

1 Kings 19

After the spectacular fire flashed from heaven in answer to Elijah's prayer, God sent rain to end the drought, which was also an answer to the prophet's prayer. Elijah hiked up his robe and raced into the city, outstripping the king's chariot. Then Elijah heard something that knocked the wind right out of him. Queen Jezebel, who had a history of murdering the Lord's prophets, vowed to kill Elijah within twenty-four hours. Elijah ran for his life—all the way to the southernmost town in the kingdom of Judah. Reaching Beersheba, he traveled into the wilderness alone, prayed that God would take his life, and fell into an exhausted sleep.

God tenderly nurtured the physically and emotionally drained prophet. During Elijah's long, restorative sleep, an angel woke him up twice and offered fresh bread and water. This heavenly food nourished Elijah for the two-hundred-mile journey to Mount Horeb. There God displayed his power with a fierce wind, an earthquake, and fire. But Elijah recognized God's presence in his gentle, whispering voice. God assured Elijah that he wasn't alone; Israel included seven thousand people who had refused to worship Baal. In addition, God had appointed three men to continue the purge of Baal worship that had begun on Mount Carmel.

After we experience God in some dramatic way, a letdown is sure to follow. Times of spiritual victory leave us vulnerable to discouragement; we may even struggle with depression. When physical, emotional, and spiritual weariness set in, we can find ourselves feeling like a failure and drained of our desire to serve God. Rather than giving up or beating ourselves up, we can turn to God and bask in his tender loving care. The same God who flashed fire from heaven will surround his exhausted, hurting children with the nurturing they need to get back on their feet. We don't have to run all the way to Beersheba—just into our Father's arms.

> *Do not withhold Your tender mercies from me, O* LORD*;*
> *Let Your lovingkindness and Your*
> *truth continually preserve me.*
>
> Psalm 40:11 NKJV

Selective Hearing

1 Kings 22:1–40

Even though Ahab was such an evil king, God made sure he was exposed to the truth. Ahab had the opportunity to learn from and be guided by one of Israel's greatest prophets; instead he hated Elijah as an enemy. Ahab preferred to take advice from his wicked wife Jezebel, who urged him on to commit more evil. He also listened to false prophets who curried his favor by telling him what they thought he wanted to hear. This tendency toward selective hearing eventually led Ahab to his death.

As Ahab persuaded Jehoshaphat, the king of Judah, to join him in battle against the Arameans, Jehoshaphat insisted that they seek God's guidance. Ahab called together four hundred prophets who unanimously predicted a military victory. Unconvinced, Jehoshaphat asked for a true prophet of the Lord. Ahab admitted that Micaiah was available, but complained that "he doesn't prophesy anything good about me, only evil" (v. 8). Sure enough, Micaiah predicted Ahab's death in the battle, after first mocking the advice of the king's "yes men." Although Ahab took the precaution of disguising himself, he died when a "random" arrow hit him between the sections of his armor.

People have a tendency to listen to those who tell them what they want to hear. Instead of learning biblical truth, many Christians look for speakers and teachers who merely validate their own preconceived ideas and opinions. They reject any interpretation of the Scriptures that makes them feel uncomfortable. Sometimes they even manage to find a church that excuses their sinful behavior. There will always be plenty of false teachers who reject the notion of absolute truth and ignore God's standards. But it's dangerous to be selective in our hearing. Sometimes it's the person we don't want to listen to who is saying exactly what we need to hear.

> *A time will come when people will not listen*
> *to accurate teachings. Instead, they will follow*
> *their own desires and surround themselves with*
> *teachers who tell them what they want to hear.*
>
> 2 Timothy 4:3

2 Kings

The Road to Self-Destruction

The LORD had said, "I will put Judah out of my sight as I put Israel out of my sight. I will reject Jerusalem, the city that I chose, and I will reject the temple where I said my name would be."

2 Kings 23:27

Second Kings continues to trace the history of the separate nations of Israel and Judah after their division a century earlier. The first seventeen chapters alternate between the northern and southern kingdoms, listing the rulers who, for the most part, led the people further and further into moral and spiritual deterioration. Israel was governed by a total of nineteen evil kings representing nine separate dynasties. Judah's single dynasty included twenty kings; only a few of them were godly.

Throughout this period of spiritual decline, God sent prophets who tried to turn the people's hearts back to him. After God whisked Elijah to heaven, Elisha had a fifty-year ministry marked by miracles ranging from solutions to everyday problems to supernatural military intervention. The leaders and the people largely ignored the prophets' warnings. Both nations continued to anger God by their sin and rebellion until his patience eventually came to an end.

The Assyrians conquered Israel in 722 BC. Judah stood another 136 years, due to periods of spiritual renewal experienced under godly kings. Eventually, Judah faced judgment through a series of three deportations to Babylon. The final wave came in 586 BC when Nebuchadnezzar destroyed Jerusalem and the temple. Despite these disasters, 2 Kings ends on a positive note. The release and kind treatment of King Jehoiachin hints that there would yet be a future for the Davidic line and for God's chosen people.

Reading 2 Kings is a good time to examine our life for any self-destructive tendencies. Are we ignoring any of God's warnings about the consequences of sinful behavior? This history encourages us to follow God instead of going along with the flow of our culture. Since we are part of God's faithful remnant, he will help us be a force for spiritual renewal in our own circle of influence.

Left Behind

2 Kings 2

Elijah and Elisha both knew that this would be the older prophet's last day on the earth. As the two men traveled together, three times Elijah urged Elisha to stay behind. Each time, Elisha refused. He had determined to stay with Elijah until the last possible moment. He did not want to miss the opportunity to spend time with his mentor and spiritual father and to receive a special blessing from him before he departed. When they came to the Jordan River, Elijah used his coat to part the waters. As they walked across, Elijah asked what he could do for Elisha before being taken away.

Elisha asked to receive a double portion of Elijah's spirit. Elijah said that if Elisha witnessed Elijah's departure, that would be a sign that his request had been granted. Shortly afterward, a fiery chariot with fiery horses came between the two men and a whirlwind swept Elijah up into heaven. After Elijah had disappeared from sight, Elisha picked up Elijah's coat from the ground. He used it to replicate Elijah's miracle of dividing the water of the Jordan River. Elisha had the confirmation he needed: God had appointed him to carry on the work Elijah began.

Materially speaking, Elijah didn't leave much behind when God whisked him away. But Elisha received a rich spiritual inheritance from his father in the faith. Unlike these two prophets, we don't usually know when we'll see a loved one for the last time. That's why it's important to think about what we'll be leaving behind when God takes us home. The best legacy to leave is a memory of a life of faithfulness that encourages others to seek God and follow him. Every day represents a precious opportunity to testify to God's love and forgiveness through our words, our attitudes, and our actions. Our daily steps of obedience and commitment will add up to a lasting legacy for those we leave behind.

Encourage each other every day while
you have the opportunity.

Hebrews 3:13

The Right Approach

2 Kings 4

After God took Elijah to heaven, Elisha passed through Bethel, the focal point of idolatry in the northern kingdom. A large gang of boys rushed out of the city to jeer at God's prophet. Elisha considered their disrespect to be aimed at the God he served, and called down a curse on them. God sent two bears out of the nearby woods to kill forty-two of the young men (see 2 Kings 2:23–24).

In 2 Kings 4 we find stories of people who responded to God in the opposite way, with faith and obedience. The penniless widow of a God-fearing prophet told Elisha that creditors planned to seize her children as slaves. Following Elisha's instructions, she borrowed containers from her neighbors and began pouring out the small amount of oil she had in the house. The oil flowed until every last container had been filled. When the widow sold the oil, she had enough to pay her debts and support her family.

Later, Elisha wanted to reward a woman in Shunem who opened her home to him. Within a year she had the son promised by Elisha even though her husband was elderly. Several years later, the boy died. The mother laid his body in Elisha's room and went straight to find the man of God, not stopping to explain her son's death to her husband. After Elisha prayed, God restored the boy's life.

All of us are responsible for how we approach God. We can choose to remain his enemy and treat him with disrespect and contempt, or we can enter into a relationship with him through faith in his Son Jesus. God is pleased when his children ask for his help because it proves that we believe in his goodness and mercy. When we approach God with the right attitude, we can rely on his promise that he will reward those who seek him.

No one can please God without faith. Whoever
goes to God must believe that God exists and
that he rewards those who seek him.

Hebrews 11:6

A Simple Prescription

2 *Kings* 5

Desperate for a cure, Naaman grasped at the suggestion from his Israelite slave girl. She claimed that a prophet in Samaria had the power to heal his skin disease. Naaman shared this information with the king of Aram, who would go to any lengths to save the life of his friend and valuable army commander. Naaman set out for Israel with gifts of gold, silver, and clothing along with a letter from the king of Aram requesting that he be cured. Joram, the Israelite king, directed Naaman to Elisha's house.

Naaman arrived in his chariot, expecting to be shown the proper respect due a man in his station. Instead, Elisha sent a messenger outside with instructions to wash in the Jordan River seven times. The commander rode off in a huff. He'd expected the prophet to perform a sophisticated healing ritual. But if he did need to bathe in a river, why couldn't he use the superior rivers in his own country?

Naaman's servants pointed out that he would have been willing to follow something more difficult. Why not try this simple remedy? Naaman changed his mind and obeyed Elisha's instructions, emerging from the river with healthy, youthful skin.

Some people want to come to God on their own terms instead of accepting his offer of salvation through faith in Jesus. Others miss out on finding their way to God because of the simplicity of his plan. Many people consider the gospel to be old-fashioned and outdated; they stubbornly look for a more "sophisticated" spirituality or try to create their own belief system.

God has provided a way for us to be healed from the disease of sin and he paid a high price to make it possible. All he asks of us is that we trust him enough to follow his simple prescription.

> *They don't understand how to receive God's approval. So*
> *they try to set up their own way to get it, and they have*
> *not accepted God's way for receiving his approval.*
>
> Romans 10:3

An Invisible Army

2 Kings 6:8–23

The king of Aram became convinced that he had a traitor in his midst. How else could the Israelite army know exactly when and where he planned to attack them? One of the officers explained that a prophet named Elisha kept the Israelite king informed, even sharing the Aramean king's most private conversations. The Aramean king found out Elisha's location in Dothan and dispatched horses, chariots, and a large fighting force to capture him. During the night, the army secretly approached and surrounded the city.

The next morning, Elisha's servant stepped outside and saw the enemy forces that hemmed them in. He cried out in terror to his master. Elisha calmly assured his servant that there was no reason to be afraid; they had more forces on their side than the Arameans had on theirs. He prayed that God would open his servant's eyes.

Suddenly, the servant could see that the hillside around Elisha was full of fiery horses and chariots. Then Elisha asked God to confuse the sight of the Aramean soldiers. When Elisha convinced them they had come to the wrong location, the soldiers allowed him to lead them inside the city of Samaria, where God restored their clear sight.

Elisha and his servant had the privilege of seeing what is normally invisible to the human eye. God has a host of angels at his beck and call, ready to protect and minister to his children. No matter where we go, God's heavenly army surrounds us like a shield; nothing can get through this barrier without his permission. It may seem as though our enemies have us at their mercy, but that's only because our sight is so limited. If our human eyes could see the protection that surrounds us in the spiritual realm, we would understand that we never really have anything to fear.

As the mountains surround Jerusalem,
so the LORD surrounds his people now and forever.

Psalm 125:2

Mass Murder in the Palace

2 Kings 11

When King Ahaziah of Judah was assassinated after ruling for only one year, his mother decided to seize the throne for herself. But first, Athaliah would need to get rid of any possible heirs in order to secure her place. Without hesitation, the queen mother set out to assassinate all of her grandsons. If she had succeeded, she would have wiped out David's royal line. Fortunately, two courageous women risked their lives and managed to save one of Ahaziah's sons from the bloodbath. Jehosheba hid her one-year-old nephew Joash and his nurse in her bedroom. Later, she secretly took them to the temple where her husband Jehoida served as high priest.

Athaliah ruled Judah for six years, promoting Baal worship while oblivious to the fact that a legitimate heir to the throne was growing up in Yahweh's temple. At the beginning of Athaliah's seventh year of rule, Jehoida summoned certain military commanders and guards who didn't support the queen. He showed them Joash, the legitimate ruler, and enlisted their help in arranging a coronation. When Athaliah investigated the celebratory noise coming from the temple, she saw the newly crowned seven-year-old king. Athaliah screamed out, "Treason!" even though she was the one who had committed it. Officials arrested and executed Athaliah in the streets.

God expects believers to be ready to protect innocent people. We may not be involved in a dramatic rescue as Jehosheba was, but we might get the opportunity to defend someone whose character is being unjustly assassinated. We can stay informed about worldwide persecution and human rights issues and get involved in promoting justice. We can speak up for those who often have no voice in our society, including unborn children and the homeless. If we're willing, God will show us what part we can play in defending those facing persecution or danger—people who are very close to his heart.

Speak out for the one who cannot speak,
for the rights of those who are doomed.

Proverbs 31:8

Israel Goes Down

2 Kings 17

God had been waiting for the northern kingdom of Israel to change its ways for more than two hundred years, ever since the nation divided. But the people persisted in doing the very things God had clearly forbidden. While they sometimes outwardly worshiped the Lord, they also bowed down to an assortment of idols and false deities. They imitated the detestable practices of the pagan nations God had judged when he allowed the Israelites to conquer the Promised Land. The Israelites even let themselves be drawn into practicing magic and offering child sacrifices.

Prophet after prophet repeated God's warnings to turn away from evil and obey his commands. The people refused to listen. Finally, God judged their sin. Although the king of Assyria had made the Israelite king his vassal, Hoshea tried to make a treaty with Egypt. When Hoshea refused to pay the annual tribute, Assyria besieged Israel until it fell. Many of the people were deported from the land that God had given them and dispersed throughout the Assyrian kingdom. The Assyrian king repopulated the Israelite cities with a mixture of foreign people groups in order to prevent revolt. In essence, the northern kingdom of Israel had now ceased to exist.

If it wasn't for God's divine patience, the world would have ceased to exist soon after its creation. But even God's patience has limits. Since he's a holy God, he cannot tolerate sin forever. God will do all he can to draw people into a relationship with himself. He will put people and circumstances in the life of wayward believers to turn them away from disobedience.

Eventually, however, he *will* judge sin. The history of the northern kingdom demonstrates how dangerous it is to presume on God's patience. It also reminds us that we have a choice. We can either listen to God and obey him now, or later experience the consequences of ignoring his warnings.

If only you would listen to him today!

Psalm 95:7

Our First Line of Defense

2 Kings 18—19

In contrast with his evil father, King Hezekiah of Judah displayed faith in God and a commitment to bring the people back to obedience and true worship. After a few years, Hezekiah boldly rebelled against the Assyrian king and refused to pay the tribute money as his father Ahaz had done. However, when the coalition of neighboring countries failed and King Sennacherib captured the fortified cities of Judah, Hezekiah wasn't as bold.

Hezekiah's first reaction to the threat was to try to bargain his way out. He sent a message to Sennacherib apologizing and offering to pay a penalty if the Assyrian king would withdraw. In order to get the huge sum that Sennacherib demanded, Hezekiah took all the silver out of the temple and stripped the gold plating off the doors and door frames. But Sennacherib changed his mind and sent a delegation to pressure Hezekiah into surrendering.

Hezekiah sent word for Isaiah to pray for their hopeless situation, and the prophet relayed a promise that God would deliver the city. When Hezekiah received another message from the Assyrians, this time he went directly to God in prayer.

Spreading out the insulting letters, the king acknowledged God's sovereignty and beseeched him to deliver Judah so that other nations would recognize him as the true God. That very night God intervened and forced the Assyrian army to withdraw.

Whenever we face a problem or crisis, many of us attempt to handle things on our own, sometimes even trying to bargain our way out. We may not think of going to God until the situation seems hopeless. God wants us to see prayer as our first line of defense, not as a last resort when everything else has failed. We can go to him at the first sign of trouble and trust that he will be even more concerned about our situation than we are. Just as Hezekiah spread out his threatening letters before God, we can lay out our anxieties before him.

Turn all your anxiety over to God because he cares for you.

1 Peter 5:7

Judah Falls

2 Kings 25

The nation of Judah had a lot going for it. Israel's greatest king, David, had ruled from the city of Jerusalem and built the Lord's temple there. The people had easy access to the sacred place ordained by God for worship, offerings, and sacrifices. Ancient prophecies pinpointed Judah as the birthplace of the Messiah, a ruler from the Davidic line whose reign would last forever. In contrast to Israel's long line of evil rulers, Judah benefited from the reigns of several godly kings such as Hezekiah and Josiah. Judah also had the advantage of witnessing firsthand the consequences of sin when God judged the northern kingdom by letting Assyria conquer it.

Sadly, Judah refused to learn from the example of Israel. God delayed judgment because of temporary spiritual reforms and revivals instituted by Hezekiah and Josiah. But the leaders and people of Judah persisted in rebelling against God and ignoring his laws. They worshiped idols and indulged in the evil practices of other nations. Eventually, Judah fell to Babylon, the new world power. The Babylonians looted the temple, burned Jerusalem, tore down the walls, and deported most of the people.

Some people rely on their spiritual heritage or church connections to make them right with God. But having godly parents or even coming from a long line of pastors and Christian leaders isn't enough. We can't depend on baptism, communion, a confirmation ceremony, or any other ritual to curry God's favor.

Regardless of our background, each one of us must make the choice whether or not we will accept God's offer of salvation through Jesus Christ and live as his obedient child. When we stand before God one day, our connections with other Christians or with a "religious" institution won't matter; our relationship with Christ will be the only thing we have going for us. If we have that, it will be more than enough.

All of us will have to give an account of ourselves to God.

Romans 14:12

1 Chronicles

Still God's Special People

I will place him in my royal house forever, and his throne will be established forever.

1 Chronicles 17:14

It looked as though the nation of Judah ceased to exist when the Babylonians destroyed Jerusalem in 586 BC and deported most of the people. But in 538, Babylon fell to the Persians, who favored a policy of allowing exiled people to return to their homeland and rebuild their cities. The small remnant of Jews who returned from captivity to live in what had become a province in the Persian Empire must have wondered: Had they lost their unique place as God's chosen people?

The author of 1 Chronicles reminded his readers of their spiritual foundation. The first nine chapters list genealogies tracing Israel's roots from Adam down to the captives who returned to Jerusalem. The last nineteen chapters recount David's reign, highlighting his triumphs and successes. The content of 1 Chronicles serves as a supplement to 2 Samuel, viewing the same events from a spiritual perspective. The author uses a selective approach in order to encourage his readers and to draw out moral and spiritual lessons.

In spite of their past failures and present reduced circumstances, 1 Chronicles makes it clear that God's plans for humanity still center on the Jewish people. They can face the future because of the thread of God's grace woven throughout their history. This hope is based on the priesthood, the temple, and especially the promise God made to David concerning his descendant, a messianic king who would rule forever. The Jewish people had lost much because of sin and rebellion, but they had not lost their special identity as God's chosen people.

Reading 1 Chronicles encourages us to trace our own spiritual roots and reflect on God's grace woven throughout our personal history. We may have missed opportunities and blessings because of disobedience, but we can still face the future with hope. Along with the Jewish remnant, we can rejoice in our special identity as God's chosen, all because of the Messiah.

A Striking Contrast

1 Chronicles 13; 15

David had a worthy goal, the best of intentions, and a zeal for his mission. But it ended in disaster. The ark was the Jewish people's most sacred object since it represented God's presence and his promise, but it had been ignored during Saul's reign. David gathered Israel and proposed bringing the ark to a permanent resting place in Jerusalem. He either didn't know or ignored God's detailed instructions for handling the ark as laid down in Exodus 25. The Israelites loaded the ark on a cart and started off, praising God as they traveled. Suddenly the oxen stumbled, and Uzzah instinctively reached out to protect the ark. God, who had forbidden the touching of the ark, killed Uzzah on the spot.

Uzzah's death angered and frightened David. He waited three months before making a second attempt to bring the ark to Jerusalem. This time he followed God's guidelines, with a strikingly different outcome. After consecrating themselves, Levites carried the ark on their shoulders using special poles that slipped through the rings on the sides. Other Levites sang and played instruments as the procession joyfully made its way to Jerusalem. As David and the people celebrated the ark's arrival, they had learned a valuable lesson about the importance of doing things God's way.

Believers today may approach their relationship with God with passion and zeal, yet have a casual attitude toward his guidelines for everyday living. Some are ignorant of what God expects of them because they haven't studied his Word; others ignore specific commands that aren't to their liking.

It's dangerous to let ourselves develop a careless attitude toward obedience. God gave us instructions for our attitudes, our behavior, and our relationships so that we can live a life of joy and meaning according to his guidelines. What a difference it makes when we're careful to do things his way.

I find joy in the way shown by your written instructions
more than I find joy in all kinds of riches.

Psalm 119:14

David's Idea

1 Chronicles 17

As time passed, David became bothered by the fact that he lived in a beautiful palace of cedar while the ark of God stood inside a tent. He wanted to build a special house for God's presence to dwell in. However, speaking through the prophet Nathan, God refused to let David take on the project. Because of David's heavy involvement in warfare in subduing Israel's enemies and unifying the nation, the honor of building God's temple would go to another (1 Chron. 22:8). But God promised to build David a "house" in the sense of establishing a lasting dynasty through one of his sons.

Instead of resenting that God had turned down his noble idea, David humbled himself and thanked God for his goodness. He acknowledged that he did not deserve what God had already done for him or what God promised to do for his family in the future.

This poet-king expressed a similar attitude when he penned Psalm 16. There he compared God's blessings in his life to a desirable inheritance of land. David felt grateful for where his boundary lines had fallen. God had proven to be enough to satisfy his deepest longings; David was content with how God had ordained his life.

When we get excited about something we want to do for God, it's hard when he shuts down our plans. We may be motivated by a desire to honor him, but that doesn't mean our idea is part of his will for us. He may have something completely different in mind. Remembering that we don't deserve any of God's blessings will help us keep an attitude of humility. If our heart is set on God instead of some lofty idea, we'll find that he is more than enough to satisfy our longings. Then we can accept whatever he ordains for our life, and wherever our boundary lines fall will seem pleasant to us.

> *Your boundary lines mark out pleasant places for me.*
> *Indeed, my inheritance is something beautiful.*
>
> Psalm 16:6

Investing in the Future

1 Chronicles 22

Although David had his heart set on building God's temple, God reserved that honor for Solomon. Thanks to David's diligence in subduing Israel's enemies, his son would have a peaceful reign that would free him to focus more on constructing the temple and establishing systematic worship in Israel. David accepted God's decision with no trace of resentment and proceeded to do everything in his power to help Solomon succeed in such a monumental assignment.

David would never see the temple with his own eyes, but he had a vision of what it would mean to the nation of Israel—and to the world. He knew that such a great God deserved the most magnificent dwelling place that could be constructed. David set stonecutters to work and had other laborers prepare wood. He gathered huge quantities of iron, bronze, and other building materials. He put these at Solomon's disposal, along with the staggering amounts of gold and silver he had accumulated. Perhaps most importantly, David instructed Solomon and encouraged him for his task ahead. He also urged Israel's leaders to dedicate themselves to the project.

David's example reminds us not to be shortsighted about our service to God. Our most important assignment may be to contribute to work that will reap dividends well after our own lifetime. We don't always witness results from spiritually training a child, sharing the gospel, or financially supporting missions work. But any time we pour our time, energy, or resources into the future of God's kingdom, we prove that we have a faith with long-range vision. God will reward our investment in future generations and our desire to leave a positive impact on the world after we leave it. And one day, he will show us what we can't see with our eyes right now.

> *There will be descendants who serve him,*
> *a generation that will be told about the Lord.*
> *They will tell people yet to be born about his righteousness—*
> *that he has finished it.*

Psalm 22:30–31

2 Chronicles

Lessons from the Past

However, if my people, who are called by my name, will humble themselves, pray, search for me, and turn from their evil ways, then I will hear their prayer from heaven, forgive their sins, and heal their country.

2 Chronicles 7:14

The book of 2 Chronicles picks up the history of Judah after David's death and continues through the period of captivity under the Babylonians and Persians. The first nine chapters highlight Solomon's peaceful and prosperous forty-year reign. The rest of the book reviews Judah's succession of mostly evil rulers as they reigned over a people persistently drawn to foreign gods. The narrative ends with the proclamation from Cyrus inviting the Jewish people to return to their homeland.

The content parallels that in 1 and 2 Kings but offers more detailed accounts of Judah's five kings who brought about spiritual reforms. Asa, Jehoshaphat, Joash, Hezekiah, and Josiah all destroyed illegal places of worship and urged the people back to true worship of Yahweh. These transformations proved to be short-lived because their children turned away from God when they came to power. Second Chronicles reminds the Jewish people of their history in order to demonstrate the disastrous consequences of idolatry.

Equally important is the message of hope and restoration based on the Davidic covenant. The temple features prominently in 2 Chronicles as a symbol of this covenant. The book opens with a description of Solomon's glorious temple. Later, a few godly kings repaired the neglected building and restored temple worship. The Babylonians had destroyed the temple, but Cyrus's decree opened the way for it to be rebuilt. The original readers of 2 Chronicles worshiped in the rebuilt temple. Although it paled in comparison to the original, the building itself testified to God's desire to forgive and restore those who return to him in repentance.

Reading 2 Chronicles can prompt us to examine our own life. Have we let ourselves be drawn away from true worship of God? Do our actions or attitudes reveal a need for spiritual reforms? Along with the original readers, we can rejoice in God's promise to hear the repentant prayers of those called by his name.

Solomon's Greatest Building Project

2 Chronicles 3–4

God gave David detailed plans for the construction and furnishing of his temple. David dedicated his later years to gathering and preparing building materials and organizing the personnel for such a massive undertaking. By the time Solomon ascended to the throne, much of the groundwork had been laid, but it was up to him to initiate the actual work. Solomon knew that no earthly structure could contain God or be worthy of his glory. But he set out to build the best temple humans could construct using the finest materials and most skilled craftsmen.

Solomon didn't have to concern himself with selecting the location for the temple because God had already made that choice. When David sinned by taking an unauthorized census, God sent a plague on Israel as judgment. God later stopped the plague and instructed David to offer sacrifices at the threshing floor where he had seen the Lord's messenger.

David obeyed, purchasing the threshing floor and the plot of land beside it (see 2 Sam. 24). Solomon built the foundation of the temple on this spot on Mount Moriah, the same place where Abraham had offered up his only son when God tested his commitment.

Our life is like a building project. God has given us detailed instructions in his Word and provided everything we need. He has already purchased the foundation for us to build on. Like Solomon's temple, the foundation of our life must be built on a place of sacrifice: God's sacrifice of his only Son, which paid for our sins, and our sacrifice of self-will and the desire to do things our own way.

We can never live a life that honors God in the way he truly deserves, but we can put our best efforts into pleasing him. It all starts with making sure that we're building on the right foundation.

> *After all, no one can lay any other foundation than the one that is already laid, and that foundation is Jesus Christ.*
>
> 1 Corinthians 3:11

The Glory of the Lord

2 Chronicles 5—7:10

After seven years of labor, the temple had been constructed and furnished. Two huge decorated pillars in front hinted at the opulence inside. The finest gold shimmered everywhere the eye looked—on the walls, rafters, doors, and utensils. Precious gems studded the walls along with carvings of palm trees, decorative chains, and cherubim. The main hall held ten gold lamp stands, ten tables, and ten gold bowls. Marking off the most holy place was a curtain woven from blue, purple, and dark red yarn and linen. But none of the magnificent objects in the temple compared with what entered it during the dedication service.

After Solomon had everything arranged, he summoned the leaders and tribal heads to accompany the most indispensable item to the temple: the ark that represented God's covenant with Israel. The priests carried the ark with poles and placed it on the specially prepared table in the most holy place. After they completed this task, the singers and musicians praised and thanked God. Suddenly, God's glory filled the temple in the form of a cloud. Solomon knelt and prayed a prayer of dedication, and God responded by consuming the offerings and sacrifices with fire. Seeing the fire from heaven and the cloud of God's glory filling the temple, the Israelites fell to their knees in worship.

In the Old Testament, the temple represented God's presence among his people and the focal point of his contact with them. Because of Jesus's sacrifice, believers today have something infinitely more precious than a building studded with gold and gems. We have God's Spirit living inside us; our point of contact with God is prayer based on our relationship with his Son. If we dedicate ourselves to loving, serving, and obeying God, his glory will fill our life. And people can't help but notice it.

> *God wanted his people throughout the world to know the glorious riches of this mystery—which is Christ living in you, giving you the hope of glory.*
>
> Colossians 1:27

Preparing for War

2 Chronicles 14

God had promised the Israelites that obeying his laws and commands would bring them peace and prosperity. When Asa became king, he did "what the Lord his God considered good and right" (v. 2). Asa destroyed pagan altars and commanded the people of Judah to worship God and follow his teachings. As a result, the nation enjoyed ten years of peace. Asa recognized this period as the perfect opportunity to strengthen Judah's defenses.

Asa built fortified cities surrounded by walls with towers and strong doors that could be barred. He amassed an army of 300,000 Judeans and 280,000 Benjamites armed with shields, spears, and bows. By making the most of Judah's time of peace, Asa ensured that the nation would be ready for an attack when it came—and it did come.

Zera from Sudan set out to attack Judah with three hundred chariots and a million fighting men. Asa and his army marched out to face the enemy. Once they assumed their battle positions, Asa prayed a simple prayer. He acknowledged his army's dependence on God for help in facing such impossible odds. God answered that prayer and gave Judah a stunning victory. Asa returned to Jerusalem in triumph with much plunder.

The principle of preparing for war during times of peace also applies to our spiritual life. When our life seems to be going smoothly, we may be tempted to slack off in the spiritual disciplines. But these times are not for being idle; they allow us to prepare for times of trouble. The moment when temptation or trials strike is too late to build up our defenses. We need to strengthen our faith during the peaceful times by keeping in close communion with God through Bible study and prayer. Then when an attack does come, we'll be ready to assume our battle position: on our knees asking God for help.

> *Keep your mind clear, and be alert. Your opponent*
> *the devil is prowling around like a roaring*
> *lion as he looks for someone to devour.*
>
> 1 Peter 5:8

Strong Start, Weak Finish

2 Chronicles 14—16

Asa began his forty-one-year reign over Judah determined to abolish idol worship and turn the people's hearts back to God. This zealous king not only destroyed altars and objects associated with foreign gods, he even deposed his grandmother from her position as queen mother because of her involvement with the pagan goddess Asherah. When Asa faced off against the Ethiopian army, he turned to God in prayer and gained a victory over forces that vastly outnumbered his own. Asa listened to the prophet Azariah who urged him to remain strong and dedicated to the Lord. He responded by stepping up his destruction of idols, making repairs in the temple, and leading the people to renew their covenant with God.

Sadly, in his later years Asa got off-track. When King Baasha of Israel invaded Judah, Asa didn't turn to God as he had earlier. Instead, he bribed the king of Aram to attack Israel. Judah escaped the danger, but a prophet named Hanani rebuked Asa for not relying on God and predicted future wars as judgment for his actions. Instead of repenting, the enraged king threw Hanani in prison and mistreated some of his subjects. Later, Asa suffered from a serious foot disease, but again failed to ask God for help.

Asa is remembered as a godly king, but his last five years stand out as a testament to how easily we can get off-track in our relationship with God. The Christian life is more like a marathon than a sprint. No matter how well we start out, we can never afford to slack off.

If we let our passion toward God cool, other influences can pull us away from obeying and trusting in him alone. Eventually, we may find that we're running in the wrong direction—away from God and his will for our life. Nurturing our relationship with God and depending on him is the only way we'll find the endurance to finish our race well.

We must run the race that lies ahead of us and never give up.

Hebrews 12:1

Dangerous Alliances

2 Chronicles 18—20

Asa's son Jehoshaphat succeeded him as king and continued the fight against idol worship. Jehoshaphat also initiated a program to educate the people about God's laws; he even traveled throughout Judah personally encouraging people to turn back to the Lord. Jehoshaphat fortified Judah's defenses and earned respect and honor from leaders of the surrounding nations. Unfortunately, Jehoshaphat made some poor choices when it came to relationships and alliances. He made a tragic mistake when he arranged for his son to marry the wicked Ahab's daughter Athaliah, a decision that brought nothing but grief.

Jehoshaphat also ignored a warning from the prophet Micaiah and let Ahab, Israel's king, persuade him to go to war with him against the Arameans. When Jehoshaphat returned to Jerusalem, a prophet there rebuked him and warned that he had incurred God's wrath by aligning himself with the ungodly Ahab.

The king failed to learn the lesson. He later entered a business venture with Ahab's son Ahaziah. God destroyed their ships before the project got off the ground. But these consequences pale in comparison with the mass murder later committed by Jehoshaphat's daughter-in-law when she tried to destroy the royal line of David.

Many believers who love God and try to follow him have a blind spot when it comes to relationships. We may find ourselves drawn into ungodly alliances because we feel responsible to share our faith. Other times we get entangled in inappropriate relationships because we give in to our personal desires, ignoring God's warnings. God never commands us to avoid associating with unbelievers. He does warn us not to enter into a close partnership where we could be influenced or controlled by someone who doesn't know him. Such situations make us more vulnerable to sin and the temptation to compromise our faith—and they will bring nothing but grief.

> *Stop forming inappropriate relationships with*
> *unbelievers. Can right and wrong be partners? Can*
> *light have anything in common with darkness?*
>
> 2 Corinthians 6:14

Josiah's Cleanup Campaign

2 Chronicles 34:1–21

King Josiah chose not to follow in the footsteps of his father and grandfather, who were especially wicked kings. At the age of sixteen, Josiah dedicated himself to serving God. Four years later he initiated a sweeping campaign to abolish idolatry in Judah and in territories of what had been the northern kingdom. In his purge of the land, Josiah destroyed pagan altars, Asherah poles, and idols, grinding them into powder. The king also turned his attention to cleaning and repairing the Lord's temple. After several years, God rewarded Josiah's efforts with a remarkable discovery—or rather a rediscovery of something that had been lost and largely forgotten.

One day the priest Hilkiah found a copy of the book written by Moses to record God's laws and teachings for Israel. (Most scholars believe the scroll contained Deuteronomy, or a portion of it.) When the secretary began to read the book to Josiah, the king tore his clothes in distress. Josiah understood how far the nation had strayed from God's commands, inviting God's righteous anger. The king commanded several officials to investigate the book and the Lord's opinion about it.

If we examine our life, we may find that we need to do a little purging ourselves. We may have slipped into habits, attitudes, and behavior patterns that aren't pleasing to God. Or we may have allowed something or someone to become an idol to us, pulling our devotion away from God. An honest evaluation of how we measure up to God's standards will reveal what we need to clean up. And God will reward our efforts by leading us into a deeper knowledge of him. We may rediscover something we didn't even realize we had lost: the joy of an intimate relationship with our Lord.

I pray that the glorious Father, the God of our Lord
Jesus Christ, would give you a spirit of wisdom
and revelation as you come to know Christ
better. Then you will have deeper insight.

Ephesians 1:17–18

Temporary Fixation or Lasting Change?

2 Chronicles 34:22–33

When Josiah ordered his officials to look into the matter of the book found in the temple, they went to the prophetess Huldah. She confirmed that Judah would suffer the curses written in the book as judgment for disobedience and idolatry. Then she delivered a somewhat more positive message: because of Josiah's devotion to the Lord, the disaster would be postponed until after his death. The officials reported Huldah's words to Josiah, who summoned Judah's leaders.

After leading the people to the temple, Josiah read the book aloud and made a promise to faithfully obey God's instructions with all his heart and soul. Then Josiah had the people renew their covenant with God and pledge to live by the terms of it. From that point, the people throughout Israel obeyed God and worshiped him alone—as long as Josiah lived. In the thirty-first year of his reign, Josiah died from wounds he received in a battle. After his death, the people of Israel returned to their former practices of idolatry and pagan worship.

The fact that the Israelites reverted to their old ways shows that they were following Josiah but not truly following God. We all probably know someone who seemed to embrace Christianity, but after a while they slipped back into their old lifestyle. In 1 John 2:19, John addressed the issue of some people who had left the church. He explained that the fact that they left proved that "they were never really part of us."

Sometimes people make a show of following Christ and then drift away when it becomes hard or when they lose interest. Jesus said that his true followers will remain loyal to him even when they experience hardship or persecution. Perseverance doesn't earn our salvation; it's a sign that our faith is genuine. With God's help we will endure to the end no matter what—and show that the change in us is permanent, not just a temporary fixation.

But the person who patiently endures to the end will be saved.

Matthew 10:22

Ezra

Going Home

> May God be with all of you who are his people. You may go to Jerusalem (which is in Judah) and build a temple for the LORD God of Israel.
>
> Ezra 1:3

Judah endured seventy years of Babylonian captivity as judgment for sin and idolatry. After the Persians conquered the Babylonians, God prompted the Persian king to allow the Israelite exiles to return to Judah. The book of Ezra opens the same way that 2 Chronicles ends: with the invitation from Cyrus for the Jewish people to return to their homeland and rebuild God's temple. Out of perhaps two or three million, less than fifty thousand chose to leave the comparative comfort of their lives in Babylon and make the risky nine-hundred-mile trip to a destroyed city.

Just as there had been three deportations to Babylon, three separate groups of exiles returned to Israel. The first six chapters of Ezra focus on the group led by Zerubbabel and the rebuilding of the temple amid severe opposition. After a gap of fifty-eight years, chapters 7–10 pick up the story of the exiles who returned with Ezra, and his efforts to reform the people's worship and lifestyles. The story of the third group of returning Jews is told in Nehemiah.

The remnant who returned to Judah faced many struggles. Ezra wrote to encourage them to stay faithful to the Lord and fulfill their covenant obligations to him. Chapters 9 and 10 give us examples to follow as Ezra confronts the people about sin in their midst and they respond in the proper way.

Ezra also offers encouragement to believers whose fellowship with God has been broken by disobedience or rebellion. No matter how much we've lost due to our foolish choices, our position in Christ is secure. We may suffer the consequences of our actions or experience our Father's discipline, but through repentance and obedience we can once again enjoy intimate fellowship with him. Ezra reminds us that because of God's mercy and grace, his children can never stray so far that they can't go home again.

Remembering What Was Lost

Ezra 3

As soon as the first group of returning Jews settled in, they repaired the broken altar at the temple site. Following the law of Moses, the people offered the prescribed sacrifices and celebrated the festivals. By the second year after their return, preparations had been made to begin rebuilding the temple itself. Zerubbabel appointed priests to supervise as the workers laid the foundation on the site of the original temple. The completion of this first phase of the building project was marked by a dedication service filled with praise and celebration, but with mixed emotions.

As the priests played instruments and sang about God's goodness, the people shouted in joyful praise. But many in the group had a different reaction. Those who were old enough to remember the temple Solomon had built wept out loud. They recalled the ornate building lavishly decorated with gold and precious stones, surrounded by a spacious courtyard and set in a thriving city. These people understood that the new temple, erected amid ruins, would never match the old temple's splendor. The loud sounds of joy and sorrow mingled together and could be heard from far away.

Sometimes problems and adversity make us yearn for the "good old days" when life seemed more glorious—or perhaps easier or simpler. Dissatisfaction with our present circumstances may color our memory and make the past seem better than it actually was. But whether we are remembering accurately or not, this mindset is a trap that keeps us from seeing God's present blessings. It makes us vulnerable to discouragement or depression; we may start to believe that our life is no longer worthwhile. If we belong to God, he has a purpose for every stage of our life, even when we see nothing but ruins. Instead of falling into the comparison trap, we can look forward to what he has planned for our future.

> Don't ask, "Why were things better in the old days than
> they are now?" It isn't wisdom that leads you to ask this!
>
> Ecclesiastes 7:10

Facing Opposition

Ezra 4:1—5; 5—6:15

Not everyone was anxious to see the temple rebuilt. Zerubbabel and the returning Jews faced stiff opposition from their neighbors. When the king of Assyria had conquered the northern tribes, he brought in other people groups to intermarry with the Israelites he had left in the land. The descendants of this mixed group now did everything they could to stop the building project.

First, they tried to infiltrate the group by offering to help, claiming that they also worshiped Yahweh. The Jewish leaders refused their "help" since they knew these people worshiped pagan gods as well. Then the antagonists resorted to intimidations, threats, false accusations, and bribery. The work on the temple came to a standstill for about fifteen years, until God sent the prophets Haggai and Zechariah to encourage Zerubbabel.

When the Jews resumed building, a Persian governor named Tattenai questioned their authority in a letter to Darius, then-ruler of Persia. His plan backfired. Darius found Cyrus's original decree and ordered Tattenai to avoid interfering. He also commanded him to help finance the project and provide for the Jewish sacrifices with his own resources. With renewed commitment and zeal, the Jews completed the temple in four years.

We can expect stiff opposition when we're doing God's work. This may come in the form of people claiming to be fellow believers who try to sidetrack us. Or we may be the victim of outright hostility, persecution, or false accusations. When we begin to feel discouraged, it helps to remember that the Holy Spirit within us is more powerful than any antagonist we'll ever face. Instead of letting our enemies intimidate us, we can move forward in confidence and know that God will help us finish whatever project he has assigned us.

> *Dear children, you belong to God. So you have won*
> *the victory over these people, because the one who is*
> *in you is greater than the one who is in the world.*
>
> 1 John 4:4

The King's Favor

Ezra 7–8

Eighty years after the first wave of exiles returned to Judah under Zerubbabel, Ezra led a second group home. Their number represented only a fraction of the size of the first group, but included Levites to minister in the temple and a leader who was committed to teaching God's laws in Israel. King Artaxerxes not only decreed that any Jews who wished to return could accompany Ezra, he also donated silver and gold for the temple. He also authorized Ezra to obtain additional resources as needed from the royal treasuries, and he returned articles that the Babylonians had seized from the temple when they conquered Judah.

Ezra praised God and gave him the credit for the favor he received. He acknowledged that God had put the idea in the king's and his officials' minds to treat him kindly and contribute to the temple. Ezra understood the truth expressed in Proverbs 21:1 that the king's heart is "under the LORD's control" and he turns it in "any direction he chooses." Decades earlier, when Cyrus issued the original decree freeing the Jews to return home, he admitted that his decision was in obedience to Israel's God, although he simply acknowledged Yahweh as one among many gods.

Whenever we enjoy special favor from someone or receive a positive answer to a request, hopefully we'll remember whom we really have to thank for it. Even though God gives people the freedom to choose, he still holds ultimate control over the hearts and minds of everyone. That includes unbelievers who don't know him personally and who have no desire to obey him. At times our fate seems to be in the hands of someone who holds power or authority over us. We can trust God to carry out his will regarding us no matter what. After all, we already enjoy the favor of the King of kings.

The LORD grants favor and honor.
He does not hold back any blessing
from those who live innocently.

Psalm 84:11

True Repentance

Ezra 9—10

When Ezra returned to Jerusalem, the temple had been standing for almost sixty years. The people followed God's laws concerning sacrifices and offerings, but they failed to obey his instructions for living. Ezra had come to Judah to teach God's laws and standards; he soon discovered he had his work cut out for him. Ezra heard a disturbing report that some of the Israelites had married women from pagan cultures, ignoring God's warning. Even some of the leaders and priests had intermarried, making the people vulnerable to idolatry—the very sin that had brought about their seventy-year captivity.

As soon as Ezra heard the news, he tore his clothes and ripped out some of his hair to express his deep grief and shock. That evening he knelt before the temple, weeping and praying. Although Ezra had not taken a pagan wife, he acknowledged his nation's guilt and implored God to be merciful even though they deserved his wrath. The people responded to Ezra's grief and realized their desperate need to correct the situation. Three days later, Ezra led the guilty parties to confess their guilt and pledge to separate from their foreign wives.

When people do something wrong, they may feel sorry for the consequences of their behavior—or for getting caught—while feeling no real shame for their actions. This response is a far cry from the genuine repentance that these Israelites demonstrated. Godly sorrow over sin is more than tears or strong emotions; it leads to a change of mind toward sin that results in changed behavior.

When we confess our sins to God, he expects us to turn away from them. This may mean leaving a habit, behavior, or relationship behind; in some cases restitution may be called for. Whether we need to settle a debt, offer an apology, perform some act of service, or make changes in our lifestyle, true repentance always involves action.

*To be distressed in a godly way causes people to change
the way they think and act and leads them to be saved.*

2 Corinthians 7:10

Nehemiah

Rebuilding the Walls

Then I told them that my God had been guiding me and what the king had told me. They replied, "Let's begin to rebuild." So they encouraged one another to begin this God-pleasing work.

Nehemiah 2:18

Under Zerubbabel's leadership the Jews had rebuilt the temple, the center of their fellowship with God. It was obvious that God had moved on behalf of his people. When Ezra arrived in Judah around eighty years later, his teaching ministry led to a great spiritual revival among the people. But there was still work to be done. Almost a hundred years after the first group of exiles returned to Judah, God brought a third group home. They were led by Nehemiah, a man who felt burdened to restore Jerusalem's broken walls.

The book of Nehemiah tells the story of how God prompted the Persian king's cupbearer to lead the third and final group of exiles back to their homeland and to oversee the rebuilding of Jerusalem's ruined walls and gates. Nehemiah had to deal with opposition, false accusations, and death threats from outsiders. He faced conflict and betrayal from among his fellow Jews. But Nehemiah persevered and led his countrymen to repair the wall in an unbelievably short amount of time. After that, he put his organizational and leadership skills to use while serving as Jerusalem's governor for twelve years.

The part of the book written in first-person is considered by many to be Nehemiah's autobiography. Also included are copies of letters, decrees, and registers. Nehemiah is the last of the historical books and is the ending point for the Jews' history as covered in the Old Testament. This historical narrative encouraged its original readers by highlighting how God reestablished his people in their homeland. Nehemiah's life also provides examples of character traits we can imitate. Like him, we can learn to face every obstacle with a combination of prayer, courage, and hard work, depending on God's power. Then when God gives us a burden for something he wants done, we will be ready to begin our own "God-pleasing work."

Prayer before Plans

Nehemiah 1–2

Nehemiah had lived his entire life in Babylon, but he loved the homeland of his people. He was shocked and grieved to hear that Jerusalem's walls and gates still lay in ruins, leaving the city disgraced and defenseless. Nehemiah broke down and wept. As he mourned and fasted for days, he poured out his heart to God. By the end of his prayer, Nehemiah knew what he needed to do. King Artaxerxes had stopped the rebuilding years earlier (see Ezra 4:17–23); only he could reverse the edict. And since Nehemiah served as the royal cupbearer, he had access to the king.

After four months, Nehemiah's opportunity finally came when Artaxerxes asked him why he looked sad and troubled. Nehemiah held a trusted position as the person responsible for ensuring the safety of the king's wine, but for a servant to show negative emotion could jeopardize his life. Even so, Nehemiah explained the reason for his sadness: the city of his ancestors lay in ruins.

"What do you want?" Artaxerxes asked. Although Nehemiah had prepared for this question, he shot up a quick prayer for God's help. God gave Nehemiah the words to say, and the king offered Nehemiah everything he needed to travel to Jerusalem and oversee the restoration of Jerusalem's walls.

When faced with a problem, we often react in one of two extremes. We may let our distress paralyze us and do nothing, or we may rush into action without first thinking things through. Many of us make the mistake of formulating a plan and then asking God to bless our efforts as we pursue it. The best approach is to begin with honest, heartfelt prayer, sharing our concerns and feelings with God. As we talk with him about our problem, God will clarify our situation and reveal what part he wants us to play in the solution. If we want our plan to be successful, it needs to be built on a solid foundation of prayer.

> *Commit to the* Lord *whatever you do,*
> *and your plans will succeed.*
>
> Proverbs 16:3 NIV

Confronting Evil

Nehemiah 5:1–13

With the support of King Artaxerxes, Nehemiah traveled to Jerusalem to oversee the rebuilding of the city's wall. He spent several days secretly assessing the damage and developing his strategy. When Nehemiah shared his vision with his fellow Jews, they wholeheartedly joined in the project. But there were enemies in the area who did not want to see Jerusalem rebuilt. They ridiculed and threatened the workers, made false accusations, and plotted attacks to stop the work. Nehemiah prayed and devised a plan of defense. Then in the midst of external opposition, a problem arose from within.

Focus on the building project, along with a food shortage, had forced many men to either mortgage their property or borrow money. Jewish lenders were charging their countrymen interest even though God had forbidden it; their actions forced some families to sell their children into temporary slavery. Nehemiah could have focused on his God-given project and ignored the situation. But this news infuriated him. His compassion and love for justice required him to speak up. After first taking time to think and pray, Nehemiah confronted the offenders and exposed their guilt. They promised to make restitution and change their ways.

We may be tempted to overlook injustice and sin in the hopes that someone else will take care of it. It's especially hard when the offender is from within our circle of family or friends. But God wants us to have the courage to speak out against evil, especially when it's perpetrated by someone claiming to know him. It's never easy to confront someone about their behavior. But we can learn from Nehemiah's godly approach. It's crucial that we take time to let our emotions cool, and to think and pray about the situation. Then, with God's help we can lovingly but firmly speak the truth in hopes that God will prompt the offender to change their ways.

> *Have nothing to do with the useless works that darkness*
> *produces. Instead, expose them for what they are.*
>
> Ephesians 5:11

An Impressive Feat

Nehemiah 3—6

Faced with the enormous task of rebuilding Jerusalem's wall, Nehemiah put his expert organizational skills to work. He divided the wall into sections, assigning people to work near their own homes whenever possible. This saved time, plus ensured the workers' motivation and personal involvement. When the threats of terrorist attacks increased, Nehemiah arranged for a rotating shift of armed guards to stand watch. The work progressed rapidly in spite of the circumstances. When the Jews' enemies heard that the only task remaining was to set the doors in the gates, they grew more desperate.

Sanballat and Tobiah tried several times to lure Nehemiah away from the city in order to harm or kill him. When that didn't work, they tried to turn the people and local officials against him by using slander and false reports. They even hired a priest to discredit Nehemiah. Their efforts failed and the project was completed in only fifty-two days. Afterward, even the Jews' enemies and the surrounding nations had to admit that such a feat could only have been possible with God's help. No one could accomplish so much by mere human strength.

God wants his children to accomplish many amazing feats that make the rest of the world take notice. He may assign us our own little section to work on, or he may appoint us to oversee a grand project. We may not feel like we're capable of doing very much for God, but we all have important roles to play. Because of that, we all face opposition from God's enemies. No matter what hurdles we encounter, we have God's power working for us and in us. He will help us do things we couldn't possibly achieve on our own. Then God will receive glory when everyone has to admit it could only have been done with his help.

> *You will also know the unlimited greatness of his power*
> *as it works with might and strength for us, the believers.*
>
> Ephesians 1:19

Esther

God's Perfect Timing

> The fact is, even if you remain silent now, someone else will help and rescue the Jews, but you and your relatives will die. And who knows, you may have gained your royal position for a time like this.
>
> Esther 4:14

Even before the exile began, God had commanded the Israelites to return to their homeland when they got the chance (speaking through the prophets Isaiah and Jeremiah). But the vast majority chose not to leave their settled life to face the hardships of the journey and the work of rebuilding. The book of Esther tells the story of two Jews who remained in the Persian Empire, living in Susa, the capital city under King Xerxes. Chronologically, the events fit between chapters 6 and 7 of Ezra, after the first exiles returned under Zerubbabel and before the second group returned with Ezra.

An unusual feature of Esther is that the anonymous author never refers to God by name. Still, Yahweh's presence is evident throughout the book as he orchestrates events for the preservation of his chosen people, even when they are disobedient. God's sovereignty intersects with human will as what seems like a series of coincidences accomplishes his purposes. In God's perfect timing, a beauty pageant, a king's insomnia, and a distraught man falling on a couch all fit perfectly together to deliver the Jews from an enemy who longed for their annihilation.

For us today, the book is much more than a thrilling tale of intrigue, romance, and suspense, with a heavy dose of irony. It's more than an explanation of the origin of Purim, which Jews still celebrate today. Esther's story comforts us with the knowledge that even when God seems hidden, he is actively working on our behalf. The story also reminds us that God has placed each one of us in a position where he can use us in some special way, whether our circumstances are pleasant or difficult. If we stay alert for God-given opportunities and wait for his perfect timing, we'll understand what God wants us to do in "a time like this."

The Mother of All Beauty Pageants

Esther 1–2

King Xerxes deposed Queen Vashti when she refused to obey his drunken order to appear at his banquet so he could show her off to his guests. He soon regretted his rash decision. The king's staff suggested gathering all the beautiful young women in the kingdom together so he could choose a new queen. This idea pleased Xerxes, who sent scouts into each of his 127 provinces to bring the most gorgeous women into his already extensive harem. A young Jewish woman named Esther was included in this group.

Even after these women were selected and brought to the palace, they weren't ready to be considered by the king. First, they had to go through an entire year of special beauty treatments with oils, perfumes, and cosmetics. After that, each woman awaited her turn to spend one night with Xerxes. The next morning, she would be sent to the second harem. There she would live out her days among all the other concubines, unless the king requested her by name. Most of these women would probably never see the king again; only one would be crowned as queen.

Thank goodness we don't have to win a beauty contest in order to be accepted by God. We don't need to spruce ourselves up to win his approval. There's no extensive beauty treatment that would cover the ugliness of our sin anyway. We don't become God's child because of our efforts to make ourselves worthy. He accepts us just the way we are, and then he begins to transform us into the image of his Son. When this lifelong process ends, we will finally be the beautiful creation God intended us to be. Until then, no matter what we look like, we can rejoice that we've already been chosen by the King of kings.

> *He saved us, but not because of anything we had done to gain his approval. Instead, because of his mercy he saved us through the washing in which the Holy Spirit gives us new birth and renewal.*
>
> Titus 3:5

Haman's Hatred

Esther 3:1—4:3

King Xerxes promoted Haman to second-in-command and ordered all his officials to kneel and bow before him. One man who usually sat at the king's gate ignored this command. Mordecai, Esther's older cousin and guardian, refused to bow to Haman. This infuriated Haman, who decided it wouldn't be enough just to kill Mordecai. When he learned Mordecai's nationality, Haman plotted to wipe out every single Jew in the Persian Empire.

By casting lots, Haman settled on a date about a year away for the massacre to take place. Then he told Xerxes a "certain nationality" scattered throughout the kingdom refused to obey his royal decrees. Haman urged the extermination of this group and offered to donate a staggering amount of silver to the royal treasury in return. Easily influenced by his officials, Xerxes gave Haman permission to do whatever he wanted with these rebellious people.

Haman didn't waste time; he promptly sent out proclamations to every province ordering the murder of all Jews, including young and old, women and children, on the thirteenth day of the twelfth month. Haman then sat down to toast the future massacre with the king, satisfied that he would soon get what he wanted. Later, however, Haman decided he couldn't wait that long to kill Mordecai, so he erected a seventy-five-foot pole on which he planned to execute his enemy (5:13–14).

Jesus said we shouldn't be surprised if people hate us when we take a stand for him. Sometimes people feel uncomfortable around us because we don't bow down and worship the things of this world. Others hate us simply because of our allegiance to the One they have rejected. No matter how much hatred we encounter, staying true to our Lord is always worth the price we pay. Other people may plot against us and long to see our downfall, but God is in control. And as Haman would soon discover, God protects his own.

> *[Jesus said] "Everyone will hate you because you are committed to me."*
>
> Matthew 10:22

Esther's Risky Move

Esther 4

When Mordecai heard about Haman's death decree against the Jews, he instructed Esther to appeal to Xerxes for mercy on behalf of their people. Esther reminded Mordecai of a certain law: anyone who approached the king in his throne room without being summoned would be put to death; however, if Xerxes held out his golden scepter to that person, his or her life would be spared. But everyone knew Xerxes was a man of capricious moods and unpredictable temper. To make matters worse, he hadn't requested Esther's presence in a month. If the king's affection for her had begun to fade, how could she hope for a favorable response when she approached him in the throne room?

Mordecai warned Esther that being in the palace would not protect her from the edict. Deep down he believed that even if Esther refused to act, God would still preserve his chosen people somehow. But Mordecai also suspected that God had put Esther in a unique position to be a part of his divine plan. Esther relented and sent a request for all the Jews in Susa to join her in fasting. After that, she would approach the king. Knowing that such a move could very well result in her death, Esther declared, "If I die, I die."

Sometimes we act like God is an unpredictable tyrant; we feel hesitant to approach him and fearful of how he will react. But God makes it clear that he desires our company; he even reaches out to us and tries to draw us closer to himself. In Revelation 3:20 Jesus portrayed himself as standing and knocking at the door of our heart. If we respond to his invitation, we will enjoy intimate fellowship with him. As long as we come to God with the proper attitude, we never have to worry about getting a favorable response in his throne room. He's always glad to see us.

> *Look, I'm standing at the door and knocking.*
> *If anyone listens to my voice and opens the*
> *door, I'll come in and we'll eat together.*
>
> Revelation 3:20

Waiting for the Right Moment

Esther 5

After three days of fasting, Esther dressed in her royal robes and stood in the entrance to the throne room. Xerxes looked up and felt pleased with his queen. Relief must have washed over Esther when the king stretched out his scepter, guaranteeing her safety. Considering the life-or-death nature of the circumstances, Esther's first instinct may have been to blurt out her request. But three days of fasting and prayer had prepared Esther for handling a delicate situation and a temperamental tyrant. Despite the urgency of the circumstances, she sensed it was not yet time to plead for the lives of the Jewish population.

In answer to the king's question, Esther simply invited him, along with Haman, to attend a special dinner she had prepared. During the meal, Xerxes questioned her a second time. Following God's guidance, Esther promised to reveal her request when Xerxes and Haman attended a second dinner the next day. In the meantime, God worked quietly behind the scenes through what seemed like a series of coincidences. By the next day, the stage had been set for Esther to play her role in God's plan to save the Jews and crush their enemy.

Whether we're facing a difficult problem or dealing with a difficult person, we need to exercise restraint, even when the situation seems urgent. Speaking or reacting too quickly can make matters worse if we do or say the wrong thing or use bad timing. Our best approach is to first strengthen ourselves with focused prayer, and then stay tuned in to God's leading. His Spirit may prompt us to delay responding so that he can arrange events and set the stage for the best possible outcome. If we trust God for discernment, we can count on him to show us the right moment to speak or act.

The heart of a righteous person carefully
considers how to answer,
but the mouths of wicked people pour
out a flood of evil things.

Proverbs 15:28

Just Deserts

Esther 6–7

Esther may have planned the dinner, but God arranged for Haman to get his just deserts. The night before Esther's second banquet, King Xerxes had trouble sleeping and asked a servant to read from the official records. The servant happened to pick a section that recorded how Mordecai had uncovered an assassination plot against the king five years earlier. When Xerxes learned that Mordecai had not been rewarded, he decided to seek someone's advice on how to repay such a heroic act. Ironically, Haman was just outside waiting to ask for Mordecai's death. When Xerxes asked his advice, Haman assumed the king meant to honor *him* and recommended an elaborate scheme—which Xerxes then instructed him to carry out on Mordecai's behalf.

After being forced to publicly honor the man he hated, Haman rushed home in humiliation. During Esther's dinner later that day, she asked Xerxes to spare her life and the lives of her people, identifying Haman as the perpetrator of the planned massacre. The enraged king stomped off into the garden. Moments later, he returned just as a panicked Haman fell onto the queen's couch while begging for mercy. Xerxes's assumption that Haman was trying to assault Esther sealed his doom. A servant mentioned that Haman had erected a pole in his yard to execute Mordecai, the man who had saved Xerxes's life. Soon Haman's body hung on it instead.

What seemed like poetic justice was really divine retribution. In God's timing, the tables turned. Mordecai received his long-overdue reward for his good deed, and Haman got the death sentence he wanted to impose on Mordecai and all the Jews. As the Judge of all the earth, God will see that people get what they deserve sooner or later. We may get impatient waiting for justice to be done, and we may never see it in our lifetime. But God promises to reward the godly for all the good they do to serve him, and also to repay those who choose to pursue evil.

> *God alone is the judge.*
> *He punishes one person and rewards another.*
>
> Psalm 75:7

Job

When Life Isn't Fair

But I know that my defender lives, and afterwards, he will rise on the earth.

Job 19:25

Job is the first of the Bible's five poetical books. The author and setting are unknown, but many consider it to be the oldest book in the Bible. Both Ezekiel (see 14:14, 20) and James (see 5:11) referred to Job as a real person. The uncertain aspects of its origins seem to be fitting, since the book itself addresses a great mystery: why godly people experience undeserved suffering. The message of this ancient text speaks to every person who has ever lived or who will be born in the future.

The first chapter is set in heaven, with God giving Satan permission to afflict his faithful servant Job. Within minutes, Job loses his possessions, his extensive flocks and herds, and all of his children. Then Satan attacks Job with a painful disease. As Job wrestles with the natural question "Why?" his bereaved wife offers no support. His friends try to convince him that his own sin has caused his suffering.

During his ordeal, Job questions his circumstances and he questions God, but he never renounces him. After several lengthy debates between Job and his four "counselors," God himself speaks. He reveals his power and majesty to Job, leaving him speechless and fully submitted to God's sovereignty. In the end, God restores Job's health and gives him ten children and more wealth than he had before.

The book of Job reminds us that we live in a world distorted by the effects of sin. Although God is in control, we may face adversity that has nothing to do with our own actions. If we lost everything today, would our relationship with God be enough? Will we trust him even when we don't understand the reasons for our suffering? Can we ask "why" without challenging God's authority by demanding an explanation? When we're hurting and confused, the best thing to focus on is what we do know. Along with Job, we can say with confidence, "But I know that my defender lives."

Solid or Superficial Faith?

Job 1–2

When God praised Job's faithfulness and exemplary character, Satan was not impressed. He countered that Job only followed God because of the lavish blessings God had given him. Satan predicted that if God took those away, Job would curse him. God granted Satan permission to strike all that Job had. In one day, Job lost everything he owned plus all ten of his children. Job tore his robe and shaved his head to express his deep anguish. But still, he worshiped God. "The LORD has given, and the LORD has taken away!" he said. "May the name of the LORD be praised" (Job 1:21).

Satan persisted in questioning Job's motives. He argued that if Job had to suffer physically, he would surely deny God. With permission from God, Satan struck Job with a painful disease that caused skin sores from head to toe, along with other symptoms.

Seeing her husband's misery, Job's grieving wife wondered if it wouldn't be better for him to curse God and die. But even in his agony, Job clung to his trust in God. "We accept the good that God gives us," he pointed out. "Shouldn't we also accept the bad?" (2:10).

Job proved Satan wrong: he served and worshiped God because he loved him, not because of how God had blessed him. Sooner or later, each one of us will experience similar opportunities to prove our motives for following God. Whether caused by our actions or undeserved, adversity is the ultimate test of whether our faith is solid or superficial. It reveals whether we worship and love God for who he is, or for what he can give us.

When times of hardship and loss come, will we walk away from the Christian life? Or will we cling to a belief in God's goodness even in the midst of suffering? Like Job, will we choose to worship God even in the midst of pain?

May the name of the LORD be praised.

Job 1:21

The Great Debates

Job 4–37

Three of Job's friends heard about his calamities and gathered to comfort him and offer their sympathies. Appalled by Job's horrific appearance, they ripped their clothes and wept. Following Jewish custom, Eliphaz, Bildad, and Zophar sat in silence, waiting for their mourning friend to speak first. After seven days and nights, Job finally began to talk about his grief and pain. Job expressed a wish that he had never been born—or that he could die at that present moment. Shocked by this, his friends proceeded to correct his thinking.

What followed was a series of lengthy but futile discussions concerning Job's troubles. His friends argued that suffering is always caused by sin in someone's life. They urged Job to pinpoint the wrongdoing in his own life, confess it, and repent. Job maintained his innocence while acknowledging that God had brought about his affliction.

Job's friends may have had good intentions, but they failed to be of any real help to the bereaved man. Job wondered if their "long-winded speeches" would ever end. He suggested that they imagine themselves in his place to get an idea of how their words affected him. Instead of feeling consoled, Job felt condemned. "You are all pathetic at comforting me," he told his friends (Job 16:2).

Many people can relate to Job's frustration at having well-meaning friends make insensitive remarks during times of distress. When someone we care about is troubled or grieving, we naturally want to offer encouragement and support. But too often we feel the need to explain their circumstances or to say something profound. We can't help a hurting friend by giving pat answers or spouting off clichés. It may not help to quote Scriptures at that moment—or even to talk at all. The most important thing is simply our presence, or practical acts that show we care. If we end up talking just for the sake of talking, we risk being "pathetic" comforters like Job's friends.

> *Be happy with those who are happy. Be*
> *sad with those who are sad.*
>
> Romans 12:15

God Joins the Discussion

Job 38:1—42:6

Job continued to defend himself against his friends' accusations that some hidden personal sin had brought on his suffering. As the dialogue heated up, Job complained that God allowed wicked people to prosper while punishing him. He repeatedly called on God to answer him, or to at least provide an intercessor to plead his innocence. Job's attitude began to resemble self-righteousness. Finally, God stepped into the discussion, speaking out of a storm.

Instead of answering Job's charges, God interrogated *him* by asking more than seventy questions about the universe and its workings. Job could answer none of them, but the quiz reminded him that God has all the forces of nature at his disposal and every detail of creation under his control. Job got the point: If he had such limited knowledge of the physical world, how could he expect to comprehend God's actions? In the light of God's majesty and power, Job saw that he had no right to question his Creator. "I have stated things I didn't understand," he admitted, "things too mysterious for me to know" (42:3).

God chose not to explain his purposes to Job concerning his suffering, but he did reveal more of himself to Job. That proved to be enough to satisfy Job and help him accept his devastating circumstances. Whenever we struggle to understand God's actions, or his seeming failure to intervene in our situation, we need to remember that he never owes us an explanation for what he does.

Meditating on the wonders of the universe and God's sovereignty over his creation can help us keep things in perspective. Any complaints we have seem insignificant in light of the fact that such a God not only cares about us, but took on human form and died for us. If we truly want to grow in our understanding, we'll resist demanding answers from God and simply ask him to reveal *himself* to us.

> O LORD, *what are humans that you should care about them?*
> *What are mere mortals that you should think about them?*
>
> Psalm 144:3

Restoration

Job 42:7–17

When God finished his two speeches, Job humbled himself and confessed his ignorance and pride. In response, God cleared Job's name by rebuking his friends for their presumptuous words. God also asked Job to intercede for them in prayer. Because of Job's repentance and his willingness to forgive his friends, God transformed his life. Job lived another 140 years and enjoyed even greater blessings than in his younger years.

Job's relatives and friends who had initially forsaken him during his troubles now visited him, bringing comforting words and material gifts. God gave him twice as much wealth and livestock as he owned before. Although nothing could replace the ten children he had lost, God gave Job ten more sons and daughters. Job had the privilege of living to see four generations of his descendants.

The greatest blessing of Job's new life must have been his deeper relationship with his Lord. By clinging to his faith, Job walked away from his horrifying ordeal with a greater understanding of himself and of God's infinite wisdom and power. "I had heard about you with my own ears," Job acknowledged, "but now I have seen you with my own eyes" (see Job 42:5).

Sometimes we experience loss because God wants to refine our faith or use our life as a witness to others. Other times he asks us to give up something in order to follow and serve him. Whatever the purpose, God promises that we will be compensated. We don't know if that will be in material form or in spiritual blessings; we don't know at what point it will come. We may not experience our full restoration in this earthly life, but we can be sure that one day God will give us far more than we ever lost.

> *Anyone who gave up his home, wife, brothers, parents,*
> *or children because of the kingdom of God will*
> *certainly receive many times as much in this life and*
> *will receive eternal life in the world to come.*
>
> Luke 18:29–30

Psalms

The Bible's Songbook

My mouth will speak the praise of the LORD, and all living creatures will praise his holy name forever and ever.

Psalm 145:21

At the center of the Bible stands its longest and most diverse book, and the one most often quoted. *Psalms* is a Greek word referring to music accompanied by stringed instruments. This collection of 150 prayers, poems, and songs served as the Jewish people's temple hymnbook and devotional guide. Although the psalms cover the complete range of human experiences and emotions, the overarching theme is worship. Individual psalms focus on specific elements of worship including praise and adoration, thanksgiving, petition, and expression of repentance.

The psalms were written over a period of about a thousand years, from the time of Moses (c. 1410 BC) to the time of the exiles returning from Babylonian captivity (c. 430 BC). Approximately half were penned by David, who also helped organize the collection into five separate groupings. Other identified authors include Asaph, the sons of Korah, Solomon, Ethan, Heman, and Moses. Some of the psalms include superscriptions that pinpoint a correlated historical event, while others relate prophecies of the coming Messiah.

With such a diverse range of subject matter, Psalms is relevant to our life at any given moment, regardless of our circumstances or mood. When we don't know how to express our feelings to God, we can let the psalmists help us out. And since almost every psalm contains some note of praise, reading the appropriate passage fixes our thoughts on God and his attributes more than on our problems.

Whether we use Psalms for our personal devotional time or hear it read in a church service, the book can teach us to worship God the way he desires. Psalms can also deepen our prayer life by encouraging us to have honest communication with God as its authors did, while acknowledging his sovereignty and goodness. As we meditate on passages from Psalms, we'll discover that these ancient words can breathe new life into our relationship with God.

The Good Shepherd

Psalm 23

David wrote one of the most beloved psalms using two images that were familiar to his readers. The first part of Psalm 23 pictures a shepherd faithfully caring for the needs of his flock, providing food, shelter, protection from danger, and guidance. The last two verses use the metaphor of a gracious host offering hospitality to a guest, even while that guest is surrounded by his enemies. Both of these images beautifully portray the Lord's tender loving care of his people.

David wrote about what he knew. He had plenty of experience tending sheep in his earlier years; later in life he frequently knew what it felt like to be surrounded by enemies. These years taught David to depend upon God to meet his needs regardless of his circumstances. David's words assure us that we can trust in God's presence and protection even when we walk through times as dark as the valley of death.

In John 10, Jesus identified himself as the "good shepherd" who gives his life for the sheep. In biblical days, the shepherd sometimes slept in the doorway of the sheepfold to guard his flock from wild animals or thieves. Christ submitted to death on the cross so that he could offer us safety and security. Now he wants to guide, protect, and nurture us. But he lets us choose whether or not we will follow his lead. We must decide whether we will listen to our Shepherd's voice and entrust ourselves into his care, or ignore his call and follow another path.

Only obedient followers can fully enjoy God's blessings. We'll never find contentment when we rebel and go our own way. Whether we need rest, renewal, protection, nourishment for our soul, or guidance, Psalm 23 tells us where to find it. We'll never lack for anything when we let the Good Shepherd lead us. And one day he will safely guide us home, where we'll live with him forever.

> *[Jesus said] "I am the good shepherd. The good shepherd gives his life for the sheep."*
>
> John 10:11

Raw Honesty

Psalm 142

If two friends want to get to know each other, they must be willing to honestly share their thoughts and feelings. But many people only experience shallow relationships marked by superficial communication. This tendency often carries over into our relationship with God. We may feel as though God expects us to always be upbeat or focus on the positive when we pray. The book of Psalms makes it obvious that he doesn't require us to suppress our negative emotions when we talk with him.

The 150 psalms run the gamut of every human emotion or impulse. The writers freely expressed what they were feeling, from the lowest depths of depression and despair to the heights of rejoicing and gratitude. They laid their souls bare before God, describing their doubts, fears, and disappointments. They never hid their yearning to be closer to him, or their desire to be vindicated and see their enemies fall. When they felt as though God was keeping himself distant, they told him about it. And God included all these expressions—the good, the bad, and the ugly—in his Word.

Our relationship with God has to be based on honest communication. While we do need to approach him with the reverence and respect that he deserves, God doesn't want us to sugarcoat our true feelings no matter how negative they are. He already knows exactly how we're feeling anyway, so trying to put on a happy face and hide our true feelings is ridiculous.

Some people are taught to mask their negative emotions during childhood; others develop a fear of being transparent and vulnerable because of past hurtful relationships. When we approach God that way, it shows a lack of trust in him and in his character. God wants us to experience the freedom that the writers of the psalms knew. He also wants our relationship with him to move to a deeper level—and that requires raw honesty.

I pour out my complaints in his presence
and tell him my troubles.

Psalm 142:2

Managing Our Moods

Psalms 13; 42

The writers of the psalms never held back from expressing their true feelings, no matter how needy or depressed they felt. But they also never wallowed in self-pity or despair. Even in their low moods, they always ended on a high note. After the psalmist expressed his feelings, he reminded himself of how God had helped him or his people in the past, how God loved and cared for him in the present, or how he would one day enjoy eternal life in God's presence.

Sometimes the writer reminded himself to deliberately praise God in spite of disheartening circumstances. For example, in Psalm 13, David complained that he felt oppressed by his enemies and forgotten by God. He ended by declaring, "But I trust your mercy" and vowed to "sing to the LORD" who had been good to him (vv. 5–6). The writer of Psalm 42 encouraged himself with a little self-talk: "Why are you discouraged, my soul? Why are you so restless? Put your hope in God, because I will still praise him. He is my savior and my God" (v. 5).

We all have to deal with discouragement, bad moods, and sadness. Sometimes we struggle with depression. Ignoring such emotions doesn't help. Neither does the other extreme of getting bogged down in nursing our negative feelings. The psalmists demonstrate a healthy way to manage our emotions. After honestly expressing our thoughts and feelings to God, we can remind ourselves of God's character and make a conscious choice to praise him.

It's amazing how our perspective—and our mood—changes when we shift our focus from our problems to who God is, what he's done for us in the past, and what he promises to do in the future. There may be times when we require professional help in the form of counseling or medication. But for many of our negative emotions, the prescription found in Psalms is exactly what we need. The best antidote to feeling bad is to meditate on God's goodness.

But I will always have hope.
I will praise you more and more.

Psalm 71:14

The Right Ingredients ·

Psalm 19

Besides teaching us how to worship God, the book of Psalms also shows us how to have a powerful prayer life. Various psalms focus on different elements that are crucial in our communication with God: praise and adoration, thanksgiving, confession of sins and repentance, and presenting our requests.

Psalm 96 is a song of pure adoration to God. In Psalm 148 the writer calls on people, angels, animals, mountains, trees, heavenly bodies, and forces of nature to praise the Lord. Psalm 136 focuses on God as the Creator and urges us to thank him for his mercy. The writer of Psalm 107 offers thanksgiving to God while reviewing how God had worked on the nation's behalf in the past.

In Psalm 5:3 David tells God, "In the morning I lay my needs in front of you, and I wait." His petition took on a different tone in Psalm 70 as he calls himself "oppressed and needy" and calls on God to "come quickly to rescue me!" (see vv. 1, 5). Psalm 51 is David's poignant confession of sin after a prophet confronted him about his adultery. He asks God to create a clean heart in him so that he could rejoice in his salvation once again.

Sometimes we leave out one or more of these elements and then wonder why we don't have a dynamic prayer life. Maybe we rush into a recitation of our needs and requests without thanking God for what he's already done for us. Or we may focus on praising him but never get around to examining our heart and confessing our sins.

We may find it helpful to incorporate the psalmists' words into our own prayers, personalizing them to fit our specific needs and situation. Whether our conversations with God are Scripture-based or simply inspired by the words of one of the psalmists, we need to include all the ingredients if we want a balanced prayer life that is pleasing to God.

> *May the words from my mouth and*
> *the thoughts from my heart*
> *be acceptable to you, O LORD, my rock and my defender.*
>
> Psalm 19:14

God's Character

Psalm 145

One of the things that makes the book of Psalms special is the character study of God we find there. As we read the psalmists' praise of God's attributes, we gain a deeper understanding and appreciation for who he is. Many individual psalms focus on a single character trait of God, often one that speaks to a specific setting or situation. Psalm 34:8 invites us to "taste and see that the LORD is good." Psalm 139 celebrates him as our all-knowing and ever-present Lord. The writer of Psalm 33 declares that "everything he does is trustworthy. The LORD loves righteousness and justice" (vv. 4–5).

Psalm 145 encompasses a number of God's traits, including his greatness, majesty, and faithfulness. David wrote that God is "merciful, compassionate, patient, and always ready to forgive" (v. 8). He is "good to everyone and has compassion for everything that he has made" (v. 9). As David considered how God had worked in his life, he often burst out in praise. "O God, who is like you?" he asked (Ps. 71:19). In Psalm 40:5 he answered his own question: "No one compares to you!" David knew that words are not adequate to describe God, but he vowed to talk about God's qualities for as long as he lived.

Meditating on God's character traits strengthens our faith and deepens our personal relationship with him. It encourages us to acknowledge him in good times and helps us to trust him in hard times. No matter what we're going through, thinking about God's attributes reminds us that we always have reason to praise him.

The more we concentrate on who he is rather than on our own circumstances, the more motivated we'll be to tell other people about our compassionate, merciful, patient, forgiving God. And even though there are no words to adequately describe him, we just might end up doing a little psalm-writing of our own.

No one compares to you!

Psalm 40:5

God's Word

Psalm 119

It seems fitting that the longest psalm, and also the longest chapter in the Bible, has God's Word as its topic. The unknown writer penned a collection of prayers and meditations about the beauty and power of God's Word and the blessings of obeying it. The psalm is arranged according to a strict pattern, divided into twenty-two sections with each one corresponding to a letter of the Hebrew alphabet. Within each stanza, each of the eight verses begins with the same letter. Almost every one of the 176 verses mentions God's Word, often using synonyms such as commandments, laws, precepts, teachings, regulations, written instructions, and guiding principles.

The writer's choice of words shows that God's written Word is closely tied to God himself. The psalmist describes the Word as righteous, true, reliable, trustworthy, and miraculous. He professes his love and longing for God's teachings. As he reflects on them and obeys them, he finds joy, comfort, hope, new life, and the assurance that he will never feel ashamed. He asks God for increased understanding of the Scriptures so he can obey them more fully.

God's Word has the power to shape our character and our behavior as it guides us through every stage of our life. Reading Psalm 119 is a good opportunity to check our own attitude toward the Bible. Do we feel some of that same love and yearning for God's Word that the psalmist expressed? Have we committed to faithfully following God's instructions? Do we find joy, comfort, and hope in his Word?

If we sense our attitude toward the Bible growing cold, we may need to spend some time in Psalm 119. God encourages us to meditate, memorize, and apply his Word to our life. He also invites us to ask for greater understanding. If we're being obedient to what we already know, God will open our eyes so we can discover more miraculous things from his Word.

Uncover my eyes
so that I may see the miraculous things in your teachings.

Psalm 119:18

Jesus in Psalms

Some of the psalms are classified as "messianic psalms" because they anticipate the coming of Israel's long-awaited Messiah. Some even prophesy specific details that were later fulfilled perfectly in Jesus Christ's life, ministry, and death. Old Testament writers sometimes quoted from messianic psalms or used similar wording when discussing the Messiah (compare Zech. 9:10 with Ps. 72:8). New Testament writers referred to certain verses in Psalms as depicting Christ (for example, Acts 4:11 and 1 Pet. 2:7 both quote Ps. 118:22). More importantly, Jesus applied Psalm 118:22 and other verses to himself (see John 13:18).

David apparently wrote Psalm 22 during a time of intense suffering, but through the Holy Spirit's guidance his words accurately described what Jesus would endure centuries later. During his crucifixion Jesus quoted the opening lines of Psalm 22 as he cried out to God for strength. While he hung on the cross, onlookers insulted him and shook their heads (v. 7); some mockingly challenged him to have God save him (v. 8). His hands and feet were pierced (v. 16) and he suffered intense thirst (v. 15). Soldiers at the foot of the cross gambled for his clothing (v. 18).

Other psalms fill in additional details. Jesus was betrayed by a friend (41:9) and accused by false witnesses (35:11). He was offered vinegar for his thirst (69:21). He prayed for his enemies (109:4). Not one of his bones was broken (34:20). He rose from the dead (16:8–10) and ascended into heaven (68:18).

Although the Gospels record the events surrounding Jesus's crucifixion and death, Psalm 22 allows us to glimpse his thoughts and feelings. It's a difficult passage to read, knowing that he endured such agony for us. Jesus suffered so that we can live with him for eternity if we accept the salvation made possible by his sacrifice. When we go through suffering, we can find strength to endure by meditating on the closing words of Psalm 22: "He has finished it" (v. 31).

This is a statement that can be trusted: If we
have died with him, we will live with him.

2 Timothy 2:11

Proverbs

God's Textbook for Wise Living

A wise person will listen and continue to learn, and an understanding person will gain direction.

Proverbs 1:5

Proverbs is a prime example of Jewish wisdom literature and perhaps the most practical book in the Old Testament. This collection of maxims, pointed questions, short poems (mostly in the form of couplets), and brief parables covers a broad range of subjects, sharing God's advice on all aspects of day-to-day living. The purpose is clearly stated in the opening verses of the first chapter: to explain and impart wisdom that is based on a right relationship with God and that influences every area of a person's life.

Solomon wrote the largest portion of Proverbs; other authors mentioned include Agur, Lemuel, and a group called "the wise." Solomon probably collected and edited most of the material before the later years of his reign when his character began to decline. The stages of Solomon's life illustrate the distinction that Proverbs makes between knowledge (having the facts) and wisdom (applying knowledge to our life). The moral and ethical instructions in Proverbs show us how to live a wise, godly life by applying spiritual truth to our relationships and our conduct. They also teach us how to avoid the negative consequences of ungodly choices.

Proverbs is as relevant today as it was in Solomon's time. It offers something for everyone, whether we need counsel on relationships, business matters, anger, parenting, manners, or almost anything else. Whatever issue we're struggling with, we can find helpful advice on how to handle it in a way that pleases God. Or we may need to use certain passages as guidelines to evaluate our attitudes, our behavior, or our character traits. But we need to do more than read; we need to meditate on the wisdom found in Proverbs until it becomes ingrained in our thinking and affects our daily life. God has given us a treasure trove of practical advice; if we're wise, we'll spend the rest of our life applying it.

The Cast of Characters

Proverbs 1

We're all familiar with caricatures, those drawings that exaggerate one or more of a person's features. Proverbs makes use of literary caricatures as powerful object lessons for its readers. We're shown positive character traits that serve as models for our own behavior or attitudes, while negative traits warn us to watch for these weaknesses in ourselves and make needed corrections. The opening chapter introduces the main characters.

The "wise" person represents someone who listens and obeys God. This person lives a disciplined life and continues to learn and grow in understanding. The "fool" is a person who is opposed to God and rejects his wisdom. Proverbs 13:20 warns us that it can be dangerous to associate with fools. The "simple" or "gullible" person is not firmly committed to anything. This type of person makes no effort to gain self-discipline and can be easily deceived or misled (14:15).

Within these three major groups, specific strengths and weaknesses are highlighted throughout Proverbs. The "diligent," the "prudent" or "sensible," and the "upright" or "decent" provide positive examples for us to imitate. In contrast, the "lazy," the "wicked," and those "without sense" show us some actions to avoid. Other negative examples are the "mocker" or "scoffer" (21:24) and the "person who thinks he is wise" but is really worse off than a fool (26:12).

Our attitudes and actions reveal our character more than our words do. An honest self-examination will show us which character in Proverbs we most resemble. If we don't like the answer, we can do something about it. We often hear the cliché that people don't change, but Proverbs 8:5 says that even a fool is not beyond hope. What sets the wise person apart in Proverbs is a teachable spirit. If we make the choice to listen to God and respond to his wisdom, we can move away from foolishness and step into a more positive role.

Whoever listens to me will live without worry
and will be free from the dread of disaster.

Proverbs 1:33

The Key to Wisdom

Proverbs 2–4; 8

Several chapters in Proverbs are devoted to the application of truth to our decisions, our relationships, and every aspect of our daily life. Chapters 2–4 portray a father extolling the benefits of wisdom including long life, fulfillment, honor, peace, safety, health, success, and a good reputation. Chapter 8 personifies wisdom as a virtuous woman calling out in the streets to offer something described as far better than fine silver, pure gold, or precious jewels.

Although wisdom is a gift from God (2:6), it requires effort on our part. We're instructed to pursue God's wisdom as if we're looking for hidden treasure. Proverbs 9:10 reveals the key to unlock this treasure and expresses the central truth of the entire book: the beginning point of wisdom is the fear of the Lord. We can't grow in our understanding if we don't have an attitude of proper respect and reverence for God. The more we revere God, the more wisdom we gain; the more we grow in wisdom, the greater our reverence of God will be.

How does God's wisdom play out in a person's life? It motivates us to pursue knowledge and understanding more than material riches. We'll respond to correction in a spirit of humility, and find favor with God and other people (3:4). We will hate evil and love what is right. When we face decisions, we'll trust in God more than in our own human reasoning.

Our culture prizes higher learning but places little value on the wisdom that springs from a personal relationship with God. If we're not careful, this attitude can affect our thinking and make us lose our sense of reverence for God. We may end up chasing after worldly knowledge instead of the wisdom that Proverbs describes. As long as we hold on to the key God has shown us, we can expect to find lifelong treasure and enjoy the many benefits of godly wisdom.

> *The fear of the Lord is the beginning of wisdom.*
> *The knowledge of the Holy One is understanding.*
>
> Proverbs 9:10

Guarding Our Purity

Proverbs 5; 6:20–7:27

Proverbs 5–7 makes it obvious that true wisdom will motivate us to guard our sexual purity. Solomon uses graphic words to illustrate a seductive but dangerous woman who lures men. What seems sweet at first turns out to be a bitter experience. Too late her victims regret ignoring correction and spurning self-discipline. Solomon urged his sons to find satisfaction and delight in their wives, especially since God saw everything they did. He warned that adultery leads to self-destruction, often ending in disgrace, sexually transmitted diseases, or violence from a jealous husband.

The narrative in chapter 7 relates how a naïve young man fell into adultery by allowing himself to be in the wrong place at the wrong time. Ignoring the warning to "stay far away from her," he strolled near an immoral woman's house at night. The seductively dressed woman met him with flattery that fed his ego, and she boldly kissed him in public. She enticed him by talking about the sensual pleasures they could enjoy, while assuring him that her husband would never know. The man blindly followed, not realizing that he had been trapped like an animal in a snare.

Books, movies, and television shows often portray extramarital relationships as not only acceptable, but as something beautiful. Proverbs sets the record straight. God designed sex solely for the marriage relationship. Whether we're male or female, single or married, God expects us to guard against sexual temptation. A large part of that is making sure we don't stray into the wrong place at the wrong time.

Preserving our sexual purity while living in this world can only be done with supernatural power. God wants to help protect us from the sad consequences of sexual sin. If we depend on him and follow his wisdom, we won't find ourselves caught in the trap of immorality.

> *Stay away from sexual sins. Other sins that people commit*
> *don't affect their bodies the same way sexual sins do.*
> *People who sin sexually sin against their own bodies.*
>
> 1 Corinthians 6:18

How to Disgust God

Proverbs 4:20–27; 6:12–19

The book of Proverbs gives a lot of advice on what to do—and on what *not* to do. Chapter 6 shows us some attitudes and behaviors to avoid through a description of what God considers a "good-for-nothing scoundrel" (also translated as "worthless," "wicked," or "villain"). The passage uses a numeric literary device also found other places in Proverbs. The "six things that the LORD hates, even seven that are disgusting to him" (v. 16) are not meant to be a complete list, but a representative grouping that draws attention to the last item.

God hates a haughty look, a lying tongue, hands that murder, a mind that plots wicked plans, feet that are ready to move toward sin, and a mouth that gives false testimony against someone. This type of person spreads conflict and discord wherever he goes, even among family and friends. In contrast, Proverbs 4 tells us how to be the kind of person who pleases God. We're advised to keep our mouth free from dishonesty and deceptive speech, keep our eyes focused on the path of God's commands, and use our feet to walk away from evil.

We may not consider ourselves a worthless or good-for-nothing scoundrel, but we can easily slip into habits and attitudes that God finds disgusting. He hates any form of self-pride, dishonesty, wicked thoughts, and readiness to contribute to conflict. The only way to protect ourselves from these tendencies is to carefully guard our heart, since it determines our life's direction. In Proverbs the heart denotes our inner life, or the center of our thinking, feeling, and decision making.

If we internalize God's wisdom, it will shape our values according to his and guide us on the right path. Then we can evaluate everything we see, say, and do according to whether it's something that pleases God, or something that fits on his hate list.

Guard your heart above all else,
for it determines the course of your life.
Proverbs 4:23 NLT

An Ideal Woman—or Man

Proverbs 31:10—31

The book of Proverbs closes with a description of a person who embodies all of the wisdom found in the book, and who lives it out on a day-by-day basis. Although many illustrations in Proverbs use a male figure, this acrostic poem portrays a wife and mother. The Proverbs 31 woman seems to be a composite of desirable character traits rather than a single person. As such, the character study of this ideal woman is pertinent to all of us, whether male or female, young or old.

This wife and mother works diligently and plans her time wisely. She not only takes care of her family's needs, she also reaches out to help the poor and needy in practical ways. Besides being a homemaker, she makes wise business investments. She speaks with wisdom and conducts herself with dignity and nobility. Her husband trusts her with all his heart; she contributes to his high reputation. She smiles at the future rather than stressing out about what might happen. What is the secret of this outstanding woman? Her life is based on Proverbs 1:7: she fears the Lord.

The example of the Proverbs 31 woman helps us examine our own life and pinpoint which areas we need to work on. Do we use wise planning to make the most of our time and resources, investing in things that have eternal rewards? Do we place high priority on our family's needs, but also use God-given opportunities to minister to the needy? Do we give our spouse reason to trust us implicitly? Are we a source of good in the lives of our family, friends, and neighbors? Do we worry about the future or do we entrust it into God's hands? We'll never be perfect while we live on the earth, but if we fear God and do our best to live his way, we can be sure that we're moving toward his ideal of what a woman or man should be.

Blessed are all who fear the LORD
and live his way.

Psalm 128:1

Ecclesiastes

What's It All About?

After having heard it all, this is the conclusion: Fear God, and keep his commands, because this applies to everyone. God will certainly judge everything that is done.

Ecclesiastes 12:13–14

What's the meaning of life? Almost three thousand years ago, a great king shared his insights on that universal question. Solomon had it all—wealth, fame, power, and more wisdom than any man on earth. Late in his reign, he looked back at his frantic search for purpose and fulfillment after his heart had strayed from God. Even with the immense resources at his disposal, Solomon discovered that it's impossible to find happiness apart from God. He shared his conclusion in hopes of sparing his readers the grief that his own disobedience had caused: the only way to make sense of life is to honor and obey God.

Ecclesiastes has several unique features that can make it difficult to read and interpret. Solomon used a common technique of wisdom teaching by stating two apparently contradictory principles so that the reader can apply the one that fits his or her situation. Rather than state general truths, Solomon used a provocative style that often focused on specific deviations from what would normally be expected. Since Ecclesiastes examines the end result of human philosophy that leaves out God, certain verses naturally contradict statements found elsewhere in Scripture.

Ecclesiastes opens and ends with a concise description of life spent without God: "Everything is pointless!" (1:2; 12:8). Yet despite a sometimes negative, pessimistic tone, the book ends with a positive message for those who choose to obey God. Yes, life is short, but we can live in the light of eternity. When life seems unfair and filled with unexplainable inconsistencies, we can look forward to God's future judgment when he will set everything right. We can accept each day as it comes as a gift from his hand. Then we'll be able to enjoy all the good things in our life—as long as we don't try to find our significance or meaning in them.

Seasons of Life

Ecclesiastes 3:1–8

Solomon experimented with every possible means of searching for meaning and fulfillment in life. He didn't find long-term satisfaction from his extensive building, planting, or gathering of wealth (Eccles. 2:4–8). He didn't find lasting joy when he dedicated himself to pleasure and laughter (2:1–2). Solomon figured out the hard way that any human endeavor is worthless if it's done apart from God's will and outside of his timing. Chapter 3 contains Solomon's well-known poem that reminds us there is an appropriate time for every event, activity, and emotional response "under heaven."

Solomon's list of fourteen opposites begins with birth and death, things we have no control over. The precise meaning of some of the activities isn't clear; others are obvious. There are appropriate times to laugh and to cry, to mourn and to celebrate, to display affection and to refrain from it. It may be the right time to search for something, or it may be time to give it up as lost. Sometimes we need to plant; other times we need to uproot and start over. There are times for healing, but also for killing in self-defense or to protect others. We should love at the appropriate times, but also feel hate and righteous anger toward sin.

Every season that God allows us to go through has a purpose and represents an opportunity for us to grow spiritually. We can learn to be content by accepting our circumstances as part of God's plan and by looking for what he wants to teach us or accomplish through us. If we begin to doubt God's goodness or resent what we're experiencing, we can remember that God has also determined the duration of each season of our life. Times of crying and mourning are inevitable, but they won't last forever. Neither will the times of laughing and dancing. We bring glory to God when we live to the fullest in every stage of our life.

> *Everything has its own time, and there is a specific
> time for every activity under heaven.*
>
> Ecclesiastes 3:1

Life under the Sun

Ecclesiastes 9

Many passages in Ecclesiastes are depressing and rightfully so, since they come from the viewpoint of living life without God. Solomon asserted that the person who hasn't been born yet is better off than the living or the dead because he hasn't seen "the evil that is done under the sun" (4:3). He complained that he had observed wickedness where justice and righteousness should be found (see 3:16). Righteous people sometimes suffered for the actions of wicked people, and wicked people got what the righteous deserved (see 8:14). A race was not necessarily won by the fastest runner, or a battle by the mightiest soldier. Intelligent and skilled people didn't always get the recompense they deserved.

Ecclesiastes points out that life on earth is filled with inconsistencies and can seem like a string of random events, with death the only certainty. "So I came to hate life because everything done under the sun seemed wrong to me," Solomon concluded (2:17). As believers, we have a keen sense of life's contradictions and injustices. But we also know that Christ died on the cross to redeem us and all of creation from the effects of sin. When he returns to the earth one day, he will set all things right. Only then will the world operate as God intended it to.

Our physical existence is on a fallen planet heavily influenced by the effects of sin. But spiritually speaking, we already live in a different realm where Christ is seated at God's right hand. When life seems random or contradictory, we can choose to focus on God's future judgment when he will reward righteousness and punish evil. We may have to dwell "under the sun" for a while longer, but if we belong to the Son, we know that one day we will live in a perfect world where everything will make sense.

*Since you were brought back to life with
Christ, focus on the things that are above—
where Christ holds the highest position.*

Colossians 3:1

19

How to Enjoy Life

Ecclesiastes 5:18–20; 12:9–14

King Solomon undertook impressive building and landscaping projects. He amassed flocks, herds, slaves, silver, and gold; he acquired singers, musicians, and concubines. Solomon became the greatest person in Jerusalem and his fame spread throughout the earth. With all the vast resources at his disposal, Solomon did whatever appealed to him and allowed himself to have any pleasure he desired (2:10). Yet when he surveyed everything that he had accomplished, accumulated, and experienced, Solomon concluded that it was all pointless, like "trying to catch the wind" (1:14).

Solomon began his reign with a desire and commitment to honor and obey God. But he ignored God's command and married hundreds of women from pagan nations. Just as God had warned, Solomon's heart was turned toward idolatry and immorality. Late in his life, Solomon looked back at the wasted years he'd spent away from God. He had done it all and seen it all, but it all meant nothing. Solomon couldn't turn back the clock, but God led him to record his life lessons to show us how to find fulfillment and enjoy life.

The final chapter of Ecclesiastes reveals that Solomon finally discovered the answer he was seeking. We will find meaning and purpose only through knowing God and obeying him. Once we understand that God is good and in control even when life seems confusing and unpredictable, we can freely enjoy the blessings he gives us.

God wants us to enjoy the good things he provides without making them our end goal or trying to find our self-worth in them. Whether we're eating, drinking, or reaping the benefits of our labor, we can gratefully accept it all as gifts from his hand. Our culture may urge us to chase after wealth, power, knowledge, or pleasure, but we'll never truly find happiness in life until we learn to trust in God. Any other approach is like trying to catch the wind.

> *They should place their confidence in God who*
> *richly provides us with everything to enjoy.*
>
> 1 Timothy 6:17

Song of Songs

The Greatest Love Story

I am my beloved's, and my beloved is mine.
Song of Songs 6:3

Is it historical narrative, a fictional story, or an allegory? Is it a single unified poem or a collection of love songs? Are there two or three main characters? Song of Songs is one of the Bible's most difficult books, with a long history of debate and diverse interpretation. Most scholars consider Solomon the author, but they disagree over his motivation for writing. Was he recounting his own early romance and marriage before he amassed a harem of a thousand women, or did he simply want to present an idealized portrayal of marital love?

Some people believe the song tells the actual story of Solomon wooing and wedding a shepherdess from Shulam. Others see three main characters, with either King Solomon trying to lure the Shulammite away from her lover, or a young shepherd trying to turn her heart away from the king who has married her.

Despite the many questions about its structure and characters, the topic of Song of Songs is crystal clear. The sensuous dialogue between the couple makes some people uncomfortable, but God included this song in his Word to celebrate the joys of love and marriage and to show the proper context for sexual intimacy. Song of Songs provides guidelines to help us view marriage and sex according to God's perspective rather than the world's distorted view.

On a deeper level, Jews have seen the book as a portrayal of God's love for Israel. Christians view it as an expression of Christ's love for his bride, the church. Just as the young couple yearned to be united with each other, Christ longs for the day when we can live with him in a new relationship unhindered by the presence or power of sin. Whether or not we ever experience the ideal marital relationship depicted in Song of Songs, we can rejoice in the knowledge that Christ has claimed us as his own. And one day we will be united with our beloved.

Was That a Compliment?

Song of Songs 4:1–7; 5:9–16

The groom in Song of Songs declared his bride to be "beautiful in every way" and proceeded to praise her figure and facial features in glowing terms. However, once we get past her eyes "like doves," the metaphors sound strange to our modern ears. He compared his lover's hair to a flock of goats, her lips to scarlet thread, and her temples to slices of pomegranates. Her teeth reminded him of sheep about to be shorn. He described her neck as a tower and her breasts as fawns or gazelles.

The bride announced that her groom stood out among ten thousand men. She admired his eyes like doves bathing in milk, his head like fine gold, his cheeks like a garden of spices, and his lips like lilies. And how could she resist a chest like a block of ivory covered with sapphires, legs like columns of marble, and hands like disks of gold set with emeralds? We might never use such expressions, but we can understand that her groom appreciated being compared to costly building materials and precious stones.

Men and women in the early stages of a romantic relationship usually don't hesitate to compliment each other. As the years pass, they often drop the habit, which can make the other person feel neglected or unappreciated. In a similar way, parents often lavishly praise their children during the early years. When adolescence hits, they may forget to let them know how special they are—just when their kids are struggling with self-esteem issues.

We're all hungry for words of affirmation from our loved ones. Song of Songs reminds us not to hold back from expressing our love and appreciation. Sincere praise, especially of a person's character, can transform a relationship. We don't have to refer to goats or pomegranates to say the words a family member or friend longs to hear.

How beautiful are your expressions
of love, my bride, my sister!
How much better are your expressions of love than wine.

Song of Songs 4:10

X-Rated Talk

Song of Songs

Since the Bible contains a number of prohibitions and warnings about sex, some people act as though God forbids it. They seem to forget that our Creator is the one who thought of sex in the first place. Song of Songs portrays sexual intimacy as God intended, within the context of a loving, committed marriage. God designed the act of sex not only to produce children, but to be a source of mutual comfort and pleasure between a husband and wife. An unselfish, loving approach to the sexual dimension in marriage is one way for the couple to honor God and each other.

Biblical guidelines for sex are necessary since we live in a fallen world. Sin has damaged the relationship between men and women, and God's gift is often distorted into something focused on selfish gratification. Our culture even tries to portray lust and all kinds of unnatural perversion as forms of sexual intimacy. Many people never experience the sense of security and joy from sex that God designed it to bring to the marital relationship.

Some people feel embarrassed reading the passages where the betrothed man and woman in Song of Songs describe their desire for each other and their longing to be united. Yet most of us no longer blush at the sexual innuendos and crude humor so prevalent in television shows, movies, and songs on the radio. Obscene language and jokes have become commonplace even in public settings.

Such talk has no place in a believer's life. When we cheapen the concept of sex, we dishonor the God who created it as something beautiful to be celebrated by married couples. Any other view of sex is X-rated and should be censored from our conversation, our thoughts, and our attitudes.

> *Don't let sexual sin, perversion of any kind, or greed even be*
> *mentioned among you. This is not appropriate behavior for*
> *God's holy people. It's not right that dirty stories, foolish talk,*
> *or obscene jokes should be mentioned among you either.*

> Ephesians 5:3–4

The Prophets

Speaking for God

The Bible mentions a number of prophets who left no surviving written records. These include Nathan, Elijah, Elisha, Huldah, Iddo, Shemaiah, and others. The works of the writing prophets make up a quarter of the Scriptures. The books of Isaiah, Jeremiah, Lamentations, Ezekiel, and Daniel are known as the Major prophets because of their longer length, with the exception of Lamentations. The remaining twelve books of the Old Testament are called the Minor prophets. The prophetical books were written between the ninth and fifth centuries BC.

Also called seers, watchmen, or messengers, prophets were divinely appointed to proclaim God's message. He communicated with his representatives through dreams, visions, forces of nature, and sometimes an audible voice. In Deuteronomy 18:18–20, God promised the Israelites that he would put his words in the mouths of his prophets. He explained that a genuine prophet would speak in the name of Yahweh and whatever he predicted would come true.

God's prophets came from different backgrounds with distinctive personalities and writing styles, but they were all committed to sharing his truth. They exposed sin and warned people to repent and make needed corrections, reminding them of God's holiness and his laws. They warned of coming judgment if people continued to rebel against God. They also testified about the coming Messiah, sometimes relating specific details about his life and work.

As believers today, God has called each one of us to be his representative to the rest of the world. He expects us to confront sin, reflect his holiness, and share his message of love and forgiveness by testifying about the Messiah who has come and who will return someday. Through the Bible, God has already communicated the truth that he wants us to share with others. Whether we are sharing God's perspective on future events or his plan of salvation through Christ, we are called to speak for him like the Old Testament prophets did.

Therefore, we are Christ's representatives,
and through us God is calling you.

2 Corinthians 5:20

Isaiah

God Always Keeps His Promises

> Turn to me and be saved, all who live at the ends of the earth, because I am God, and there is no other. I have bound myself with an oath.
>
> Isaiah 45:22–23

Generally considered the greatest of the Old Testament prophets, Isaiah had a sixty-year ministry under four of Judah's kings. Little is known about his personal history, but the literary quality of his writing indicates that he was well-educated and perhaps born into an aristocratic home. Isaiah's name means "Yahweh is salvation," which seems appropriate since he recorded the clearest, most comprehensive account of the future Messiah and his saving work.

The book of Isaiah has been called a miniature Bible because of the content within its two major divisions. The first thirty-nine chapters correlate to the Old Testament, stressing God's holiness and justice, and announcing his judgment for sin on Judah, the surrounding nations, and the rest of the world. The last twenty-seven chapters relate to the New Testament as they highlight God's compassion and unearned favor. This section also prophesies about the Messiah who would come first to suffer and die on a cross, and later return to rule as the world's sovereign king.

In Isaiah's time, many Israelites had stopped believing the promises God made concerning Abraham's descendants. They preferred to depend on human strength and power instead. Isaiah taught that God's promises still stood in spite of Judah's sin and unbelief. God would refine his people through judgment, but their repentance would bring restoration and renewal. And one day, the Savior would come from among the tribe of Judah to bless the entire world.

Isaiah's beautiful writing offers us glimpses of God's holiness and righteousness against a background of sin and unbelief. We also see a clear picture of God's compassion in his plan to send a Savior to die, not just for Judah's sin but for the entire world's. Isaiah reminds us that we can depend on God to keep his promises no matter what.

Ready to Serve

Isaiah 6

Isaiah had a vision of God that radically changed his perspective and prepared him to be God's special messenger. In the temple, God's presence resided above the cover of the ark of the covenant. But Isaiah saw him seated on a high and lofty throne, with the train of his robe filling the temple. Heavenly beings flew above him, calling to each other and proclaiming the Lord's holiness. At the sound of their voices, the doorposts shook and the temple filled with smoke.

In the face of God's majesty and holiness, Isaiah saw the sinfulness of himself and his people. Grief overwhelmed him. "Oh, no!" he cried. "I'm doomed." One of the angels touched Isaiah's lips with a burning coal from the altar. "Your guilt has been taken away, and your sin has been forgiven," he told Isaiah (v. 7). After Isaiah had been cleansed of sin, God offered him an opportunity to serve. "Whom will I send?" he asked. Isaiah answered without hesitation, "Here I am. Send me!" (v. 8). Regardless of the people's response, Isaiah would take God's words to those whose hearts had hardened against the truth.

The more clearly we see God in his holiness, majesty, and power, the more clearly we see our own sinfulness, weakness, and inadequacy. Once we get to that point, God can use us in his work in a mighty way. Sometimes we act as though we can't do much for God until we become a giant in the faith or an expert on the Bible or theology. But his prerequisites for service are an attitude of humility and an awareness of our dependence on him. Knowing that our sins have been forgiven by a holy God motivates us to share that message with others. When God asks "Whom will I send?" how can we hesitate to give the answer that God wants to hear?

> *Then I heard the voice of the Lord, saying,*
> *"Whom will I send? Who will go for us?"*
> *I said, "Here I am. Send me!"*
>
> Isaiah 6:8

Comforting Words

Isaiah 40

The first thirty-nine chapters of Isaiah deal mostly with warnings of God's judgment on Israel and the surrounding nations for their sin. Chapter 40 represents a major shift in focus as the theme moves from condemnation to comfort. When Isaiah first shared these messages, Judah still had a hundred difficult years ahead plus seventy years of captivity. But God allowed his prophet to see ahead to the period of restoration that would come after Judah had received the full punishment for her sins. "Comfort my people!" God instructed Isaiah. "Speak tenderly to Jerusalem and announce to it that its hard time of labor is over and its wrongs have been paid for" (vv. 1–2).

While God's holiness requires him to judge sin, he stands ready to comfort and restore those who turn to him in repentance. Jesus demonstrated this side of God's nature when he agonized over Jerusalem's refusal to respond to God. "How often I wanted to gather your children together the way a hen gathers her chicks under her wings!" he cried. "But you were not willing!" (see Matt. 23:37). The people of Israel had condemned themselves by ignoring the prophets God had sent; now they rejected their Messiah. God longed to shelter and protect them, but they refused to run to him.

Trouble and hardship can drive us to our knees in prayer, or it can make us turn away from God in bitterness. Whenever we suffer the consequences of our wrong choices and actions, God is disciplining us to purify us and draw us back into a restored relationship with him. Sometimes our pain keeps us from hearing the tender words he longs to speak to us. Reading the Scriptures and spending quiet time in prayer will help us run under his sheltering wings. We'll also find comfort in remembering that if God disciplines us, it's because we're his child and he wants what is best for us.

> *The Lord disciplines everyone he loves.*
> *He severely disciplines everyone he accepts as his child.*
>
> Hebrews 12:6

Long-Range Vision

Isaiah 44:28–45:8

The prophecies in Isaiah cover the major points of God's plan for world history: the Babylonian captivity and the remnant who would return to Judah; God's judgment on Israel's persecutors; the blessings brought to the Gentiles through the Messiah's redemptive work; the Messiah's suffering and humiliation and his second coming to rule the world as David's Branch; the new heavens and earth. Many of the messages have a twofold nature, predicting a soon-to-occur event while also referring to an event in the distant future. This distinction of prophetic Scriptures makes it especially important to heed the warning in 2 Peter 1:20 that prophecy is not a matter of our own interpretation.

Isaiah 44 and 45 include a prophecy that is impossible to misinterpret. God shared his plan to raise up a pagan emperor named Cyrus to deliver his chosen people from captivity and arrange for the rebuilding of Jerusalem. Almost 150 years later, the ruler of the combined Medo-Persian Empire conquered Babylon. The very next year, Cyrus issued the decree (recorded in 2 Chron. 36:22–23 and Ezra 1:1–4) that freed the Jewish people to return to Judah. Cyrus also fulfilled his predicted role in carrying out God's judgment on Israel's enemies.

God called Cyrus by name and predicted his actions to demonstrate his sovereignty and to remind us that he controls the future. On a personal level, it's reassuring to know that God already sees how our own life story will play out. He sees the disappointments and heartaches we'll face, along with the joys and triumphs. He knows every action we'll take, including our mistakes and wrong choices. And he's already planned how to use it all for our good and his glory. We may wish we could see into the future and know what to expect, but we're better off learning to trust the only One who has such long-range vision.

Every day of my life was recorded in your book
before one of them had taken place.

Psalm 139:16

Jesus in Isaiah

Of the three hundred Old Testament prophecies about the Messiah's first coming, many are found in the book of Isaiah. Jesus's virgin birth is referred to in Isaiah 7:14, while 11:1–2 specifies his lineage and anointing by God. In 9:1–7 we see an example of a passage that blends together prophecies concerning the Messiah's first and second comings. We also learn a few descriptive names that shed light on Jesus's identity and character: Wonderful Counselor, Mighty God, Everlasting Father, and Prince of Peace. While we usually associate these familiar verses with the celebration of Christ's birth, they also include the promise of his future eternal reign.

Other chapters focus on the glorious period when Christ will rule the earth, a time of such peace and harmony that animals now considered dangerous will be harmless (11:6–8). Chapter 53, however, describes the suffering that the Messiah would endure before entering his rightful place of honor and glory. This "man of sorrows" would be despised and rejected by people. Despite his innocence, he would be arrested and condemned as a criminal, and endure an agonizing death as he carried the burden of our sins and paid the price to set us free from condemnation.

Isaiah gives the most comprehensive picture of Christ found in the Old Testament. The messianic prophecies also offer an accurate portrayal of the Christian life. We've been blessed with all the spiritual blessings that heaven has to offer (see Eph. 1:3). We've already received the gifts of God's forgiveness and eternal life, and we look forward to enjoying the glories of heaven. But living as God's child also means being willing to endure abuse, false accusations, and persecution. God often calls us to follow Jesus's example by giving up our rights and personal desires in order to serve others. Being identified with Jesus holds the promise of a glorious future; it also includes times of hardship and suffering before we get there.

If we are his children, we are also God's heirs.
If we share in Christ's suffering in order to share
his glory, we are heirs together with him.

Romans 8:17

Transformation

Isaiah 60

Isaiah is a book of contrasts, moving from the depths of Israel's sin and depravity to the heights of God's glory and majesty. Warnings of God's wrathful judgment on Israel for her rebellion are followed by promises of restoration and assurances of his tender loving care. Chapter 35 shows the transformation that will take place in the land and people when the Messiah begins his millennial reign. Because of Christ's healing power, the blind will see and the deaf will hear. The mute will shout for joy and the lame will leap like deer. Streams of water will gush in the parched desert; the wilderness will blossom like a lily.

In chapter 60 Isaiah contrasts the spiritual darkness that now covers the earth with the light of God's glory that will dawn when Christ returns to rule the world. That light and the spiritual blessings it brings will attract all nations and they will flock to its source. Israel will become the predominant culture of the world, with other countries bringing their wealth to enrich the nation. Even countries that formerly despised or oppressed Israel will honor God's people and acknowledge Jerusalem, or Zion, as God's holy city and his dwelling place on earth.

If we're believers, then we have had our own darkness-to-light experience. The moment we trusted Christ as our Savior, God delivered us from Satan's kingdom of darkness and transferred us into his kingdom of light and truth. Because of that change, people should see a contrast between our old way of living and our present attitudes and actions.

As we grow to be more like Christ, the people around us will be attracted to the source of the light that shines in our life. We naturally look forward to the glorious way that God will transform the world in the future, but we want to make sure that we're allowing his Spirit to change our life today.

> *God has rescued us from the power of darkness and has
> brought us into the kingdom of his Son, whom he loves.*
>
> Colossians 1:13

Jeremiah

A Messenger in Troubled Times

"Your own wickedness will correct you, and your unfaithful ways will punish you. You should know and see how evil and bitter it is for you if you abandon the LORD your God and do not fear me," declares the Almighty LORD of Armies.

Jeremiah 2:19

One of Judah's greatest prophets, Jeremiah lived and served during his nation's darkest days. As world powers shifted, Judah sank further into idolatry, apostasy, and moral decay. During his forty-year ministry, Jeremiah warned of God's terrible judgment if the people refused to repent and turn to him. When the people rejected his message (including his neighbors, friends, and family), Jeremiah began prophesying about Jerusalem's fall. Throughout his life, Jeremiah endured deprivation, ridicule, beatings, and persecution. He was thrown in prison and into a cistern. During the Babylonian invasion, his countrymen forced him to go to Egypt against his will, where he presumably died.

Jeremiah did not arrange his material in chronological order; some of his early prophecies are placed near the end of the book. He mingled sections of narrative with poetic and prose passages, often using symbolism. The autobiographical portions of the book get very personal. Jeremiah admits his feelings of inadequacy when he received his call from God as a youth (see 1:6), and a later moment of doubt about God's justice (see 12:1–2). Most of all, Jeremiah agonized over the messages he had to deliver and his people's hardhearted response. He wept over the coming destruction of his beloved nation, but he still faithfully carried out his calling.

God has called each of us to be his messenger, especially in times of trouble and upheaval. People want to hear about God's love, but warnings about his judgment of sin will not make us popular. Reading Jeremiah encourages us to be faithful in sharing a balanced view of God's character. The writings of this "weeping prophet" also remind us that even as we share God's message, our heart should break over the fate of those who choose to reject him.

Promiscuous Sisters

Jeremiah 2:1–3:13

God didn't mince words when he confronted the people of Judah about their idolatry. He compared their chasing after foreign gods to animals in heat during mating season. He said it would be hard to find a high hill or a large tree where they had not worshiped the Canaanite gods. God had set the nation of Israel apart and planted them like a choice grapevine. They turned against him to worship idols of wood and stone by offering animal sacrifices and committing unspeakable acts of sexual immorality. No amount of soap or detergent could wash away the stains of their wickedness.

In chapter 3 God used a parable about two promiscuous sisters to describe Israel and Judah. They waited by the roadside for lovers, acting like cult prostitutes. As Israel continued to commit spiritual adultery by uniting herself with false gods, God waited for her to return to him. Eventually, he "divorced" Israel by sending her into Assyrian captivity. Instead of learning from her sister's fate, Judah also acted like a prostitute and polluted the land with idol worship. Adding hypocrisy to her sin of spiritual adultery, Judah made an outward show of faithfulness to God but never changed her behavior.

We probably see no comparison between our lifestyle and the shocking behavior described by God in this passage. But if we honestly examine our heart, we may discover we've been chasing after something other than God. The idols people worship today may not be as visible as objects of wood or stone, but they still offend God just as much. Our heart can be pulled away from God when we place too much importance on things of this world like wealth, knowledge, prestige, or relationships. Anytime we give someone or something the priority that God deserves, we're guilty of spiritual adultery.

> *You unfaithful people! Don't you know that love for*
> *this evil world is hatred toward God? Whoever wants*
> *to be a friend of this world is an enemy of God.*
>
> James 4:4

In the Potter's Hand

Jeremiah 18:1—19:12

One day God sent Jeremiah to the potter's house and promised to give him a message there. As Jeremiah watched the potter working at his wheel, he saw that when a pot had a defect or didn't develop properly, the craftsman reworked it into a new pot. God explained how this process illustrated his relationship with his chosen people.

As Judah's Creator, God had the right to shape the people according to his purposes and plans. If they repented of their sins, he would rework the nation into a usable vessel; otherwise, they would be worthless. On another occasion, God warned them of the consequences of refusing to repent by having Jeremiah smash a clay pot at the city dump.

Isaiah used the same imagery in a prayer expressing the returning remnant's need to be submissive to God. "You are our Father," he wrote. "We are the clay, and you are our potter. We are the work of your hands" (64:8). In the New Testament, Paul employed the same familiar symbolism to show how ludicrous it is to question God's choices (see Rom. 9:19–21). Just as a potter uses clay to make different types of objects, God shapes people for different purposes according to his plan.

Sometimes we're tempted to question why God made us a certain way or why he placed us in our present circumstances. Dissatisfaction can make us forget that we owe our very existence to God. He has the right to deal with all of his creation as he sees fit. Rather than give God our suggestions and ideas, we need to focus on yielding to his good and perfect will for our life. When we become soft and pliable in our Potter's hands, we can be sure that he will shape us into something far greater than anything we could ever have imagined.

> *A potter has the right to do whatever he wants with his clay. He can make something for a special occasion or something for everyday use from the same lump of clay.*
>
> Romans 9:21

Great News

Jeremiah 31:31—40

Although most of Jeremiah's messages focused on condemnation and judgment, they weren't all doom and gloom. He also prophesied about the day when a remnant of the Israelites would return to Judah to rebuild the city. But Jeremiah had much greater news than that to share. God revealed to the prophet that in the future he would make a new covenant with his people. Under the old covenant, God had written his commandments on stone tablets but the people found they were not able to keep them; this time he would engrave his teachings on people's hearts, giving them the power to understand and obey.

The night before his crucifixion, Jesus shared the Passover meal with his disciples. Passing around a cup of wine and some bread, he announced the beginning of this new covenant. The blood he would shed on the cross the next day and his broken body would usher in God's new promise.

All the promises of the new covenant won't be fulfilled until Jesus sets up his millennial kingdom and all of Israel believes in him. But as Christians living in the church age, we live under the new covenant and enjoy its blessings. No longer condemned by written laws that we're unable to follow, we have God's Spirit living in us, guiding and empowering us to obey his will.

The new covenant sets Christianity apart from all other religions and philosophies. We don't follow a list of rules or complicated steps to get right with God. He offers us a personal relationship with him through faith in Jesus Christ. Once we choose to accept him as Savior, God sends his Spirit to dwell in us and give us the ability to live in a way that pleases him. God even paid the price of the new covenant with his own blood. With such great news to share, why should we ever be timid about discussing our beliefs?

> *[Jesus said] "This cup is the new covenant
> in My blood, which is shed for you."*
>
> Luke 22:20 NKJV

Total Commitment

Jeremiah 35

God used a family descended from Moses's father-in-law as a visual aid to point out Judah's sin. He had Jeremiah invite the whole family of Rechab into a side room in the temple and offer them wine. God knew the men would refuse to drink on the basis of their forefather's command. Two hundred years earlier, their forefather Jonadab had ordered his family to abstain from wine and to live a simple, nomadic lifestyle instead of building houses and planting fields. His descendants had obeyed his instructions to the letter. They had recently moved to Jerusalem, but only because of the threat from the Babylonians.

God contrasted Judah's behavior with the example of Rechab's family. The Rechabites considered themselves bound to their human ancestor's command; Judah ignored the commands of their heavenly Father. The Rechabites obeyed a onetime command, while God had sent prophets time and again to remind his people of their covenant obligations. For two hundred years, the Rechabites had unwaveringly held to their oath; Judah had consistently broken God's commands and refused to listen to him. God promised to reward Rechab's family for their faithfulness to their ancestor's command; the people of Judah would be punished for their unfaithfulness.

God is looking for the kind of commitment the family of Rechab demonstrated when they refused Jeremiah's offer of wine. But sadly, we often show more loyalty to worldly things than to our heavenly Father. We may honor our allegiance to our flag, a political party, or membership in a social or professional organization more than our relationship with Christ.

Thankfully, God's faithfulness to his children doesn't depend on their fidelity. Even when we're disobedient or waver in our faith, God will not deny us or turn his back on us. Since God is so committed to our relationship, how could we ever treat it lightly? Our goal is to be as steadfast as a Rechabite.

If we are unfaithful, he remains faithful
because he cannot be untrue to himself.

2 Timothy 2:13

Lamentations

A Funeral Song for Jerusalem

The reason I can still find hope is that I keep this one thing in mind: the LORD's mercy. We were not completely wiped out. His compassion is never limited. It is new every morning. His faithfulness is great.

Lamentations 3:21–23

Jeremiah lived to see many of his prophecies come true. Shortly after Jerusalem fell in 586 BC, he wrote an eyewitness account of that horrifying event. The Babylonians reduced the city to rubble and tortured, killed, or carried off most of the inhabitants. Overwhelmed by the suffering and devastation he witnessed, Jeremiah wrote the book of Lamentations in the style of ancient Jewish funeral songs or chants. Each of its five chapters represents a separate lament poem, with Jeremiah switching between three points of view: himself, the captives, and the personified city of Jerusalem.

As the brokenhearted prophet mourned the fate of his people, he acknowledged that they had brought this destruction on themselves. For forty years, God had used Jeremiah to warn Judah of his coming judgment, yet they ignored God's calls to repent and turn from their sins. Even in the midst of his suffering and grief, however, Jeremiah testified to God's mercy and goodness. God had not wiped out the entire nation of Judah. Just as he had kept his promise of righteous judgment for sin, he would restore Judah because of his great faithfulness and unlimited compassion.

When we suffer the painful consequences of our sins, Lamentations has a few reminders for us. It's appropriate to grieve over our past mistakes and the pain and losses our disobedience caused, but God doesn't want us to wallow in self-pity or despair. After acknowledging that we've brought the suffering on ourselves, we need to remember that God promises restoration and blessing when we confess and repent of our sins. Even if our eyes are "worn out with tears" as Jeremiah's were, we can look forward to a future overflowing with God's unlimited compassion and faithfulness.

Ezekiel

Unusual Object Lessons

"I will reveal the holiness of my great name, which has been dishonored by the nations, the name that you have dishonored among them. Then the nations will know that I am the LORD, because I will reveal my holiness among you as they watch," declares the Almighty LORD.

Ezekiel 36:23

During the second invasion of Jerusalem in 597 BC, Nebuchadnezzar carried off ten thousand captives, including a young priest named Ezekiel. While the much older Jeremiah prophesied to the people who remained in Judah, Ezekiel ministered to a group of exiles living in Babylon. At first, he preached about God's coming judgment of Jerusalem (chapters 1–24) and seven surrounding nations (chapters 25–32). After Jerusalem fell, God gave Ezekiel messages of hope involving the future restoration of God's people (chapters 33–48).

One of the most complex books in the Bible, Ezekiel is an anthology of writings using a mixture of literary devices. Ezekiel included poetry, allegories, parables, symbolism, and apocalyptic visions. He also shared six visions containing vivid imagery that are difficult to interpret. God gave Ezekiel some unusual instructions to illustrate his messages, such as lying on his side for 180 days while eating one small meal a day cooked over manure.

At age thirty, Ezekiel received his calling as a prophet along with a vision of God's glory; he sprinkled references to God's glory throughout the book. Through Ezekiel, God frequently emphasized his priority of revealing his character and holiness, not just to Judah but to the entire world. More than sixty times, God explained that his actions were designed to let people know "that I am the LORD."

We may struggle to understand some passages in Ezekiel, but the book can give us a renewed appreciation for God's character and glory, and a reminder that he still desires to make himself known. As believers, we are called to reflect his holiness and compassion to the world. If we focus on honoring and obeying him, our life will be an object lesson that points people to the Lord.

The Duties of a Watchman

Ezekiel 3:16—21; 33:1—9

In ancient times, watchmen often stood guard on hilltops, in towers, or atop city walls to be on the lookout for enemies. The watchman's warning gave those outside the city walls time to flee to safety and alerted the people inside the walls to secure the gates and prepare for attack. If a watchman failed to warn of approaching danger, he paid for his negligence with his life.

God appointed Ezekiel to be a spiritual watchman for Judah and warn them of God's approaching judgment. If Ezekiel didn't share his God-given messages, God would hold him accountable. If he faithfully carried out his duty, he would be cleared of any guilt when people chose to ignore his warning. (Later, after the destruction of Jerusalem, the content of Ezekiel's messages changed and God repeated his commissioning as a watchman.)

Centuries later, Paul wrote to Timothy about his duties as a young pastor. Similar to a watchman, Timothy was to proclaim the truth that people needed to hear by correcting those in error, warning those involved in blatant sin, and supporting those who needed encouragement to persevere. Whether it was convenient or not, and whether he expected people to respond or not, Timothy had duties to carry out.

God has appointed each one of us to be his watchman. Even if we don't have a public ministry of preaching or teaching, God has placed us within a circle of family, friends, neighbors, and acquaintances. We're responsible to tell others about his coming judgment of sin and his offer of forgiveness to anyone who chooses to accept it.

If we keep silent when God wants us to share his truth with someone, we will regret it someday. But as long as we're obedient, we'll be cleared of any guilt if they choose to reject his offer of salvation. We know what our duties are; the question is, will we carry them out?

> *Be ready to spread the word whether or not the time is right. Point out errors, warn people, and encourage them.*
>
> 2 Timothy 4:2

A Portrait of Satan

Ezekiel 28:1–19

Chapters 26 and 27 contain messages of God's judgment of the city of Tyre and his plan to use the Babylonians against them. In chapter 28, the message focuses on Tyre's ruler and his coming punishment. Ethbaal III (who ruled Tyre at the time) believed himself to be a god. He took great pride in his wisdom and shrewdness that had made him rich. As his wealth increased, so did his arrogance. Ezekiel prophesied that Ethbaal III's pride would doom him to a shameful death at the hand of his enemies.

The lament in verses 12–19 includes phrases that could not be applied to a mere human. God seems to be identifying the true ruler of Tyre, the motivating force behind the human king. The description fits well with other passages referring to Satan. God created him to be a model of perfection, filled with wisdom and beauty, and appointed him to a high position in the angelic realm. Satan was in the Garden of Eden and had free access to God's holy mountain. He was sinless until his splendor and beauty went to his head and corrupted his heart. Satan lost his place in heaven; someday he will be cast into the lake of fire at his final judgment.

Satan and the king of Tyre both present chilling examples of the danger of pride and where it can lead us. If we place too much emphasis on our accomplishments, our abilities, or the positive things about ourselves, we can grow self-centered and arrogant. We begin to believe that we deserve the good things in our life—and so much more. Such thinking puts us in opposition to God, who values an attitude of humility. We can keep things in perspective by remembering that everything we have and all that we are comes from God's hand. If we fully give the credit to God, then our portrait won't look like Satan's, who is a perfect picture of pride.

Scripture says,
"God opposes arrogant people,
but he is kind to humble people."

James 4:6

The Valley of Bones

Ezekiel 37:1–14

"Son of man, can these bones live?" God's question must have sounded strange to Ezekiel as he looked over the scattered, dried-out bones filling the valley. "Only you know, Almighty LORD," he answered (v. 3). Then God commanded Ezekiel to prophesy to the bones, promising them that their bodies would be rebuilt and they would be brought back to life and know their Lord. Ezekiel obeyed and began to preach to the bones in the valley.

Suddenly, a rattling noise echoed through the valley as the bones began lining up and attaching to each other. Ezekiel watched as ligaments formed, muscles developed, and skin covered the bodies. Next, God told Ezekiel to call for breath to enter the corpses; as he obeyed, the bodies stood up on their feet.

God explained that the dried bones represented the Jewish people in their present condition. Scattered and living in exile, with Jerusalem and the temple destroyed, most of them felt hopeless. But God would give them new life by putting his Spirit in them. One day he would bring them back to their homeland like bringing bodies back from the grave.

Ezekiel's vision in the valley of bones served as a vivid reminder of God's promise to restore the nation of Israel. It can also encourage us as we share the message of God's love and forgiveness. We may hesitate to witness to someone who seems as unresponsive as dried-out bones. But we can't expect to always see instantaneous acceptance of the gospel. When the bones in the valley came to life, they went through a process as a result of Ezekiel's prophesying. People usually hear about God's salvation a number of times before they understand and accept Christ as Savior. Even if it feels like we're talking to bones, we want to be obedient to share the message that can bring faith and new life to a spiritually dead person.

> *So faith comes from hearing the message, and the
> message that is heard is what Christ spoke.*
>
> Romans 10:17

Daniel

Staying Faithful under Pressure

He changes times and periods of history. He removes kings and establishes them. He gives wisdom to those who are wise and knowledge to those who have insight. He reveals deeply hidden things. He knows what is in the dark, and light lives with him.

Daniel 2:21–22

In 605 BC Nebuchadnezzar attacked Jerusalem and deported young Israelite men from the royal family and the nobility, including Daniel and his friends. The teenager quickly rose to a prominent position in Babylon; he continued to serve in the government after the Medo-Persians conquered the Babylonians. Daniel's ministry lasted at least seventy years. Even though he was captive in a pagan nation that promoted self-indulgence and idolatry, Daniel held fast to his faith. His determination to follow God even under the worst of circumstances made him an example for his fellow exiles.

In the second half of the book, Daniel recorded the apocalyptic visions God gave him. This section provides a panoramic view of history and highlights the central truth of the book: God alone directs history. Because he controls the rise and fall of nations, God will carry out his promise to preserve his people. One day he will restore Israel's glory under the messianic kingdom that will last forever. Daniel understood God's sovereignty and trusted that no matter what happened, God was working out his plan for Daniel's life, for the Jewish race, and for the world at large. An understanding of the book of Daniel is necessary in order to fully comprehend the culmination of God's plan for history outlined in Revelation. All but two chapters in Revelation have some background in Daniel.

Besides Daniel's prophetic contributions, the book is rich in practical applications for believers today. Reading Daniel helps us remember that no matter how confusing, current events are moving the world toward fulfillment of God's plan for history. The courage, integrity, and commitment to prayer that Daniel modeled inspire us as we live in a culture opposed to God's truth. Like him, we can learn to stay faithful regardless of the pressures we face.

No Compromise

Daniel 1:1—16

When Nebuchadnezzar invaded Jerusalem, he followed the usual Babylonian practice of carrying off the best and brightest inhabitants to assimilate them into Babylonian culture. Then his chief of staff selected the best-looking, smartest, and most talented young men to undergo an intensive three-year training program to prepare them to serve in the king's palace. As a starting point for their new identities, the chief of staff changed the names of Daniel, Hananiah, Mishael, and Azariah. Their old names acknowledged and honored Yahweh; their new ones (Belteshazzar, Shadrach, Meshach, and Abednego) reflected the names of Babylonian gods.

During this indoctrination period, the captives were assigned a food allowance from the king's table. Daniel and his friends determined not to indulge in the strong wine and extravagant royal diet, which would not have been prepared according to Jewish laws. So Daniel requested a trial period during which he and his friends would consume only vegetables and water. After ten days, they would be compared with the men eating the king's food. The supervisor agreed, and when Daniel and his three friends ended up looking healthier and stronger than the others, he released them from the requirement.

Like Daniel, we're surrounded by a culture that encourages self-absorption and extravagance, one that values beauty and intelligence more than character. Every day we're bombarded with attempts to pull us away from God's truth and temptations to adopt the world's way of thinking. In order to withstand the pressure to compromise and accept the standards of those around us, we need more than beliefs—we need conviction and a conscious decision to obey God regardless of our circumstances. Even when others exercise control over us, we can depend on God to help us find solutions. Instead of compromising and conforming to the culture around us, we can let God transform us. Then we'll be able to influence others with his truth.

Do not conform any longer to the pattern of this world,
but be transformed by the renewing of your mind.

Romans 12:2 NIV

Golden Opportunities

Daniel 1:17–21

It's hard to imagine Daniel's emotions as his captors wrenched him from family and home, forcing him to march hundreds of miles to Babylon. Once there, the teenager could have been dazzled by the city that represented the center of world power and commerce. However, instead of being seduced by the luxury, worldliness, and idolatry that surrounded him, Daniel determined to live for God. Rather than despair at being separated from Jerusalem and the temple, he adjusted to his situation while refusing to do anything that would break one of God's commands.

When Daniel requested to abstain from the assigned diet, he did so respectfully. As he and his friends went through training in Babylonian arts and language, they excelled, learning everything they could about their new culture. After the three-year period ended, Nebuchadnezzar examined all the young men. He found that Daniel and his friends were unequaled. They knew ten times as much as all the magicians, sorcerers, and wise men in his kingdom.

Because Daniel trusted God with his life, he accepted his situation and made use of the opportunities it afforded. Nebuchadnezzar appointed Daniel to serve in the palace and later promoted him to a high position. During his long career as a civil servant under pagan kings, Daniel served to the best of his ability while maintaining his integrity. He became a witness for God in a culture of godlessness.

God has placed each one of us in a unique position to influence our culture. If we simply rail against the evils of our society or avoid any aspect of culture that's not specifically Christian, we may overlook opportunities to impact lives for Christ. God never wants us to do anything that would go against his Word. But when we submit to authorities, treat others with respect, and make the most of our opportunities, who knows the difference we can make in the lives of unbelievers watching us?

> *Be wise in the way you act toward those who are outside*
> *the Christian faith. Make the most of your opportunities.*
>
> Colossians 4:5

Nebuchadnezzar's Dream

Daniel 2

When Nebuchadnezzar had a disturbing dream one night, he called on his wise men as usual. They approached the king confident that their interpretations would satisfy him as in the past, but this time proved to be different. Nebuchadnezzar demanded that they first describe his dream, and *then* explain the meaning of it. When they protested that his request was humanly impossible, Nebuchadnezzar flew into a rage and ordered the deaths of all his advisers and wise men. Daniel heard about the edict and knew it included him and his friends.

Instead of panicking, Daniel approached the king and requested time to find the answer. Then he asked his three friends to join him in prayer. God revealed the dream and its meaning to Daniel in a nighttime vision. When Daniel went back to Nebuchadnezzar to interpret the dream, he first emphasized that he had received the information from the true God in heaven, the only One who could reveal such a mystery. Daniel went on to describe the king's dream of a giant statue made of different types of material. He explained that God had shown Nebuchadnezzar four world powers that would rule for a time until God established a kingdom that would last forever.

Daniel demonstrated great faith by telling the king he would interpret the dream even before God revealed it to him. After the king agreed to postpone the executions, Daniel prayed in full confidence that God would answer. God is pleased when we approach prayer expecting our needs to be met.

Sometimes he may ask us to take an action step before we see the answer to our request. He may call us to move to a new location before we have a job there, or pledge money to his work before it's in our bank account. As long as our requests line up with his will, we can be confident that the answer is on its way.

Have faith that you will receive
whatever you ask for in prayer.

Matthew 21:22

Three Men and a Furnace

Daniel 3

Each time the loud music cued, the people bowed down before the ninety-foot-tall gold statue as Nebuchadnezzar had commanded. One day, some astrologers reported to the king that "certain Jews," captives whom he had elevated to positions of authority, were ignoring his order. Enraged, Nebuchadnezzar summoned Shadrach, Meshach, and Abednego. He reminded them of the penalty for refusing to worship the gold statue: they would be thrown into a blazing furnace to be burned alive. The three young men answered that their God could save them from the furnace, but even if he chose not to, they would never worship the statue.

The furious king ordered the furnace to be heated seven times hotter than usual. The intensity of the heat killed the soldiers who threw the bound Hebrews into the fire. A moment later, Nebuchadnezzar sprang to his feet. "Didn't we throw three men into the furnace?" Through the opening in the furnace, he could see the Hebrew men walking around in the middle of the fire, untied and unharmed. He also saw that a fourth man accompanied them, one who had the appearance of a heavenly being. When Nebuchadnezzar examined Shadrach, Meshach, and Abednego, he found that the fire had not harmed the men's bodies or clothes, singed their hair, or even left a smell of smoke on them.

The fourth man in the furnace could have been an angel sent by God to strengthen the young Hebrews or a physical appearance of Christ before his earthly birth. In either case, God's message is clear: he has promised to never leave those who trust and obey him, no matter what we go through. Sometimes he delivers us from a fiery trial; other times he chooses to let us go through it to accomplish his purpose. But even when we're not aware of his presence, he is right there, walking through it with us.

> *He will be with you. He won't abandon you or*
> *leave you. So don't be afraid or terrified.*
>
> Deuteronomy 31:8

The Writing on the Wall

Daniel 5

One night during Belshazzar's reign, he threw a lavish banquet. As the party progressed, Belshazzar called for the golden utensils that Nebuchadnezzar had taken from the temple in Jerusalem. The guests drank wine from these sacred objects, all the while praising their idols. Suddenly, the fingers of a hand appeared and began writing on one of the walls. Filled with terror, Belshazzar screamed for his psychics, astrologers, and diviners. He promised to richly reward anyone who could explain the meaning of the mysterious writing. When none of his advisers could do so, Belshazzar grew more frightened.

The commotion brought the queen mother into the banquet hall. She told Belshazzar about Daniel's ability to interpret dreams, explain riddles, and solve difficult problems. Brushing off the king's offer of reward, Daniel explained that Belshazzar had failed to humble himself before the God of heaven even though he had heard about him from Nebuchadnezzar. Drinking from the temple vessels had showed his utter contempt for God.

Now God had sent Belshazzar a message: "Numbered, Numbered, Weighed, and Divided" (v. 25). God had numbered the days of Belshazzar's kingdom. He had weighed the king and found him wanting. His kingdom would be divided and given to the Medes and Persians. That very night the Persian army diverted the Euphrates River, walked into Babylon, and conquered the city without a fight.

Every day we're surrounded by examples of people treating God with contempt. Using his name as profanity is commonplace. Television shows and movies are filled with irreverent humor that ridicules God and those who believe in him. There are times when we can speak out against such blasphemy, but often we're helpless to do anything. It may be hard to stand by and hear God mocked, but we can be sure that he will vindicate his name when he's ready. Eventually, those who oppose him will see the writing on the wall.

Make no mistake about this: You can
never make a fool out of God.

Galatians 6:7

In the Lions' Den

Daniel 6

Daniel served under the Persian ruler Darius with his usual diligence and integrity, distinguishing himself among all the other officials. When Darius decided to put Daniel in charge of the entire kingdom, the other administrators grew jealous. They examined Daniel's job performance, looking for grounds to bring charges against him. Finding nothing, they decided to use his religious practices to orchestrate his downfall. The officials talked Darius into signing a decree that flattered his ego: for a period of thirty days, people could only pray to the king. Anyone who disobeyed would be executed by being thrown into a lions' den.

The decree didn't stop Daniel from following his customary routine of praying to his God three times a day; he made no effort to hide his actions. When the officials reported this to Darius, he desperately searched for a way to save his most trusted official from certain death. But the law of the Medes and the Persians could not be revoked; Darius reluctantly gave the order.

After a sleepless night, he rushed to the sealed lions' den. In answer to his call, Daniel explained that God had shut the lions' mouths so they couldn't harm him. The overjoyed king sent a proclamation throughout his empire telling people to fear and revere the living God who had saved Daniel from the lions.

Since Daniel's conduct and character were blameless, his enemies had to use his faith as the basis to accuse him. When someone attacks us in this manner, it seems unfair. But God may allow us to be punished or persecuted even when we're innocent of wrongdoing so that we can be witnesses of his power. Other people will watch to see how we react when we suffer for doing good. Whether God delivers us in a miraculous way, or simply gives us the strength to endure, they won't be able to deny his presence and his power in our life. Everyone will know who was with us in our own lions' den.

*If it is God's will, it's better to suffer for
doing good than for doing wrong.*

1 Peter 3:17

Unseen Battles

Daniel 9–12

Daniel was a man who took prayer seriously. In his later years, he read in Jeremiah's writings that Jerusalem would lie in ruins for seventy years. Realizing that the period of captivity had almost ended, Daniel began to fast and pray. Daniel confessed his and his nation's sin and pleaded for God's mercy and the restoration of his people. His prayers were interrupted by a visit from the angel Gabriel, who had previously visited Daniel to interpret his vision of the ram and goat (see Dan. 8). Gabriel explained that God had dispatched him to give Daniel insight into Israel's future as soon as Daniel began making his request.

Later, after the Jewish captivity ended and some of the exiles had returned to Jerusalem, Daniel saw his final vision. Disturbed by the images of a great war involving Israel, Daniel spent three weeks mourning, fasting, and praying. Then a heavenly being showed up whose brilliant appearance made Daniel faint. The angel told Daniel that God had heard everything he said from the moment he decided to pray for understanding. But his arrival had been delayed for three weeks while demonic spirits tried to stop him. He resumed his mission when Michael, another chief angel, came to help him fight. The angel had come to interpret Daniel's vision of what would happen to the Jewish people in the last days.

Unfortunately, Satan takes prayer more seriously than some Christians do. He does his best to keep us from praying; when that doesn't work, he tries to oppose God's answer. He tempts us to feel discouraged when we don't see an immediate response to our request. If Satan can't keep us from praying, he hopes we'll be satisfied with shallow or repetitive prayers. Anytime we engage in fervent prayer regarding God's will, we participate in the unseen struggle between angels serving God and the fallen angels who do Satan's bidding. And that is serious business.

> *We are wrestling with rulers, authorities, the powers*
> *who govern this world of darkness, and spiritual*
> *forces that control evil in the heavenly world.*
>
> Ephesians 6:12

Jesus in Daniel

God allowed the prophet Daniel to see several visions of the future, including glimpses of the Messiah. In one vision, Daniel saw the Son of Man approach the Ancient of Days to receive power, honor, and a kingdom (see Dan. 7:13–14). Chapters 9 and 10 record the revelation that God gave Daniel to explain his plan for the Jewish people, sometimes called the "vision of seventy weeks" or "seventy sevens." Many people believe that the second segment of this time period (sixty-two "sevens," or 434 years) pinpoints the Messiah's triumphal entry into Jerusalem on March 29, AD 33.

Jesus Christ is also revealed in Nebuchadnezzar's first dream. The giant statue made of different metals represented major world powers that would rule for a time. Nebuchadnezzar then saw a stone cut, but not by human hands. The stone smashed the statue so completely that not a trace of it could be found. Then the stone became a great mountain that filled the whole world. The king's dream pointed to the time when the Messiah will crush all earthly powers and set up his everlasting kingdom.

Other Old Testament passages also refer to Jesus as a rock or stone, and New Testament writers often echo these prophecies. Peter quoted Isaiah 28:16 when he called Jesus the precious cornerstone that God laid as the foundation for his church. Just as a building depends on its cornerstone for support and stability, believers can trust Christ and rely on him.

In contrast, for those who reject him, Jesus becomes "a stone that people trip over, a large rock that people find offensive" (1 Pet. 2:8, quoting Isa. 8:14). If someone refuses to believe the gospel, they stumble over the message of Christ and his redemptive work on the cross. God has laid the cornerstone; he gives us the choice of building on it or tripping over it. If we have Jesus Christ as our foundation, God promises that we will never be ashamed.

> *That is why Scripture says,*
> *"I am laying a chosen and precious cornerstone in Zion,*
> *and the person who believes in him*
> *will never be ashamed."*
>
> 1 Peter 2:6

Minor Prophets with a Major Message

The last twelve books of the Old Testament were originally joined together in one scroll and referred to as "The Twelve." Late in the 4th century AD they became known as the Minor prophets, since for the most part they are shorter in length than the five books of the Major prophets. These messages may be more concise, but they contain the same powerful themes as the writings of the Major prophets. As God's spokesmen, these twelve prophets exposed sin, called people to repent and turn back to God, warned of coming judgment, and pointed to the coming Messiah.

Taken together, the Minor prophets span a period of four hundred years. God sent three of the Minor prophets to the northern kingdom (Jonah, Amos, Hosea) and six to the southern kingdom (Obadiah, Joel, Micah, Nahum, Zephaniah, Habakkuk). The remaining three (Haggai, Zechariah, Malachi) prophesied during the postexilic period.

Although little is known about most of the Minor prophets, it's obvious that they represent a range of different backgrounds and personalities just as the Major prophets do. But each man shared a desire to obey God's call on his life and to see people brought into a right relationship with him.

The label "Minor prophets" is based solely on the length of the books, not because they are less important. Each one is a vital part of God's Word. In a similar way, each believer has a vital role to play in God's work. We often focus on those who are most visible in the body of Christ, trying to categorize Christians into "major" and "minor" players. God doesn't think in those terms. Whether we are speaking to an audience of thousands or quietly sharing God's truth with our neighbor, our ministries are equally important in his eyes. We are all members of the same team with a common purpose. There's nothing minor about being God's co-worker.

> *The one who plants and the one who waters have*
> *the same goal, and each will receive a reward for*
> *his own work. We are God's coworkers.*
>
> 1 Corinthians 3:8–9

Hosea

A Cheating Heart

The LORD says, "I will cure them of their unfaithfulness. I will love them freely. I will no longer be angry with them."

Hosea 14:4

Hosea prophesied during the latter half of the 8th century BC. The northern kingdom had enjoyed a period of political and economic prosperity, but they failed to acknowledge God as the source of those blessings. The final days of Israel (sometimes referred to as Ephraim, its largest tribe) were a time of chaos, upheaval, and moral corruption. During Hosea's ministry, four kings were assassinated while in office. God accused the people and the priests of arrogance, hypocrisy, ingratitude, social injustice, and violent crimes including murder. Their most serious offense, however, was spiritual adultery.

Israel had adopted the worship of Baal, the Canaanite god thought to control agriculture, fertility, and the weather. Baal worship centered on ritual prostitution along with degrading sexual practices. In turning to Baal, the nation had forsaken their covenant with God and broken their promises to worship him alone and obey his commands. God called Hosea to illustrate his message with his personal life. He commanded the prophet to marry a woman who would be unfaithful to him. Just as Gomer abandoned her husband Hosea, Israel had acted as an adulterous wife and abandoned God.

Hosea's pain over his wife's adultery helped him better understand the grief of God over his people's sins. For forty years, Hosea warned the people that continued unfaithfulness would rouse God's anger. He specifically named Assyria as the nation God would use to punish them (see 11:5). Yet sprinkled throughout the book are messages of hope. Hosea bought back his unfaithful wife, just as God promised to purify and redeem Israel one day.

The graphic messages in Hosea encourage us to examine our relationship with God. Have we stayed true to our covenant with him, worshiping him alone and obeying his commands? If we remember the high price God paid to redeem us from the slave market of sin, he won't see any traces of cheating in our heart.

Unconditional Love

Hosea 3

The third chapter in Hosea is short, but its five verses communicate the core message of the book and also the gospel. God instructed Hosea to buy back his adulterous wife and love her instead of divorcing her. After Gomer deserted her husband, she either sold herself as a slave or became a prostitute or mistress to another man. Hosea paid silver and barley that amounted to thirty shekels in value, the typical price for a slave. He brought Gomer home and told her that her former lifestyle was over. After a lengthy period of isolation at home, Gomer would be restored in her relationship with her husband.

Hosea's actions served as an object lesson for Israel. His merciful, forgiving spirit toward his unfaithful wife illustrated that God would still love Israel and be willing to take her back after she repented of her sins. But first, the people would go into a lengthy period of isolation. For a long time, they would be separated from the former practices they had used as means of cultic activity and Baal worship. Israel would lose its national sovereignty for a time until God restored the glory of the nation.

As powerful as Hosea's example is, we have the ultimate demonstration of God's forgiveness and love in Jesus Christ. Jesus willingly suffered torture and a painful death in our place, not because we deserved it but simply because he loves us. God sent Jesus to redeem us from sin when we were ungodly and living in rebellion against him.

At the very moment God accepts us as his child, he can see ahead to all the times we will fail and slip into sin. Yet he stands ready to restore us when we repent. How can a human mind comprehend such unconditional love? The only logical response is to do our best to stay faithful and obedient to our loving Father, and to try and show that same merciful, forgiving attitude toward others.

> *Christ died for us while we were still sinners.*
> *This demonstrates God's love for us.*
>
> Romans 5:8

Joel

A Locust Invasion

"But even now," declares the LORD, "return to me with all your heart—with fasting, crying, and mourning." Tear your hearts, not your clothes. Return to the LORD your God. He is merciful and compassionate, patient, and always ready to forgive and to change his plans about disaster.

Joel 2:12–13

Fields, orchards, and vineyards lay in ruins. Wave after wave of locusts had swarmed across the land like a vast army, stripping trees and grapevines and devouring vegetation until nothing was left. The destruction of the crops left the nation bereft of grain, wine, and olive oil, signs of God's covenant blessing (see Deut. 7:13). The formal worship system suffered since priests lacked the necessary ingredients for certain offerings. With nothing to harvest, a great famine loomed ahead for the people of Judah.

The prophet Joel used this national disaster to urge his country to return to God. The people had grown complacent and self-centered, falling into sin and idolatry. Joel warned that the devastation caused by the locusts was nothing compared to the terrible judgment of the day of the Lord, when God would punish his own people along with other nations.

Judah had a choice: they could listen to God now or face his anger later. God longed for his people to return to him in heartfelt repentance so that disaster would be averted. Yet even so, he promised that great blessing would come after judgment, both materially and spiritually.

Believers have no need to fear the terrible day of the Lord when God will punish sin and vindicate his name. But as his children, we still risk being disciplined when we disobey or turn away from him. Jesus paid the penalty for our sin, but if we deliberately indulge in sinful behavior, we can expect God to do something about it. Like Judah, we have a choice each time we sin: we can listen to God and repent now, or face his discipline later.

Amos

A False Sense of Security

"The days are going to come," declares the Almighty LORD, "when I will send a famine throughout the land. It won't be an ordinary famine or drought. Instead, there will be a famine of hearing the words of the LORD."

Amos 8:11

Under Jeroboam II the northern kingdom reached the pinnacle of its power and prosperity. Israel's territory had been expanded; the nation seemed secure from outside threats. Businesses were thriving and many people enjoyed extravagant lifestyles. But while the Israelites offered sacrifices and went through the motions of worshiping God, they had grown coldhearted and indifferent toward him. They oppressed and exploited the poor, and engaged in sexual immorality, all the while claiming that God had blessed them.

In the southern kingdom, Amos herded sheep and grew fig trees—until God called him to preach in Israel. Amos relayed the visions of God's coming judgments on the surrounding nations, on his homeland of Judah, and finally on Israel. At that point, his message became highly unpopular. The Israelites expected a day of reckoning when their enemies would be punished; they didn't expect judgment to fall on them as well.

As Amos continued preaching and condemning Israel's sins, Amaziah the priest tried to intimidate and silence him. Amos spent about a year warning of judgment and calling for repentance, often using vivid metaphors drawn from his farming life. His pleas fell on deaf ears. Since the people rejected God's words, there would come a time when they would no longer hear him speak.

Amos means "Burden" or "Burden Lifter." He didn't consider himself a prophet by profession (7:14), but he left his occupation and his homeland to obey God's call. God also wants us ready to leave our comfort zone to share his truth, even when the message is unpopular. He may give us a concern for a group of people in a foreign land or a family next door. But if we are God's child, we should have a burden for those who don't know him.

Obadiah

An Old Feud

> Because of the violence you did to Jacob, your relative, you will be covered with shame. You will be destroyed forever.
>
> Obadiah 10

The struggle between Jacob and Esau began while they were still in the womb (see Gen. 25:21–26). Years later, Jacob took advantage of Esau's hunger to get his older brother's birthright. When Jacob tricked their father into giving him the blessing of the firstborn, Esau wanted to murder his twin. The hostility between these brothers passed down to their descendants. Although Judah (descended from Jacob) and Edom (descended from Esau) were neighboring countries and blood relatives, they lived as bitter enemies.

As Israel journeyed to the Promised Land, Edom refused to let them pass through its territory (see Num. 20:14–21). Later, the Edomites joined Israel's enemies whenever they attacked instead of rushing to Israel's aid. When Babylon captured Jerusalem, Edom celebrated. Finally, God sent an obscure prophet to announce his judgment on Edom for their cruel treatment of his chosen people.

Obadiah's message to Edom included no call for repentance; their actions had sealed their fate. Despite Edom's pride in their "impregnable" cliffs, one day the nation would become extinct. Ironically, Obadiah's prophecy was fulfilled when the Edomites (then known as the Idumaeans) joined together with the Jews in the rebellion against Rome in AD 70. After the destruction of Jerusalem, this group of people faded from history.

Obadiah is the shortest book in the Old Testament; we know nothing about the author except his name. Yet this single chapter holds a powerful twofold message for believers today. It reminds us not to persecute or hold a grudge against another believer. God doesn't want his children acting like enemies, turning people away from the faith instead of drawing them in. On the other hand, the second half of Obadiah gives us a glimpse of what it means to be one of God's chosen and under his protection. Whether we're treating another believer as an enemy or someone is attacking us, God takes either scenario very seriously.

Jonah

God's Compassion

So he prayed to the LORD, "LORD, isn't this what I said would happen when I was still in my own country? That's why I tried to run to Tarshish in the first place. I knew that you are a merciful and compassionate God, patient, and always ready to forgive and to reconsider your threats of destruction."

Jonah 4:2

God told Jonah to take a message of impending judgment to Nineveh, an Assyrian city well-known for brutality, wickedness, and wartime atrocities. When Jonah boarded a ship going in the opposite direction, God arranged for the prophet to have some time to think—in the belly of a huge fish. Jonah jumped at a second chance to obey, the evil city repented, and God spared them.

Disappointed, Jonah admitted that he had been afraid such a thing would happen. He didn't want the Assyrians saved; he wanted them to get what they deserved. God then focused his attention on the angry prophet and taught Jonah some lessons about himself and about the God he served.

Many people have tried to label Jonah as a myth or an allegory. But the book mentions actual cities and 2 Kings 14:25 refers to Jonah as a prophet. More importantly, Jesus recognized the book as historical and literal, referring both to its author and its events. He compared Jonah's three days in the fish to his own death, burial, and resurrection.

Jonah is historical narrative with a special message for Israel and also for us today. The Jews had been reluctant to carry out their mission to share God's love and forgiveness with the rest of the world. Through Jonah, God made it clear that his compassion extends to all people groups and every nation. As we read this book, we can reflect on how much we share God's compassion for the world. Are we willing to share his message with those outside our circle, even with those who seem least likely to respond? Or like Jonah, are we more interested in seeing people get what they deserve?

A Reluctant Messenger

Jonah 1–2

According to 2 Kings 14:25, Jonah had the privilege of prophesying prosperity for Israel under Jeroboam II. But when God told him to go and preach condemnation to the great city of Nineveh, Jonah's new assignment didn't suit him. Instead of going northeast, Jonah boarded a ship going in the opposite direction, to Tarshish. His disobedience endangered the lives of the ship's crew when God sent a violent storm. Terrified, the pagan sailors lightened the ship's load and cried out to their gods. They decided to throw dice to identify the person responsible for the storm. God intervened and pinpointed Jonah.

Jonah admitted his guilt and advised the sailors to throw him overboard to end the storm. At first they tried to row harder, but the storm worsened. Finally, the sailors threw Jonah into the sea after praying for forgiveness from his God. As Jonah sank to the bottom and felt his life ebbing away, he cried out to God for help.

God sent a huge fish to swallow him. Jonah offered a prayer of thanksgiving to God for not letting him drown. During three days and nights inside the fish, Jonah's perspective changed dramatically. God then commanded the fish to spit Jonah out on the shore. Jonah was now ready to obey.

Jonah discovered he couldn't run away from God. He also learned that we pay a price whenever we disobey God's commands. When God gives us an assignment that seems too difficult or distasteful, we may try to run away from our responsibilities as Jonah did. God might do something drastic to get our attention or he may choose to use someone else in our place. In any case, our disobedience can hurt those around us and bring us unnecessary trouble and pain. How much better it is to obey God the first time he asks, without taking any painful detours.

Lead me on the path of your commandments,
because I am happy with them.

Psalm 119:35

A Pouting Preacher

Jonah 3–4

After living in the stomach of a huge fish for three days, Jonah jumped at a second chance to obey God. He traveled to Nineveh and walked through the city announcing that in forty days Nineveh would be destroyed. Surprisingly, the people believed his message and repented, fasting and wearing sackcloth. The king ordered everyone to turn away from their violence and wicked ways and to cry out to God in hopes that he would turn from his anger. Sure enough, God decided not to destroy them.

God's decision to spare Nineveh infuriated Jonah so much that he asked God to kill him. "What right do you have to be angry?" God asked (4:4). Instead of answering, Jonah sat down outside the city to nurse his resentment and wait to see what would happen. God provided a plant to shade Jonah, but the next day he sent a worm to kill the plant and a scorching wind. Nearly fainting from the heat, Jonah again declared that he wanted to die.

Once again God asked Jonah what right he had to be angry; Jonah insisted that he had every right. God exposed his selfishness. Jonah hadn't made the plant grow, but it had made him comfortable for a day. Now he mourned the plant's loss while being angry that God had spared the lives of thousands of people whom he had created.

We can get so focused on our self-centered interests that we miss the bigger picture of God at work. If our emotions are controlled by the presence or absence of personal blessings, we won't have room in our heart for compassion for others. Sometimes we may feel disappointed with how God handles a situation; we may be tempted to pout when we don't get what we want. But just as God has shown us mercy, he wants us to look beyond our selfish ambitions to the lost and hurting people around us—people he created and died for.

> *Don't act out of selfish ambition or be conceited. Instead,*
> *humbly think of others as being better than yourselves.*
>
> Philippians 2:3

Micah

Speaking Up against Injustice

You mortals, the LORD has told you what is good. This is what the LORD requires from you: to do what is right, to love mercy, and to live humbly with your God.

Micah 6:8

Micah prophesied during the ministry of Isaiah, and their writings share many similarities. But since Micah came from a small, rural town in southern Judah, he didn't have the awareness of politics and worldwide affairs that Isaiah displayed. Instead, God gave Micah a burden for people suffering from social injustice and abuse. Micah denounced the corruption that pervaded every level of society, including rulers, priests, and false prophets. He warned that God would judge both Israel and Judah for their sins, specifically naming Assyria and Babylon as the nations God would use to punish them.

Like a lawyer, Micah laid out God's case against his people, accusing them of fraud, theft, oppression, extortion, lying, hypocrisy, murder, and other offenses. He reminded them that God desired more than rituals and empty expressions of religion. God wanted his children to display the marks of a true relationship with him by practicing justice, mercy, and humility before God. If they refused to repent and change their ways, judgment would come.

Even though Micah predicted the fall of Israel and Judah, all three of his messages end on a note of hope. The book closes with a beautiful portrayal of God's forgiving nature. In a wordplay on his name ("Who is like Yahweh?") Micah explains that God's anger doesn't last because he delights in showing mercy. If we come to God in repentance, he promises to "throw all our sins into the deep sea" (7:19).

Many people focus solely on God's loving nature and try to ignore his anger over sin. Micah reminds us to keep a balanced view of God, not forgetting that his holiness requires him to hate sin and expose it. He also urges us to get involved with the culture around us, having enough compassion to speak out against injustice whenever we see it.

Jesus in Micah

Like other Old Testament prophets, Micah blended predictions of events in the near future with visions of the distant future. He often prophesied about the time when the Messiah would return to judge sin, vanquish Israel's enemies, and reign over the earth as described in 2:12–13, 4:1–8, and 5:4–5. One of the most exciting messianic prophecies, however, is found in Micah 5:2 and relates to the Messiah's first coming. Although Jerusalem prided itself on being a powerful and wealthy city, Micah pinpointed an obscure village in the region of Ephrathah as the birthplace of the Messiah. Christ would be born seven hundred years later in Bethlehem, the hometown of his ancestor David.

Seven centuries later, wise men from the east arrived in Jerusalem looking for "the one who was born to be the king of the Jews." Herod summoned the chief priests and scribes to question them about where the Messiah was supposed to be born. The Jewish scholars knew the answer: they paraphrased Micah 5:2, giving the precise location of Christ's birth (see Matt. 2:1–6).

About thirty years later, people debated whether Jesus was the Messiah. Since Jesus had grown up in Nazareth in Galilee, many people rejected him based on the prophecy in Micah (see John 7:41–42). When Nicodemus defended Jesus, the other Pharisees challenged him to study the Scriptures and see that no prophet came from Galilee (see John 7:52).

Those who refused to accept Jesus as the Messiah would not take the trouble to verify his birthplace. They could have studied the Scriptures and learned that Jesus fulfilled three hundred Old Testament prophecies about the Messiah; instead they formed an opinion based on their prejudices and preconceived ideas. Their example reminds us to approach the Scriptures with a mind open to receiving God's truth; otherwise, we could miss something as plain as the nose on our face, just like those who rejected the Messiah even when he stood in front of them.

You, Bethlehem Ephrathah,
are too small to be included among Judah's cities.
Yet, from you Israel's future ruler will come for me.
His origins go back to the distant past, to days long ago.

Micah 5:2

Nahum

The Offer Has Expired!

The LORD is good. He is a fortress in the day of trouble. He knows those who seek shelter in him. He will put an end to Nineveh with a devastating flood. He will pursue his enemies with darkness.

Nahum 1:7–8

God had spared the city of Nineveh in Assyria when the people responded to Jonah's preaching; their repentance, however, proved to be short-lived. Around 745 BC Assyria became the leading world power in the Near East, its vast empire attained through bloodshed and shocking brutality. Written records included Assyrian rulers' boasts about massacring groups of conquered people. They gloated over their torture and horrible mutilation of captured leaders. In 722 BC the Assyrians destroyed Samaria and exiled the northern kingdom of Israel. Treated as a vassal kingdom, Judah also suffered attacks from this evil empire.

About a hundred years after Jonah's mission, God gave Nahum a vision of the coming fall of Nineveh and destruction of Assyria. Similar to Obadiah's message to Edom, Nahum's proclamation included no plea to repent. God's judgment of the evil city was certain and irrevocable at this point. Nahum's detailed prophecies were fulfilled less than fifty years later. Nineveh fell to the Babylonians, Medes, and Scythians in 612 BC. Just as Nahum predicted, Nineveh's destruction was complete and final; the city was never rebuilt.

Nahum's name means "comfort" or "consolation." Although the bulk of his book centers on Nineveh's wickedness and coming judgment, he assured Judah that God shelters those who trust in him. Judah must certainly have been comforted by the knowledge that God would soon put an end to the evil nation that threatened them.

Nahum reminds believers today that kingdoms built on wickedness and tyranny will eventually fall. God may delay his judgment but it is certain to come. One day he will rid the world of every trace of sin and evil—and we can certainly take comfort in that.

31

Habakkuk

Age-Old Questions

Look at the proud person. He is not right in himself. But the righteous person will live because of his faithfulness.

Habakkuk 2:4

Habakkuk lived in Judah during its final days, a period of moral and spiritual decline. Deeply troubled by the rampant violence, injustice, and idolatry, Habakkuk cried out to God. Why did God tolerate wrongdoing? How long would evil triumph and righteous people be downtrodden? Why didn't God do something about it? God responded that he planned to use Babylon to punish Judah for her sins.

This answer added to Habakkuk's confusion and created a moral dilemma in his mind: Why would God use an even more ungodly nation to judge his people? Habakkuk declared that he would wait expectantly for God's answers like a guard stationed in a watchtower. God assured Habakkuk that in due time, Babylon and all ungodliness would be punished. In the meantime, the righteous would live by their faith.

After hearing God's response, Habakkuk developed a new appreciation for God's wisdom and power. He moved from complaining and questioning God to affirming his confidence in God's purposes. Habakkuk closed his book with a beautiful psalm praising God and declaring his trust in him. Even when faced with the terrifying prospect of Judah's invasion, he vowed to find his joy and strength in the God who saved him.

The book of Habakkuk is unique since it represents a dialogue between God and the poet-prophet. Their interaction assures us we don't have to be afraid to ask God questions. We can all identify with the urge to cry out, "Why don't you do something?" All of us will struggle to understand God's ways at some point. If we try to ignore our doubts or if we dwell on them, we can become cynical and bitter. When we focus on the joy of knowing God, we can wait patiently for him to work out his plan. Even with our limited understanding, we can learn, as Habakkuk did, to live by faith.

Zephaniah

Judgment Day

Search for the LORD, all you humble people in the land who carry out his justice. Search for what is right. Search for humility. Maybe you will find shelter on the day of the LORD's anger.

Zephaniah 2:3

It's not hard to pick up on the theme of Zephaniah; although the prophet sometimes used different phrases, these three chapters refer to the day of the Lord twenty-three times, more than any other Old Testament book. Zephaniah described God's judgment of sin as a time of darkness, devastation, and anguish. Unless Judah repented, it would face God's fury along with the other nations. Correction was badly needed as the priests led the way in mixing worship of Yahweh with worship of nature and pagan gods. The rulers were corrupt. The people had become so indifferent toward God that they didn't expect him to do anything at all, either good or bad.

Zephaniah is not only a book of doom and gloom. Whether he's addressing the coming Babylonian invasion of Judah or the final day of the Lord, Zephaniah shows the dual nature of God's judgment/blessing. After the exile, God would gather a remnant back to their homeland. And someday, after he cleanses the world of sin, God will fully restore and renew Israel and all those who trust in him. The dark day of God's judgment will lead to a bright and glorious future for his people.

Zephaniah traced his lineage back four generations, unlike other Old Testament prophets. He appears to be the only prophet known to be of royal descent, the great-great-grandson of Hezekiah. This would have given him freer access to the court of Josiah, his distant relative. If Zephaniah prophesied early in Josiah's reign, his ministry helped prepare the people for the bursts of revival that occurred under Judah's last godly king.

Many people today are indifferent toward God. They don't want to think about his judgment or his blessing. If we're faithful in sharing God's truth, as Zephaniah was, God may use us to help someone avoid the anguish of judgment day.

Haggai

Putting God First

> Is it time for you to live in your paneled houses while this house lies in ruins?
> Now, this is what the LORD of Armies says: Carefully consider your ways!
>
> Haggai 1:4–5

Ezra records how Zerubbabel led the first group of Jews out of Babylonian exile back to Jerusalem. After erecting an altar for sacrifices and offerings, the group began to rebuild the temple, laying the foundation in the second year. Then political opposition and harassment from their neighbors brought the work to a standstill. The group's initial optimism and high hopes dissolved into discouragement and spiritual apathy. They lost their sense of purpose and became preoccupied with building and beautifying their own homes instead of finishing the temple.

Fifteen years later, God gave several short but pointed messages through Haggai, urging the Jews to get their priorities straight. God demanded to know why the people lived in luxurious homes while his own house stood in ruins. Because they were more concerned with their own needs than with doing God's will, they were not enjoying his blessings. The drought, crop failures, and impoverishment they suffered stemmed from their selfishness and disobedience.

God exhorted Zerubbabel, the high priest Joshua, and "everyone in the land" to be strong and get back to work. A restored temple would please the Lord and bring blessings on his people. God assured them of his presence and promised to fill the completed temple with his peace and glory. This promise would be ultimately fulfilled during Christ's millennial reign on earth, but for now, the Jews had work to do.

Haggai's prophecies are dated from August to December 520 BC, yet their message speaks to us twenty-five centuries later. God still calls us to get our priorities straight and to seek first God's kingdom and his righteousness, as Jesus put it (see Matt. 6:33). Anytime we pursue our own selfish interests above God's will, we suffer. If we heed Haggai's call to put God and his work first, we can enjoy God's blessings of joy, peace, and prosperity.

Zechariah

The King Is Coming

Rejoice with all your heart, people of Zion! Shout in triumph, people of Jerusalem! Look! Your King is coming to you: He is righteous and victorious. He is humble and rides on a donkey, on a colt, a young pack animal.

Zechariah 9:9

A couple of months after Haggai began prophesying, he was joined by a much younger colleague, Zechariah. Like Haggai, Zechariah addressed the need for the Jews to remain faithful in their service to God and to keep themselves pure and undefiled. But Zechariah's messages went far beyond the present concerns and physical work facing the remnant. He encouraged them to finish rebuilding the temple by reminding them of its future importance: one day the Messiah's glory would inhabit it. Through a series of apocalyptic visions filled with symbolism and graphic imagery, Zechariah outlined God's plan for his chosen people until the Messiah comes to renew them and reign over the earth.

Among the prophetical books, Zechariah is second only to Isaiah in the number of messianic prophecies it contains. References to the Messiah are sprinkled throughout the nine chapters. He is portrayed as the angel of the Lord (3:1–2), the righteous branch (3:8; 6:12–13), and a cleansing fountain (13:1). Other passages offer specific details of the Messiah's life such as being sold for thirty pieces of silver (11:4–13), being pierced (12:10), and his sheep scattering when he is struck (13:7). Chapter 9 paints the picture of Christ's triumphal entry when he rode into Jerusalem on a donkey as the people shouted and rejoiced.

Unlike Zechariah's original audience, we can read the New Testament and see how Christ's life perfectly fulfilled these prophecies five hundred years later. But the references to Christ's return at the end of this age are still in the future. Reading Zechariah encourages us to look beyond our present concerns to our ultimate hope. We can find motivation to be faithful in our service to God and to keep ourselves pure when we remember the heart of Zechariah's stirring message: our King is coming!

Malachi

Last Wake-up Call

"Certainly the day is coming! . . . All arrogant people and all evildoers will be like straw. The day that is coming will burn them up completely," says the Lord of Armies.

Malachi 4:1

A hundred years had passed since the first group of Jews returned to their homeland. The temple had been rebuilt, the priesthood reestablished. But the Jews had grown tired of waiting for signs of the glorious future described by the prophets. Judah was nothing more than a small, insignificant province in the Persian Empire. The land seemed cursed by drought, pestilence, and crop failure. God's presence had not come to inhabit the rebuilt temple. Disappointed and disillusioned, the leaders and people began to doubt God's love and justice. They wondered if it was really worth serving God at all.

As their cynicism deepened, the people grew morally and spiritually corrupt. They were guilty of many of the sins that had led to their captivity in Babylon, yet they had become so insensitive they wondered why God wasn't blessing them. God sent Malachi to try to break through the people's apathy and hardened hearts. Using a series of questions and answers, God demonstrated that their circumstances were due to their own disobedience, not his lack of concern.

God accused them of showing contempt for him by sacrificing defective animals. They had robbed him by withholding tithes and offerings. He condemned their indifference to his laws, their widespread divorce, and their intermarriage with pagans. This dialogue between a holy God and his unfaithful people proved Judah's guilt. But along with the coming judgment came a note of hope: for those who revered God, "the Sun of Righteousness will rise with healing in his wings" (Mal. 4:2).

Reading Malachi gives us an opportunity to have our own question and answer session. Do disappointments and failures make us doubt God's love for us? Have we allowed a spirit of cynicism to creep into our attitude toward him? Have we grown indifferent and careless toward God's commands? If we answer "yes," then we, too, need a wake-up call.

Four Hundred Years of Silence

The time gap between the close of the Old Testament and the birth of Christ is referred to as the "intertestamental period" or "the silent years." For centuries, God had sent his people a succession of prophets to speak his words. After the ministries of Nehemiah and Malachi, not a single prophet recognized as a divine spokesman appeared in public for four hundred years. (Luke 2:36 applies the term "prophetess" to Anna, an elderly woman who stayed at the temple fasting and praying.)

God seemed silent; in reality, he was setting the stage to unveil his Son, the Savior who would offer salvation and eternal life to the world. Soon he would speak to Jews and Gentiles alike, and it would be the best news they had ever heard.

For the Jews, this four-hundred-year period included war, uprisings, internal strife, and, except for a brief period of independence, oppression under foreign rulers. God used elements from this dark era to arrange the perfect setting for Christ's work and for the birth of the Church. Greek became the common language during the period that Greece held power; as a result, the New Testament was written in a language that almost everyone could understand. By the time Christ was born, the Jewish people were subjects of the Roman Empire, but free to worship and to enjoy a measure of stability. The highway system constructed by the Romans made it easier to spread the gospel.

Sometimes it may seem as though God is not active in our life. We question whether he hears our prayers; we wonder if he sees our circumstances. The Bible assures us that our Father is involved in every detail of our life. During the good times and the bad—and in those "in-between" times, God is always busy at work, weaving together our good and bad experiences, setting the stage to use us for his purposes. Just when it seems as though nothing is happening, God may be preparing to unveil something spectacular in our life.

We know that all things work together for the good of those who love God—those whom he has called according to his plan.

Romans 8:28

Slight Variations but Still the Gospel Truth

Appropriately, the New Testament begins with four accounts of the life and death of Jesus: the books of Matthew, Mark, Luke, and John. These four Gospels comprise almost half of the New Testament and serve as a link that points back to the Old Testament promises of the coming Messiah; they also lay the foundation for the rest of the New Testament.

Matthew, Mark, and Luke are referred to as the Synoptic ("seeing together") Gospels because they overlap in many places. John is sometimes called the supplemental Gospel since the majority of his material is unique to that book. The first three Gospels have a historical slant and focus more on Jesus's public ministry; John has a theological slant and includes more of Jesus's private interactions. The Synoptic Gospels emphasize Jesus's moral and practical teachings, while John focuses more on the person of Christ and is more explicit about his identity.

These four books are not biographies but topical narratives of Christ's life. Each author arranged his material to fit his particular theme, including some details while omitting others. Critics have noted apparent contradictions, especially in the accounts of Christ's death and resurrection. A careful study shows that each author fills in additional details; taken together, they give a composite picture of these events.

When four different people describe the same event, their accounts won't match up perfectly. Each person will see what happened from their unique viewpoint. Some will miss details that others notice, but that doesn't discount them as eyewitnesses. Similarly, God included four different Gospels in order to give testimony of independent witnesses to the life, death, and resurrection of Jesus.

Human testimony will always be flawed, but the Bible assures us that every single verse in it is inspired, or God-breathed. Much debate centers on how much the Gospel writers relied on oral tradition, written documents, and each other's material. But since God's Holy Spirit directed these authors, we can be sure that every word is the gospel truth.

Every Scripture passage is inspired by God.

2 Timothy 3:16

Matthew

The Silence Is Broken

When Jesus came near, he spoke to them. He said, "All authority in heaven and on earth has been given to me."

Matthew 28:18

Matthew (also know as Levi) held the detested position of tax collector for the Roman government. When Jesus invited Matthew to follow him, Matthew walked away from his booth. Later, he threw a banquet in his home to honor Jesus, inviting many other tax collectors (see Luke 5:27–32). As one of the twelve disciples, Matthew wrote his eyewitness account of Jesus's ministry to convince his fellow Jews that the long-awaited King of Israel had come at last. He frequently quoted Old Testament passages to show how Jesus fulfilled prophecies about the Messiah.

After beginning with a genealogy stressing Jesus's royal heritage traced through Joseph, Matthew relates how the long period of silence on God's part is broken by a baby's cry in the night. Later, God speaks loud and clear through a wild-looking man shouting for people to repent. During the three years of Jesus's earthly ministry, we hear God's voice teaching crowds hungry for spiritual truth, offering healing and hope to the hurting, commanding evil spirits, and even calling people back from death. Scripture shows that some people recognized God's voice, while others did not.

Sometimes even believers can fall into the second category. We all experience times when God seems silent and uninvolved in our life. From a human standpoint, we feel ignored. We can let discouragement make us question God's presence and his interest in our situation. If unchecked, we may become so cynical and wrapped up in our own perceptions that we fail to notice when God does speak to us.

Our best response in spiritual dry times is to trust in God's character and his promises instead of our emotions. If we continue in consistent prayer and study of God's Word, our ears will be more attuned to him. Then when he does break the silence, we'll be sure to recognize his voice, no matter what form it takes.

AUGUST

8

Skeletons in the Closet?

Matthew 1:1—18

As a Jew writing to a Jewish audience, Matthew naturally opened his book with a genealogy, something very important in that culture. In order to introduce Jesus as the fulfillment of Old Testament prophecies about the Messiah, Matthew had to prove that Jesus was a direct descendant of David with a rightful claim to the throne. He traced Jesus's ancestry through Joseph, his legal father, and ended at Abraham, verifying that Jesus was one of God's chosen people. (Luke traced Jesus's ancestry all the way back to Adam through Mary, also a direct descendant of David through another son.)

Matthew condensed Jesus's genealogy by skipping some generations, but he proved Jesus's credentials and also revealed something about God's love and mercy. The list of forty-six people includes a motley crew ranging from ordinary men to flawed heroes and from adulterers to evil kings. Jewish genealogies normally did not include women's names since ancestry was traced through men; however, God had Matthew include Mary, Jesus's mother. The genealogy also names four women from the Old Testament, all of them either foreigners or of questionable character.

Tamar disguised herself as a prostitute and had sex with her father-in-law; Bathsheba committed adultery with King David. Rahab was originally a prostitute in Jericho and Ruth came from Moab, whose people according to Deuteronomy 23:3 could not "join the assembly of the LORD." Yet God allowed Ruth and the others the privilege of being ancestors of his Son.

God wanted to make it clear that his mercy and grace extend to the entire world, not just to one group of people. There is nothing that can cut us off from his forgiveness—not our past mistakes, our questionable background, or our present failures. Only one thing can keep us from being a part of God's family: our choice not to believe in his Son, Jesus Christ.

God loved the world this way: He gave his only Son so that everyone who believes in him will not die but will have eternal life.

John 3:16

A Virgin Gives Birth

Matthew 1:18—25

The marriage between Joseph and Mary had been arranged. Although they lived in their parents' homes during the one-year waiting period before their actual marriage, their betrothal could only be broken by divorce or death. The news of Mary's pregnancy must have shocked and grieved Joseph. He could have let her be exposed to public scandal or even had her stoned for sexual infidelity; instead, Joseph decided to try to protect her by opting for a quiet divorce.

One night an angel appeared to Joseph in a dream and told him to go ahead and marry his betrothed. The angel assured Joseph that Mary had not been unfaithful to him; her baby had been conceived through God's Holy Spirit. She would give birth to a son named Jesus who would save people from their sins.

At the end of his genealogy of Jesus, Matthew made it clear that Jesus was the son of Mary but not Joseph (v. 16). In his account of Jesus's birth, he reminded his readers of the prophecy in Isaiah 7:14: a virgin would give birth to a son named *Immanuel*, or "God is with us." Being born of a woman made Jesus a human being, yet the Savior of the world had to be free from any trace of sin. With God as his father, Jesus was also fully divine.

Jesus's virgin birth is more than a supernatural event that taxes our brains when we try to understand it. It has a practical side that Hebrews 4 explains. Being human, Jesus experienced the same physical limitations and the same temptations that we do, although he never gave in and sinned. We can find comfort knowing that Jesus fully understands the pull of sin that we face daily. The fact that he can sympathize with our weaknesses and struggles gives us confidence to go to him when we need help, knowing that he alone has the power and authority to help us stand firm.

> *We have a chief priest who is able to sympathize*
> *with our weaknesses. He was tempted in every*
> *way that we are, but he didn't sin.*
>
> Hebrews 4:15

A Surprise Visit

Matthew 2:1–12

Sometime before Jesus's second birthday, his family had a surprise visit from unexpected guests. "Wise men" or *magi* (perhaps astronomers) from an eastern country journeyed hundreds of miles or more to look for the king of the Jews. When they stopped in Jerusalem, they learned that the Messiah was to be born in Bethlehem. The star or bright light they had seen in their own country then reappeared and led them to the very house where Mary and Joseph lived.

Upon entering the house, these men of high station bowed down and worshiped little Jesus. They opened their treasure chests and gave him gifts fit for a king: gold, frankincense, and myrrh. After God warned them in a dream not to obey King Herod's instructions to report back to him, these wise men returned home by a different route.

The identity of these surprise visitors is shrouded in mystery. Although "wise men" originally denoted experts in mysteries in Persia and Babylon, the term later came to be applied to those involved in astrology, dream interpretations, magic, and the pursuit of wisdom. We don't know if the revelation these men received came from watching the sky or from interaction with Jews and their Old Testament prophecies. We can't be sure if they had any understanding of Jesus's divine origins, but we can be certain that they understood the true meaning of worship.

These men were willing to embark on a long, uncomfortable journey to seek Jesus out, acting on the knowledge they had been given. They humbled themselves to bow down before a little child and worship him simply for who he was. They gave him generous gifts, the best they had to offer. Their example challenges us to examine our own attitudes. Have we allowed our worship to become self-centered or halfhearted? Do we focus more on music or other elements of a church service than on the One we are supposedly worshiping? If we're wise, we'll learn to honor Jesus as the Magi did.

So they bowed down and worshiped him.

Matthew 2:11

A Messenger in the Desert

Matthew 3:1—12

About thirty years after Jesus was born, the first true prophet in four hundred years appeared on the scene in Judea. John the Baptist traveled throughout the wilderness area around the Jordan River preaching a radical message. In anticipation of the coming Messiah, John called the people to move beyond mere words and rituals. He baptized them as an outward sign that they had asked God's forgiveness for their sins and committed to living a holy lifestyle. John confronted the religious leaders' hypocrisy and ridiculed the idea that Abraham's descendants would automatically be granted entrance into the Messiah's kingdom. God demanded true repentance made evident by godly behavior.

John showed no interest in bringing glory to himself. He lived a simple lifestyle, eating the diet of poor nomadic desert people. He dressed as Elijah did, in clothes made from camel hair and a leather belt. John fully understood his role: to be a messenger who helps prepare the people to receive their Messiah. Just as Isaiah 40:3 prophesied, John's voice cried out in the desert, "Clear a way for the LORD!" Later, when some of his disciples left to follow Jesus, John knew that he was doing his job. He explained that according to God's plan, Jesus must become greater while John himself became less important.

God expects each one of us to help smooth the way for people to receive their Savior. He may give us an opportunity to explain who Jesus is and how God offers forgiveness of sins to those who repent. Or he may place us in a position where someone needs to see an example of an obedient, godly lifestyle. Sometimes our ego gets in the way of our role as a messenger for Christ. When that happens, we can become an obstacle that keeps people from knowing him instead of one who helps make the way straight. Like John the Baptist, our job is to become less important so that Jesus can be magnified and more people will know him.

> *He must increase in importance, while*
> *I must decrease in importance.*
>
> John 3:30

The Mystery of the Trinity

Matthew 3:13—17

Even as John baptized people as a sign of repentance, he explained that someone would come soon who would baptize people with the Holy Spirit and with fire. One day Jesus showed up and asked John to baptize him. Knowing that Jesus was the Messiah, John protested that he himself needed to be baptized by Jesus. Although Jesus had no need for repentance, he insisted that it was God's will for John to baptize him. Through this symbolic act, Jesus identified with the sinful people he came to save and also inaugurated his own public ministry.

As Jesus came up out of the water, God's invisible Spirit took on a physical dovelike form and came to rest on Jesus. A voice from heaven said, "This is my Son, whom I love—my Son with whom I am pleased" (v. 17). Earlier, God had told John the Baptist, "When you see the Spirit come down and stay on someone, you'll know that person is the one who baptizes with the Holy Spirit" (see John 1:33). God sent the sign so the messenger preparing the way for the Messiah would know without a shadow of doubt that he had arrived.

Although the word *Trinity*, a term that means "three-in-one" or "one-in three," is never used in the Bible, the concept is foreshadowed in the Old Testament in passages where God uses a plural pronoun to refer to himself (such as Gen. 1:26 and Isa. 6:8). Matthew 3:16–17 is the first of a number of passages in the New Testament that show God the Father, God the Son, and God the Spirit active and present at the same time. (Other passages that refer to all three persons of the Godhead include John 14:16–17, 26; 2 Cor. 13:14; Eph. 4:4–6.)

We may find it impossible to fully comprehend the idea that God is three distinct Persons but one in essence, but we can appreciate the way the Trinity is involved in our salvation. God the Father sent the Son to save us from sin; Jesus the Son sent the Holy Spirit to fill us with his power to live a godly life. Thinking about the three-in-one nature of God gives us all the more reason to worship him.

God the Father knew you long ago and chose you to live
holy lives with the Spirit's help so that you are obedient
to Jesus Christ and are sprinkled with his blood.

1 Peter 1:2

Resisting Temptation

Matthew 4:1–11

After Jesus was baptized, God's Spirit led him into the desert for a time of testing. When Jesus had fasted for forty days, Satan came and urged him to satisfy his hunger by turning stones into bread. Jesus knew that the fasting was God's will, so he quoted Deuteronomy 8:3: "A person cannot live on bread alone but on every word that God speaks." Next, Satan challenged Jesus to display his identity by jumping off the highest point of the temple. Satan quoted Psalm 91:11–12 as proof that Jesus would not be harmed. Jesus responded that it would be wrong to test God (see Deut. 6:16).

Finally, Satan tried to lure Jesus into sin by offering him a shortcut. Showing Jesus a vision of all the kingdoms of the earth in their splendor, Satan promised to give them to Jesus if he would bow down and worship him. Jesus could bypass the path of suffering and the cross and still be King of Kings. Jesus countered with a core truth of Scripture: "Worship the Lord your God and serve only him" (Matt. 4:10). Defeated, Satan then left Jesus alone.

Satan is still active today, trying to lure people into sin. He often attacks when we're most vulnerable, appealing to our physical appetites, our materialism, or our pride. He may tempt us to go outside God's plan by taking a shortcut or a path that avoids suffering. Satan may even use people who twist or misquote Scripture to influence our thinking.

Although God allows us to go through times of testing, he promises to help us withstand them. And Jesus has given us an example to follow. To be ready for temptation, we need to be thoroughly familiar with the Bible, so we can tell Satan what Scripture really says.

> *The temptations in your life are no different from what others experience. And God is faithful. He will not allow the temptation to be more than you can stand. When you are tempted, he will show you a way out so that you can endure.*
>
> 1 Corinthians 10:13 NLT

Reeling in Four Fishermen

Matthew 4:18–22

After John the Baptist was imprisoned, Jesus went back to Galilee and began his ministry of teaching, preaching, and healing. Along the shores of the Sea of Galilee, Jesus called two sets of brothers to become his disciples. Jesus had already met Andrew and Peter (see John 1:35–42); now he challenged them to leave their profession behind and become a part of his ministry. "Come, follow me!" he said. "I will teach you how to catch people instead of fish" (v. 19). The brothers immediately left their nets. Farther down the shore, Jesus extended the same invitation to James and John, who left their boat and their father to follow him.

Jesus made it clear that following him would not be easy; he urged people to count the cost before making a commitment. "Foxes have holes, and birds have nests, but the Son of Man has nowhere to sleep," he pointed out to a would-be disciple (Matt. 8:20). Jesus also promised rewards for his faithful followers. When a rich man wasn't able to obey Jesus's instruction to give all his money away, Peter thought about how much the disciples had left behind. "We've given up everything to follow you," he asked. "What will we get out of it?" (see Matt. 19:27). Jesus explained that anyone who gives up something for him will be more than compensated with blessings in this life in addition to their inheritance of eternal life.

Following Jesus doesn't necessarily mean a life of comfort and security. He expects us to be willing to leave everything behind and make him our highest priority. We may be called to give up material wealth, our reputation, certain relationships, our leisure time, or cherished habits in order to serve him. But whatever sacrifice we make for Jesus will be worth it. We have his promise that we will be repaid a hundredfold—and that's a wise investment.

> *[Jesus said] "Everyone who gave up homes, brothers or sisters, father, mother, children, or fields because of my name will receive a hundred times more and will inherit eternal life."*
>
> Matthew 19:29

Choice of Rewards

Matthew 6:1—18

The term *hypocrites* originally referred to Greek actors who changed masks as they played various roles. Jesus often used the label for the religious leaders of his day, especially the Pharisees. Although these men prided themselves on their righteousness, Jesus saw their true motivation. He knew they did the right things for the wrong reasons.

When the Pharisees gave money to the needy, they made sure everyone knew it. They turned prayer into a public performance, using long repetitive phrases to try to impress listeners. When they fasted, they made it obvious so everyone would see how spiritual they were. Jesus pointed out that the praise they garnered from other people would be their only reward for their "good deeds."

In contrast, Jesus urged his followers to take the opposite approach. Whether in a public or private setting, our prayers should be honest and sincere, and directed toward God alone. Instead of a shallow repetition of words or phrases, we can imitate the attitudes expressed in the model prayer that Jesus demonstrated (vv. 9–13). Giving to the needy should be done in secret with no thought of how it might benefit us. Our fasting should be a private matter between us and God. When we do these things in secret, God will see it and reward us (a promise Jesus repeated three times).

We have a choice in how we express our faith. We can do it in a way that draws attention to ourselves and wins admiration from other people. Or we can do our acts of service and good deeds to bring glory to God. It's not always easy to do the right thing if no one will see it and recognize our sacrifice. But our heavenly Father sees everything done in secret. We can test our motives by asking, "Would I be doing this if no one except God knew about it?" If the answer is "yes," then we can expect a reward from him.

Your Father sees what you do in private. He will reward you.

Matthew 6:4

The Saddest Words in the Bible

Matthew 7:15–29

False prophets who pretended to speak for God were prevalent in the Old Testament; apparently they still posed a problem in Jesus's day. He warned that people should evaluate a person's words by examining their lifestyle. Jesus also explained that just because someone calls him "Lord" doesn't mean they will enter the kingdom of heaven. On judgment day, many people will protest that they prophesied, forced out demons, and performed miracles—all in his name. Then Jesus will speak the saddest words they've ever heard: "I've never known you. Get away from me, you evil people" (v. 23).

Today we have no shortage of false teachers and leaders, people who look religious but have no personal relationship with Jesus. Their spiritual talk deceives many people but they are motivated by something other than glorifying God. Even if they seem to exhibit supernatural power by performing miracles, their power comes from some source apart from God. One day Jesus will expose these false teachers as imposters, along with anyone else who looked like a Christian but never accepted him as Savior.

At that time, many churchgoers who deceived themselves into thinking they were believers will be shocked to hear Jesus call them evildoers. They may point to their good deeds or religious accomplishments, but they will lack the necessary credentials; Jesus doesn't know them as his children. Sadly, they will discover their self-deception too late.

At the end of our life, what will matter most is whether we had a personal relationship with Christ. Did we place our faith in him as our Savior and Lord, as evidenced by a life of obedience to his commands? Did we merely know *about* him, or did we truly know him? If the latter is true, then we can look forward to being welcomed into Jesus's presence; we don't have to worry about hearing the saddest words that can fall on human ears.

> *[Jesus said] "Then I will tell them plainly, 'I never knew you. Away from me, you evildoers!'"*
>
> Matthew 7:23 NIV

Wrestling with Doubts

Matthew 11:2—19

John the Baptist had a unique place in history. Before John's supernatural birth to elderly parents, the angel Gabriel designated his name and announced that he would minister in the "spirit and power of Elijah" (see Luke 1:17). John's role was to be the messenger who prepared the way for the coming of the Messiah; he had the privilege of baptizing the Son of God. Even so, John the Baptist had a moment when he needed reassurance about God's plan.

As a prophet, John had publicly denounced the sinful marriage between Herod and his sister-in-law. While John languished in prison, awaiting possible execution, he struggled with confusion. Perhaps he wondered why Jesus had not freed the world of injustice and sin as the Messiah was expected to do. Maybe he wondered why God had allowed his own ministry to be halted. Whatever thoughts John struggled with, he took his doubts to the right person.

John sent his disciples to Jesus with a question: "Are you the one who is coming, or should we look for someone else?" (v. 3). Jesus told the men to report back to John what they had observed: sick people healed, dead people brought back to life, and the spreading of the Good News. Then Jesus praised John as far more than a prophet and said that no one born on earth was greater than John.

While we live our earthly life, our faith will always be mixed with times of questioning and uncertainty. If we try to ignore those feelings, they can become a barrier that makes God seem distant from us. Instead of growing spiritually, we can become paralyzed by guilt over our imperfect faith. God wants us to bring our doubts and questions to him so he can help us work through them. We may not understand everything that we want to, but wrestling with our doubts can make our faith grow stronger.

> *The father instantly cried out, "I do believe,*
> *but help me overcome my unbelief!"*
>
> Mark 9:24 NLT

Jesus's Teaching Methods

Matthew 13

As Jesus faced increasing opposition, he began to focus more on instructing his disciples. Jesus still spoke to crowds, but he began to use metaphors and stories on those occasions. Matthew 13 includes seven of Jesus's parables, short stories that use familiar objects or experiences to illustrate spiritual truths and principles. A farmer sowing seeds illustrated different ways people react to hearing God's Word. A net full of fish and a field of wheat and weeds growing together pictured believers and unbelievers living side by side. A mustard seed and yeast represented the growth of the kingdom of heaven; its value was compared to treasure and to a fine pearl worth selling everything to own.

Noticing the change in Jesus's teaching methods, his disciples privately asked him why he spoke to the people in parables. Jesus explained that he did it to teach them truth, to reveal mysteries about his kingdom that had been hidden before. Those receptive to the truth would gain understanding from the parables, but the truth would be concealed from those who were spiritually lazy or who refused to believe in Jesus. They would miss the meaning of Jesus's parables.

There are many creative ways to share God's truth with people. But we need to remember that until a person accepts Jesus as their Savior, they won't have the ability to truly understand the things of God. Without the Holy Spirit living inside and revealing truth to them, God's Word can seem irrelevant, meaningless, or even foolish. Bible verses, stories, and songs won't hold the same meaning for them as they do for us. We need God's wisdom to know when and how to share our faith with those who need to hear the truth. And they need our prayers that God will help them reach the starting point for understanding it.

> *A person who isn't spiritual doesn't accept the teachings of God's Spirit. He thinks they're nonsense. He can't understand them because a person must be spiritual to evaluate them.*
>
> 1 Corinthians 2:14

Walking on Water

Matthew 14:22–36

When Jesus went to pray alone on a mountainside, his twelve disciples rowed out onto the Sea of Galilee. A few miles from shore, they found themselves in the middle of a fierce storm. The ferocious wind tossed their boat around for hours until they were exhausted. In the early morning hours, they looked up and saw a figure walking on the water. Thinking of evil spirits, the men screamed in terror. Then they heard Jesus's familiar voice speaking to them: "Calm down! It's me. Don't be afraid!"

Peter blurted out, "Lord, if it is you, order me to come to you on the water." Jesus invited him with a simple, "Come!" (vv. 27–29). Peter stepped out of the boat without hesitation. He began walking toward Jesus—until he got distracted by the raging waves all around him. He felt himself sinking and cried out for Jesus to save him. Immediately, Jesus lifted Peter up out of the water. "You have so little faith!" he said. "Why did you doubt?" (v. 31).

Chances are, we'll never try to walk on water, but we can probably identify with that sinking feeling Peter must have had. Sometimes God asks us to do something that goes beyond our comfort zone; other times he allows us to land in a situation that seems to challenge us beyond what we can endure. Even though we start out with good intentions, our faith can waver if we look only at our circumstances.

Peter got to experience a thrilling demonstration of God's power, but he learned the dangers we face whenever we take our eyes off Jesus. If we focus on our inadequacies or on what's happening around us, we may miss the joy of doing something that seems impossible in our own strength. Jesus stands ready to reach out when we need his help, but who knows what God will do through us if we learn to keep our eyes where they belong?

We must focus on Jesus, the source and goal of our faith.

Hebrews 12:2

The Transfiguration

Matthew 17:1–13

As Jesus talked to the disciples about his second coming, he told them that some of them would be allowed to see the Son of Man in his kingdom before they died (see 16:28). Six days later, he led Peter, James, and John up on a mountain. There Jesus's appearance changed before their eyes. His face shone like the sun and his clothes looked like a white light. Suddenly Moses and Elijah appeared in heavenly glory and began talking with Jesus about his approaching death (see Luke 9:31).

Peter suggested erecting three shelters, but God interrupted him. From a bright cloud, a loud voice spoke, "This is my Son, whom I love and with whom I am pleased. Listen to him!" (v. 5). The terrified disciples fell to the ground; when they looked up, Jesus was alone.

The transfiguration was a special revelation to Jesus's inner circle of disciples. The presence of Moses and Elijah confirmed Jesus's messianic mission to fulfill the law and the prophets. Jesus's transformed appearance served as a reminder of both his glory in heaven before he became human and his future exaltation. Years later, Peter would refer to this event and assure his readers that his message was not based on myths he made up. He and the other apostles were eyewitnesses of Jesus's majesty and glory (see 2 Pet. 1:16–18).

We can receive a revelation of Jesus's glory and majesty by reading the Gospel accounts of his life, death, and resurrection. He may have walked the earth long ago, but the Bible assures us that Jesus never changes. The same Savior who gave three disciples a foretaste of his kingdom wants to make our life radiate with his glory as he transforms us into his image.

There's not much we can count on in this temporary, earthly life. Relationships dissolve, material wealth disappears, promises are broken. But we can find security in a relationship with the One who never changes, and in knowing that one day we will be transfigured too.

Jesus Christ is the same yesterday, today, and forever.

Hebrews 13:8

No Limits

Matthew 18:15—35

As Jesus taught about the proper way to handle conflicts between believers, Peter asked a question: "Lord, how often do I have to forgive a believer who wrongs me? Seven times?" (v. 21). Traditional rabbinic teaching held that a person should forgive someone who offended them up to three times. Thinking that he was being exceptionally generous, Peter must have been shocked by Jesus's answer.

Jesus responded, "I tell you, not just seven times, but seventy times seven"—in other words, forgive without keeping count. Then Jesus told a parable to illustrate the motivation behind this command. A servant and his family were saved from being sold into slavery when his master canceled his huge debt. Yet that servant turned around and showed no mercy for someone who owed him a much smaller amount. Jesus's point was that since God has forgiven our sins, he expects us to show forgiveness to others.

The principle of forgiving those who wrong us is woven throughout the Bible. As God gave the Israelites laws for living, he instructed them to not bear grudges against each another (see Lev. 19:18). Jesus explained that one condition for answered prayer is being willing to forgive those who have hurt us (see Mark 11:25). In his letters, Paul often stressed the importance of forgiving others.

When we've been deeply or repeatedly hurt by someone, this command seems to go against logic and human nature. We can only obey with supernatural help. God knows that we can be damaged physically, emotionally, and spiritually by nursing a grudge against someone. When we withhold forgiveness from another believer, we can't be in a right relationship with God or with the body of Christ. God wants us to know the joy and freedom that comes from letting go of old hurts and wounds. If we remember how much God has forgiven us, we can make the difficult choice to extend forgiveness to others—with no limits.

> *Be kind to each other, sympathetic, forgiving each*
> *other as God has forgiven you through Christ.*
>
> Ephesians 4:32

Mark

Jesus the Servant

Whoever wants to be most important among you will be a slave for everyone. It's the same way with the Son of Man. He didn't come so that others could serve him. He came to serve and to give his life as a ransom for many people.

Mark 10:44–45

Mark is the shortest, simplest, and probably the earliest of the four Gospels (written between AD 55–65). Although not an apostle, Mark had a close relationship with Peter. Mary, Mark's mother, had a house in Jerusalem that was used as a meeting place for believers. Peter must have been a frequent guest because the servant girl recognized his voice at the gate (see Acts 12:12–16). Peter referred to "my son Mark" in 1 Peter 5:13. Most likely, Mark drew from Peter's preaching and eyewitness accounts as his primary source, which would explain why descriptions of incidents involving Peter are especially vivid.

Written to an audience of Gentile Christians, this Gospel omits some material that would be of special interest to Jews. Mark emphasizes action above words, including few of Jesus's parables while recording more of his miracles than the other Gospels. He offers more detailed descriptions of parallel events found in Matthew and Luke and records more of the emotional reactions of Jesus and those he interacts with.

Mark's brisk, fast-moving account portrays Jesus as the divine Servant at work, busily ministering to others through his teaching and healing. A large portion of the book focuses on the last week of Jesus's life, when he made the ultimate sacrifice for those he came to serve.

Many people failed to recognize Jesus as Messiah because they didn't understand his role as the suffering Servant who came to give his life for the world's sins. We can miss out on the joys and blessings of the Christian life if we don't understand *our* role as a servant. God doesn't call us to be popular or successful according to the world's definition, but to follow Jesus's example of self-sacrifice and service to others.

A Healing Touch

Mark 1:21—45; 2:1—12; 3:1—12

The first chapter of Mark quickly zeroes in on Jesus's healing ministry and the impact it had on the people who witnessed him at work. One day, Jesus forced an evil spirit out of a man in the synagogue and healed Peter's mother-in-law from a fever. That evening it seemed as though the whole city of Capernaum had gathered at the door, bringing their loved ones who had a wide range of diseases and demon possession. Jesus "healed many," a Hebrew expression that means "all who were brought."

Later, Jesus healed a man from a serious skin disease and a paralytic whose friends made a hole in the roof in their desperation to get him to Jesus. As news of the miracles spread, Jesus couldn't travel without being surrounded by people who needed his compassionate touch. But not everyone appreciated his healing ministry.

The religious leaders hated the fact that Jesus frequently healed on the Sabbath. On one occasion, a synagogue leader told the crowd, "There are six days when work can be done. So come on one of those days to be healed. Don't come on the day of worship" (see Luke 13:14). Jesus rebuked this uncaring attitude and refused to put restrictions on his healing. He cured those who begged for help and also those who were mute or unable to ask.

Some people restrict Jesus's work in their life by simply not asking for his help. Even though medical attention is often necessary, why shouldn't we automatically go to the Great Physician when we need healing? On the other hand, some go to the opposite extreme and think a believer should never have to suffer pain or sickness at all if they only have enough faith. Although God does allow us to go through times of sickness and suffering, it only makes sense to ask him to heal us. Whether or not he removes our physical ailments, Jesus has already healed us of the deadliest disease—the curse of sin.

Heal me, O Lord, *and I will be healed.*

Jeremiah 17:14

A Calming Influence

Mark 4:35–41

Sudden, violent storms were common on the Sea of Galilee due to its location and the surrounding geography. Even though Jesus's twelve disciples included experienced fishermen, they panicked during one windstorm that threatened to swamp their boat. Jesus slept in the back of the boat, exhausted from teaching the crowds. The men woke him up, asking, "Teacher, don't you care that we're going to die?" (v. 38). Jesus commanded the wind and the sea to be still. The storm didn't just die down gradually—it instantly stopped. Turning to the amazed disciples, Jesus rebuked them for their lack of faith.

The men's fear may seem like a normal reaction to their situation, but Jesus expected more from his followers. Tranquility may seem impossible during life's sudden crises, whether we're in the middle of an external storm or dealing with turbulent emotions that wreak havoc with our mind. But like the disciples, we are in the presence of the One who has authority over weather, nature, and our mind. God offers us a peace that can withstand any onslaught.

In the Old Testament, David displayed this kind of childlike trust in God, recording his experiences in many of the Psalms. Although he endured a lot of turbulence in his life, David knew that God was in control and placed himself in his loving hands. Even when his enemies pursued and surrounded him, David declared that he could sleep in peace because "you alone, O LORD, enable me to live securely" (see Ps. 4:8).

The secret to achieving this kind of peace in spite of our circumstances is explained in Philippians 4:4–9. Instead of worrying, we are to pray about everything. As we talk to God about our needs and concerns, we are to thank him for all that he's done for us. If we follow these guidelines, God promises that his peace will guard our heart and mind, no matter what storm is raging around us—or within us.

> *Then God's peace, which goes beyond anything*
> *we can imagine, will guard your thoughts*
> *and emotions through Christ Jesus.*
>
> Philippians 4:7

A Timid Touch

Mark 5:21–34

Weaving her way through the crowd, the woman inched closer to Jesus. If the people she brushed against knew her problem, how horrified they would be! For twelve years she had suffered from chronic bleeding, a condition that made her and anyone she touched ceremonially unclean. Besides the pain of being shut out from formal worship of God and normal social contact, the woman had wasted all her money searching for a cure only to see her condition worsen. Now, she had found reason to hope again. She had heard about Jesus's power to heal all kinds of diseases. *If I can just touch his clothes, I'll get well*, she assured herself.

Finally, the woman got close enough to reach out and touch Jesus's cloak. Instantly, she felt the bleeding stop. Jesus suddenly turned around and demanded to know who had touched his clothes. The woman trembled with fear, wondering how he would react if he knew. When Jesus continued to search the crowd, she fell down before him and confessed. Jesus addressed her with a term of endearment and assured her that she had been cured.

The woman planned to touch Jesus's robe and then slip away, but he knew that she needed more. Jesus wanted to make it clear that she had been healed because of her faith that had led her to seek him out, not from a magical touch of clothing. He wanted to see her healed not just from her medical condition, but from the humiliation of her painful past.

Shame and guilt over our failures or past mistakes can make us hesitant to approach our heavenly Father. We may have trouble believing that he wants an intimate relationship with us after what we've done. But once we become God's child, we have his acceptance and unconditional love. Nothing can ever change that. How could we let anything make us feel too ashamed to come before such a loving Father face-to-face?

> *Because of Christ and our faith in him, we can now*
> *come boldly and confidently into God's presence.*
>
> Ephesians 3:12 NLT

An Amazing Picnic

Mark 6:30—44

One day Jesus tried to get away with his disciples to a quiet place for some much-needed rest, but the excited crowds had anticipated his destination. Five thousand men, plus women and children, had gathered to await his arrival. Instead of being annoyed, Jesus felt compassion and began to teach the crowd.

Late in the day, his disciples made a logical suggestion. Since they were in a remote area, why not dismiss the people so they could buy food in the surrounding villages? The disciples weren't prepared for Jesus's response: "You give them something to eat" (v. 37). They pointed out the impossibility of the task: it would take eight months of a laborer's wages to feed such a multitude.

Jesus sent the disciples out into the crowd to see how much food was available. They reported a meager supply of five small loaves of bread and two fish. After having the people sit down in orderly groups on the grass, Jesus looked up to heaven and prayed a blessing over the food. As he broke the bread and fish, the disciples served portions to the people—and kept on serving. The crowd of thousands ate until they were full. Picking up the leftover pieces, the disciples gathered enough to fill twelve baskets.

We may be surprised to sense God asking us to do some impossible task that defies human logic. If we feel like we lack the resources, the skills, or the strength to obey, we need to remember how God can multiply our meager offerings. Like Jesus, we can look toward heaven to acknowledge the source of our provision. Then we can pray for God's blessing over our need and watch to see how he will work. What looks to be impossible through human eyes may simply be a perfect opportunity for God to display his power in ways that we could never have imagined.

> *Glory belongs to God, whose power is at work in us. By this power he can do infinitely more than we can ask or imagine.*
>
> Ephesians 3:20

The Right Answer

Mark 8:27–30

When Jesus taught his twelve disciples, he often began with a question. One day he asked them, "Who do people say I am?" (v. 27). The disciples told Jesus what they had heard the people saying about him. Some believed him to be John the Baptist come back to life after being beheaded by Herod. Others said he must be Elijah; still others thought he was one of the other prophets. Then Jesus made the question more personal: "But who do you say I am?" Peter spoke up and answered for the group: "You are the Messiah!" (v. 29).

Peter's declaration showed that the twelve disciples recognized Jesus's identity, unlike the crowds who had witnessed miracle after miracle. But the disciples' understanding was far from complete. Jesus was preparing to correct their commonly held misconceptions about the Messiah's role. Since they didn't understand the true meaning of the title, Jesus commanded them to not tell anyone he was the Messiah.

Jesus's question has echoed down through the centuries, igniting countless arguments, conflicts, and debates. It's a question that each one of us must answer today. Some people who either ignore or don't know what Jesus said about himself call him one of the greatest teachers or philosophers who ever lived, or simply a good, moral man who taught about God. If we're familiar with the biblical accounts of Jesus's life, then we have to decide if he was self-deceived, a deceiver, or who he claimed to be: God in human form, who came to earth to die for our sins.

Mark records this conversation at the center of his Gospel because it represents a turning point in his narrative and in Jesus's ministry. Our answer to Jesus's question will be the turning point of our life. If we accept everything that Jesus said about himself, we will submit to him as Savior and Lord. Our relationship with God and the eternal destiny of our souls depend on what we believe about Jesus's identity. We can't afford to get the answer wrong.

He asked them, "But who do you say I am?"

Mark 8:29

The Road Ahead

Mark 8:31–38

No more parables or veiled allusions. Jesus knew the right time had come to prepare his disciples for what lay ahead. Calling himself the Son of Man, he clearly explained what would happen to him. The religious leaders, the chief priests, and the scribes would all reject him. He would be killed, but after three days he would come back to life. Later, Jesus revealed further details about the near future. He would be betrayed and handed over to the authorities (9:30–31). He would be ridiculed, spit on, and whipped (10:32–34).

The disciples could not square Jesus's words with the commonly held belief that the Messiah would come to set Israel free from Roman rule and set up an earthly kingdom. How could it be part of the divine plan for God's Anointed One to suffer and be killed? Peter took Jesus aside and began to reprimand him for saying such things.

"Get out of my way, Satan!" Jesus answered (v. 33). He rebuked Peter and the others for not thinking about God's purposes, but only about their own feelings and desires. Addressing the crowd along with his disciples, Jesus explained what was required from those who choose to follow him: self-denial and total submission to God's will.

From a human standpoint, we would love to enjoy the benefits and blessings of the Christian life without the self-denial part, but the Bible clearly explains that our path will not be easy. Every believer's life will include sacrifice, suffering, and persecution to some degree. As long as we live in this world, we will face our share of troubles. But the night before his crucifixion, Jesus explained that his death on the cross represented a victory over sin and death. The road ahead may include pain and suffering as part of God's plan, but thanks to Jesus's sacrifice, it ultimately leads to the glory of eternal life with him.

> *[Jesus said] "Here on earth you will have many trials and sorrows. But take heart, because I have overcome the world."*
>
> John 16:33 NLT

Settling an Argument

Mark 9:33—37

After Jesus and his disciples traveled to Capernaum, he asked them what they had been arguing about on the way. At first, the men were silent, too embarrassed and ashamed to answer his question. Finally, the disciples admitted that they had argued about which one of them was the greatest. Rank and position were important to the Jews, and in light of the messianic kingdom they expected Jesus to set up, they probably dreamed about status and honor. Jesus gave them a new perspective on greatness and leadership in the form of a paradox.

To be important in God's eyes, he explained, a person must voluntarily become a servant to other people. The goal is not to be first, but rather to take the last place. The highest positions in God's kingdom go to those who are willing to be lowly enough to serve the needs of others. To illustrate this concept of service, Jesus put his arms around a little child, considered an insignificant person in that culture. He said that when anyone welcomed or showed kindness to a little child in his name, it was the same as doing it for Jesus himself.

There's nothing wrong with ambition or pursuit of excellence as long as they don't become a source of pride. When we try to achieve greatness by chasing after positions of power, physical strength, popularity, or worldly success, we're going in the wrong direction. God evaluates us on the basis of humility and service.

If we look for opportunities to serve others and put their needs ahead of our own, if we never consider ourselves above doing tasks that seem menial, if we build others up instead of ourselves—that's when we're on the track to greatness in God's eyes. And we just might discover that last place is the best place to be after all.

> He told them, "Whoever wants to be the most
> important person must take the last place
> and be a servant to everyone else."
>
> Mark 9:35

The Most Important Commandment

Mark 12:28–34

The Jewish scribes, or teachers of the law, had turned the Mosaic law into more than six hundred individual commands. Although they considered all of the laws binding, some scribes liked to debate over which ones held lesser or greater importance. They also tried to find a single, fundamental command that would sum up the entire law. Impressed by how Jesus handled a trick question from the Sadducees, one scribe brought his question to Jesus: "Which commandment is the most important of them all?" (v. 28).

Drawing from Deuteronomy 6:5, Jesus answered that the greatest commandment is to love God with all our heart, soul, mind, and strength. Then he added a second, complementary command, found in Leviticus 19:18: to love others as we love ourselves. The scribe recognized the wisdom in Jesus's response. He agreed and added that to wholeheartedly love God and other people is more important than all the burnt offerings and sacrifices. Jesus commended the scribe for his growing spiritual understanding.

If we follow these two principles from Jesus, then we will be fulfilling all of the Ten Commandments along with the other Old Testament laws. We can be busy with Bible studies, prayer, church activities, and ministry to others yet fall short in one area. While correct doctrine and service are crucial components of the Christian life, they can't make up for a lack of love in our heart. If we are committed to obeying God, then we will be growing in our love for him and for the people around us.

On the night before he was crucified, Jesus told his disciples that he had a new command to give them: they were to love each other the same way he had loved them. He explained that the world would recognize them as his followers by their love for each other (see John 13:34–35). The kind of love God calls us to is a tall order. It becomes easier when we reflect on how he showed his love for us.

We love because God loved us first.

1 John 4:19

Luke

Jesus the Savior

Indeed, the Son of Man has come to seek and to save people who are lost.

Luke 19:10

Luke's Gospel is the longest, most comprehensive of the four; most of the material in 9:51–19:27 is not found in any other Gospel. As a physician and a man of science, Luke gave a more complete account of Jesus's miraculous birth. As a Greek, he paid attention to detail and accuracy. Luke opened his narrative by explaining his intention to present a carefully investigated, chronological account of the life of Christ. Since Luke was a close friend and traveling companion to the apostle Paul, he could have easily interviewed eyewitnesses, including the apostles, to corroborate the written historical documents available to him.

While Luke specifically addressed his Gospel to Theophilus (probably a man of high social standing), he also wrote for a wider Gentile audience. Therefore, Luke took the time to explain Jewish customs and localities and seldom made references to Jesus's fulfillment of prophecy, which would have been of less interest to non-Jewish readers. He often substituted Greek words for Aramaic ones, and in his few Old Testament quotations, he used the Greek translation. When Luke traced Jesus's genealogy, he didn't stop at Abraham; he went all the way back to Adam.

The book of Luke emphasizes that Jesus came to be the Savior for the entire human race. It highlights the stories of outcasts from Jewish society coming to faith in Jesus—sinners, beggars, lepers, and Samaritans. Women and children are given a prominent place. Thanks to Luke's keen interest in people and his eye for detail, we find vivid portraits of people barely mentioned or left out of the other Gospels.

Luke accomplished his goal of demonstrating that faith in Jesus Christ is based not on hearsay or myths, but on a solid foundation of historical fact. Reading his passionate narrative challenges us to make sure we've moved beyond merely accepting the facts about Jesus. Have we also accepted him as our Savior who came to seek and save us?

SEPTEMBER

1

Two Birth Announcements

Luke 1

When God sent Gabriel to announce two future miraculous births, the angel's words elicited two very different reactions. He paid his first visit to an elderly priest named Zechariah. For years he and his wife Elizabeth had lived with the humiliation of barrenness, considered a curse in their culture. One day as Zechariah burned incense in the temple, Gabriel appeared and announced that Zechariah would have a son. John would be a great man who would bring many Israelites back to God and prepare the people for their Messiah. Despite the detailed description, Zechariah found the news too good to be true. Thinking only of his and Elizabeth's advanced age, Zechariah asked for proof. Gabriel told Zechariah that he would be unable to speak until John's birth since he hadn't believed the message.

Several months later, Gabriel paid a visit to a young woman in Nazareth. Every Jewish woman dreamed of giving birth to the long-awaited Messiah, but the angel's sudden announcement startled Mary since she was a virgin. She felt confused and wondered how this would be accomplished. Gabriel explained that God would perform the miracle through the power of the Holy Spirit. Mary didn't comprehend it all, but her response reveals her desire to submit to God's will: "Let everything you've said happen to me" (v. 38). Mary understood that God had a special assignment for her, and that was enough.

We may think that age, physical limitations, lack of education, or low social standing can hinder us from being used in a special way by God. But there are no barriers to what he can do in our lives as long as we make ourselves available and submit to his will even when we don't understand how things will play out. When God tells us something too good to be true, how will we react? Will we doubt his words as Zechariah did, or can we show the trust and submission that Mary displayed?

Mary answered, "I am the Lord's servant. Let everything you've said happen to me."

Luke 1:38

God's Unexpected Plan

Luke 2:1—40

No one could have foreseen how the greatest event in history would happen. A Roman census forced Joseph and Mary to travel to Bethlehem even though she was near the end of her pregnancy. With the town crowded with visitors, they were unable to get a room in the inn—not even for the most important birth ever to take place. Mary had her baby in a stable, probably a dark cave outside the inn used to shelter animals. A feeding trough served as a bed for Jesus, God come down to earth in human form.

God sent an angel to announce the birth of the Savior of the world, but not to the religious leaders, the Jewish dignitaries, or the powerful Roman rulers. A group of humble shepherds out in the fields received the first invitation to worship the Lamb of God. Then, forty days after Jesus's birth, Mary and Joseph went to Jerusalem to present him to the Lord and offer a sacrifice according to Mosaic law. Only two people recognized the presence of the Messiah—Simeon and Anna.

Most people would have expected the King of Kings to be born in luxurious surroundings, with crowds coming to worship him instead of a handful of shepherds. But God often doesn't work as we expect him to. Just when we think we have him figured out, he does something that we would never have dreamed.

Our human mind will never fully comprehend God; some days we may wonder what in the world he's thinking. The required trip to Bethlehem seemed to come at an inconvenient time, but God used the emperor's decree to have Jesus born in the town prophesied in Micah 5:2. The overcrowded inn was a nuisance, but God wanted shepherds to worship the Lamb of God in a stable. We can trust that God is perfectly wise in everything he does, and that he's always in control even when he carries out his plans in unexpected ways.

> *"My thoughts are not your thoughts,*
> *and my ways are not your ways," declares the* LORD.
>
> Isaiah 55:8

Jesus at His Father's House

Luke 2:41–52

When Jesus was twelve years old, his family made their annual sixty-five-mile journey from Nazareth to Jerusalem for the Passover celebration. After the festival ended, Joseph and Mary left for home with their caravan. They traveled a day before discovering that Jesus was not with any of their friends or relatives. Frantic with worry, Joseph and Mary hurried back to Jerusalem. Three days later, they finally found their son, and their anxiety was replaced with astonishment.

Jesus sat in the temple courtyard among the teachers, listening to them and asking questions. His intelligence and understanding stunned those who heard the discussions. Mary told Jesus that she and Joseph had been worried sick about him and asked why he had treated them in such a manner. Jesus seemed surprised that they would not instinctively know to find him at the temple. "Why were you looking for me?" he asked. "Didn't you realize that I had to be in my Father's house?" (v. 49).

Jesus's response indicates that even at age twelve, he understood that he was the Son of God. Perhaps he felt an obligation to seize every opportunity to learn and prepare for his future mission. It seemed only natural for him to be in his Father's house. As children of God, we should feel the same way about our places of worship. God wants us to be part of a community of believers who worship, pray, study, and serve together. Within our church family, we can find encouragement, comfort, practical help, and opportunities to work together to share the gospel.

When some early Christians gave up the habit of meeting together, the writer of Hebrews urged them to go back to regular gatherings. We may be tempted to "skip church" because of a busy lifestyle. But there are joys and learning opportunities that can only be found within a local church family. Why wouldn't we want to be in our Father's house?

> *We should not stop gathering together with*
> *other believers, as some of you are doing.*
>
> Hebrews 10:25

Jesus's Hometown Reception

Luke 4:14–30

After Jesus had gained a reputation as a popular teacher, he returned to his hometown of Nazareth for a visit. The synagogue leader invited Jesus to read from the Scriptures and teach. Jesus read from the first two verses of Isaiah 61, a prophecy that the Messiah would come to tell the Good News and announce the year of the Lord's favor. Jesus then sat down to comment on the verses. "This passage came true today when you heard me read it," he told his audience (v. 21).

The people couldn't help noticing how graciously Jesus spoke, but how could he refer to himself as the Messiah? They all knew he was Joseph's son; after all, hadn't they watched him grow up in their village? Jesus sensed their doubt and opposition to his authority. He reminded them of two instances during the ministries of Elijah and Elisha when God performed special miracles for Gentiles while Israel was in unbelief. The implication that God would bless Gentiles over Jews infuriated the people. They rushed out of the synagogue and forced Jesus to the edge of a cliff. But it was not his time to die. Jesus simply slipped through the crowd unharmed.

The people of Nazareth had been familiar with Jesus all of his life. They knew his family and which house he grew up in. As a result, they didn't see his true identity. They didn't recognize the Messiah when he was standing in front of them. Their lack of faith limited his miracles and healing ministry in Nazareth (see Matt. 13:58).

In a similar way, our familiarity with Christianity can dull our vision of God and hinder his work in our life. If we find that we're rattling off Scriptures, songs, and platitudes without thinking about their meaning, we need to ask God to give us a renewed sense of wonder at who is standing in front of us.

I keep asking that the God of our Lord Jesus Christ,
the glorious Father, may give you the Spirit of wisdom
and revelation, so that you may know him better.

Ephesians 1:17 NIV

SEPTEMBER

5

The Testimony of an Evil Spirit

Luke 4:31—41

People were amazed at the inherent authority with which Jesus spoke; soon they witnessed his authority over sickness and demons. One day as Jesus taught in the synagogue in Capernaum, a man with an evil spirit began shouting at him. The demon recognized Jesus's true identity and knew that God's Son held the power to destroy demonic forces. "Have you come to destroy us?" the spirit yelled. "I know who you are—the Holy One of God!" (v. 34).

"Keep quiet, and come out of him!" Jesus ordered (v. 35). The demon threw the man down on the floor but came out of his body without harming him. Many of the people there had probably witnessed exorcisms involving strange rituals and incantations. They were amazed that Jesus simply spoke a few words and the evil spirit obeyed him. Later that evening, many people brought their sick loved ones for Jesus to heal. As Jesus laid hands on them, demons came out of many, shouting, "You are the Son of God!" (v. 41).

While the majority of people did not recognize Jesus as the Messiah, demonic spirits knew who he was. They understood his power and obeyed his commands. This shows that it's not enough to simply know the facts about Jesus since even demons know his true identity. In order to have a personal relationship with Jesus, we have to move beyond intellectual acceptance of his deity and receive him as Savior.

The biblical use of the word "believe" implies a personal confidence and trust in Jesus's sacrifice for our sins. As a result, we submit to his authority over us and do our best to live a holy lifestyle. In order to be God's child, we have to believe that Jesus is who he says he is, and then receive the gift of forgiveness that he died to offer us. If we stop at the first step, then we've done nothing more than demonic spirits do.

But as many as received Him, to them He
gave the right to become children of God,
even to those who believe in His name.

John 1:12 NASB

A Shocking Dinner Party

Luke 7:36—50

Simon could not believe what he was seeing. The Pharisee had invited Jesus to his dinner party, but he didn't welcome the presence of that woman with the bad reputation. Yet there she knelt behind the couch where Jesus reclined. As her tears fell on his feet, she dried them off with her hair, constantly kissing them. Then she opened a bottle of expensive perfume and poured it over his feet. *Aha!* Simon thought. *If Jesus really were a prophet, he would know she's a sinful woman and wouldn't let her touch him.*

In answer to Simon's thoughts, Jesus told a parable about two men whose debts to a moneylender were canceled. Jesus asked which man would love his benefactor most, the one who owed him fifty silver coins or the one who owed ten times as much. Simon answered correctly: the one who had the larger debt canceled.

Jesus then contrasted the woman's behavior with that of his self-righteous host. Simon had failed to offer Jesus the common courtesy of providing for his feet to be washed; he didn't extend a kiss of greeting when Jesus entered his house. The woman had realized her sinful condition and lavished Jesus with demonstrations of her love and gratitude for the forgiveness he offered.

Like Simon, we may think of ourselves as good, moral people who love God. It would be better to identify with the sinful woman who showed a deep awareness of how much she had been forgiven. We can't appreciate God's forgiveness until we understand the depth of our sin. Paul reminds us that before we accepted Christ, we were God's enemy and had no hope (see Eph. 2:12). Yet Christ gave his life for us. If we reflect on how much our forgiveness cost God and how little we deserve it, we'll think that no expression of love is too lavish for such a Savior.

> *Once you were separated from God. The evil things you did showed your hostile attitude. But now Christ has brought you back to God by dying in his physical body.*
>
> Colossians 1:21–22

Elevated Status

Luke 8:1–3

During New Testament times, some Jewish men began their day by thanking God they had not been born as a Gentile, a slave, or a woman. Women were not allowed to learn from rabbis; some even taught it would be better to burn the words of the Law than to teach them to a woman in public. In light of such prejudice, Jesus's behavior must have seemed scandalous. As he traveled between cities and villages spreading the Good News about God's kingdom, Jesus allowed a number of women to accompany him and his closest disciples.

This group included Mary, a former social outcast from Magdalene whom Jesus had healed of demon possession. Also present was Joanna, who represented the highest level of society as the wife of one of Herod's palace officials. These and many other women traveled with Jesus and his twelve disciples, financially supporting them out of their own means.

While the culture around him treated women and certain other members of society as inferior, Jesus demonstrated that all people are of equal value in God's eyes. Everyone is welcome to join in the fellowship and service of God's family.

Regardless of cultural prejudices and preferences, we are all on an equal footing. Each one of us was born as a sinner in need of God's saving grace. Yes, there are different roles and distinctions within a family, a church, and a society. Paul gave different advice to slaves and masters, to husbands and wives. But he made it clear that in terms of spiritual position and privilege, no one is superior to another person.

Some people pull a verse out of context and claim that Christianity is degrading to women, or that it condones slavery. In reality, Jesus elevated us all to a new status. By dying to pay the penalty for our sins, he made it possible for anyone to become God's child. What higher status could there be than that?

There are neither Jews nor Greeks, slaves nor free people,
males nor females. You are all the same in Christ Jesus.

Galatians 3:28

The Main Thing

Luke 10:38—42

Martha and Mary both loved Jesus and wanted to serve him wholeheartedly. But when Jesus was a guest in their home, the two sisters focused on different aspects of his visit. As a meticulous hostess, Martha wanted to serve the best meal she could. Her mind was filled with all the details and preparations needed for a successful dinner party. Mary, on the other hand, made the most of the opportunity to simply sit at Jesus's feet and soak up his words. She was oblivious to anything else—until Martha's resentment about the situation boiled over.

"Lord," Martha asked, "don't you care that my sister has left me to do the work all by myself? Tell her to help me" (v. 40). Jesus lovingly corrected Martha for being so distracted by household chores to the point that she could not enjoy his presence. He told her there was only one thing she truly needed to be concerned about. "Mary has made the right choice," Jesus added, "and that one thing will not be taken away from her" (v. 42).

Every day we make the choice of where our focus will be. Will we allow ourselves to get so caught up in the busyness of life that we neglect to spend time with God? Or will we put aside other responsibilities in order to first give him our undivided attention, soaking up his words as we study the Bible, enjoying his presence as we worship him and pray?

Household chores, nurturing our family, career advancement, and service to others are all important, but we don't want to let those things crowd out what matters most. Time spent with Jesus always reaps eternal rewards, and that's a good reason to make him our first priority every day. No matter how long our to-do list is, God calls us to choose the most important thing, as Mary did—the thing that can never be taken away from us.

There is only one thing worth being concerned about.

Luke 10:42 NLT

257

How to Pray

Luke 11:1–13

During his time on earth, Jesus modeled a life of ongoing communication with his Father. He prayed at the time of his baptism and during his forty-day fast that preceded his ministry. Jesus sometimes went off by himself to pray alone, but he also prayed in front of others. He prayed in the garden just before his arrest and on the cross as he died. When one of his disciples asked, "Lord, teach us to pray," Jesus taught them a prayer often referred to as "The Lord's Prayer."

In this model prayer, Jesus began with worship, expressing a desire for God's name and reputation to be honored and revered. The second request centered on the advancement of God's kingdom, demonstrating that prayer should focus on God's interests before our personal wishes. This was followed by a petition for daily provision of physical needs.

The fourth request asked for forgiveness of sins, not for salvation but for daily confession and cleansing. Along with this request is an acknowledgment that since God has forgiven us, we are obligated to forgive others who wrong us. The model prayer ended with a request that Jesus's followers be protected from situations that would lead them into sin.

Jesus then told his disciples a parable to illustrate the importance of being persistent in prayer. Surprised by an unexpected guest, a man wanted to borrow bread from a friend. That friend wouldn't get out of bed until the man pestered him by continuing to knock at his door. In contrast with the friend who was unwilling to help, God delights in meeting his children's needs. Through this parable, Jesus encourages us to keep bringing our requests to God, while trusting that he knows what is best for us. We may not get everything we ask for, but we can be certain that our Father will give us good gifts.

> So I tell you to ask, and you will receive. Search, and you
> will find. Knock, and the door will be opened for you.
>
> Luke 11:9

Parables of Lost Things

Luke 15

The Pharisees and teachers of the religious law felt disgusted by Jesus's association with people they considered to be hopeless sinners. Going beyond the law, they took great pains to avoid anyone or anything that might make them "unclean." Jesus challenged the religious leaders' thinking by telling them three parables that demonstrated God's attitude toward sinners. The first story involved a man who left ninety-nine sheep in the field to go off and search for the missing one. In the second parable, a woman turned her house upside down looking for a lost coin. In both cases, there was great rejoicing and celebration when the lost object was found.

In the third parable, a younger son demanded his rightful inheritance and left his father's house. After squandering his money in wild living, the son hit rock bottom; he found himself longing to eat the food of the pigs he tended. Swallowing his pride, he decided to return home and ask his father to hire him as a servant. The father spotted his son when he was still a long way off, ran out, and welcomed him home with hugs and kisses. Then he ordered his servants to prepare a feast to celebrate the fact that his lost son had been found.

All three parables show how highly God values each individual who doesn't yet know him (although some interpret this parable to represent an errant believer's restoration to fellowship with God). He doesn't merely stand ready to offer forgiveness when a sinner comes to him—he goes out seeking the lost, drawing them to him, and running to meet them.

God wants us to share his concern for those who are outside his family, even for people considered to be "hopeless sinners." We can ask God to give us a heart for the lost, then pray and share our faith as opportunities arise. Then we can rejoice along with heaven whenever a person who has been lost is found through God's amazing grace.

> *[The father said] "My son was dead and has come back to life. He was lost but has been found." Then they began to celebrate.*
>
> Luke 15:24

A Tax Collector Makes Change

Luke 19:1—10

The Romans levied heavy taxes on the nations under their control in order to support their empire. In Palestine these taxes were collected by Jews who agreed to work for Rome, which made them traitors in the eyes of their countrymen. These men were hated all the more because they often grossly overcharged people and pocketed the difference. In Jericho the chief tax collector, Zacchaeus, had made himself rich from the misery of his fellow Jews. But Zacchaeus would soon become a philanthropist.

When Zacchaeus heard that Jesus was passing through his town, he wanted to get a good look at him. Because of his small size, Zacchaeus couldn't see over the heads of the crowd. He ran ahead and climbed up in a sycamore-fig tree. When Jesus came by, he looked up into the tree and called the tax collector by name. "Zacchaeus, I must stay at your house today," Jesus announced (v. 5).

Zacchaeus joyfully welcomed Jesus into his home. During dinner, Zacchaeus vowed that he would give half his possessions to the poor; in addition he would repay anyone he had cheated by four times the amount. Jesus pointed out that this transformation in Zacchaeus indicated he had entered into a right relationship with God.

The Bible doesn't record the full conversation between Jesus and Zacchaeus, but we do know that it led to a change of heart on Zacchaeus's part—which led to a changed life. A person who accepts God's offer of forgiveness and salvation doesn't stay the same. Instead of following our own selfish desires, we do our best to live in a way that pleases God. That might include making needed restitution as Zacchaeus did, changing the way we perform our jobs, or even switching vocations. One thing is for sure: when Jesus calls us by name, we will be a changed person.

> *Because you are children who obey God, don't live the kind of lives you once lived. Once you lived to satisfy your desires because you didn't know any better.*
>
> 1 Peter 1:14

John

Is Jesus Really God?

[Jesus said] "The Father and I are one. . . . The person who has seen me has seen the Father."

John 10:30; 14:9

Among the twelve apostles, Peter, James, and John belonged to an inner circle whom Jesus often drew aside. John seemed to have an especially close relationship with Jesus. During the Last Supper, he reclined next to Jesus. As Jesus hung dying on the cross, he entrusted the care of his mother to John. Leaving behind his nickname "Son of Thunder," John came to refer to himself as "the disciple whom Jesus loved." Sometime late in the first century, this beloved disciple wrote the fourth Gospel, considered by many to be the most profound and powerful.

The book of John provides a rich supplement to the Synoptic Gospels; more than 90 percent of the material is original. Written in a distinctive style, each of the twenty-one chapters depicts an aspect of Jesus's character or work. John skips an account of Jesus's birth; instead he begins with a prologue attesting to his deity. He selects seven of Jesus's miracles, or signs, that proclaim him as the Son of God. While omitting the parables, John includes a series of "I am" statements made by Christ that contain metaphors revealing his identity and his relationship with believers. John's blend of historical narrative and theological interpretation offers what many consider to be the clearest portrayal of Jesus found in the Bible.

John explicitly states his purpose for writing: "so that you will believe that Jesus is the Messiah, the Son of God, and so that you will have life by believing in him" (John 20:31). In fact, the Greek word usually translated "believe" occurs ninety-eight times in the book. John's Gospel is a powerful resource to use in sharing God's offer of salvation and eternal life for those who accept the forgiveness made possible by Jesus's death and resurrection. For believers, reading the book can also strengthen our faith and remind us that the only life worth living is found in a close relationship with the One who was God in the flesh.

The Living Word

John 1:1–18

John didn't begin his Gospel with Jesus's genealogy or an account of his birth; he went back much further than that—even earlier than the "In the beginning" of Genesis 1:1. Before sharing his account of the life, death, and resurrection of Jesus, John launched into a theological discussion of his identity. John affirmed that before Jesus appeared on the earth, he already existed. He was "with God" and he "was God"—two Persons in communion with each other, yet one God.

When John called Jesus "the Word" (*Logos*), he used a term familiar to both Greek and Jewish readers. Greek philosophers applied *logos* to the principle of reason that they believed governed the world and accounted for the orderliness of nature. John gave that impersonal term life by identifying Christ as the Creator and Sustainer of everything that is seen. The Jews used "the Word" as another way of referring to God. John's prologue introduced Jesus as the God-Man who lived on the earth for a while and revealed the Father's glory, similar to the way God's glory temporarily resided in the temple in Old Testament times.

It's fitting that John opened by testifying to Christ's humanity and deity because that truth is the foundation of all that follows in the book. If we can't accept Jesus as God in the flesh, then his miracles and teachings don't have much meaning; neither do his suffering, death, and resurrection. The basis for Christianity and for our personal faith is found in the first chapter of John.

Because Jesus took on human form and came down to earth to live for a while and then die for our sins, we have the choice to be forgiven and have God's Spirit come to live within us. Then, just as Jesus revealed the Father's glory to the world two thousand years ago, he can reveal the Father's glory in our own life.

> *The Word became human and lived among us. We saw*
> *his glory. It was the glory that the Father shares with*
> *his only Son, a glory full of kindness and truth.*
>
> John 1:14

Water into Wine

John 2:1–12

Despite numerous so-called "gospel stories" from sources other than the New Testament, the Bible indicates that Jesus did not perform miracles as a child or young adult. Only John includes the first of Jesus's thirty-five recorded miracles. Jesus's first miracle was witnessed solely by his mother, his early disciples, and some servants. (John later informs us in 21:25 that his book contains only a fraction of what Jesus did during his few short years of ministry; in fact, he says the whole world could not contain the books needed to tell all that Jesus did.)

While attending a wedding in Cana, Mary mentioned to her son that the hosts had run out of wine. This wasn't just embarrassing; to run out of wine during the weeklong wedding feast represented a serious breach of the hospitality code. Although Jesus's response is hard to understand, Mary trusted him to solve the problem. She told the servants to do whatever Jesus instructed them.

Jesus had the servants pour water into six huge stone jars used for ceremonial washing. As the servants dipped the water out, it became fine wine. The master of ceremonies expressed amazement when he tasted it. Hosts customarily served their best wine at the beginning of a celebration and saved the cheap wine for later, when the guests had drunk so much they wouldn't notice the difference. The master of this banquet complimented the groom on saving the best wine for last.

Jesus would later heal incurable diseases, command storms, and even raise the dead. His first miracle, however, was done quietly and behind the scenes. He used his divine power to save a newly married couple from humiliation and to bring joy to a celebration. If we only expect Jesus to work in obvious, dramatic ways, we can miss what he is doing in our own life. He often works quietly behind the scenes to bring us blessing and joy. But first, we have to trust him and follow the advice that Mary gave the servants at a wedding in Cana so long ago.

His mother told the servers, "Do whatever he tells you."

John 2:5

Jesus Does a Little Housecleaning

John 2:13–17

The fact that all Jewish males were expected to attend the annual Passover in Jerusalem made the temple especially crowded during that weeklong celebration. The booths of the merchants and moneychangers in the temple courtyard made the situation worse. The religious leaders allowed their presence because their business helped fund the temple upkeep and because they offered a convenience for those who had traveled from far distances. Foreigners had to pay the temple tax in local currency, which the moneychangers provided for a fee. Out-of-town Jews could also buy the required animals for sacrifices on-site instead of bringing them on their journey.

These services had degenerated into exploitation of the people. The moneychangers charged steep exchange rates and the merchants' prices for sacrificial animals were higher than found elsewhere. Jesus was angered by their dishonesty and greed, and by their presence in the outer courtyard where non-Jews worshiped. Their businesses hindered the very purpose of the temple. Making a whip out of ropes, Jesus drove the people and animals out of the courtyard and turned over the tables. He ordered the merchants and moneychangers to stop making his Father's house a marketplace.

Near the end of his public ministry, Jesus again cleansed the temple. At that time, he accused the merchants of turning the temple into "a gathering place for thieves" (see Luke 19:46).

Jesus never displayed anger over personal insults or wrongs, but he was filled with righteous indignation when people made a mockery of God's house. He saw the actions of the merchants and moneychangers as an insult to God. While uncontrolled rage can lead us into sin and cause much damage, there is a right time to be angry. Our indignation should be directed at sin and injustice, not petty offenses committed against us. When someone mocks or insults God, then it's time to speak up.

Indeed, devotion for your house has consumed me,
and the insults of those who insult you have fallen on me.

Psalm 69:9

A Curious Man

John 3:1–21

Nicodemus was a highly respected teacher and a member of the Sanhedrin, the Jewish governing body. Although the Pharisees generally opposed Jesus, one night Nicodemus went to talk with him one-on-one. Nicodemus politely addressed Jesus as "Rabbi" and acknowledged that his miracles proved God had sent him. Jesus skipped over small talk and began explaining *why* God had sent him. For all his learning and prestige, Nicodemus had a difficult time understanding Jesus's words.

Jesus told Nicodemus that in order to see the kingdom of God, a person must be born from above, or born again. The religious leader asked how an old man could be born a second time. Jesus explained that entrance into the kingdom requires one thing: a spiritual rebirth, which can be accomplished only by the Holy Spirit. Jesus chided Nicodemus for being a well-known teacher to Israel and yet not understanding this transformation. Being thoroughly familiar with the Scriptures, Nicodemus should have connected Jesus's words with Old Testament references to the new covenant when the Spirit would give people new hearts.

Nicodemus may have come to Jesus out of curiosity, but the conversation proved to be life-changing. Later, when the chief priests and Pharisees tried to have Jesus arrested, Nicodemus boldly spoke up for him (see John 7:50–51). After the crucifixion, Nicodemus joined with Joseph of Arimathea, another Sanhedrin member, in arranging for Jesus's burial.

Some people treat their birthday like a big deal, but believers have an even more important anniversary to celebrate: our rebirth. When we placed our faith in Jesus as our Savior and Lord, God placed his Spirit within us. At that moment, we were born a second time, as God's child and a brand-new creation. Our first birthday is important because we received the gift of life; our second, spiritual birthday is even greater because we accepted God's gift of eternal life.

Jesus replied to Nicodemus, "I can guarantee
this truth: No one can see the kingdom of
God without being born from above."

John 3:3

A Thirsty Woman

John 4:1–42

She was a Samaritan, a race despised by Jews. Her ancestors came from intermarriage between Jews who remained in the northern kingdom after it fell and foreigners brought in by the Assyrians. Her people had built their own temple on Mount Gerizim where they worshiped; they rejected all of the Old Testament except the Pentateuch. Most Jews avoided passing through Samaria, but Jesus went out of his way to have a conversation with this woman who was an outcast even among her own people.

She felt shocked when the Jewish man waiting at Jacob's well asked her—a woman, a stranger, and a Samaritan—for a drink. Jesus's comment about water that keeps a person from ever thirsting again intrigued her. But when he exposed the details of her immoral lifestyle, the woman grew uncomfortable and changed the subject to a popular theological debate.

As Jesus explained that God must be worshiped in spirit and truth, the woman expressed a longing for the Messiah who would explain all things. Then Jesus did something unusual—he openly declared his identity. The Samaritan woman rushed off to tell people about the discovery she'd made. She left her water jar behind; she had discovered something much more satisfying.

The human soul thirsts and hungers for a relationship with its Creator. That longing will never be truly satisfied until we know him personally through Jesus Christ. Once we accept the living water Jesus offers us, we still need to drink deeply of him every day—through prayer, worship, and Bible study. We also need to take every opportunity to share what Jesus gives with the people around us. Every day we're surrounded by thirsty people who need to find the only One who can quench their thirst.

> *[Jesus said] "But those who drink the water that*
> *I will give them will never become thirsty again.*
> *In fact, the water I will give them will become in*
> *them a spring that gushes up to eternal life."*
>
> John 4:14

Caught in the Act

John 8:3—11

The woman with the disheveled hair and clothes wasn't the only one they had trapped—or so the scribes and Pharisees thought. They brought the woman who had been caught in the act of adultery and stood her in front of the crowd. Reminding Jesus of the penalty for such sin, they challenged him, "What do you say?" (v. 5). The religious leaders knew that if Jesus argued for letting the woman go free, he would be contradicting the law of Moses. But if he advocated stoning the woman to death as the law required, he would lose popularity with some people. Also, the leaders could report him to the Romans, who didn't allow the Jews to carry out executions.

Jesus seemed to ignore their question, stooping down to write on the ground with his finger. When they pestered him for an answer, Jesus stood up. "The person who is sinless should be the first to throw a stone at her," he told them (v. 7). Then he bent down and continued to write on the ground. One by one, the scribes and Pharisees slunk away, beginning with the older men. Finally, Jesus straightened up and asked the woman, "Where did they go? Has anyone condemned you?" Relieved, she answered, "No one, sir." Jesus responded, "I don't condemn you either" (vv. 10–11).

We often focus on this statement of Jesus without giving as much thought to his final words: "Go! From now on, don't sin" (v. 11). When we repent and confess something wrong that we've done, God's forgiveness lifts a heavy burden of guilt and shame from our spirit. But as recipients of his mercy and grace, we have a responsibility to take sin seriously.

God doesn't forgive us to simply let us off the hook; he wants us to learn from our moral failures and depend on his power to help us stand strong against future temptation. Jesus's words remind us that even as God forgives us for a sin we've committed, he urges us to turn away from it and not do it anymore.

> *Jesus said, "I don't condemn you either.*
> *Go! From now on don't sin."*
>
> John 8:11

The One and Only

John 6:35; 8:12; 10:7, 9, 11, 14; 14:6; 15:1

Jesus used a series of "I am" statements to help explain his identity and his mission on earth. For the most part, these drew from everyday images and familiar biblical allusions. After reminding his listeners about the manna that rained down from heaven to feed the Israelites in the desert, Jesus called himself the bread of life. He explained that anyone who comes to him will never get hungry and will live forever.

During the Feast of Tabernacles, while the large lamps were being lit, Jesus told the Pharisees, "I am the light of the world. Whoever follows me will have a life filled with light and will never live in the dark" (8:12).

Later, Jesus described himself as the gate for the sheep and as the good shepherd. While others enter the sheep pen by some other way to steal and kill, Jesus has the right to enter through the gate. His sheep respond to his voice and find security and safety. In contrast to a hired hand who runs away at the first signs of danger, the good shepherd willingly lays down his life to protect his sheep. Jesus also called himself the true vine. Genuine believers are like branches. As long as we stay connected to Christ, our life will produce fruit.

These analogies underscore another of Jesus's "I am" statements: "I am the way, the truth, and the life. No one goes to the Father except through me" (14:6). Jesus made it clear that there is only one way to have access to God and receive salvation. We may try to find spiritual nourishment elsewhere, but Christ is the only bread of life. We can try to have a fruitful life, but without being connected to the true vine, we'll wither. We may follow some other shepherd, but only the good shepherd gave his life for us. The only way to God is through his one and only Son; any other path will lead us to a dead end.

No one has ever seen God, but God the One and Only,
who is at the Father's side, has made him known.

John 1:18 NIV

"I Am"

John 8:25–59; 10:22–39

If there had been any doubt about what Jesus meant in his other "I am" revelations, the confusion was cleared up in the conversations recorded in John 8 and 10. The Jews understood exactly what Jesus was saying, and they wanted to kill him for it. As Jesus taught in the temple courtyard, the religious leaders challenged his earlier statements about himself. In the exchange that followed, Jesus told the Pharisees that whoever obeyed his words would never die.

At this remark, the Jews accused Jesus of being demon possessed. Abraham and the prophets had died; did Jesus think he was greater than them? Jesus told the Jews that their ancestor Abraham had joyfully looked forward to Jesus's day. They demanded to know how Jesus could possibly have seen Abraham, who had lived two thousand years earlier. His answer stunned them: "Before Abraham was ever born, I am" (8:58).

These Jews were familiar with the passage in Exodus where God spoke with Moses from a burning bush. When Moses asked whom he should say had sent him to the Israelites, God answered, "I Am Who I Am" (3:14). He instructed Moses to say that "I Am" had sent him. Jesus used the equivalent of that Hebrew expression, applying God's holy name to himself. The Jews picked up stones to carry out the death penalty prescribed in Leviticus 24:16 for anyone blaspheming and claiming to be God.

Anyone familiar with the Bible cannot ignore Jesus's claims of deity. Such statements demand a response from us. We can react like the unbelieving Jews and be stunned by the audacity of what we see as outlandish assertions. Or we can take Jesus at his word and worship him as the eternal God, the same One who spoke from a burning bush to Moses and who later taught in the temple courts. While Abraham looked ahead to Jesus's day with joy, we can look backward and rejoice that "I Am" came to earth to die for our sins.

Jesus told them, "I can guarantee this truth:
Before Abraham was ever born, I am."

John 8:58

The Ultimate Healing

John 11:1–44

Martha and Mary knew that Jesus loved their brother; they also knew he had the power to heal him. The sisters sent Jesus a message as soon as Lazarus grew ill. But Jesus waited two days before setting out for Bethany, informing his disciples that Lazarus had already died. By the time Jesus arrived, Lazarus had been in the tomb for four days. The sisters were surrounded by Jews who had come to mourn with and comfort them.

When Jesus told Martha that her brother would live again, she assumed that he referred to the resurrection at the end of time. Jesus told her that anyone who believed in him would live even if they died, but Martha could not grasp his full meaning. As Jesus saw Mary and the other mourners, their grief and the horror of death deeply moved him. He wept with them.

Then Jesus ordered the stone rolled away from the tomb. Martha protested, knowing that the body would have begun decomposing. After the stone was moved, Jesus said a prayer of thanksgiving and shouted in a loud voice, "Lazarus, come out!" The dead man immediately stepped out of the cave; Jesus ordered his burial cloths to be removed.

Jesus could have healed Lazarus from a distance; he could have kept his beloved friend from getting sick in the first place. He could have promptly responded to the sisters' message and spared them the grief of four days of mourning. But God had a purpose in his timing. The miracle displayed Jesus's power, strengthened the disciples' faith, and led to many Jews believing in him.

God doesn't always heal or restore someone's health when we ask him. But he wants us to trust that he has a purpose and to remember that if our loved one knows him, they have left a sinful world and joyfully entered into his presence. And whenever we read John 8, we can find comfort knowing that God is weeping along with us as we mourn.

*We don't want you to grieve like other
people who have no hope.*

1 Thessalonians 4:13

·

The Danger of Self-Confidence

John 12:12—50; 13:21—38

The news about Jesus raising Lazarus from the dead spread quickly. The huge crowd that was gathered in Jerusalem for Passover week met Jesus as he neared the city and hailed him as the Messiah. Surely this would be the time when he would use his powers to free their nation from Roman rule and set up his eternal kingdom. Waving palm branches, the people praised him and shouted "*Hosanna!*" (Hebrew for "Save" or "Save now"). But Jesus knew what lay ahead; later that day, he told his disciples that he felt deeply troubled (12:27). A few days later, he made remarks that deeply troubled his disciples.

As Jesus shared the Passover meal with the twelve disciples, he announced that one of them would soon betray him. Such a concept was unthinkable in the disciples' minds. How could someone in their close-knit group be a traitor? Later in the conversation, Peter proclaimed, "Lord, I'll give my life for you" (13:37). Jesus countered by telling Peter that before the night ended, he would deny knowing Jesus three times. The disciples were shocked by Jesus's predictions. They had no idea that within hours, Judas would betray Jesus to the Roman authorities with a kiss, the other eleven would desert their Master, and Peter would repeatedly lie about knowing Jesus in order to protect himself.

We may think we have a good understanding of our strengths and weaknesses; we may be confident of our ability to resist certain temptations. But in reality, we have no idea how we will react to situations we've never faced before. Trusting in our own moral or spiritual strength can be an extremely dangerous attitude. Whenever we think we're safe from Satan's attacks, that's when we're especially vulnerable to his deceptions and temptations. Even the most mature believers can fall into sin at any moment if they let down their guard. We're only safe when we remember how much we depend on God's power to help us stand.

> So, people who think they are standing firmly
> should be careful that they don't fall.
>
> 1 Corinthians 10:12

Extreme Obedience

John 18:1—19:16

After the Passover meal ended, Jesus led his disciples into a garden. The quietness was soon broken by a large crowd of Roman soldiers and temple guards carrying torches and weapons, led by Judas, who had left the group after Jesus had predicted his betrayal. Jesus's arrest triggered a series of horrifying events over the next several hours. After being bound, Jesus was shuttled back and forth between Jewish and Roman authorities for hearings and trials. In the process, he endured false accusations, humiliation, and cruel physical abuse. In the end, Roman soldiers nailed Jesus to a cross to suffer one of the most painful deaths imaginable.

With hosts of angels at his beck and call, Jesus could have put a stop to his torment at any moment. He knew that God had put everything under his control (see John 13:3), but he also knew that events were unfolding according to God's plan. As Jesus prayed just before his arrest, he expressed a desire to be spared the agony that lay ahead; yet his death was a necessary part of God's plan to redeem the human race from sin. Jesus surrendered to that plan, saying, "However, your will must be done, not mine" (see Luke 22:42).

Earlier in his ministry, Jesus had predicted his death, stressing that no one would take his life from him; he would give it up of his own free will (see John 10:18). His sacrifice represents the ultimate act of obedience to God's will. With such an example before us, how can we not be ashamed when we struggle with obeying even the simplest commands? Following God's will often involves sacrificing our own desires and plans, our material wealth, or our personal comfort. When we look at the point where Christ's obedience took him, surely we can find encouragement to obey whatever God calls us to do.

> *Have the same attitude that Christ Jesus had. . . .*
> *He humbled himself by becoming*
> *obedient to the point of death,*
> *death on a cross.*
>
> Philippians 2:5, 8

SEPTEMBER

24

Extreme Love

John 19:17–37

Even as his time of suffering and death drew near, Jesus kept his focus on ministering to others. In the room where he celebrated the Passover meal with his disciples, Jesus took on the role of a servant and washed his disciples' feet. He tried to prepare his disciples for his death and for the troubles they would soon face. Although Jesus felt deeply troubled, he offered them comfort, promising to send the Holy Spirit in his place. He assured the disciples that they would be together with him again one day. Just before his arrest, Jesus prayed not only for himself, but for his disciples and all who would follow him in the future.

Even while dying on the cross, Jesus focused on the needs of others—even to the point of asking God to forgive those who were killing him. One of the criminals being crucified beside him acknowledged Jesus as the Messiah and asked for forgiveness. Jesus assured him they would be in Paradise together that very day (see Luke 23:39–43). As he looked down and saw his grieving mother nearby, Jesus entrusted Mary's care and provision into the hands of John, who stood with her.

Jesus submitted himself to the most degrading and excruciatingly painful form of execution known at that time so we would not have to pay the penalty for our sin. His sacrifice represents the ultimate act of love. One of his final instructions was for his followers to love each other as he had loved them. How can we hope to meet such a standard when our natural instinct is to think of ourselves first?

The only way to win the struggle with our selfish human nature is to allow God's Spirit to control how we respond to others. When we remember that Jesus spent his final hours on earth putting others' needs ahead of his own, we can find encouragement to love those around us in a more Christlike way.

> *[Jesus said] "Love each other as I have loved you.*
> *This is what I'm commanding you to do."*
>
> John 15:12

An Empty Tomb

John 20:1—21:14

All four Gospel writers focus on different details surrounding the discovery of the empty tomb, but each one testifies to the shock that Jesus's followers felt at finding his body gone. The first to hear the news were Mary Magdalene and the other women who had gone early in the morning to anoint Jesus's body with spices. When they reported to the disciples that an angel had told them Jesus had risen, Peter and John raced to the grave. The sight of the burial clothes lying as though the body within had disappeared perplexed them. When the others left, Mary Magdalene stayed behind at the tomb, crying. Suddenly Jesus stood before her. Mary mistook him for the gardener until he spoke her name.

After Jesus died, the Jewish leaders had asked for Roman soldiers to guard the tomb in order to prevent Jesus's disciples from stealing his body and deceiving the people. After Jesus rose, these soldiers reported what they had witnessed to the chief priests, who bribed them to say that the disciples had indeed taken the body while the guards slept. Even as the Jewish leaders tried to spread this story, Jesus appeared to his followers many times over the next forty days.

In 1 Corinthians 15 Paul wrote that one appearance was witnessed by more than five hundred believers, most of whom were still living at the time of his writing. He went on to explain how Jesus's bodily resurrection forms the basis of the Christian faith. If Jesus didn't rise from the dead, then our faith has no meaning and we have no hope of life after death.

Jesus's resurrection is a historical fact witnessed by many people who went on to lay down their lives for their belief in his deity. The cross is the usual symbol of our faith, but the empty tomb proves that God accepted Jesus's perfect sacrifice for the world's sins. It also reminds us that if we believe in him, we will also rise from the dead one day.

But Christ has indeed been raised from the dead,
the firstfruits of those who have fallen asleep.

1 Corinthians 15:20 NIV

Restoration

John 21

Even after seeing that Jesus had risen from the dead, Peter probably felt like a miserable failure. He'd been so sure of himself when he vowed to stand by Jesus even to the point of death. Then, only hours later he had lied about even knowing Jesus, just to protect himself. Peter wondered what his future held, until a nighttime fishing trip led to an encounter with Jesus that changed his life. After breakfast on the beach, Jesus began asking Peter if he loved him. Peter had denied Jesus three times; Jesus gave him three chances to affirm his love and commitment. With each response, Jesus urged Peter to feed and take care of his sheep. Through this simple conversation, Jesus reinstated Peter and helped prepare him for his role as an early leader of the church.

Like Peter, Judas realized that he had made a terrible mistake. The Bible doesn't explain what Judas expected would happen when he betrayed Jesus, but Matthew records his remorse over the outcome. When Judas saw that Jesus had been condemned, he went back to the chief priests and tried to return the money they had paid him. Judas admitted that he had betrayed an innocent man. The priests retorted, "What do we care? That's your problem." Overcome by guilt, Judas threw the silver into the temple, went out, and hanged himself (see Matt. 27:1–5).

Both of these men deeply regretted their actions, but Judas stopped short of repentance. He could have turned to God and received forgiveness and reconciliation; instead, his life ended tragically. By accepting the forgiveness that Jesus offered, Peter was restored to full fellowship and became a stronger leader because of his past mistakes. Their stories remind us of the choice we face whenever we realize that we have sinned. We can allow our regret and guilt to overwhelm us, creating a barrier between us and God. Or we can repent of our actions and confess them to the One who is waiting to offer forgiveness and restoration.

> *The LORD is compassionate, merciful, patient,*
> *and always ready to forgive.*
>
> Psalm 103:8

Acts

The Birth of the Church

> But you will receive power when the Holy Spirit comes to you. Then you will be
> my witnesses to testify about me in Jerusalem, throughout Judea and Samaria,
> and to the ends of the earth.
>
> Acts 1:8

Acts is Luke's sequel to his Gospel and provides us with the only eyewitness account of the church's beginning and early growth. Although not a comprehensive history, the book highlights important events during the first thirty years of the Christian faith, after Jesus returned to heaven. The last words that Christ spoke to his followers, known as "the Great Commission," outline the content of Acts. According to God's plan, the disciples proclaimed the good news about the risen Savior first to the Jews in Jerusalem. The majority of Jews rejected the gospel, but it spread throughout Judea and Samaria, and eventually to the remotest corners of the Roman Empire.

Most scholars believe that Luke wrote Acts around AD 62–63 since the narrative ends abruptly with Paul's imprisonment in Rome. The Greek physician demonstrated his usual careful investigation and attention to detail, citing eighty geographical locations and referring to more than a hundred people by name. As Paul's traveling companion, Luke witnessed firsthand many of the events; he would have been able to interview Peter and John for other events.

Traditionally called "The Acts of the Apostles," the first twelve chapters focus on Peter's ministry, while the rest of the book recounts Paul's missionary journeys. One unique feature of Acts is its inclusion of dozens of speeches and sermons in its twenty-eight chapters. Interspersed with these are narratives that read like adventure stories, along with occasional progress reports as the newly birthed church grows and Christ's faithful followers carry the gospel to "the ends of the earth."

Acts gives us more than an exciting look at how God's church was born. As we watch how first-century believers took every opportunity to share the gospel even in the face of suffering and persecution, we can find encouragement to do the same in our own little corner of the earth.

Jesus Goes Up

Acts 1:1–11

During the forty days after Jesus's resurrection, he showed his disciples undeniable proof that he was physically alive. Jesus also spent time teaching them more about the kingdom of God. During one of these gatherings on the Mount of Olives, he instructed his disciples to stay in Jerusalem until they received the gift the Father had promised to send. Jesus explained that in a few days they would be baptized with the Holy Spirit. Connecting this idea to Old Testament promises, the disciples asked Jesus if the time for Israel's restoration had come.

Jesus explained that the disciples did not need to be concerned about dates God had set for future events, but should instead focus on the assignment they had been given. This band of apostles would be Christ's witnesses to the world after they had received the supernatural power of the Holy Spirit. After Jesus spoke these words, he began rising toward heaven. The apostles kept staring upward even after Jesus left their sight. Suddenly two angels in human form appeared and asked, "Why are you standing here looking at the sky?" They assured the apostles that Jesus would one day return to the earth in the same way he had departed.

As Jesus prayed on the night of his arrest, he affirmed that he had glorified the Father by finishing the work God had given him to do. After he returned to heaven, his apostles still had work to do: spreading the gospel throughout the world. That assignment is still ongoing and each believer today has an important role to play. Jesus doesn't want us standing around "staring up at the sky." He wants us to look around and see the people nearby who need to hear the gospel. We have the same commission as the apostles, and we have the same supernatural power to carry out that work until Jesus returns.

I thank Christ Jesus our Lord that he has
trusted me and has appointed me to do his
work with the strength he has given me.

1 Timothy 1:12

The Holy Spirit Comes Down

Acts 2:1–40

The Old Testament includes examples of God's Spirit temporarily coming upon people to empower them to utter prophecies or perform specific tasks. Jesus knew that once he returned to heaven, the role of the Holy Spirit would change. The night before his crucifixion, Jesus prepared his closest followers. Jesus told the troubled disciples that it was actually a good thing that he was going away, because then God would send another Helper who would be with them forever. This Helper would guide them into the full truth and help them understand Jesus's words (see John 16:5–15).

Ten days after Jesus ascended into heaven, all the believers were gathered together. Suddenly the sound of a violent, rushing wind filled the house. Something that looked like tongues of fire settled on each believer, giving them the power to speak in other languages. Jews from various nations, who had come to Jerusalem to celebrate Pentecost, were dumbfounded to hear their native tongues spoken by Jews from Galilee. Peter stood up and, quoting Joel 2:28–32, explained that the crowd had just witnessed the fulfillment of prophecies that God would pour out his Spirit. After Peter also explained how Jesus had fulfilled prophecies about the Messiah, three thousand people came to faith in Christ.

Christians have differing viewpoints on the Holy Spirit, but Paul unequivocally stated that all believers have God's Spirit living inside them. If we allow the Holy Spirit to control us instead of our corrupt human nature, he will give us supernatural power to carry out the work God has planned for us to do. Just a few weeks before Pentecost, Jesus's disciples had deserted their master and cowered in fear behind locked doors. The Holy Spirit transformed them into fearless witnesses for Christ. That same Spirit wants to transform us so that we, like those first-century believers, can change the world around us.

> *But if God's Spirit lives in you, you are under the control*
> *of your spiritual nature, not your corrupt nature.*
> *Whoever doesn't have the Spirit of*
> *Christ doesn't belong to him.*

> Romans 8:9

Peter and John Get in Trouble

Acts 3:1—4:31

When Peter and John passed a lame beggar at the temple gate, Peter healed him in the name of Jesus Christ of Nazareth. A crowd gathered as people rushed over to get a look at the man who had been lame since birth. Peter seized the opportunity to preach a sermon, giving credit for the healing to Jesus's power. He went on to explain how Jesus's life and death had fulfilled prophecies about the Messiah. Peter's message also caught the attention of some priests and Sadducees. After being arrested by the temple guards, he and John spent the night in jail.

The next morning, the Sanhedrin summoned them for questioning. Filled with the Holy Spirit, Peter put the council on the defensive by proclaiming that they had crucified the only One who can save people from sin. The rulers were astonished that uneducated fishermen could speak so powerfully. Since the council could not deny the miracle, they threatened Peter and John and ordered them to stop speaking about Jesus.

Peter and John asked the Sanhedrin if they thought it would be better to obey them instead of God. After their release, Peter and John joined the other apostles in prayer. They asked God to demonstrate his power and allow them to speak in his name even more boldly. God's affirmative answer caused the meeting place to shake.

Whenever we talk about Jesus, we can expect to get some negative reactions. But we can't let embarrassment or fear of rejection keep us from obeying God's command to share his message of love and forgiveness. Like the apostles, we can ask God to show his power through us and help us speak boldly for him. We can trust God to give us the right words to say, as Jesus promised the apostles in Matthew 10:19. And we can meditate on all that God has done for us. Then we will have plenty to talk about.

We cannot stop talking about what we've seen and heard.

Acts 4:20

Liar, Liar

Acts 4:32—5:11

The early church attracted attention because of their unity and their generosity in sharing with each other. No one suffered from poverty, because from time to time members would voluntarily sell property or possessions and bring money to the apostles, who would then distribute it among the needy. When a respected leader named Barnabas sold his land and turned the money over to the apostles, a husband and wife came up with a plan to look just as generous. Ananias and Sapphira sold a piece of property and pretended to donate all the proceeds to the church, but they secretly held back a portion of the money for their personal use.

Peter confronted Ananias and accused him of letting Satan make him lie to the Holy Spirit and keep some of the money. Peter pointed out there had been no need for the deception, since Ananias had the right to use the money from his property as he wished. When Peter told Ananias he had lied to God, Ananias dropped dead. A few hours later, Sapphira arrived and Peter questioned her about the price for the land. Sapphira also lied, and Peter asked how she and her husband could agree to test the Lord's Spirit. She also dropped dead and was buried beside her husband.

God may have dealt harshly with this couple to provide an example for the developing church, and to protect the believers' unity and witness to the world. He doesn't always judge lying so severely, which is fortunate for us since lying is so ingrained in our culture. Even if we avoid telling outright falsehoods, we can still lie by the way we present or withhold certain information; sometimes we allow our behavior to deceive others.

When we're dishonest in our speech or actions, we are being guided by Satan, whom the Bible calls "the father of lies" (see John 8:44). If we allow the Holy Spirit to keep us free from lies and deception, God will find us delightful instead of disgusting.

> *Lips that lie are disgusting to the LORD,*
> *but honest people are his delight.*
>
> Proverbs 12:22

Joy from a Beating

Acts 5:12—42

Jesus had promised that his apostles would be given divine power to heal the sick and afflicted and to force demons out of people (see Mark 16:17–18). God's Spirit worked so powerfully through these early believers that the church grew at a phenomenal rate. Everyone spoke highly of them—except for the religious leaders. Out of jealousy, the chief priest and the Sadducees arrested the apostles and threw them in jail. That night, an angel led the apostles out of the prison and told them to keep preaching in the temple courtyard.

The next morning, authorities discovered that the locked and guarded cells were empty and learned that the apostles were again speaking at the temple. The Sanhedrin wanted to sentence the apostles to death until Gamaliel, a respected leader, suggested that they wait and see if this "movement" would fizzle out as others had done. The council took his advice and let the apostles go after beating them and again ordering them to stop talking about Jesus. The apostles left bloodied and bruised, but rejoiced that they'd been considered worthy to suffer for Jesus's name.

It's hard to think of false accusations, unjust punishment, and persecution as being privileges. But the Bible warns us to expect such treatment from a world that treated Jesus the same way. It also reminds us that God has special blessings in store for those who are mistreated for their commitment to Christ. When we identify with Jesus's suffering, we are drawn closer to him as he gives us strength to endure. Our life becomes a powerful witness for him as others watch our actions. And we can look forward to a great reward someday. It truly is an honor to be dishonored for being a Christian.

> *Blessed are you when people hate you, avoid you,*
> *insult you, and slander you*
> *because you are committed to the Son of Man.*
> *Rejoice then, and be very happy!*
> *You have a great reward in heaven.*
>
> Luke 6:22–23

The First Martyr

Acts 6:8—7:60

As the church increased in size, the sharing of provisions required more organization. Stephen was one of seven well-respected men chosen to oversee the daily food distribution to the widows. Besides serving as an administrator, Stephen did amazing miracles and signs among the people. He also spoke about the gospel with power from the Holy Spirit. His greatest speech, however, prompted his execution.

Members of a particular synagogue argued with Stephen but were no match for his God-given wisdom. So they slandered him and bribed witnesses to lie about him before the Sanhedrin. Stephen's enemies accused him of blasphemy and of speaking against Moses's teachings. Before Stephen responded, all seventy-one members of the council were awestruck at the angelic look on his face, which glowed with glory as Moses's had when he communed with God.

Instead of defending himself, Stephen summarized the Jews' history and cited Scriptures to prove that they had killed the Messiah. He ended by accusing his accusers of failing to obey Moses's teachings. Stephen looked toward heaven and exclaimed that he saw Jesus at God's right hand. Infuriated, his listeners dragged him out of the city and stoned him. Stephen died with a prayer of forgiveness for his killers on his lips.

At first glance, some people might see Stephen's death as a senseless waste. He served God in powerful ways yet his life and ministry were cut short. But his death triggered persecution against Christians that led to the gospel being spread beyond Jerusalem. It also had a lasting impact on a man who would become one of the greatest witnesses for the gospel the world has ever known: the apostle Paul. Whether God calls us to give up our time, our wealth, or our life, it won't be a waste. And we can be sure that if we speak words given to us by the Holy Spirit as Stephen did, they will have a lasting impact.

[My word] will not return to Me empty,
Without accomplishing what I desire,
And without succeeding in the matter for which I sent it.

Isaiah 55:11 NASB

Philip Gets Around

Acts 8:26—40

Stephen's martyrdom triggered persecution that forced many believers to leave Jerusalem. Philip (a Grecian Jew, not the apostle) went to Samaria, where he accompanied his proclamation of the Messiah with miraculous healings and signs. Crowds responded to the good news and two apostles traveled to Samaria to sanction Philip's ministry there. But soon an angel commanded Philip to go down a different road—the desert highway that led to Gaza.

Traveling that same road was a high-ranking Ethiopian official on his way home after worshiping in Jerusalem. God's Spirit instructed Philip to stay close to the man's chariot. When Philip heard the Ethiopian reading from the book of Isaiah, he asked, "Do you understand what you're reading?" (v. 30). The official welcomed Philip into his chariot. Having just read Isaiah 53:7–8, he asked Philip if those verses referred to Isaiah or to someone else.

Philip seized the opportunity to explain how the passage identified Jesus as the Savior of the world. The Ethiopian official believed the gospel message and asked to be baptized as the chariot passed by a watering place in the desert. As soon as they stepped out of the water, God's Spirit whisked Philip away. The official went on his way rejoicing. Philip found himself at Azotus, an ancient Philistine capital. From there he traveled to Caesarea, preaching the gospel along the way.

As Philip followed the Spirit's leading, God put him exactly where he was needed. The Ethiopian "just happened" to be struggling with a key messianic passage. The chariot "just happened" to be passing by water at the right time. This incident helped the gospel spread to the ends of the earth. In a similar way, God may use us to explain a Bible passage, to witness a person's decision to accept Jesus as Savior, or to help prepare someone to receive him at a later date. If we're willing, we'll find ourselves in the right place at the right time to help with God's harvest.

> *[Jesus said] "I'm telling you to look and see*
> *that the fields are ready to be harvested."*
>
> John 4:35

Saul Sees the Light

Acts 8:1–3; 9:1–21

The young man who guarded the cloaks of Stephen's executioners turned out to be a key player in the persecution against believers. Saul set out to destroy the church, dragging men and women out of their homes and throwing them into prison. He had such hatred for the church that he obtained authorization from the high priest to track down believers in Damascus, a six-day journey by foot. On the way, however, Saul had a change of heart.

Just outside the city, a brilliant light suddenly flashed around Saul, causing him to fall to the ground. He heard a voice call his name and say, "Why are you persecuting me?" In response Saul asked, "Who are you?" The voice answered, "I'm Jesus, the one you're persecuting" (9:4–5). Jesus commanded Saul to go into Damascus to await further instructions. Unable to see, Saul had to be guided into the city, where he fasted and prayed for three days.

The Lord then appeared in a vision to a believer named Ananias, telling him to find Saul and place his hands on him to restore his sight. Knowing Saul's reputation, Ananias protested—until God assured him that Saul was his chosen instrument. After regaining his sight, Saul became such a powerful witness for Christ that the Jews in Damascus tried to murder this person who formerly wanted to kill Christians.

We may not have had a "blinding light" conversion experience as Saul did, but that doesn't mean we can't shine for Christ. Whether God reveals himself to us in a dramatic way or we quietly come to faith in Jesus, our life will bear witness that we have been chosen by him. Like Saul, we will find that God has changed our desires, our attitudes, and our actions in such a way that those around us can't help but notice. People may refuse to listen to our words, but a transformed life is hard to argue with.

You will shine like stars among them in the world
as you hold firmly to the word of life.

Philippians 2:15–16

Barnabas, the Encourager

Acts 9:22–31

Three years after his conversion, Saul went to Jerusalem and tried to join the apostles there (see Gal. 1:17–19). Remembering his former violence against Christians, the believers in that city naturally felt skeptical and suspicious. How could they trust this man who had been such a zealous enemy of the church? For all they knew, Saul could be putting on an act in order to trap and capture more believers. The apostles were too afraid of Saul to believe that he had truly become a follower of Jesus.

The apostles' attitude changed when another believer interceded on behalf of Saul. Joseph was a Jewish convert from the island of Cyprus whom the Jerusalem Christians had nicknamed Barnabas, or "Son of Encouragement." He brought Saul to the apostles and explained how Saul had seen the Lord Jesus on the road to Damascus and heard his voice. Barnabas also affirmed how boldly Saul had spoken for Jesus in that city.

Barnabas's testimony convinced the apostles that Saul had indeed become a believer, and they accepted him into their group. Saul traveled with the apostles throughout Jerusalem, fearlessly speaking and teaching about Jesus. Barnabas's willingness to speak up for Saul and connect him with other believers played a crucial role in the spread of the gospel and development of the early church.

If we look around us, we will likely find someone who needs a Barnabas to come alongside and offer encouragement. A new believer might be looking for someone to mentor them and help them become grounded in their faith. A Christian who is new to the area would probably welcome help in getting connected with other believers and spiritual resources. Or we may find a case similar to Saul's, where our intervention could help clear up serious misunderstandings. Everyone needs encouragement from time to time; if we're alert to opportunities, we can all be a Barnabas to somebody.

*Then Barnabas took an interest in Saul
and brought him to the apostles.*

Acts 9:27

Peter Dreams of Food

Acts 10

Cornelius was a Roman centurion who worshiped Israel's God. He gave generously to the poor and lived a godly life filled with prayer—but he didn't know about Christ. Since Cornelius needed to hear the gospel, God had an angel instruct him to send for Peter, who was staying in Joppa. Cornelius explained his vision to two of his servants and a military aide, then sent them on the thirty-three-mile journey. In the meantime, God did a little preparation work with Peter.

The next day, Peter was praying on the roof and became hungry. In a vision, he saw a large sheet full of animals, reptiles, and birds being lowered to the ground. A voice commanded him to kill and eat them. Peter argued that he couldn't do that; he had never eaten anything unclean in his life. God rebuked him, "Don't say that the things which God has made clean are impure" (v. 15). The same vision was repeated two more times.

As Peter puzzled over the dream's meaning, the Holy Spirit instructed him to go with the men who were downstairs looking for him. Peter traveled to Cornelius's house, despite his Jewish bias that considered Gentiles unclean. As he shared the news about Jesus, his eager audience believed and received the Holy Spirit. Previously, the Jewish-Gentile conflict had hindered the spread of the gospel; that barrier had now been broken.

We may tend to view certain nations, races, or groups of people as outside of God's reach. Maybe our neighbor, co-worker, or friend practices a religion that is so far removed from Christianity it seems hopeless to attempt to witness to them. God desires to see everyone come to faith in Christ. If someone is seeking him, he will go to any lengths to get the gospel to that person. We might be the one God wants to send, after we overcome the barrier of our prejudice and bias.

> *Now I understand that God doesn't play favorites.*
> *Rather, whoever respects God and does what is*
> *right is acceptable to him in any nation.*
>
> Acts 10:34–35

Too Good to Be True

Acts 12:1–19

During the persecution against the church in Jerusalem, King Herod executed the apostle James. Since this pleased the Jews, Herod threw Peter in a heavily guarded prison cell, planning to bring charges against him after Passover. Herod must have known about Peter's earlier escape; the night before his trial, Peter was sleeping between two Roman soldiers, his hands bound with chains. Two other soldiers guarded the door. Suddenly, bright light filled the cell and an angel woke Peter. The chains fell from his hands. Peter followed the angel in a daze until he found himself alone on the street.

When he realized what had happened, Peter went to a house that served as a gathering place for Christians. Many believers were there earnestly praying on Peter's behalf. When a servant named Rhoda responded to the knock on the door, she recognized Peter's voice. But she was so overjoyed that she rushed off to tell the good news without first opening the door to let him in.

The other people told Rhoda she was crazy; when she insisted, they said it must be his angel. When Peter kept knocking, the believers opened the door and were shocked to see him standing there. Peter told them of his supernatural escape and urged them to share the news with the other believers.

The people at the house couldn't believe that Peter was at the door—even though they had most likely been praying that God would deliver him from prison as he had done before. Like those early believers, we may be shocked when God performs a miracle, even though we know that nothing is impossible for him. Jesus taught that we should pray with faith, believing we've already received what we ask for. As long as we pray with the right motives and according to God's will, nothing is too good to be true.

> *That's why I tell you to have faith that you have already received whatever you pray for, and it will be yours.*
>
> Mark 11:24

New Directions

Acts 13

Acts 13 represents a turning point in Luke's narrative, in Saul's life, and in the spread of the gospel. Saul replaces Peter as the central figure in the book. While Jerusalem is still home to the mother church, the church at Antioch becomes Saul's base of operations. God commands the church leaders there to set Barnabas and Saul apart for a special work. The two men set off on a missionary journey that concentrated on several cities in Galatia. During the trip, Saul soon emerges as the dominant leader and chief spokesperson. Since he is now working in Gentile territory, Saul begins using his Roman name, Paul.

Paul's three missionary journeys take up most of the remaining chapters in Acts. His combined land and sea trips totaled thousands of miles as he worked tirelessly to spread the gospel throughout much of the Roman Empire. Paul faced many hardships; on his first journey, he was stoned and left for dead by a mob in Lystra.

In later trips, he endured beatings from the Jews and from the Romans, as well as death threats, imprisonment, and three shipwrecks. Through it all, Paul pressed on with the same single-minded devotion that he had displayed when he was hunting down and persecuting believers.

Paul always kept the main goal of his life in mind: to tell others the good news about Jesus Christ. Despite his strong personality, he stayed sensitive and obedient to the Holy Spirit's leading. Paul offered everything to God and God used it all: his education, his training, his Roman citizenship, and even his weaknesses. Aside from Jesus, no single person contributed more to the spread of Christianity.

How can we live with that same fervent devotion to God's call on our life when it's so easy to get distracted by the cares of life and by worldly pursuits? Paul reminds us that we will only know true fulfillment when we give all we have for the goal of knowing Christ and making him known.

For to me, to live is Christ and to die is gain.

Philippians 1:21 NASB

Second Chances

Acts 13:13; 15:36—41

When Barnabas and Paul set off on their missionary journey, they took along John Mark as a helper. The group sailed across the Mediterranean to Cyprus; after preaching there, they sailed to Perga in Pamphylia. At that point, John Mark left the group and returned to Jerusalem. Many reasons have been suggested as motives for his desertion, including homesickness, fear, illness, unwillingness to face the dangers or the rigorous travel, disillusionment at the emphasis on witnessing to Gentiles, or resentment when leadership shifted from his cousin Barnabas to Paul. Whatever the reason, Paul did not take John Mark's defection lightly.

Some time later, Paul suggested a return trip to visit the churches established during their first journey. Barnabas again wanted to take Mark along, but Paul refused. The two men disagreed so sharply that they went on separate journeys. Paul chose Silas as his partner; Barnabas took his cousin Mark. However, Paul's later letters reveal that his attitude toward Mark changed drastically at some point.

Mark eventually became Paul's close friend, a valued co-worker, and a trusted Christian leader. As Paul sat in a dungeon awaiting execution, he asked Timothy to bring Mark when he came to visit. Paul desired the company of this man he once labeled as untrustworthy, but now considered helpful in his ministry (see 2 Tim. 4:11–12).

We all make mistakes, but we wouldn't want others to define us by our past failures. Yet we often write someone off because they once made a poor choice. The Bible is full of people who made serious errors in judgment, learned from their mistakes, and ended up being used by God in powerful ways. Their stories remind us that, with God's help, people *can* change. If we refuse to believe that, we may miss out on relationships and cut others off from ministry. Since God is willing to give someone a second chance, why shouldn't we do the same?

> *Be humble and gentle in every way. Be patient with*
> *each other and lovingly accept each other.*
>
> Ephesians 4:2

Lydia's New Business

Acts 16:1—15

As Paul started out on his second missionary journey, the Holy Spirit prevented him from going into certain cities. God had arranged for these areas to hear the gospel at a later date. After Paul landed in Troas, God gave more positive direction. One night Paul had a vision of a man begging, "Come to Macedonia to help us" (v. 9). Paul and his companions boarded a ship headed for Philippi, a leading city in Macedonia. Since Philippi had no synagogue, on the Sabbath the missionaries went outside the city to a place along the river, where they expected to find a place of prayer. They began speaking to the small group of women assembled there.

Lydia was a Gentile convert to Judaism and a successful merchant of costly purple cloth. God opened Lydia's heart as she listened to Paul's message about Jesus; she became Paul's first convert in Europe. After being baptized, Lydia begged the missionaries to stay at her house. "If you're convinced that I believe in the Lord, then stay at my home," she told them (v. 15). She continued to offer her house as a meeting place for the believers in Philippi, playing a crucial role in the development of the church there.

This first-century businesswoman modeled an important principle of the Christian life: regardless of our occupation, we should make it our business to do good to other believers. God expects us to use our resources to meet needs within the body of Christ. A part of that ministry is hospitality. We may have the opportunity to offer housing to someone with an emergency need. Or we can make our home available for small group meetings, extend an invitation to someone who needs encouragement, or host visiting missionaries.

Lydia considered it a privilege, not a burden, to play the host. With our busy lifestyles and emphasis on having picture-perfect homes, the art of hospitality has faded. But when we obey God in this area, we'll find that the blessings far outweigh the effort involved.

Always be eager to practice hospitality.

Romans 12:13 NLT

A Prison Concert

Acts 16:16—40

When Paul forced an evil spirit out of a slave girl, it infuriated her owners. Her ability to predict the future had made them rich; now their source of income had vanished. The girl's owners accused Paul and Silas of stirring up trouble and promoting customs unacceptable to Roman citizens. The authorities had Paul and Silas severely beaten with wooden rods and jailed in an inner cell with irons clamped around their ankles. Despite their bleak situation, Paul and Silas used the time to pray and to sing praise to God as the other prisoners listened.

Around midnight a violent earthquake shook the jail. Doors flew open and all the prisoners' chains fell off. When the jailer woke up, he assumed the prisoners had escaped. Knowing that he would be held accountable, he drew his sword to kill himself. But Paul and Silas had seen the situation not as a chance to escape, but as an opportunity to witness for Christ. Paul shouted out, assuring the jailer that all the prisoners were still there.

The shocked jailer knelt and asked what he needed to do to be saved. Paul and Silas shared the gospel message with the jailer and his family, who all believed and became Christians that night. The Bible doesn't tell us how the other prisoners responded, but they had certainly been exposed to a powerful example of the Christian faith.

Whenever we find ourselves in a difficult situation, we have a choice to make. We can either dwell on our circumstances, or we can focus on the One who controls them. We may not feel like praising God during times when our first instinct is to be depressed, upset, or angry. But making a conscious choice to praise him in spite of what we're facing changes our perspective and pleases God as it demonstrates our trust in him. Plus, someone watching our response to troubles may be prompted to respond to the gospel.

*Sing to the L*ORD*! Praise his name!*
*Day after day announce that the L*ORD *saves his people.*

Psalm 96:2

The Bereans Check Paul Out

Acts 17:1–13

In Thessalonica, the capital city of Macedonia, Paul spent three consecutive Sabbaths in the synagogue discussing how Scripture revealed Jesus as the Messiah. Some Jews accepted the message, mostly Greek converts and wives of prominent men. After a while, the Jews grew jealous of Paul's and Silas's popularity. They rounded up some questionable characters who formed a mob and instigated a riot in the city. When the unruly crowd couldn't find the two missionaries, they dragged out Jason, the man who had provided them housing. As soon as it got dark, the believers sent Paul and Silas to Berea, fifty miles away.

Among the Bereans, Paul found a more open-minded, thoughtful, and discerning audience. They eagerly listened to Paul's message about Jesus, but they didn't take what he said at face value. Each day the Bereans searched the Scriptures for themselves to make sure what Paul taught was true. After carefully verifying his claims about Jesus based on God's Word, many of the Bereans became believers and accepted God's gift of salvation. Although Jewish unbelievers from Thessalonica again forced Paul to flee, Timothy and Silas stayed in Berea to nurture the newly founded church.

The Bereans' example reminds us how important it is to evaluate anything we read or hear against the standard of God's Word. Many people try to represent man-made philosophies or their own ideas as God's truth. Books, television programs, and movies often claim to reveal the "real truth" about Jesus or Christianity. If we're not thoroughly grounded in the Bible, we can be taken in by stories that touch our emotions or by reasoning that sounds correct to our ears but contradicts the Scriptures. We can only distinguish between the real and the phony when we do what the Bereans did—spend time in the Word every day, verifying what *God* says.

> *They were very willing to receive God's message,*
> *and every day they carefully examined the*
> *Scriptures to see if what Paul said was true.*
>
> Acts 17:11

Plenty of Diversity, Not Enough Truth

Acts 17:16–34

As Paul walked through the city of Athens, the statues and magnificent temples deeply grieved him. Everywhere he looked, he saw evidence of the city's idolatry. Paul followed his usual practice of going into the synagogues to talk with Jews and Gentile converts. He also took advantage of the fact that Athenians loved to discuss and debate the latest ideas. Every day he held discussions in the public square with whomever happened to be there. When Paul talked about Jesus and the resurrection, some philosophers called him a babbling fool; others noted that he seemed to advocate foreign gods.

Paul soon got a chance to speak to the Areopagus, the city's high council, whose members were eager to hear his beliefs. Instead of beginning with a review of Jewish history and Scriptures, Paul began by acknowledging that the people of Athens were "very religious." He used an inscription on an altar he'd seen as his starting point.

The Athenians were so afraid of overlooking some deity they didn't know about that they had erected an altar and dedicated it "To an unknown god." Athens represented the world's intellectual center, yet with all their education, they knew nothing of the one true God. Paul jumped at the chance to introduce them to this God and his Son.

Just like ancient Athens, our culture prides itself on being open to new ideas and philosophies. Many people consider one set of beliefs as good as any other. If we start talking about the gospel, we can expect the same response that Paul received. Some may laugh at us—even call us a "babbling fool." But if we follow Paul's example and look for a starting point to establish common ground with our listeners, we may be able to introduce them to the one true God and the only way to salvation.

> *And there is salvation in no one else; for there is*
> *no other name under heaven that has been given*
> *among men by which we must be saved.*

Acts 4:12 NASB

Sensitivity Training

Acts 18:1–3, 24–28

Aquila and Priscilla fled from Rome when the emperor Claudius expelled the Jews in AD 49. Paul met the couple in Corinth during his second missionary journey and learned that they shared the same vocation: tentmaking. Aquila and Priscilla opened their home to the apostle and the three worked together, allowing Paul to support himself instead of depending on the Corinthian believers for support. We're not told if Aquila and Priscilla were believers before they met Paul, but they surely benefited from his store of wisdom shared on a daily basis as well as from his formal teaching.

Paul formed a close relationship with this couple, who dedicated themselves to serving Christ. In his letter to the Roman believers, Paul sent greetings to his "co-workers" Priscilla and Aquila who "risked their lives" to save him (see 16:3–4). Paul even said that, besides the house church that met at their home, all churches everywhere were grateful to Priscilla and Aquila. The last few verses of Acts 18 give us a glimpse into the character of this godly couple.

While they were staying in Ephesus, a popular and eloquent speaker named Apollos came to town. He knew the Scriptures thoroughly, and his teaching about Jesus was accurate—but deficient. He knew only about the baptism commanded by John for repentance of sin. Rather than correcting Apollos in the synagogue, Aquila and Priscilla invited him into their home. There they shared the full story of Jesus's death, burial, and resurrection that made salvation possible, and the giving of the Holy Spirit.

This couple's example provides a lesson in sensitivity training that many Christians need. Priscilla and Aquila were more interested in sharing their knowledge than in showing it off. It's important to be loving and sensitive to other people's feelings when we share God's truth, even if their views are way off base. If we correct them in a way that embarrasses them, they won't be interested in hearing what we know.

But while knowledge makes us feel important,
it is love that strengthens the church.

1 Corinthians 8:1 NLT

Finishing the Race

Acts 20:13—21:14

During Paul's third missionary journey, he sensed the Holy Spirit compelling him to go to Jerusalem. Hoping to get there by the day of Pentecost, Paul sent messages for the church leaders in Ephesus to meet him in Miletus. He confided that the Spirit had warned him that suffering and imprisonment waited for him in Jerusalem. For that reason, he did not expect to see them again. "But I don't place any value on my own life," Paul insisted. "I want to finish the race I'm running" (20:24). His remarks led to a tearful good-bye as the elders accompanied him to his ship.

Next, Paul sailed for Tyre, where he stayed a week. The believers there had learned through the Spirit that Paul would face grave danger in Jerusalem. Concerned for his safety, they urged him to change his plans. While Paul and his companions visited Philip in Caesarea, a prophet from Judea named Agabus showed up. He used Paul's belt to tie up his own hands and feet as an illustration of how Paul would be bound by the Jews in Jerusalem.

Hearing this prophecy, the believers and Paul's traveling companions, including Luke, begged him not to go to Jerusalem. Paul asked the group why they were crying and breaking his heart. He proclaimed that he was ready not only to be tied up, but to die for Jesus. Finally, the believers dropped the matter, saying, "May the Lord's will be done" (21:14).

Paul never shrank from where God's Spirit led him, and neither should we. Like Paul, we may have people concerned about our safety and welfare who unknowingly try to dissuade us from obeying God. Or we may be the ones trying to change the mind of a loved one. But each one of us must run the race God has laid out for us, even when it means facing possible danger. If our first priority is for God's will to be done then, like Paul, we will be willing to do whatever it takes to finish our race well.

*I have fought the good fight. I have completed
the race. I have kept the faith.*

2 Timothy 4:7

Seizing the Day

Acts 21:15—28:31

Soon after Paul arrived in Jerusalem, some Jews accused him of violating the temple and started a riot against him. Even after Paul was arrested, the Jews plotted his murder. A heavy guard of Roman soldiers escorted Paul to Caesarea, the Roman headquarters for the area. There, Paul spent two years in prison until he appealed his case to Caesar. Following a grueling two-thousand-mile trip to Rome, Paul lived in confinement in that city for two more years.

Paul didn't allow his arrest to halt his ministry—he simply changed audiences. During his imprisonment in Caesarea, Paul preached and gave his testimony before Governor Felix numerous times. He also testified before Felix's successor Festus, King Herod Agrippa and his wife, and an untold number of military officials and city leaders who would have also been present.

While traveling to Rome, Paul witnessed to sailors and officers during a harrowing shipwreck. He preached and healed many sick people during the three months the crew stayed on the island of Malta. Paul spent two years in Rome under house arrest, but he kept busy writing letters to several churches along with personal letters like Philemon. Paul counseled, taught, preached, and witnessed to those who came to see him, as well as to the entire Roman guard (see Phil. 1:13).

The book of Acts ends here, but according to records written by early church fathers, Paul was released and he visited several countries. However, after a second Roman imprisonment he was executed under the emperor Nero around AD 67–68.

Paul wasn't about to let false accusations, imprisonment, or being stranded on an island keep him from doing what God had called him to do. He saw his difficulties as new opportunities to tell people about Jesus. His example encourages us to view our own troubles and trials in a new light. Instead of giving in to discouragement or despair, we can look for ways that our circumstances might contribute to the one thing that matters most.

> *But what does it matter? Nothing matters except that, in one way or another, people are told the message about Christ.*
>
> Philippians 1:18

A Collection of Letters

Of the twenty-seven books in the New Testament, twenty-one are letters, also called Epistles. Paul wrote thirteen of these during his journeys and times of imprisonment. Paul's letters are titled according to their recipients; the remaining eight Epistles (except Hebrews) are titled according to their authors. The apostle John wrote three Epistles and Peter wrote two. Two of Jesus's brothers, James and Judas (or Jude), each wrote one; the author of Hebrews remains unknown. Most of the letters include an opening that names the sender and recipients, and offers a salutation and prayer. This is followed by the body and closing, which varies greatly among the letters.

Within each Epistle, every single part is necessary for an accurate interpretation of the letter. Our understanding will be hindered if we merely read one or more sections without considering the document in its entirety. It's also important to read with a view of the specific circumstances faced by the recipients, although it's impossible to fully grasp the setting the way its original readers did. Other keys for understanding the Epistles are found in their references to Old Testament Scriptures and to Christ's teachings. These allusions shed light not only on the letter itself, but on the Bible as a whole.

Most of the Epistles address specific problems and situations within a church, often arising from dangerous doctrines and false teachings that had infiltrated the body of believers. Although filled with doctrine, each letter is much more than a theological discussion or treatise. The writings are geared toward practical application and filled with concrete examples of living out the Christian faith.

Like the early believers, we have questions about how to handle problems within our churches. Today we face the same dangers from false teachings and the same struggle to apply Scripture to everyday living. These twenty-one letters are addressed to us as well as to the original recipients. Through them, God has provided what we need to keep our doctrine pure and our lifestyle pleasing to him.

Watch your life and doctrine closely.
1 Timothy 4:16 NIV

Romans

The Case for the Gospel

I'm not ashamed of the Good News. It is God's power to save everyone who believes, Jews first and Greeks as well.

Romans 1:16

Paul had never been to Rome, but he longed to visit the large group of believers there. Near the end of his third missionary journey, around AD 57, Paul wrote a letter to be carried to Rome by Phoebe, a leading member of a church near Corinth where Paul was staying. Besides introducing himself and informing them of his plan to visit, Paul wanted to build the believers up in their knowledge and understanding and to encourage unity between Jews and Gentiles. The resulting letter arguably represents the most detailed and systematic presentation of doctrine anywhere in the Bible.

Like a skillful lawyer, Paul builds his case using a question and answer format as he confronts hypothetical objections to his statements. Paul begins by demonstrating the sinfulness of the human race and our need for God's intervention. Then he moves on to the forgiveness and reconciliation possible through faith in Jesus Christ. Speaking to a mixed group, Paul explains how both Jews and Gentiles fit into God's plan, addressing specific comments to each side. Romans would be a masterpiece as a theological treatise if it ended there, but it proves to be much more.

After thoroughly examining the basic doctrines of the Christian faith, Paul explores the basic principles of the Christian life. He offers practical instructions for godly living, noting that the freedom we have in Christ comes with responsibilities. After we accept his offer of salvation, God expects us to genuinely love others, live as good citizens, and use our spiritual gifts to build up his body.

Romans provides guidelines for us to evaluate our doctrine and lifestyle in light of God's truth and standards. It also reminds us that our beliefs and behavior need to match. Do we cling to the biblical tenets of the Christian faith while also living out the realities they represent? If so, our own life is building a case for the gospel.

Guilty as Charged

Romans 1:18–3:20

After Paul opened his letter, he launched into a discussion of God's plan of salvation by showing why it's needed in the first place, starting with the Gentiles. From the beginning of time, God has displayed his divine nature through the beauty and complexity of the natural world he created. In addition, his presence is revealed by each person's conscience, or innate sense of moral standards. Yet instead of responding to the clear evidence of a Creator, people refused to acknowledge or worship him. As they suppressed the truth, their minds became darkened and pulled them into a downward spiral leading to idolatry and all kinds of evil behavior.

Paul then addressed the Jews, refuting the idea that their special covenant relationship with God automatically assured their good standing with him. Even the most moral and religious Jews failed to meet God's standard, which is perfection. Although God had given them his law, they didn't obey it; yet they criticized others for committing the very same sins they practiced. Paul made it clear that people have no excuse for failing to respond to the light that God has given them concerning himself. Every single person stands condemned before a holy God and deserves his wrath, Jews and Gentiles alike.

Today we have more evidence of God's presence and divine character; we possess the complete Scriptures, including records of his most personal revelation of himself through Jesus Christ. Yet people still rebel against the truth and refuse to honor God, choosing instead to worship themselves or invisible modern idols.

In our society we can easily see the end result as people grow more morally insensitive and futile in their thinking. It may be unpopular to teach concepts of condemnation and God's righteous anger at sin, but people need to understand the bad news before they can accept the good news. And thankfully, that good news is also for everyone.

Because all people have sinned, they
have fallen short of God's glory.

Romans 3:23

299

God's Offer: A Full Pardon

Romans 3:21—4:25

Paul built an airtight case for the charges against us. God's holiness demands a penalty for sin; his justice requires him to punish all wrongdoing. Our own efforts at being a good person can't save us since God's standard is perfection. Following the law can't make us right with him because no one can obey it perfectly; when we break one law, we're as guilty as if we broke them all (see James 2:10). Each one of us stands convicted and condemned, facing a death sentence. Thankfully, Paul then delivered the good news: God has provided a way for us to be declared "not guilty." The same One who is our Judge is also our Savior.

Jesus took the penalty for our sin upon himself by dying in our place. His resurrection showed that God accepted Jesus's sacrifice as full payment and that his righteous anger against sin has been satisfied, or *propitiated*. By believing in Jesus's work on the cross in our behalf and receiving God's gift of salvation, we are freed from our death sentence. Just as a person found innocent in a courtroom has his record cleared of the charges against him, God wipes our record clean when we accept his offer of forgiveness and reconciliation by placing our faith in what Jesus did for us.

Paul spoke specifically to his Jewish readers by using the Old Testament examples of Abraham and David to stress that salvation has nothing to do with good works, circumcision, or any other human effort. In this way, Christianity is unique from other religions and philosophies, which depend on following rules or rituals to earn right standing with God. The fact that our relationship with God comes as a result of his undeserved favor, or grace, leaves no room for human pride—only deep gratitude for the price he paid so that we can be fully pardoned.

> *God saved you through faith as an act of kindness.*
> *You had nothing to do with it. Being saved is*
> *a gift from God. It's not the result of anything*
> *you've done, so no one can brag about it.*
>
> Ephesians 2:8–9

A Daily Struggle

Romans 7:14–25

Paul often examined the past, present, and future aspects of our salvation experience. Through Christ's death we have been saved from the penalty of our sin, or *justified*. Someday we will be saved from the very presence of sin when we see God face-to-face and receive our glorified body. In the meantime, as we mature spiritually and allow God to transform us into the image of Christ, we are being saved from the power of sin, or *sanctified*. Since sanctification is a lifelong process, as long as we're on this earth we will face a daily struggle. Paul graphically described this struggle in chapter 7.

Paul declared that in his mind, he loved God's commands and desired to obey them. But his old corrupt nature fought to control him and pull him into sin. As a result, Paul often found himself not doing the good that he wanted to do, but doing the evil things that he did not want to do. This internal war made Paul feel miserable and prompted him to cry out, "Who will rescue me from my dying body?" (v. 24). He immediately answered his own question: Jesus had died to pay the penalty for his sin and someday would free him from sin's presence. Until then, Paul knew he could depend on Jesus to empower him in the daily conflict with his old sinful nature.

When we become a believer, that doesn't mean we'll be immune to temptation and never do anything wrong. We're still vulnerable to sin and Satan works as hard as he can to make us give in to sinful impulses. Every day we'll face the same struggle that Paul wrestled with as our sinful human nature battles against our desire to live according to God's standards.

Paul showed us where to go for help in the daily conflicts we face. It does no good for us to fight against sin with our own strength and willpower; we need the Spirit's help. The same One who rescued us in the past wants to help us in our daily fight against sin's power.

I thank God that our Lord Jesus Christ rescues me!
Romans 7:25

Life in the Spirit

Romans 8

If believers still have to contend with their old sinful nature, how is it possible to live a victorious Christian life that pleases God? Paul answers that question powerfully in chapter 8. He begins by assuring us that once we believe in Christ, we never have to worry about condemnation from any source. Our enemies, Satan, or our own conscience may convict us, but those charges will not stick. Christ not only died to pay for our past, present, and future sins; he now sits at God's right hand interceding for us.

Paul goes on to describe our new life of freedom and righteousness made possible by the Holy Spirit indwelling us. His presence assures us that we have been adopted into God's family. As his dearly loved children, we are no longer slaves to sin; we can draw on the Spirit's power to resist sinful tendencies and impulses. Every day we can choose to be controlled by God's Holy Spirit instead of by our sinful nature.

Being God's child means that we will someday share in Christ's glory; it also involves sharing in his sufferings in this life. But the glorious future that awaits us is so wonderful it makes any suffering and trials we experience seem meaningless in comparison. In the meantime, the Holy Spirit helps us by interceding when we don't know how we should pray. We also have God's promise that he will cause all our experiences, including adversity, to work together for our ultimate good.

Paul ends his summary of the victorious Christian life with a reminder of God's deep love for us. God didn't spare his own Son, but handed him over to death for us. How can we doubt that he will give us all we need to live a godly life? Nothing in all of creation can ever separate us from God's love. With such safety and security, how can we not live in victory?

The one who loves us gives us an overwhelming
victory in all these difficulties.

Romans 8:37

Wild Olive Branches

Romans 11

Romans 9–11 contain Paul's lengthy discussion on God's relationship with the nation of Israel and what that means for Gentile believers. To some, it seemed that God had rejected his chosen people; in reality they (except for a small remnant) had turned away from him by rejecting the Messiah. Because of their unbelief, God set the Jews aside temporarily. He used their hardened hearts and closed minds to accomplish his divine purpose of offering salvation to the rest of the world. Although Israel stumbled, the fall is not permanent. God is faithful to his covenant promises and will one day restore the nation as most of the Jewish people accept their Messiah.

Paul noted that Israel's failure did not give Gentile believers reason to gloat. In Romans 11:16–24 he used the familiar analogy of the olive tree to represent Israel. God had broken off some branches of the cultivated tree and grafted in wild olive branches (believing Gentiles). But those grafted-in branches derived their nourishment and support from the roots of the original tree. With such indebtedness to the Jewish race through whom Jesus said salvation came (see John 4:22), the non-Jewish believers had no reason to feel arrogant or superior.

The book of Romans stresses that God is sovereign and answers to no one concerning his actions. At the same time, it shows that people are responsible for the consequences of their decision to either accept or reject Christ. Sometimes it's hard to see how these two concepts fit together, but Paul states unequivocally that "God's choice does not depend on a person's desire or effort, but on God's mercy" (9:16).

We can never consider ourselves chosen because of our heritage, our ethnic background, or our family. We never have reason to feel superior to any other group of people. We do have plenty of reason to thank God for his mercy and grace, even when we don't fully understand how it works.

God's riches, wisdom, and knowledge are so deep that it is impossible to explain his decisions or to understand his ways.

Romans 11:33

A Living Sacrifice

Romans 12

The first eleven chapters of Paul's letter to the Roman church focused on God's love and mercy as revealed through his plan of salvation. Paul began the practical portion of his letter by looking at how we should respond to such great compassion. Old Testament sacrifices required a person to bring an animal without blemish to be slaughtered as a picture of payment for sins. Through his death on the cross, Jesus fulfilled the symbolism of the old system; now God calls us to offer a new type of sacrifice: our life.

To live a life that pleases God, we must offer up every area to him—our body, soul, mind, personality, and energy. This means refusing to let our thinking and behavior be shaped by the culture around us, whose standards and values often oppose God's. Instead, we allow God to transform us from the inside out as our mind is daily renewed through Bible study, prayer, and fellowship with other believers. As our thinking changes, we begin to desire God's will above all else.

Our transformed lifestyle will be evident in the way we treat believers and unbelievers alike. We will humbly and enthusiastically use our gifts to serve God and his body, being hospitable and generous with other believers. We will empathize with others in their joy and sorrow. When someone hurts us, we won't pay them back with evil but will leave vengeance up to God. Instead of being conquered by evil, we will conquer evil with good.

Thankfully, we don't have to be involved in bloody animal sacrifices, but Paul urges us to participate in a much more demanding kind of worship. Every day God expects us to offer him our personal goals, dreams, and desires in favor of doing his will. It may be difficult to learn to submit, but once we experience being a living sacrifice, we'll discover we weren't really living before.

> *I encourage you to offer your bodies as living*
> *sacrifices, dedicated to God and pleasing to him.*
> *This kind of worship is appropriate for you.*
>
> Romans 12:1

Law-Abiding Citizens

Romans 13:1–7

Although Paul wrote in Philippians 3:20 that believers are "citizens of heaven," he explained that part of living out our faith means being good citizens on the earth. As Christians, we are responsible to obey governing authorities since God is the one who ultimately establishes them. Whether they know it or not, our civil leaders are God's servants, put in office to use their power to promote justice and punish evil. When we rebel against the authorities over us, we're actually rebelling against what God has instituted.

The Bible makes it clear, however, that God does not want us to submit to civil authorities when doing so requires us to violate his commands and moral standards. When Queen Jezebel tried to murder all of God's prophets, Obadiah hid one hundred of them in caves (see 1 Kings 18:4). Shadrach, Meshach, and Abednego refused to bow down and worship the gold statue that King Nebuchadnezzar erected (see Dan. 3:12–18); Daniel ignored the royal edict forbidding people to pray to anyone other than King Darius (see Dan. 6:10). God told the wise men to go home by a different route instead of reporting back to Herod about their visit with the King of the Jews (see Matt. 2:12).

It's difficult to have a submissive attitude toward our government at a time when our country has moved so far away from God's standards. It couldn't have been any easier for the original readers of Paul's letter, considering that the madman Nero ruled Rome from AD 54–68 and delighted in torturing and massacring Christians.

Even when it goes against our nature, God expects us to pay our taxes and support our government. Even when we can't admire a leader, we can show them honor and respect for their position, remembering that God put them there. And we can pray for those in authority as well as for the outcome of elections, hoping that we will gain leaders we *can* admire.

> *Every person should obey the government in power. No government would exist if it hadn't been established by God.*
>
> Romans 13:1

Pick Your Battles

Romans 14:1—15:7

Is it a sin to have a glass of wine with dinner? Can I go shopping on Sunday? Would it be wrong to see that R-rated movie? Scripture identifies certain activities as sin while remaining silent on others. This opens the door for people to form judgments based on their backgrounds or personal opinions. Conflicts arise when one person tries to impose their rules on another, or when believers judge each other for being either "too permissive" or "too legalistic."

Believers in first-century Rome also had divisive issues. Many Christians had a problem with the idea of eating meat that had been part of a sacrifice to an idol and later sold in the market. Believers coming from a Jewish background sometimes felt compelled to still observe the Jewish holy days. In both cases, Paul urged believers to enjoy their freedom in Christ while being sensitive to others' views.

If our actions would offend another Christian, it is better to act out of love and give up our liberty. For example, when the Jerusalem council later advised Gentiles in Antioch to avoid eating food offered to idols, Paul agreed with the decision because the practice offended many Jewish believers (see Acts 15).

With believers coming from so many different backgrounds and levels of maturity, differences of opinion are to be expected. Some issues are worth fighting for, but when a behavior isn't forbidden by the Bible we can prayerfully examine our conscience on the subject. Our responsibility doesn't end there, however. We need to take into account the feelings of other believers.

God calls us to avoid actions that could hinder a fellow believer's spiritual growth. He also wants us to refrain from criticizing the behavior of other Christians who exercise freedom in ways that would make us uncomfortable. Of course we should take a stand against sin, but it's always best to look at gray areas through grace-colored glasses.

Therefore, accept each other in the same way that Christ accepted you.

Romans 15:7

1 Corinthians

Living It Out

> Don't you know that your body is a temple that belongs to the Holy Spirit? The Holy Spirit, whom you received from God, lives in you. You don't belong to yourselves. You were bought for a price. So bring glory to God in the way you use your body.
>
> 1 Corinthians 6:19–20

First-century Corinth was a worldwide commerce center in southern Greece, and a hotbed of paganism, materialism, and immorality. Shrines and temples to various deities filled the city, including Aphrodite, the "goddess of love." Vice and debauchery became so widespread that "acting like a Corinthian" became a well-known cliché. Paul planted a church in Corinth around AD 51 when he spent eighteen months there during his second missionary journey.

During Paul's third missionary journey, troubling reports reached him concerning quarrels among the Corinthian believers. Soon a delegation of three men brought a letter from the church asking his advice on a number of issues. Around AD 56 Paul sent the Corinthians his answer. He analyzed each problem and identified the root issue, then shared the necessary, biblically based correction.

Paul chided the Corinthians for their arrogant, snobbish attitudes that led to divisions and factions. He urged them to work toward unity, to use their gifts to build each other up, and to be sensitive to their fellow believers with weaker faith. Paul addressed their questions about marriage and order within public worship, and their confusion about the bodily resurrection of believers. He rebuked them for abusing the Lord's Supper and for tolerating sexual immorality within their midst. Because of the nature of the letter, Paul's tone often seemed harsh. But he concluded by assuring them that "through Christ Jesus my love is with all of you" (16:4).

First Corinthians is as relevant today as when Paul wrote it. Quarrels and divisions still plague churches, hindering our work and witness to the world. Believers still struggle against negative influences from the surrounding culture. This letter shows us how to live out our Christian faith, both within our church and on a personal level.

Tough Love

1 Corinthians 5

Paul had to deal with a serious issue within the Corinthian church—a shameful thing unheard of even in the surrounding pagan culture. One of their members was engaged in an incestuous affair with his stepmother, a relationship strictly forbidden in the Bible (see Lev. 18:8) as well as by Roman law. Instead of being grieved by such immoral behavior, the Corinthians seemed indifferent. Paul wondered how they could boast about their spirituality while allowing this blatant sin in their midst.

Paul warned that, if ignored, this sin would spread its deadly effects throughout the congregation in the same way that a little yeast works its way through a batch of dough. He instructed them to hand the guilty man over to Satan, probably meaning to exclude him from intimate fellowship with church members in hopes that he would repent. Paul impressed on them the necessity to take corrective action for the man's sake as well as for the health of the church.

In an earlier letter, Paul had warned the Corinthians against associating with someone who claimed to be a believer while engaging in behavior that Scripture explicitly labels as sin. It seemed that the Corinthians had applied this principle only to those outside the church. Paul reminded them that it wasn't their business to judge unbelievers. Their responsibility was to lovingly confront and discipline any member of their congregation living in open sin and showing no remorse.

At a time when people try to define loving others as tolerating anything they do, Paul's warnings are badly needed. If we ignore the sinful behavior of someone who claims to be a Christian, it appears to outsiders that we approve of their immorality. Taking disciplinary action may be an unpopular concept, but sometimes it's needed to restore the spiritual health of a person or a church.

After all, do I have any business judging those who are
outside the Christian faith? Isn't it your business to judge
those who are inside? God will judge those who are outside.

1 Corinthians 5:12–13

Body Parts

1 Corinthians 12

Early in his letter, Paul addressed the problem of factions within the church caused by people putting different leaders on pedestals (chap. 3). Apparently, divisions had also been created by the Corinthian believers elevating certain spiritual gifts above others. Paul reminded them that the Holy Spirit assigns one or more spiritual gifts to individuals according to his own purposes, not on the basis of human merit. They are not given for personal benefit, but for building up Christ's body. No one gift is superior to another; all are equally necessary.

The human body is comprised of many parts, each with a specific purpose necessary for the body to function properly. In the same way, Christ's body is composed of many individuals who have been given differing gifts and roles, all of which are dependent on each other. A church is effective only when each believer carries out their God-given role to contribute to the good of the body as a whole. Rather than being independent and aloof, God wants us to be so involved that when one person in his body is hurting, we all share that suffering. When someone has reason to rejoice, we share their happiness.

Believers today still struggle with attitudes that cause divisions within churches and hinder the effectiveness of Christ's body. We need to guard against letting our spiritual gifts become a source of pride, especially if they lead to roles that put us in the spotlight. On the other hand, it's equally important that we don't discount our role as minor or insignificant, feeling that we don't have as much to contribute as others do.

Instead of making comparisons, we need to remember who gave us our spiritual gifts and why. The church will accomplish all that God intends when each one of us accepts what God has given us and uses it to serve him and to build up other believers.

> *You are Christ's body and each of you*
> *is an individual part of it.*
>
> 1 Corinthians 12:27

True Love

1 Corinthians 13

By this point in his letter, Paul had discussed a number of problems within the Corinthian church. Believers were bringing lawsuits against each other. The poor were being ignored during communal meals. Overt sin was tolerated instead of corrected. Some members were exercising their newfound freedom in Christ in ways that caused disorder during worship services or offended those of weaker faith. Now Paul identified the root problem of all these issues: the Corinthians' self-centeredness and lack of love for each other.

Paul explained that genuine love exhibits patience and kindness. It is not jealous, boastful, arrogant, rude, or easily angered. Love does not demand its own way or keep a record of wrongs. It is not happy with injustice or evil, but rejoices in the truth. Love never stops believing and hoping the best for others. True love never gives up, and it never dies.

As important as spiritual gifts are, Paul insisted that love outranks them all (see 12:31). The greatest sacrifice we could make or the most spectacular display of faith would mean nothing if not motivated by love. Many people believe that certain gifts were active only while the church was being established, and other gifts will continue until Christ's return. In any case, all spiritual gifts will become obsolete one day. Love, on the other hand, will endure forever; its effects are eternal.

Like the Corinthians, we experience problems caused by a lack of genuine love. Our relationships with others are often based on physical attraction, emotional feelings, lust, or a self-centered desire to get our own needs met. The kind of love in 1 Corinthians 13 goes against our human nature. But the more we grow and become like Christ, the more we can love in a way that keeps other people's best interests at heart. Then we'll be reflecting God's unconditional love for us—genuine love that lasts throughout eternity.

> *So these three things remain: faith, hope, and*
> *love. But the best one of these is love.*
>
> 1 Corinthians 13:13

2 Corinthians

Setting the Record Straight

Therefore, we are Christ's representatives, and through us God is calling you.

2 Corinthians 5:20

In 1 Corinthians 5:9, Paul mentioned an earlier letter (now lost) he had sent to the church in Corinth. After writing to address problems and questions that had come to his attention, Paul paid the church a visit that turned out to be painful for him and the members (2 Cor. 2:1). Returning to Ephesus, Paul wrote a third letter in a harsh, disciplinary tone (now also lost) that was delivered by Titus. When Paul and Titus met up in Macedonia, Paul received both good and bad news.

At some point, false teachers had slandered Paul and turned the Corinthians against him. They tried to discredit his ministry by questioning his authority, his motives, and his character. Titus reported that while the majority of the Corinthians had shown a change of heart, a minority still opposed Paul. They accused him of being proud, dishonest, and unqualified; they complained that he was unimpressive in appearance and speech. From Macedonia, Paul wrote what we know as 2 Corinthians to defend the legitimacy of his ministry and to urge his detractors to accept his authority as an apostle of Christ.

Second Corinthians is the most personal and informal of Paul's letters. The apostle bares his heart as he shares his motives, desires, and passion. We also discover information about his life not recorded elsewhere: his persecution and hardships, details about his escape from Damascus, his vision of Paradise, and the thorn in his flesh. Paul's writing has sudden shifts in tone and occasional outbursts of sarcasm. Despite its emotional nature, the letter also discusses important doctrinal topics such as the contrast between the old and new covenants, the resurrection of believers, suffering for Christ, financial giving, and spiritual warfare.

Many churches today suffer conflict when people stir up dissatisfaction with the leaders. Second Corinthians reminds us to see past the slander and honestly evaluate our leaders' motives, conduct, and character—always giving them a chance to set the record straight.

Eternal Rewards

2 Corinthians 5:1—10

Paul had no fear of death. In fact, he sometimes confided that he felt torn between his longing to depart this life and be with the Lord, and his commitment to serving God on the earth (see Phil. 1:22–24). Although he would have preferred the first option, Paul persevered in his ministry through all kinds of hardships, persecution, and trials. It helped him to endure suffering by remembering that this earthly life is a temporary state, which he compared to a tent. His goal to "be pleasing" to God was also strengthened by knowing that one day he would stand before Christ's judgment seat, when the quality of his life and service would be evaluated.

In his earlier letter, Paul described this future evaluation of believers' work as being tested by fire (see 1 Cor. 3:11–15). We may have appeared to have a successful ministry, but if it was achieved through our own strength, it will be "burned up" like straw. If our work was motivated by selfish reasons or the desire for personal gain, it will count for nothing. Only service done for God's glory, fitting his agenda, and accomplished through his power will survive the testing. Christ will give us rewards for our acts of service that endure.

We don't need to look at Christ's judgment seat as a fearful thing; our eternal destiny was guaranteed the moment we trusted Jesus as our Savior. But thinking about this future event reminds us that how we live today will have eternal consequences. We would be wise to examine our life and Christian service now to see how it will pass the test in the future.

Are we motivated by a desire to see God glorified or by a need to win praise and admiration from others? Do we look for opportunities to serve that we would enjoy, or do we seek to obey God's leading even if it means a more difficult path? The answers will tell us whether to expect smoking ashes or eternal rewards.

All of us must appear in front of Christ's judgment seat.

2 Corinthians 5:10

Money Well Spent

2 Corinthians 8—9

For several years Paul had been organizing a collection for the poor in Jerusalem. The Corinthian church had planned to make a contribution a year earlier, but had failed to follow through. Paul encouraged the Corinthians to complete the process and have their gift ready when Titus and two other believers arrived to accept it. The Corinthians excelled in many areas; Paul urged them to excel in the area of giving as well.

Paul pointed to the sacrificial giving of the churches in Macedonia as an example to imitate. Although they suffered poverty themselves, these believers gave more than it seemed they could afford. Paul stressed that the Corinthians' giving should be voluntary, but he reminded them of the sowing/reaping principle. Those who "sow" generously out of the resources God has given them will reap a bountiful harvest of blessings.

In the Old Testament, the Israelites were required to give a tenth back to God, along with all the prescribed offerings and sacrifices. The New Testament emphasizes the attitude more than the amount. God wants us to give some of our resources back to him out of gratitude and love, not because we feel forced to give. Only then can we know the joy of helping other believers and participating in God's work. As we contribute to our local church, outreach ministries, and missions, we can know that our money is making a difference in others' lives and winning souls for Christ.

If we prayerfully decide what to give and do it with a joyful, generous spirit, God promises several things: he will multiply the amount to accomplish his purposes, our generous giving will lead to him being praised, God will provide for our needs so we can keep on giving to him, and finally, our obedience in this area will help us grow in righteousness. Now that is definitely money well spent.

> *Each of you should give whatever you have decided.*
> *You shouldn't be sorry that you gave or feel forced*
> *to give, since God loves a cheerful giver.*
>
> 2 Corinthians 9:7

Strength through Weakness

2 Corinthians 11:16—12:10

Second Corinthians 10–13 is primarily directed toward the minority in Corinth who were still rebelling against Paul's authority and leading the people away from the gospel with their false teachings. Since these men questioned Paul's credentials while exaggerating their own, Paul reviewed his heritage, his spiritual experiences, and his sufferings on behalf of the gospel in order to confirm his position as a true apostle of Christ. Several times he admitted that such talk made him feel like a fool even though in reality he was boasting about what God had done for him.

Speaking of himself in the third person, Paul told of being "snatched away" into heaven fourteen years earlier. Paul wasn't sure if he had been physically present in Paradise or given a vision, but he heard things that he could not share with others. So that Paul would not grow conceited over the great revelations he'd been given, God afflicted him with some sort of recurring problem, or "thorn in the flesh." Three times Paul begged God to take the problem away, but God replied, "My kindness is all you need. My power is strongest when you are weak" (12:9).

Unlike the false teachers, Paul bragged about his weakness. He had learned the lesson that human frailty is the most effective platform for displaying God's power. He willingly accepted mistreatment, hardship, persecution, and difficulties because they forced him to depend on God for strength. Then God could fill Paul with supernatural power, enabling him to accomplish much more than he could on his own.

Feeling weak can be a good thing if it forces us to turn to God instead of doing things through our own power and resources. Once we realize how desperately we depend on God's help, there will be no room for pride in our attitudes. And once we experience God's power working through us, we'll understand that he makes us stronger than we could ever be on our own.

It's clear that when I'm weak, I'm strong.

2 Corinthians 12:10

Galatians

The Statutes of Liberty

Christ has freed us so that we may enjoy the benefits of freedom. Therefore, be firm in this freedom, and don't become slaves again.

Galatians 5:1

During the early years of the church, a common controversy centered on a group who claimed that Gentile believers had to submit to Jewish laws and traditions in addition to believing in Christ. In Paul's absence, some of these "Judaizers" had infiltrated the churches in Galatia. The Galatians had embraced their teachings and were turning away from the freedom they'd found in Christ to go back into the bondage of Mosaic law. Paul wrote this letter to refute the false gospel that mixed law with grace and to defend the true doctrine of justification by faith alone.

The Judaizers had tried to discredit Paul as an apostle since he wasn't one of the original twelve. Paul pointed out that his message and doctrine had come through a direct revelation from Jesus, not from secondhand reports. Paul then used several lines of reasoning to prove that believers are saved by grace through faith alone and are no longer under the law. An analogy based on Abraham's two sons served to contrast law and grace. The son born to Hagar, the slave woman, represented those still enslaved to the Mosaic law; Sarah's son represented the free child of God.

Paul also warned the Galatians against the opposite extreme: antinomianism, the idea that freedom from the law gives a person license to sin. A believer is freed from the bondage of sin because of the indwelling Holy Spirit. The final two chapters of Paul's letter describe what it means to live in that power, free to love and serve others and grow in godliness.

The struggle between legalism and the gospel continues today. Many faiths teach that God's favor must be earned by following a list of rules or rituals. Believers need to guard against subtle influences that elevate good behavior above grace. Once we've accepted God's love as a gift, we can celebrate our liberty in Christ by living in a way that reflects our gratitude to him—not adherence to a list of rules.

The Purpose of the Law

Galatians 3:6—29

In essence, the Judaizers argued that Gentiles had to become Jews before they could become Christians. Paul asked the Galatians to remember their own personal experience of hearing the gospel and trusting Christ. They must have been under an evil spell when they let someone convince them their salvation experience was not complete! Then Paul used the Scriptures to show who Abraham's true descendants are. God counted Abraham as righteous because he believed in God's promises, not because of circumcision. So the Judaizers' own ancestor refuted the argument that circumcision was necessary for being accepted by God.

Since the Judaizers taught that following the Mosaic law was necessary for salvation, Paul quoted Deuteronomy 27:26 to show that the law could only bring condemnation. In order to receive approval, a person had to follow every single law perfectly all the time. Since this was impossible, the law became a curse. Christ took this curse upon himself when he hung on the cross. He paid the price so that those who believed in him could share in the blessings promised to Abraham and receive the Holy Spirit through faith.

Paul knew that his arguments would naturally cause people to wonder why God bothered to give the Mosaic laws. He explained that the law was necessary to show us what sin is and to make us aware of our need for a Savior. Originally, the law served as a tutor or guardian to guide, restrain, and regulate behavior. After Christ came, this guardian was no longer needed since believers receive the Holy Spirit to guide them.

Some people find comfort in having a strict list of do's and don'ts, but Christ died to free us from such bondage. That doesn't mean that the Ten Commandments are obsolete; they still give us a picture of the godly lifestyle that God desires. The difference now is that we have the Holy Spirit to help us live that way.

> *Before Christ came, Moses' laws served as*
> *our guardian. Christ came so that we could*
> *receive God's approval because of faith.*
>
> Galatians 3:24

The Law of Love

Galatians 5:13—6:10

Apart from being burdened by a list of rules or being controlled by our sinful desires, there is a third option: the freedom God wants us to enjoy. Christian liberty means allowing the Holy Spirit to lead us instead of our sinful nature (sometimes called "the flesh"). Paul listed sins that result from being controlled by the corrupt nature, such as sexual immorality, perversion, idolatry, witchcraft, hatred, and angry outbursts. He also included less obvious sins: selfish ambitions, conflict, factions, and envy.

In contrast, the by-products of being guided by the Spirit are love, joy, peace, patience, kindness, goodness, faithfulness, gentleness, and self-control. God's indwelling Spirit does more than suppress sins and negative traits; it produces godly attributes, all of which Jesus displayed during his earthly life. As we make the daily choice to be controlled by the Holy Spirit, we are transformed into Christ's image.

Love is not only the first character trait listed as a fruit of the Spirit; it's also the goal of the freedom we've been given. Believers are instructed to "serve each other through love" (5:13). The command to love our neighbor as we love ourselves was given in the Old Testament (see Lev. 19:18) and reaffirmed by Jesus on more than one occasion. As we love God and others, we fulfill all of God's laws ever given.

As believers, we are set free from the weight of the Mosaic law and from the tyranny of our sinful nature. Now we are called to obey the law of Christ, which can be summed up in a life of sacrificial, loving service to others. Paul gives specific examples of gently turning a sinning believer away from his error and helping carry the load of a Christian who feels overburdened. As we do our best to obey the law of love each day, we will discover what true freedom means.

> *You were indeed called to be free, brothers and sisters. Don't*
> *turn this freedom into an excuse for your corrupt nature*
> *to express itself. Rather, serve each other through love.*
>
> Galatians 5:13

Ephesians

Blueprint for the Church

> Instead, as we lovingly speak the truth, we will grow up completely in our relationship to Christ, who is the head. He makes the whole body fit together and unites it through the support of every joint. As each and every part does its job, he makes the body grow so that it builds itself up in love.
>
> Ephesians 4:15–16

One of the most prominent churches founded by Paul was located in Ephesus, an important and wealthy city in Asia. During his second missionary trip, Paul spent three years teaching and preaching there. He left when a riot broke out against him, instigated by a silversmith whose business had suffered from people turning away from worship of the goddess Artemis to faith in Christ. Paul probably wrote his letter to the Ephesians during his imprisonment in Rome between AD 60–62.

Unlike most of Paul's letters, this one doesn't address any specific problem or heresy. The overall theme is the body of Christ, with an emphasis on unity among believers demonstrated by love. Paul uses metaphors of the church as a building with Christ for its cornerstone (2:19–22) and as the bride of Christ (5:25–27). In chapter 4 he lists seven elements that all true believers have in common: one body, one Spirit, one hope, one Lord, one faith, one baptism, and one God and Father of all.

Paul's opening recounts the riches that every believer possesses through Christ. He praised God the Father, who has "blessed us with every spiritual blessing that heaven has to offer" (1:3). Believing Jews and Gentiles are co-heirs of this inheritance, having been chosen, redeemed, adopted, and sealed with God's Spirit. The final three chapters are packed with practical instructions that show what it means to be a part of Christ's body and to live a life worthy of our calling.

Ephesians can strengthen and encourage any believer who reads it. As we meditate on our spiritual riches through Christ, our natural response will be to see how our life and our church measure up to God's blueprint.

The "S" Word

Ephesians 5:22–6:9

Paul explained that living a transformed life controlled by the Spirit includes having a submissive attitude toward others. He went on to give instructions for specific relationships: husbands and wives, parents and children, and slaves and masters. Paul's advice did not mirror the cultural attitudes prevalent at that time, when the head of the household retained unlimited power and control. It also doesn't reflect the one-sided relationship that many people think of when they hear the word *submit*.

God's design for the marital relationship calls for the wife to voluntarily submit to her husband's leadership as head of the family. For his part, the husband is to put aside his own interests in order to love and care for his wife. A man's sacrificial love for his wife is compared to the way that Christ loved the church and gave up his life for it. If both partners are submitted to Jesus as Lord of their lives, then they will be able to honor and submit to each other.

Children have the responsibility to submit to their parents by obeying them. Parents are to nurture, train, and discipline their children, while avoiding unreasonable demands or actions that might exasperate them. Paul also addressed the master/slave relationship, since there were several million slaves in the Roman Empire at that time. Without condoning the system, Paul simply instructed slaves to obey their master as they would obey Christ. Masters were to respectfully care for those under their authority.

Jesus tried to teach his disciples the importance of a submissive attitude, but during his final Passover meal with them, some still argued about who was the greatest among their group (see Luke 22:24). Our human nature urges us to exalt ourselves, not to serve and build up someone else. But when we commit to obeying God and following Christ's example, the Spirit will make us willing to subordinate our rights for someone else's good. And we won't be afraid of the "S" word anymore.

Submit to one another out of reverence for Christ.

Ephesians 5:21 NIV

Armed for Battle

Ephesians 6:10—20

Paul liked to use military illustrations for spiritual principles, and that approach certainly seemed appropriate for his closing topic in his letter to the Ephesians. Paul talked about the ongoing spiritual warfare that makes the Christian life seem like a battleground. First, he instructed believers to be strong in the Lord and draw from his power, using the armor that God has provided.

Before engaging in the battle, however, it's important to know who our enemy is. This is no wrestling match with a human opponent; believers are struggling against Satan and his helpers. Paul described our enemies as "rulers, authorities, the powers who govern this world of darkness, and spiritual forces that control evil in the heavenly world" (v. 12).

Such warfare calls for supernatural weapons, and God has supplied all we need. We begin by fastening the belt of truth around our waist. (A life of integrity will help us face the "father of lies.") We strap on the breastplate of righteousness. (Having God's approval and trying to live a righteous life will protect our heart and mind from Satan's accusations.) We slip our feet into the shoes of the gospel. Then we grab our shield of faith; our mind is protected with the helmet of salvation. Finally, we pick up our sword, which is the Word of God, and we pray always and in every situation.

With such a cunning and formidable enemy, we can't afford to leave off any piece of armor or any weapon. Twice Paul emphasized the importance of using *all* the armor. Satan can spot any vulnerable area; but in reality, Christ has already defeated him and all his forces. Even though the victory has been won, every believer is called to active duty in God's army. As long as we have all our protective armor in place and prayerfully take up our sword, we'll be prepared when it comes time for us to be deployed.

> *Put on all the armor that God supplies. In this way*
> *you can take a stand against the devil's strategies.*
>
> Ephesians 6:11

Philippians

Joy to the Church

Always be joyful in the Lord! I'll say it again: Be joyful!
Philippians 4:4

Paul enjoyed a special relationship with the believers in Philippi. The church that originated from a handful of women on a riverbank in Macedonia faithfully supported Paul and, for the most part, remained a healthy congregation. When the believers heard that Paul had been imprisoned in Rome, they sent a financial gift through one of their members, Epaphroditus. Paul responded by writing the Philippians a letter to express his gratitude and deep love for them, and to urge them toward a lifestyle of holiness, humility, unity, and joy.

Philippians contains a small amount of doctrinal teaching. Paul addressed the problem of rivalry and dissension in the church, and touched on the false teachings of legalism and antinomianism. But Philippians is primarily a personal letter of love and encouragement toward spiritual growth. Besides the benefit of his instructions, Paul also offers himself as a living example as he shares thoughts about his own circumstances.

Paul declares that he has learned to be content in whatever situation he finds himself (4:11). He has the assurance that he can do all things through Christ who strengthens him (4:13). Such victorious living is possible because of his single-minded devotion to knowing Christ and sharing the gospel. Paul urged his readers to imitate Christ's perfect example of sacrifice and humility demonstrated when he temporarily set aside his rightful glory and took on human form, even submitting to a horrible death on the cross.

The concept of joy is a predominant theme in Philippians. The noun and verb form of "joy," or a synonym for it, is used sixteen times in the letter's four chapters. While happiness depends on our outward circumstances, joy is deeper, stronger, and springs from our attitudes and mindset. Joy is a steadfast, confident assurance of God's love and presence in our life no matter what we're going through. Philippians is our own personal love letter from God, reminding us that joy is a gift he wants all his children to enjoy.

Eyes on the Prize

Philippians 3:1–16

As Paul warned the Philippians about the false teaching of the Judaizers, he also listed his own impressive credentials. Paul had a spiritual heritage and list of achievements that would make any legalist feel like boasting. He was a pure-blooded Jew from the highly esteemed tribe of Benjamin. He had been a Pharisee, a member of the strictest sect among his people who scrupulously kept the laws of Moses. In his zeal for the Jewish religion, he had fought against anything viewed as heresy. But after his conversion, Paul counted all these things as garbage in comparison to the privilege of knowing Christ.

Paul also had things in his past that were a source of shame and regret. He had guarded the cloaks of the men who stoned Stephen, approving of their actions. He had dedicated himself to tracking down Christians to have them imprisoned and hopefully executed. But Paul didn't dwell on his past achievements *or* his past failures.

Like a Greek athlete in a race, Paul poured all his energy and concentration into the goal ahead of him: to know Christ more intimately and to accomplish all that God wanted him to do. He didn't let things he'd left behind drag him down and impede his progress; he also refused to let inconsequential matters sidetrack him.

Unlike some others, Paul didn't claim to have arrived at the height of spiritual maturity. He knew that as long as he lived, he would be running toward his goal. Like Paul, we all have things in our past we're ashamed of, as well as things that we can be proud of. Either category can hinder our progress in our spiritual race. Since our future hope is in Christ, it's time to let go of what is behind and look ahead to all that God has promised and everything that he wants to do through us.

> *This is what I do: I don't look back, I lengthen my stride, and I run straight toward the goal to win the prize that God's heavenly call offers in Christ Jesus.*
>
> Philippians 3:13–14

Mind Control

Philippians 4:4–20

As Paul closed his letter to the Philippians, he reminded them once again to "Be joyful!" (v. 4). Then he warned about something that can steal away our joy if we let it. Paul advised the Philippians to "never worry about anything" (v. 6). Knowing how impossible that sounded, Paul immediately shared the antidote to this destructive habit that can have serious physical, emotional, and spiritual consequences. We can learn to replace every anxious thought with prayer, requesting answers for specific needs while always giving thanks. When we practice that habit, God's peace will flood our minds, guarding our thoughts and emotions regardless of what we may be facing.

Our mind is Satan's major battleground. Worry is one way he uses our thoughts against us; he also subtly introduces fantasies, whims, and daydreams into our minds that can lead to inappropriate attitudes. Even committed Christians doing their best to serve God can have serious problems with impure thoughts. Some people struggle under a heavy load of guilt because of their thought life. Although they know it's not pleasing to God, they can't seem to get it under control.

What we put into our minds shapes our thought life. We're constantly bombarded by an endless supply of unwholesome images, television shows, movies, music, reading material, and conversation. If we allow these things to influence how we think, the results can be disastrous in our relationships with God and with other people. Philippians 4:8 gives the formula for evaluating what enters our mind. Our thought life needs to be focused on those things that are praiseworthy according to God's standards.

Since God gave us these guidelines, we don't have to leave our mind open for unwelcome intrusions from Satan or the world; we can guard it with God's Word and prayer. Then we'll have plenty of room for his peace and joy.

> *Finally, brothers and sisters, keep your thoughts on*
> *whatever is right or deserves praise: things that are true,*
> *honorable, fair, pure, acceptable, or commendable.*
>
> Philippians 4:8

Colossians

Complete in Christ

All of God lives in Christ's body, and God has made you complete in Christ. Christ is in charge of every ruler and authority.

Colossians 2:9–10

While Paul didn't start the church at Colossae, it most likely began as an outgrowth of his three-year stay in Ephesus, which was located a hundred miles away. Epaphras came to faith through Paul's ministry there and later helped found the Colossian church. During Paul's imprisonment in Rome, Epaphras brought disturbing news. The predominantly Gentile church at Colossae had been infiltrated by dangerous teachings that were causing problems. Paul wrote to confront the age-old problem of syncretism, an attempt to combine ideas from different philosophies and religions with biblical truth.

The particular mixture invading the Colossian church included elements of Jewish legalism, dietary restrictions, and rituals, along with a search for some special, deeper knowledge that could eventually lead to spiritual perfection. The false teachers also advocated asceticism, or strict discipline of the body, and visions and mystical experiences as means for spiritual growth. Angels were worshiped as mediators between God and humans, and for protection from evil spirits.

These heresies denied the deity of Christ; in rebuttal, Paul wrote one of the most Christ-centered books in the Bible. Paul displayed Christ as Lord over all creation, image of the invisible God, our Redeemer and Savior, the conqueror of sin and Satan, and head of the church. Besides leading the Colossians away from false teachings, Paul wanted to guide them toward spiritual maturity. Emphasizing the all-sufficiency of Christ, he urged them to continue their Christian life the way they had begun it. By sinking their roots deep into Christ and continuing to be built up and strengthened in him, they would not be misled by man-made philosophies and traditions.

People still try to blend Christianity with other belief systems, philosophies, or their own ideas. Colossians reminds us that Christ has already given us all we need for salvation and living the Christian life. We don't need to look anywhere else; we already have the complete picture.

Knowledge That Counts

Colossians 1:9—12; 2:1—7

The false teachings influencing the Colossian church represented a mixed bag drawing on Oriental mysticism, Jewish philosophy and legalism, pagan astrology, and other sources—with a dash of Christianity thrown in. Most scholars think these teachings had some elements of what came to be known in the second century as *Gnosticism*, taken from the Greek word for "know" or "knowledge." One of the basic tenets of Gnosticism claimed that a select few possessed superior knowledge of the deep things of God. In order to have a full spiritual experience, a person had to be "enlightened" by progressing through levels of secret, esoteric learning and rituals.

Paul used the same terms found in these heresies, but gave them different meanings. He opened his letter by assuring the Colossians that he regularly prayed that God would fill them "with the knowledge of his will through every kind of spiritual wisdom and insight" (1:9). The kind of knowledge he desired for them contrasted with what the false teachers promoted, which had only an appearance of wisdom while lacking any real value for spiritual growth (2:23).

He also pointed them to Jesus Christ, in whom "God has hidden all the treasures of wisdom and knowledge" (2:3). This source of knowledge and wisdom is available to all believers who draw upon it, not just to a select few. With such divine wisdom and understanding offered to Christians, Paul saw no need for anyone to be misled by shallow philosophies, human traditions, or superficial arguments that merely sound reasonable.

Christians today still sometimes make the mistake of looking for spiritual knowledge and understanding in sources other than God's Word. If we consistently study, meditate on, and apply Scripture to everyday situations, it will become a permanent part of us. Our thinking will be in tune with God's. And we will discover the treasures waiting for us as we draw from the true source of knowledge and wisdom.

Let Christ's word with all its wisdom and richness live in you.

Colossians 3:16

Knowledge That Transforms

Colossians 3:5–17

After Paul told the Colossians what he was praying for them, he told them why he made that specific request. He asked God to fill them with spiritual wisdom and understanding so they would be able to discern God's will and would desire to live a righteous, productive life that pleased God in every way. The starting point for spiritual knowledge that leads to a transformed lifestyle is an understanding of what Christ did for those who believe. Paul was always ready to remind people of that.

A "before and after" theme of contrasts runs throughout the letter. Paul explained that God rescued us from the power of darkness and brought us into the kingdom of his Son (1:13). Once we were alienated from God, but now we are reconciled with him through Christ's death (1:21–22). Before, we were dead in our sins because of our corrupt nature; now God has made us alive in Christ by forgiving our sins (2:13–15).

Paul described the proper response to such great love and sacrifice using Greek words that convey the idea of putting on and taking off clothes. He listed sinful habits and behaviors that we should get rid of including sexual immorality, evil desires, impurity, lust, and greed. After coming to Christ, we are to "put on" our new self with godly traits and attitudes such as kindness, patience, humility, a willingness to forgive, and a loving nature.

Learning about the Bible or theological issues simply for the sake of acquiring knowledge is not worth very much. God is pleased when we ask him for spiritual discernment, but he expects us to take the wisdom he freely gives and put it into action. The more we grow in our understanding of who Christ is and what he did for us, the more that knowledge will affect our daily walk, and our life will be transformed.

> *That you may walk worthy of the Lord, fully
> pleasing Him, being fruitful in every good work
> and increasing in the knowledge of God.*
>
> Colossians 1:10 NKJV

1 Thessalonians

Watching for His Return

We believe that Jesus died and came back to life. We also believe that, through Jesus, God will bring back those who have died. They will come back with Jesus.

1 Thessalonians 4:14

Paul established a church in Thessalonica during his second missionary journey, but severe opposition instigated by some Jews forced him to leave abruptly. Paul felt deeply concerned for this infant congregation comprised mostly of converted pagans. He'd had little time to ground them in Christian doctrine, plus the persecution against believers in Thessalonica persisted after he left. While Paul ministered elsewhere, he sent Timothy to check on the church's welfare. In response to Timothy's report, Paul wrote to the Thessalonians from Corinth around AD 51.

Calling the Thessalonians a model for other believers in the area, Paul commended their love, joy, stability of faith, and willingness to share the gospel. He defended himself against false accusations of being motivated by greed and leaving them suddenly because of cowardice. Paul encouraged the Thessalonians to stand strong in the face of persecution and to live godly lives. One of his major purposes, however, was to correct their misconceptions about the second coming of Christ.

The Thessalonians had understood from Paul that Jesus would return and take them away. When some of their loved ones died, they became confused. Would these believers miss out on the second coming? Paul comforted those grieving, and assured them that the dead in Christ would join them when all believers were caught up in the air with Christ. Besides teaching about this doctrine, Paul showed its practical effect. Every chapter ends with a reference to Christ's second coming and ties the event to some aspect of Christian living.

Reading Thessalonians reminds us to look forward to Jesus's return whenever we suffer persecution or when we lose a believing loved one. It also shows us how this hope should influence our life. If we live each day in anticipation of Jesus's coming, we'll be prepared to meet him face-to-face.

Order of Events

1 Thessalonians 4:13—5:11

Among the Jews, the Sadducees rejected the concept of a resurrection from the dead. Greek philosophers also ridiculed the idea of a bodily resurrection, since they considered matter evil. Although the Christians in Thessalonica had believed the gospel, including Jesus's resurrection, they lacked a full understanding of the resurrection of believers and what would happen to those who died before Jesus's return. Paul set out to instruct them in this area, and in doing so, he spoke words of comfort to those who were mourning the loss of loved ones.

Paul told the Thessalonians there was no reason for them to grieve like unbelievers who have no hope. Speaking from a revelation he received from Jesus, he explained that when Jesus descends from heaven, he will bring the souls of deceased Christians with him. At a loud command, the voice of the archangel, and the trumpet call of God, their bodies will be resurrected. Then believers who are alive will be caught up with them in the clouds to meet Jesus in the air.

This event is called the *rapture*, taken from a Latin word that conveys the concept of being "caught up" or "carried off" as described by the Greek text. Paul's teaching here and in 1 Corinthians 15 obviously refers to a different event from Christ's second coming to establish his earthly kingdom as depicted in Revelation and other passages. Yet people have interpreted 1 Thessalonians in various ways, debating when or if the rapture of the church will occur.

Periodically, someone makes the headlines by claiming to have calculated the date of Jesus's return. It grabs people's attention—until the date passes, then they stop thinking about it. Although we can't know the date, we can be sure that Jesus's return will happen suddenly, in an instant. Paul urged believers to be prepared by staying alert and living a life that won't embarrass us when Jesus does return.

> *Therefore, we must not fall asleep like other*
> *people, but we must stay awake and be sober.*
>
> 1 Thessalonians 5:6

2 Thessalonians

Watching for His Return (the Sequel)

Don't let anyone deceive you about this in any way. That day cannot come unless a revolt takes place first, and the man of sin, the man of destruction, is revealed.

2 Thessalonians 2:3

Within months after writing his first letter, Paul received fresh news about the Thessalonian church. He was glad to hear about their spiritual growth, increasing love for each other, and endurance in the face of persecution. But the report also troubled Paul. Rumors that the day of the Lord had begun left the Thessalonians shaken and confused. They may have even received a forged letter purportedly from Paul to this effect (2:2).

Paul had written that God didn't intend them to experience his wrath (see 1 Thess. 5:9), but the false rumors coupled with the persecution they suffered led them to believe they might be living in the tribulation period. Additionally, misunderstandings had prompted some believers to quit their jobs. While they used the excuse of waiting for Jesus's return, other church members had to support them.

Paul wrote a second letter to encourage the Thessalonians in their persecution, to correct false teachings about the day of the Lord, and to address the problem of laziness caused by their misconceptions. He reminded them that certain events will occur before the day of the Lord: a great rebellion against God culminating in the rise of the man of sin, or Antichrist, who will claim to be God. After the period of tribulation, Jesus will return to earth to defeat all of God's enemies. As for those who had quit working to wait on Jesus, Paul had a simple solution: "Whoever doesn't want to work shouldn't be allowed to eat" (3:10).

Many Christians think that studying prophecy should be reserved for scholars or mature believers who have completed years of Bible study. But according to 2 Thessalonians 2:2, Paul taught the Thessalonians about end-time events very soon after their conversion. Even though some passages may be difficult to interpret, 1 and 2 Thessalonians hold value for any believer who doesn't want to be deceived.

Order of Events, Part 2

2 Thessalonians 2:1–12

False teachers had convinced some of the Thessalonian believers that the day of the Lord had arrived and God was pouring out his judgment on the earth. But this didn't square with Paul's explanation in his letter that they would escape God's wrath by being caught up to meet Jesus. Paul corrected the error in their thinking by reminding them of specific events that must take place before the judgments of the day of the Lord. In doing so, Paul included information about end-time events found nowhere else in the Bible.

A great worldwide rebellion against God will occur as people turn away from the truth. The man of lawlessness will rise to power and deceive the world with counterfeit miracles and signs. This Antichrist will be empowered by Satan, and will eventually set himself up as God. He will try to force the entire world to worship him alone until Jesus returns and defeats him. But before the Antichrist appears on the scene, someone or something that is now restraining sin will be removed.

Verse 6 indicates that Paul had already told the Thessalonians who or what this restraining force is, but he doesn't get specific in his letter. Although interpretations vary, many people believe this refers to the Holy Spirit indwelling and working through believers, thereby holding back the tide of sin and Satan's power. If the church is raptured, that restraining force will be removed, although the Spirit will still be present on the earth, allowing people to become believers if they choose to believe in Jesus.

The thought of what will happen on the earth during the last days should motivate us to make the most of our present opportunities to share God's truth. It also encourages us to devote ourselves to prayer—for Christians to grow spiritually and work together, for the gospel to spread, and for unbelievers to receive salvation so they can escape what will happen when the floodgates holding back sin are removed.

> *The earnest prayer of a righteous person has*
> *great power and produces wonderful results.*
>
> James 5:16 NLT

1 Timothy

Instructions to a Young Leader

Pursue what God approves of: a godly life, faith, love, endurance, and gentleness. Fight the good fight for the Christian faith.

1 Timothy 6:11–12

Several comments in Paul's letter to the Philippian church (such as Phil. 2:24) indicate that he expected to be released from his Roman imprisonment. Most scholars believe that the authorities freed Paul around AD 62. After visiting several churches, he met up with Timothy at Ephesus. Paul left Timothy there while he traveled on to Macedonia. When Paul saw that his return might be delayed, he wrote Timothy a letter of encouragement and instruction. Paul knew all too well the heavy burden of responsibility that his younger, less experienced co-worker faced.

Paul instructed Timothy in combating false teachers who had infiltrated the church, as he had predicted almost five years earlier (see Acts 20:28–30). He gave directions on maintaining order in public worship and administering church discipline. Besides addressing behavior within the church, Paul advised Timothy on his personal conduct and character. As a servant of Christ, Timothy must guard his motives, keep his doctrine pure, and live above reproach. Before Paul closed, he challenged Timothy to fulfill his calling by using the spiritual gifts God had given him.

The books of 1 and 2 Timothy, along with Titus, are called the Pastoral Epistles. Paul recognized the need for structure in the growing churches; he also knew the time was drawing near when his influence would diminish and he would pass the baton on to others. But 1 Timothy is not just a leadership manual—it's also a manual for godly living. Although it and the other Pastoral Epistles are addressed solely to an individual, it's obvious that Paul wanted congregations as a whole to benefit from his words.

Whether we're a church leader, parent, grandparent, friend, or neighbor, someone is watching us. If we obey the guidelines in 1 Timothy, our speech, behavior, love, faith, and purity will serve as an example to other believers (4:12). The principles in Paul's letter apply to everyone who wants to "fight the good fight."

For Love of Money

1 Timothy 6:3–10

As Paul warned Timothy about false teachers who infiltrated churches, he explained their motivation. Their teaching and preaching didn't represent a ministry, but a moneymaking business. They considered pretending to be godly and being involved in church work as a good way to turn a profit. Paul contrasted this with the proper attitude of a true believer. While godliness doesn't necessarily bring financial gain, it is gain itself when combined with contentment.

The desire to be rich is a dangerous trap since "the love of money is the root of all kinds of evil" (v. 10). We can get pulled into an endless cycle of greed; soon we discover that the more we have, the more we want. We will find ourselves continually falling into temptation and sin. We may end up like the people Paul mentioned, whose longing for wealth made them wander from the faith and suffer much self-inflicted grief.

Many people verbally agree that money can't buy happiness while their lifestyle says otherwise. No matter how much our bank account or portfolio grows, we can never find fulfillment in money or in what it can buy. Paul pointed out that we didn't bring anything into the world when we were born; we can't take any material possessions along when we leave it. We would be better off learning to be satisfied when our basic needs are met instead of always wanting more luxuries.

These verses in 1 Timothy provide guidelines for checking the motivation of church leaders and also our own attitudes. Do our thoughts focus on ways to get more stuff that we want, or on opportunities to serve God and others? The only lasting fulfillment in life comes from making God our first priority and desire. Then, as we pursue a godly lifestyle and learn to be content with what God provides, we'll find that we're reaping huge dividends.

A godly life brings huge profits to people
who are content with what they have.

1 Timothy 6:6

2 Timothy

Staying on Course

Do your best to present yourself to God as a tried-and-true worker who isn't ashamed to teach the word of truth correctly.

2 Timothy 2:15

When a fire destroyed much of Rome in AD 64, the insane emperor Nero blamed it on the Christians. Paul's enemies in Asia took advantage of the severe backlash against believers and had him arrested once again. This time Paul wasn't in a rented house with limited freedoms and accessibility to his friends. He found himself chained like a criminal in a cold dungeon, with Luke as his only companion. When Onesiphorus visited, he had to search hard to find the apostle. Paul fully expected to be executed; he knew his life was nearing its end.

Even under these circumstances, Paul's thoughts focused on the gospel and on Timothy, his co-worker and beloved son in the faith. Paul's final letter assured Timothy of his love and prayers, and reminded the young pastor of his spiritual heritage passed down from his mother and grandmother. Paul urged Timothy to stand firm against opposition and be prepared to suffer hardship "like a good soldier of Christ Jesus" (2:3). Timothy was to guard the gospel that had been entrusted to him, preaching the Word both when it was convenient and when it was not.

Paul warned that the problem of imposters and false teachers would go from bad to worse. Many sinful people would appear to have a form of godliness while lacking its power to live a changed life. A time would come when people would desert the truth, preferring to surround themselves with teachers who said only what they wanted to hear. That made it all the more imperative for Timothy to have a solid foundation in the truth.

As we read the last words of the great apostle and missionary, we sense his loneliness as he implores Timothy to visit him one final time. We also sense the unshakeable faith that gave Paul his endurance, courage, and boldness. His example encourages us to stay on course until the end, unashamed to teach the truth at every opportunity.

Never Abandoned

2 Timothy 4:6–18

Paul knew that he faced certain execution. Using a phrase related to Old Testament sacrifices, he told Timothy that his life was being poured out as a drink offering to God. Paul wasn't afraid of death; he knew that his reward was waiting for him. He wasn't ashamed to face Jesus Christ; he had faithfully completed the work God gave him to do. But as his end drew nearer, Paul found little comfort and support from some of the churches he had sacrificed so much for.

Virtually everyone in the province of Asia had deserted Paul, although Onesiphorus had gone out of his way to be helpful (1:15), and a few others were absent because of church duties. Paul specifically mentioned a co-worker named Demas who had abandoned him because he loved this present world more than God's work. During Paul's preliminary hearing, no one had spoken up in his defense. Following the example of Jesus and Stephen, Paul asked forgiveness for those who had abandoned him.

Twice Paul urged Timothy to come visit him before winter, when it would be impossible to travel by ship. We don't know if Timothy reached his mentor before it was too late, but besides his close friend Luke, Paul did have other support. At his first hearing, the Lord stood by his side and gave him strength. Paul's fate was sealed in regard to the Roman courts; his eternal destiny was also sealed. God would take him safely home.

Before Moses died, he urged the Israelites to be strong and courageous as they crossed into the Promised Land. Their Lord would go with them and never leave them. Paul's last recorded words are another reminder that even if everyone on earth deserted us, we would still have the Lord at our side to offer comfort and strength. No matter what happens, we never have to worry about being abandoned by him.

> *The Lord your God is the one who is going with*
> *you. He won't abandon you or leave you.*
>
> Deuteronomy 31:6

Titus

Sound Doctrine Leads to Proper Behavior

Tell believers to live the kind of life that goes along with accurate teachings.

Titus 2:1

Between his first and second letters to Timothy, Paul wrote to Titus, another young co-worker and close friend. Titus was a Greek convert who had traveled and ministered with Paul, serving as Paul's ambassador to the troubled church at Corinth several times. When Paul visited the island of Crete, he left Titus behind to supervise the churches there. Knowing that Titus had his work cut out for him, Paul wrote a letter similar to 1 Timothy full of practical advice on church organization.

As in other places, the church in Crete had its share of false teachers. Paul's instructions for detecting and silencing these false teachers contribute to the overall theme of the letter: the inseparable link between belief and behavior. Although these people claimed to know God, their lifestyle indicated they didn't have a relationship with him (1:16). Paul mentioned Jewish converts who were rebellious, spoke nonsense, and deceived people (1:10). Their behavior contrasted sharply with the guidelines for Christian living given in chapters 2 and 3.

Another reason for the letter's emphasis stems from the strong pagan influence on the island of Crete. Paul quoted from one of their own, a sixth-century BC philosopher and poet, who declared that "Cretans are always liars, savage animals, and lazy gluttons" (1:12). By Paul's time, the phrase had become a general cliché to describe the low reputation of the people. The false teachers who fit this stereotype and Crete's reputation for immorality made it all the more crucial for Titus to correct and urge the members to live a life worthy of the gospel they claimed to believe.

Many churches today neglect the teaching of Christian doctrine. Some people see it as boring or unnecessary, placing more emphasis on church programs, activities, or service projects. Paul's letter to Titus reminds us that sound doctrine is at the heart of the Christian life. If we want our behavior to please God, then we need to first make sure our beliefs are in line with his truth.

Philemon

From Slave to Brother

Maybe Onesimus was gone for a while so that you could have him back forever—
no longer as a slave but better than a slave—as a dear brother. He is especially
dear to me, but even more so to you, both as a person and as a Christian.

Philemon 15–16

With slavery so widespread in the Roman Empire, some early Christians owned
slaves. Philemon was one of Paul's converts who lived in Colossae and hosted
a congregation in his home. His slave Onesimus stole from him and ran away,
an offense punishable by death. In Rome, Onesimus somehow came into contact with Paul, who was under house arrest. Onesimus embraced the gospel
message and devoted himself to helping Paul. But as a Christian, Onesimus
had a responsibility to Philemon and needed to make restitution. When Paul
sent a letter to the Colossian church by Tychicus, he also sent Onesimus along;
this made the runaway slave's return trip safer.

Although Paul's shortest letter, Philemon is a masterpiece of tactful per-
suasion. Paul never made light of the wrong committed by Onesimus, but he
acted as his advocate, urging forgiveness and reconciliation. Paul could have
used his authority as an apostle to order Philemon to do what he said; instead
he issued a personal plea for Philemon to accept Onesimus and treat him not
as a runaway slave, but as a beloved brother in Christ. Paul asked that any
financial obligation on the part of Onesimus be charged to his own account;
he briefly reminded Philemon of his own indebtedness to Paul for bringing
him the gospel.

This succinct but powerful letter pictures our relationship with Christ, who
interceded for us. He brought us reconciliation with the Father by charging
our sin debt to his own account; now we are Christ's beloved siblings instead
of slaves to sin. Paul's letter also reminds us that in addition to changing
lives, the gospel transforms relationships. When we remember what Christ
did for us, we'll be ready to welcome other believers as we would welcome
him—regardless of any barriers society tries to put between us.

Hebrews

Christ Is Greater

His Son is the reflection of God's glory and the exact likeness of God's being. He holds everything together through his powerful words. After he had cleansed people from their sins, he received the highest position, the one next to the Father in heaven.

Hebrews 1:3

Much about the book of Hebrews remains a mystery. Many early scholars considered Paul the author, although significant differences in language and style of writing seem to rule him out. More importantly, the author indicates in Hebrews 2:3 that he was not an eyewitness to Jesus, while Paul claimed personal revelation from the risen Christ. Other suggestions for authorship include Barnabas, Apollos, and Luke. Most agree that Hebrews was written before the destruction of the Jerusalem temple in AD 70 since it refers to ongoing sacrifices.

The recipients appear to be Jewish Christians who were in danger of slipping back into Judaism because of spiritual immaturity and the opposition they faced. Using an abundance of Old Testament references, the author wrote to show these believers that Christ was superior over all that came before him. Using more than twenty titles to describe Christ's attributes and work, he proved that Christ was better than ancient prophets, angels, Moses, and Aaron and his entire priestly line. How could they turn back to the old Judaic system that had been superseded by Christ in every respect?

Through his death, resurrection, and ascension, Christ offered the perfect sacrifice and became the mediator of a better covenant. He is the reality or substance of the "shadows" portrayed in the Old Testament, such as the offerings and feasts. Christ is now our High Priest, working on our behalf. Throughout his letter, the author sprinkled encouragement to endure and warnings against turning away from Christ.

Hebrews is invaluable in helping us understand the Old Testament and its symbolism as well as the supremacy of the Christian faith. The author may be unknown but his message is still relevant. When we're tempted to look elsewhere for spiritual answers, Hebrews reminds us that Christ is infinitely superior to everything else out there.

No Plateaus

Hebrews 5:11—6:3

During his lengthy discussion of Jesus's role as High Priest, the author of Hebrews paused to scold his readers for their immaturity. Such a topic would be hard to explain since they had become spiritually lazy and were slow to learn. By now they should have reached the point where they were instructing others; instead they needed someone to review the basics with them. They should be firm in the fundamental truths such as repentance, baptisms, setting people apart for special callings, the resurrection of the dead, and eternal judgment.

The author compared them to babies still on a diet of milk when they should have matured to the point of being able to handle solid food. As long as they remained in the baby stage, they would not be able to distinguish good from evil or truth from error. They would also have trouble digesting the "meat" of God's truth. Although they might be familiar with what Christ did while on earth, it would be difficult for them to understand his present priestly work in heaven.

The recipients had been believers for a long time, but they had neglected their Christian education. Some had stopped attending regular worship services. As a result, they had lapsed into spiritual apathy that kept them from progressing in their understanding and discernment. This made them vulnerable to doctrinal errors and teachings that threatened to pull them away from the Christian faith and back into the old system of Judaism.

In the spiritual life, there is no such thing as a plateau. If we aren't progressing forward, then we're losing ground. As we apply the basic truths to our lives and share them with others, we will gain more understanding and discernment. God wants us to move forward so that we won't be in danger of slipping backward; he expects us to grow up in our faith so that we can have an adult diet.

However, solid food is for mature people,
whose minds are trained by practice to know
the difference between good and evil.

Hebrews 5:14

A Greater High Priest

Hebrews 4:14—5:10; 6:19—7:28

To help his readers understand Jesus's role as High Priest, the writer of Hebrews contrasted him with Old Testament priests. The high priest was allowed to go behind the veil and enter the Most Holy Place only once a year, to stand in God's presence and atone for the nation's sins. Jesus has passed through the heavens to minister at the heavenly tabernacle. Now he sits at God's right hand, continually interceding for believers. Before making atonement for the people, Old Testament priests had to first offer a sacrifice for their own sins. Since Jesus never sinned, he had no need to do this; instead he offered himself as a sacrifice for the world.

Aaron's descendants who served as high priests died; their ministry was temporary. Jesus belongs to a higher order. The writer compared him to an Old Testament figure mentioned in Genesis 14:18–20 and briefly referred to by David in Psalm 110:4. Melchizedek served as king and priest of God in Salem (later Jerusalem) long before the nation of Israel or its priesthood existed. Since Scripture doesn't record his genealogy or death, Melchizedek is said to be a priest forever. In this way, he foreshadowed the perpetual priesthood of Jesus. Melchizedek's superiority over the Levite priesthood is also demonstrated by the fact that Abraham (Levi's ancestor) paid tithes to Melchizedek.

Although he is God, Jesus's life on earth uniquely qualified him to be a high priest who fully understands the human condition. Jesus experienced all the weaknesses and temptations that we do. As God, he never yielded to sin's pull; as a man, he felt the full force of it. He endured persecution, humiliation, false accusations, physical abuse, and an agonizing death. Our High Priest can sympathize with us in our temptations and offer compassion when we suffer. And he is always on duty.

> *But Jesus lives forever, so he serves as a priest*
> *forever. That is why he is always able to save those*
> *who come to God through him. He can do this*
> *because he always lives and intercedes for them.*
>
> Hebrews 7:24–25

A Better Covenant

Hebrews 8

As the Israelites traveled to the Promised Land, God gave Moses detailed instructions for building a portable tabernacle to represent his presence among the people and to serve as their focal point for worship. God ordained Aaron and his descendants as priests to serve in the tabernacle and later in the temple. Since Jesus came from the tribe of Judah, not Levi, technically he could not have served as a high priest on earth. Instead, he serves in the actual presence of God in heaven, of which the tabernacle was merely a shadow. His ministry is far superior to the Levitical priests' ministry as he mediates a better covenant founded on better promises.

The old covenant was based on law and depended on people's faithfulness to God. The new covenant is founded on God's faithful promises to people. Hebrews 8 quotes several of God's "I will" statements regarding the new covenant. While the law couldn't promise forgiveness, God will forgive our sins and not hold them against us. The law was written on stone tablets and focused on external behavior; the new covenant brings internal change as God inscribes his laws on our hearts and minds. Shortly after Hebrews was written, the Romans destroyed the temple, ending the old sacrificial system. The new covenant is eternal; it will never become obsolete or disappear.

As Jesus celebrated Passover the night before his crucifixion, he explained that the cup of wine represented the new covenant in his blood poured out for forgiveness of sins (see Luke 22:20). Many Christians recognize how the new covenant relates to their salvation but then try to depend on external rules and standards for growing in godliness. As we yield to the Holy Spirit's leading, he will give us the desire and power to obey the laws God has written on our hearts, leading to lasting transformation. You can't get a better promise than that.

*But the ministry Jesus has received is as superior to theirs
as the covenant of which he is mediator is superior to
the old one, and it is founded on better promises.*

Hebrews 8:6 NIV

A Perfect Sacrifice

Hebrews 9:1—10:18

The Old Testament system of sacrifices instituted by God demonstrated that forgiveness of sins required the shedding of blood. Day after day the priests stood offering sacrifices that covered the people's sins and made them outwardly clean for a time. The fact that the sacrifices had to be repeated proved that they were not enough to permanently cleanse from sin and take away guilt. These sacrifices served more as a reminder of the people's sins and as a picture of what Christ would one day accomplish.

As our great High Priest, Christ offered himself as the perfect sacrifice for sin once and for all. His sinless blood did what thousands upon thousands of animal sacrifices could not achieve. Afterward he sat down at God's right hand, indicating that his work of atonement for sin was finished. Christ's death made it possible for our sins to be permanently forgiven and our guilt removed forever. Our sins aren't just covered; they are cleansed. Our record and our conscience have been cleared.

The original readers of Hebrews were being tempted to turn back to the old system of sacrifices that had to be offered over and over. Such an action would imply that the sacrifice Christ offered wasn't enough to obtain permanent forgiveness and make us right with God. We imply the same thing when we confess our past sins over and over. Although Christ's sacrifice makes believers perfect in God's sight, our daily sins can burden us with guilt and make us feel as though we're not good enough. When we repent and confess, it's as though the sin no longer exists in God's eyes. We can live with a clear conscience if we trust in Christ's perfect sacrifice and not in our own performance.

> *Just think how much more the blood of Christ will purify*
> *our consciences from sinful deeds so that we can worship*
> *the living God. For by the power of the eternal Spirit, Christ*
> *offered himself to God as a perfect sacrifice for our sins.*
>
> Hebrews 9:14 NLT

An Irresistible Invitation

Hebrews 4:14—16; 10:19—23

Under the old system, the people were not allowed to enter the holy precincts of the tabernacle. The priests themselves were forbidden to go past the thick veil that marked off the Most Holy Place where the ark of the covenant symbolized God's throne. The high priest could only pass through this curtain once a year, on the Day of Atonement, after making elaborate preparations. Jesus's crucifixion changed all that. At the moment Christ died, the heavy curtain in the temple ripped from top to bottom (see Matt. 27:50–51). God wanted to make it clear that the barrier of sin that had separated people from himself had been removed forever.

Because of our great High Priest's perfect sacrifice and the new covenant that believers enter into, we have a standing invitation to approach God. We are not just allowed, but encouraged to come before his throne, every moment of every day. Having been cleansed inside and out by Christ's blood, there is no barrier separating us from him. We can enjoy a personal relationship with God, knowing that we are free from guilt in his eyes. For this reason, we can go to him at any time to draw from the mercy and grace Christ has made available to us.

It's important to approach God with the proper reverence for who he is, and with a clean heart that has repented and confessed any known sins. But many Christians are hesitant to be open and honest with God, too afraid or too ashamed to ask for his help when they need it. God wants his children to come to him with boldness and confidence, trusting that he will meet their needs. We can draw near to God at any time through worship, prayer, and reading and meditating on his Word. Christ didn't die so that we would be timid about approaching God's throne, but so that we could come before him often and with confidence.

> *So we can go confidently to the throne of God's*
> *kindness to receive mercy and find kindness,*
> *which will help us at the right time.*
>
> Hebrews 4:16

Hall of Faith

Hebrews 11

The eleventh chapter of Hebrews is often referred to as the "Hall of Faith." The writer begins by defining faith: a settled assurance of things that we expect and a conviction of what we cannot see. He then launches into a list of Old Testament people whose lives demonstrated this faith in the unseen reality of God and his promises. The list includes great heroes like Noah, Abraham, Sarah, and Moses, along with lesser-known personalities such as Rahab, Barak, and Jephthah. All of these people demonstrated their faith by acts of obedience or sacrifice, sometimes in dramatic ways.

In Hebrews 11:35 the author's focus shifts as he shows that not all the Old Testament saints were delivered from danger in miraculous ways like Daniel in the lions' den or the three young Hebrew men in the fiery furnace. Many were tortured and killed in various ways. But what looked like defeat in the world's eyes actually represented victory. Although God did not spare them from suffering and death, the faith of these men and women enabled them to endure with the conviction that something far better lay in store for them in the future.

To live by faith means more than believing that God exists; we must believe in his character and his promises. We trust that he will do what he says, even when we don't see any sign of those promises materializing yet. The key is to stay focused on God as the object of our faith rather than on our circumstances or emotions.

Many of the people listed in Hebrews 11 were highly flawed; some failed miserably. The fact that their names are included proves that God doesn't demand perfect performance. We will occasionally stumble and have moments of weakness, but if we trust God's Word and try to obey his will, he promises to give us enough faith to see what our eyes cannot.

> *Faith assures us of things we expect and convinces*
> *us of the existence of things we cannot see.*
>
> Hebrews 11:1

DECEMBER

4

James

Living Proof

Another person might say, "You have faith, but I do good things." Show me your faith apart from the good things you do. I will show you my faith by the good things I do.

James 2:18

The book of James may be the earliest New Testament book; it is definitely the most practical. Jesus's half-brothers didn't believe in him until after his resurrection; afterward, his half-brother James quickly became a recognized leader of the Jerusalem church. His letter is addressed to Jewish believers scattered outside of Palestine. Facing hostility and persecution, the believers had failed to put their faith into practice. As a result, they struggled with factions and conflicts, temptation to adopt a worldly lifestyle, and a double-mindedness toward God.

James encouraged these believers to live out their faith. Using many figures of speech, analogies, and vivid images drawn from nature, he urged his readers to "do" the Word and not merely hear it, to pursue heavenly instead of earthly wisdom, and to prove their faith by the way they lived instead of simply talking the talk. Then they would be able to resist Satan and their own evil desires, control their speech, treat each other without favoritism, and draw close to God. They could help each other by praying for one another and holding each other accountable.

Some scholars have claimed that James contradicts Paul's writings, especially Romans with its emphasis on justification by faith alone. In reality, James and Paul complement each other and give a full picture of faith. Both teach that salvation is obtained only by God's grace through faith, but that inward faith will naturally lead to outward actions. Otherwise, faith would be like a body without breath—dead, as James asserted in 2:26.

It's easy to claim to be God's child, but God demands more than just a verbal or mental faith. If our lifestyle doesn't match up with James's how-to manual, we need to start *doing* the Word and not just *reading* it. We may need to breathe life into our faith so that we have living proof of what we claim to believe.

Rejoicing in Trials

James 1:2–12

The New Testament makes it clear that believers can expect troubles in this life. James offered some practical advice for handling trials; he began by urging us to be glad when they come. This sounds like an impossible command, and it *is* if we view our difficulties as bad luck or punishment. James challenged us to accept the hard times God allows in our life as opportunities to grow in godliness. By persevering through trials with the right attitude, we develop patience and endurance, which help us to become spiritually mature and complete. God tests our faith so that it can become solid and steadfast no matter what we face.

Another key to handling trials is to ask God for wisdom when we need it. But we can only expect to receive his help if we ask with faith that he will answer. If our mind is filled with doubts when we pray, we're like "a wave that is blown by the wind and tossed by the sea" (v. 6).

God promises to give wisdom generously to those who ask in the right spirit. He will provide the discernment to help us not just endure trials, but to make the most of our circumstances for our good and his glory. We can even learn to see adversity as a good gift from our heavenly Father (v. 17).

Whenever tough times come, God doesn't want us to plaster a fake smile on our face and spout pious-sounding platitudes. He also doesn't want us to passively accept our circumstances while acting like a martyr. Instead of whining, complaining, and growing angry or bitter, we can trust that God loves us and wants what's best for us. Our mindset will determine the outcome of our times of testing. As long as we remember that God wants to use difficulties to build our character, we can choose to adopt an attitude of joy.

> *My brothers and sisters, be very happy when you*
> *are tested in different ways. You know that such*
> *testing of your faith produces endurance.*
>
> James 1:2–3

Equal Opportunity Faith

James 2:1—13

Magazines, books, and television shows reveal our society's fascination with the rich and famous. Many stars are held in awe and practically worshiped, regardless of their bad behavior, while poor people are often ignored. Such a shallow attitude is nothing new; James addressed the problem among first-century Christians. He imagined a scenario in which two men came to a worship service, one man decked out in fine clothes and gold jewelry and the other one shabbily dressed. The members paid special attention to the well-dressed man and gave him the best seat, but told the poor man to stand or sit at their feet.

James condemned such preferential treatment as sin. Their discrimination proved that they judged with corrupt standards and evil thoughts. He pointed out the irony in their attitude by asking several questions. Hadn't God chosen poor people and made them rich in faith? Why should they favor rich people who were often guilty of oppressing and exploiting the poor? Showing such favoritism was not only unreasonable; it violated the royal law to love your neighbor as yourself (v. 8).

One way we put our faith into practice is by treating other people as equals worthy of our attention, our courtesy, and our compassion. The world around us may be impressed by wealth, status, and power, but God expects us to look at people in a different light. He wants us to see each person as someone for whom Christ died. Evaluating people by any other standard is incompatible with our Christian faith.

Our churches should be an environment where no one ever has to worry about being judged for a less than desirable appearance. As we obey the law of love, we'll learn to look at a person's character and value them for who they are. Then we can show the world that God offers everyone an equal opportunity to become his child.

> *If you favor one person over another, you're sinning,*
> *and this law convicts you of being disobedient.*
>
> James 2:9

Mouth Control

James 3

Many Bible passages address the need for using our words wisely. The book of Proverbs especially offers lots of advice for guarding our speech. As James described the marks of a spiritually mature Christian, he also had a lot to say about this topic—and for good reason. Apparently, his readers engaged in slander against each other (4:11) and had problems with fights and quarrels among themselves (4:1). Early in his letter, James urged them all to be quick to listen, slow to speak, and to not get angry easily (1:19).

James didn't mince words when he discussed the importance of controlling the tongue. Even though the tongue is small, it holds a powerful influence over our life, just as a bit controls a horse or a small rudder directs a huge ship. Our words deeply affect others. Carelessly spoken or mean-spirited words can do a lot of damage, like a single spark igniting a raging forest fire. The tongue can set our life on fire and be used by Satan to spread destruction even after we've repented of our words.

Since the tongue is like a wild beast that no one can tame, how can we handle this "uncontrollable evil filled with deadly poison" (v. 8)? The answer is to draw from God's divine wisdom described in James 3:13–18. Depending on worldly wisdom yields jealousy, self-centeredness, disorder, and all kinds of evil. God's wisdom infuses our behavior and our words with peacefulness, gentleness, mercy, kindness, and sincerity.

James pointed out the hypocrisy when we use our mouth to praise God but also to curse or hurt people. Clean and polluted water don't flow from the same spring; neither should clean *and* polluted words come of our mouth. We need to always evaluate our words carefully. Then we need to meditate on God's Word and seek his help each day in controlling our mouth—before we set off a raging fire.

> *If a person thinks that he is religious but*
> *can't control his tongue, he is fooling himself.*
> *That person's religion is worthless.*
>
> James 1:26

1 Peter

Suffering for Christ

Dear friends, don't be surprised by the fiery troubles that are coming in order to test you. Don't feel as though something strange is happening to you, but be happy as you share Christ's sufferings. Then you will also be full of joy when he appears again in his glory.

1 Peter 4:12–13

Peter probably wrote his first letter from Rome, which he referred to figuratively as "Babylon," either shortly before or after the outbreak of Emperor Nero's cruel persecution of Christians. Peter wrote to believers in five provinces in Asia Minor (modern-day Turkey) who faced growing hostility because of their faith in Christ. He offered comfort, hope, and encouragement to help them live holy lives without wavering in their faith and to prepare them for the hard times ahead.

First, Peter reminded his readers of the riches of their salvation, both their present joy despite their circumstances and the glories of their future inheritance. He urged them to exhibit submission in all their relationships in order to foster harmony and present a strong testimony to outsiders. Three times Peter told them that if they faced suffering, it should not be for any wrongdoing on their part, but due to their stand for Christ. He pointed to Christ as both their source of hope and the ultimate example to imitate when being persecuted unjustly. Whenever they endured persecution for the right reason and in the right way, they became partners with Christ in his suffering and would receive future glory for it.

Even if we are not suffering for our faith at present, as believers we live in constant conflict with our culture. Taking a stand for Christ can make us targets for insults, ridicule, and discrimination. One day, we may face more serious persecution for our beliefs, as Christians in many countries already suffer. Reading 1 Peter can help prepare us for whatever lies ahead. Meditating on the hope we have in Christ and the example he provided can strengthen our endurance. We can also find comfort in remembering that whenever we suffer *for* Christ, we suffer *with* him.

Who We Are

1 Peter 1:13—2:12

Early in his letter, Peter wrote that believers are to be holy in every area of their lives because the God who called them is holy. Such a command sounds impossible and certainly can't be achieved in our own power. Although we'll never reach perfection in this life, every aspect of our character and lifestyle should be in the process of conforming to God's will. We'll find motivation to pursue holiness when we remember the high price that purchased our salvation. Peter pointed out that God didn't set us free from our old life of slavery to sin with a ransom payment of silver or gold, but with the precious blood of Jesus Christ.

Christ's sacrifice has given us a new identity. We are now living stones being built into a spiritual house founded on Jesus Christ, the chosen and precious cornerstone. As holy priests, we can offer spiritual sacrifices pleasing to God, such as praise, worship, and doing good deeds. God called us "out of darkness into his marvelous light" so that he could make us his "chosen people, a royal priesthood, a holy nation, people who belong to God" (2:9).

Since we belong to God, we can't also belong to this world. Our relationship with him requires us to live as foreigners and temporary residents during our earthly life. Knowing that heaven is our real home will help us resist the pull of our sinful desires and the immorality of the culture around us. It will also help us endure any hardships or suffering as we remember that this life on earth is only temporary and will pass quickly. But while we're here, God can help us live a holy lifestyle that pleases him and provides a powerful witness to unbelievers. The starting point is an understanding of what he's done for us and who we are.

> However, you are chosen people, a royal priesthood,
> a holy nation, people who belong to God. You were
> chosen to tell about the excellent qualities of God, who
> called you out of darkness into his marvelous light.
>
> 1 Peter 2:9

2 Peter

False Teachers

False prophets were among God's people in the past, as false teachers will be among you. They will secretly bring in their own destructive teachings. They will deny the Lord, who has bought them, and they will bring themselves swift destruction.

2 Peter 2:1

Three years after his first letter, Peter wrote a second one to the same churches in Asia Minor (3:1). While 1 Peter addressed the external pressures of opposition toward believers, 2 Peter focused on the internal threat of deceptive heresies arising from within the church. At the time Peter wrote this letter, Jesus had told him he would soon die (1:14); Peter was martyred sometime between AD 64–67. In his last recorded words, the great apostle warned about the danger of being seduced by false teachers and urged spiritual maturity as an antidote against being deceived.

Peter began with a reminder that God's divine power has provided believers with "everything we need for life and godliness" (1:3). Through his Holy Spirit, God allows us to share in his divine nature so we can escape sin's corruption. Believers are to work at developing character traits such as integrity, self-control, perseverance, kindness, and love. This spiritual growth must be based on the Word of God, not on subjective feelings. Peter testified to the divine origin of the Scriptures and told his readers to pay attention to them as "a light that shines in a dark place" (1:19).

In chapter 2, Peter described the false teachers within the church who brought in heresies that led people away from Christ and even encouraged sexual immorality. He called them "stains and blemishes" and "dried-up springs" (vv. 13, 17). Their lifestyles were marked by self-centeredness, arrogance, and sensuality, yet their deceptive words easily seduced "people who aren't sure of what they believe" (v. 14).

Today we have no shortage of people peddling counterfeit forms of Christianity that appeal to believers who don't thoroughly know God's Word. Peter's last lines tell us how to protect ourselves: be on guard against deception by growing in knowledge of our Lord and Savior.

Where Is He?

2 Peter 3:3—15

The false teachers that had infiltrated the churches Peter wrote to scoffed at the doctrines of future judgment and Jesus's return to the earth. By denying these events, they considered themselves free to continue their sinful lifestyles. Peter defended biblical prophecy and, in doing so, gave one of the most graphic descriptions of end-time events found in the Bible.

The skeptics based their argument on the idea that everything in the world had remained the same since the beginning of creation. Why should they expect God to intervene in human affairs? Peter reminded them of truths they had conveniently ignored. God created the world by his spoken word; he later destroyed its inhabitants with a great flood in judgment for sin. One day in the future, the heavens will disappear with a roar and God will destroy the earth with fire to make way for a new heaven and earth.

To believers longing to be delivered from persecution, it seemed that God was slow about keeping his promises. Peter explained that God doesn't operate within our framework of time; he sees events through the lens of eternity. A second reason that Jesus's return seemed delayed was because of God's patience. He longs to see as many people as possible receive salvation before the final judgment.

Like Peter, we live in the "last days," the period of time between Jesus's first and second coming. As Peter predicted, many people scoff at the ideas of Jesus's return and a future judgment on the earth. Even if we accept biblical prophecies, it's easy to get complacent and caught up in the concerns of our present life. Remembering that the earth will be destroyed will help us not get so attached to worldly possessions and pleasures. As we focus on the future from God's perspective, we'll find it easier to live the godly life he calls us to.

> *All these things will be destroyed in this way. So think of the kind of holy and godly lives you must live as you look forward to the day of God and eagerly wait for it to come.*
>
> 2 Peter 3:11—12

1 John

Living as God's Children

Consider this: The Father has given us his love. He loves us so much that we are actually called God's dear children. And that's what we are.

1 John 3:1

Paul called the apostle John one of the pillars of the church in Jerusalem (see Gal. 2:9). First-century historians indicate that John relocated from Jerusalem to Ephesus sometime before the Romans destroyed the city in AD 70. Many scholars believe John wrote his first letter from Ephesus to the Asian churches under his supervision. John wasn't addressing new believers; his readers were established in Christian doctrine taught by the apostles. But they faced two serious threats to their commitment: loving the world and what it offered, and being deceived by the lies of false teachers.

John opened his letter the same way he opened his Gospel. By affirming Jesus's deity and humanity, he immediately refuted false teachers who denied one or the other. Then John began his discussion of the relationship between God and true believers using simple language and a practical approach. John wanted his "dear children" to stand firm in the basic truths of their faith, to be assured of their salvation, and to know how to fully enjoy the benefits of being God's dearly loved child.

The letter is loosely structured, since John wrote a few lines on a topic, wandered off to a different subject, and then later returned to the original topic. Overall, 1 John presents three truths about God and how those truths affect his children. First, God is light. Since he is pure and holy, we are to walk in the light of his truth, not in the darkness of sin. Second, God is love. We show that we are God's children when we love each other, not in words alone but in action. Third, God is the source of life. Through Jesus Christ, we can be assured we have eternal life. By reminding us of these basic but wonderful truths, 1 John shows us how to have joy and confidence in our relationship with God.

What We Know

1 John 5:13–21

Some people criticize Christians for claiming to know God personally and for being so adamant about spiritual truths. Since they don't believe in a God that gets personally involved with human beings, they interpret such an attitude as arrogance. "Know" is a common theme in 1 John; the letter uses the word or an equivalent of it more than thirty times. John reminded his readers of the foundational truths of their faith to help them evaluate their lifestyle and also to safeguard them from false teachings.

Too many Christians struggle with doubts about their salvation, wondering if their conversion experience was real. One of John's purposes in writing was so that believers in Jesus can know without a shadow of doubt that they possess eternal life. We can be sure we know Christ if we obey his commands (2:3). We know we have passed from death to life if we love other believers (3:14). We know God lives in us because he has given us his Spirit (3:24). If we fail these tests, it's because either we are not saved or our fellowship with God has been broken because of sin or immaturity.

As John closed his letter, he summarized many of the points he had discussed and outlined the certainties of our faith. We know God listens to our requests and will grant those that meet his approval. We know anyone born of God does not go on sinning. Jesus protects us and Satan can't harm us, even though he has control over the world. We know God's Son has come and given us understanding so that we can know the true God.

First John offers a reassuring message that is badly needed today: in a world filled with uncertainties, we can be sure of what we know. And in a world full of fakes, we can know who is real.

> *We know that the Son of God has come and has*
> *given us understanding so that we know the real God.*
> *We are in the one who is real, his Son Jesus Christ.*
> *This Jesus Christ is the real God and eternal life.*
>
> 1 John 5:20

2 John

Watch Out for Deceivers

Everyone who doesn't continue to teach what Christ taught doesn't have God. The person who continues to teach what Christ taught has both the Father and the Son. If anyone comes to you and doesn't bring these teachings, don't take him into your home or even greet him.

2 John 9–10

John addressed his second letter to "the chosen lady and her children" (v. 1). Some interpret this literally to mean a specific woman. Others believe that John used the phrase figuratively to refer to a local church and its members, since the Greek word for "church" is feminine in gender and cities are often personified as women. Another possibility is that John addressed a woman who opened her home for a house church. That would explain the mix of singular and plural pronouns, as John sometimes spoke directly to the woman and sometimes to the congregation. In any case, John wrote about two themes that can be found in all of his writings: truth and love.

The first six verses are positive as John commended his readers for their faithfulness to obeying God's commands. He encouraged them to keep fulfilling the old commandment to love each other. But he wanted to make sure they practiced a discerning love. The last half of the letter is a negative warning against supporting those who oppose the truth about Christ and his teaching.

In his first letter, John wrote about a group of false teachers who had left the church (see 1 John 2:19). Some of these had become traveling teachers. It was customary for believers to open their homes to traveling evangelists and send them off with provisions when they left. John warned his readers not to show such hospitality to the false teachers who were infiltrating churches and spreading lies. By offering these deceivers assistance, they would be sharing in their evil work.

John's warning may sound harsh, but it reminds us that truth and love are inseparable. If we love others, we can't support those who deceive people. If we love truth, we can't encourage those who distort it.

3 John

Welcome Believers

We must support believers who go on trips like this so that we can work together with them in spreading the truth.

3 John 8

Third John is the shortest book in the Bible in the original Greek. If 2 John is addressed to a congregation rather than a specific woman, that leaves Philemon and 3 John as the only letters in the Bible addressed to individuals. John wrote this affectionate, personal note to a dear friend and devoted Christian named Gaius. John had heard how Gaius offered love and encouragement to believers, especially to traveling teachers and preachers. Gaius not only opened his home; he also extended financial and practical help to send them on their way. John assured his friend that he was doing the right thing. By supporting these missionaries who worked on behalf of the gospel, Gaius became their co-worker.

John added a few words of criticism about a domineering church leader named Diotrephes who stood in stark contrast to the faithful and generous Gaius. Diotrephes loved to be in control and was more interested in promoting himself than Jesus. He refused to have anything to do with John, one of Jesus's own apostles. Diotrephes spread malicious rumors about John and refused to welcome John's representatives. He even worked to stop others who wanted to welcome them, trying to throw them out of the church. John promised to deal with Diotrephes's behavior when he visited in person.

In his first letter, John discussed fellowship with God. In his second, he warned against fellowship with those who opposed the truth. Third John focuses on fellowship with other believers and shows us a negative example in the prideful, self-centered Diotrephes, while Gaius is a glowing model of godly love and generosity. A second positive example is found in Demetrius, who probably delivered the letter and received high praise from John. This brief letter encourages us to examine our attitudes and behavior toward other believers, whether members of our local congregation or traveling Christian workers. Would we receive praise like Gaius, or criticism like Diotrephes?

Jude

Defend the Faith

Dear friends, I had intended to write to you about the salvation we share. But something has come up. It demands that I write to you and encourage you to continue your fight for the Christian faith that was entrusted to God's holy people once for all time.

Jude 3

Although he was Jesus's half-brother, Jude humbly identified himself as "a servant of Jesus Christ and brother of James" (v. 1). He had originally intended to write a letter on the topic of salvation; instead, he felt compelled to warn his readers about immoral men who had secretly infiltrated the church in order to deceive people and distort God's truth. While many of the New Testament Epistles address the problem of false teachers, this short but powerful letter goes beyond all others with its impassioned condemnation of these dangerous men. Jude called them "dry clouds blown around by the winds" and "withered uprooted trees without any fruit" (v. 12).

These false teachers denied Christ's lordship, rejected authority, and caused divisions in the church. They equated being saved by grace with license to sin, trying to convince people that they could do as they pleased without worrying about God punishing them. Jude used a number of Old Testament examples showing God's judgment for rebellion including Cain, Balaam, Korah, fallen angels, unbelieving Israel in the wilderness, and the wicked people of Sodom and Gomorrah.

Jude's letter records the fulfillment of Peter's predictions concerning false teachers in his second letter, directly quoting 2 Peter 3:3. Now that the heretics were on the scene, Jude called his readers to action. He challenged them to be on guard against those who oppose the truth, to stay strong, and to win back those who had been deceived. Above all, they were to defend the doctrines of the Christian faith that had been entrusted to them.

Today we face the same dangers from false teachings and doctrinal errors as the first-century believers; Jude's call to action still applies. Reading his letter will help us stand firm and defend God's truth, no matter what it costs.

Revelation

The End—and a New Beginning

> Therefore, write down what you have seen, what is, and what is going to happen after these things.
>
> Revelation 1:19

Roman authorities banished the apostle John to the island of Patmos, probably during the reign of Domitian (AD 81–96). There God unveiled to John events prior to, during, and after Jesus's second coming to the earth. This final book of the Bible shows the consummation of God's plan of redemption first announced in Genesis, bringing history to its conclusion. God leaves no loose ends as he previews Christ's last battle against Satan and his allies, the final judgment of sin and Satan, and the creation of the New Jerusalem where believers will dwell with God forever.

Like parts of Ezekiel and Daniel, Revelation is written in apocalyptic form using symbolic imagery. The interpretation of John's visions has led to more disagreements and diversity of opinion than perhaps any other Bible book. It's possible to get so caught up in looking for hidden meanings and deciphering symbolism that we miss the core message: through his death and resurrection, Christ the Lamb has conquered sin, Satan, death, and hell. Because he reigns victoriously, we can look forward to a glorious future with him.

John originally wrote to seven churches in the Roman province of Asia Minor, present-day western Turkey. Through specific messages to the individual groups, Jesus offered praise and encouragement along with warnings about the danger of false teachings, materialism, and the desire for cultural approval. Since these early believers were suffering persecution, Revelation infused them with hope and the assurance that Christ will ultimately triumph over anyone who opposes him and his followers.

Studying Revelation demands commitment and diligence, but God promises to bless those who read and obey it. Knowing how history will end influences how we live today. It encourages us to keep our life pure so we can look to the future, saying, "Come, Lord Jesus!"

A Vision of Jesus

Revelation 1

The book of Revelation gives many names for Jesus, including the Lamb who was slain (5:6) and the Lion from the tribe of Judah (5:5). He's also called the faithful and true witness (3:14) and the King of Kings and Lord of Lords (19:16). The closing chapter identifies Jesus as the beginning and the end (22:13) and the bright morning star (22:16). These names address specific aspects of Jesus's character or his role in God's plan, but the most powerful portrayal of him is found in the opening chapter.

Hearing a voice, John turned and saw the Son of Man with hair as white as snow, signifying his eternal nature and infinite wisdom. His eyes were like flames of fire that see through lies and pretenses in order to judge sin. His feet glowed like bronze and his voice sounded like raging waters. His right hand held seven stars and his face rivaled the sun's brilliance. As one of the twelve disciples, John had spent three years living with Jesus during his time on earth. But the vision of Christ in his full glory struck John to the ground "like a dead man" (1:17).

Most people have a mental image of Jesus, often based on a picture that once hung in their home or in a Sunday school room. Or we may cherish a favorite portrayal of him from the Scriptures, such as the gentle Shepherd or the compassionate Healer. These images may speak to specific needs in our life, but sometimes we need a fresh vision of Jesus. When life seems too hard or confusing, the first chapter of Revelation reminds us that we belong to a resurrected Savior who holds the keys to death and hell. The world may not see his power and glory yet, but as we submit to his authority, we will see a glimpse of it in our own life.

> *Don't be afraid! I am the first and the last,*
> *the living one. I was dead, but now I am alive*
> *forever. I have the keys of death and hell.*
>
> Revelation 1:17–18

Seven Letters to Seven Churches

Revelation 2–3

When John penned Revelation, other churches existed in Asia Minor besides those listed in these chapters. Jesus used the number seven, which symbolizes completeness, to make it clear that he addressed the whole church—the entire body of believers on the earth. The instructions and warnings in each individual message were to be heeded by all of the churches, as the letters circulated and were read to each congregation. After evaluating each group's strengths and weaknesses, Jesus repeated the same phrase: "Let the person who has ears listen to what the Spirit says to the churches."

Jesus praised the believers at Ephesus for their hard work, perseverance, and diligence in guarding against false teachers. But he held one thing against them: their love for him and for each other had cooled. Thyatira, on the other hand, was strong in love but lacked discernment and tolerated heresy. Pergamum had valiantly withstood persecution, but also tolerated false teachings, especially a group called the Nicolaitans who spread sexual and spiritual adultery.

The Sardis church had a reputation for being alive but Jesus declared them spiritually dead. He urged them to strengthen the little evidence of life that remained. Only Smyrna and Philadelphia received no rebuke from Jesus, who promised to uphold them during continued testing and persecution. Jesus sent no commendation to the believers at Laodicea, who disgusted God by being lukewarm. They were content with their material wealth and unaware of their spiritual poverty.

Jesus's comments are still relevant today and remind us to use wisdom and caution when choosing a local congregation to align ourselves with. Is our church rich in material things, such as facilities and resources, yet spiritually poor? Does our congregation demonstrate a fervent devotion to Christ and love for each other? Are they careful to promote correct doctrine based on careful study of the Word? We'll never find a perfect church here on earth, but the guidelines in Revelation will help us make the best choice.

> *Let the person who has ears listen to what*
> *the Spirit says to the churches.*
>
> Revelation 2:7

Seven Letters to All Believers

Revelation 2–3

Christ's letters to the seven churches provide a good opportunity for us to examine our lives in the light of his praise and condemnation. Today we face the same dangers and temptations that these churches faced, although the cultural details may be different. With each rebuke, Jesus instructed the recipients on how to correct the situation.

The Bible stresses the importance of correct doctrine, but if we focus solely on that, we can become like the Ephesian believers. When we sense that our love and devotion for Jesus or other believers has cooled, Jesus advises us to remember the love we had early in our relationship with him. On the other hand, if we concentrate on loving others and neglect to guard our doctrine, we may be led astray by teachings that distort God's Word. Jesus gave stern warnings for the believers at Pergamum and Thyatira, whose lack of discernment led them to tolerate ungodliness.

We may be able to relate to the believers at Smyrna, surrounded by people hostile to Christ and slandered because of our faith. We can take courage from Jesus's assurance that any persecution will be for a limited time, after which he will give us the crown of life. Or we may feel like the believers at Philadelphia, as though we have only a little strength left for the fight; if so, Jesus promises to help us endure.

The message to Sardis motivates us to look past what others think of us to what Jesus sees. We may have a reputation for being a committed Christian, yet be spiritually lethargic. He urges us to wake up and breathe life into our relationship with him through obedience. If we sense that our attitude toward God has become lukewarm like the believers at Laodicea, we need to ask him to open our eyes so that he doesn't feel like spitting us out of his mouth. Our relationship with God will be transformed when we find which of the seven letters personally applies to us, and then heed Jesus's advice.

Take this seriously, and change the way you think and act.

Revelation 3:19

The Lamb and the Scroll

Revelation 4—5

During John's vision of heaven, he saw God holding a scroll in his right hand. This rolled-up parchment was affixed with seven seals that would need to be broken one by one as it was unrolled. An angel called out in a loud voice, "Who deserves to open the scroll and break the seals on it?" (5:2). No one in the universe was found worthy to open the scroll that contained God's plan for history. John wept bitterly until someone told him that the Lion from the tribe of Judah had won the victory and gained the privilege to look inside the scroll.

John looked near the throne and saw a Lamb that still bore the marks of having been sacrificed. The Lamb had seven horns symbolizing great power and seven eyes that could see throughout the earth. As Jesus Christ, the Lamb, took the scroll, the four living creatures and twenty-four elders bowed and praised him for giving his blood to purchase people to be God's own. Then the hosts of angels joined in singing to the Lamb who was slain and who deserved to receive power, wealth, wisdom, strength, honor, glory, and praise. Finally, John heard every inhabitant of heaven and throughout the earth praising God and the Lamb.

Because Jesus shed his blood to gain victory over death and the powers of evil, he is the only One who shares the privilege of knowing God's agenda for the world. Jesus not only has the authority to control events during the end times, he also has ultimate control over the events of our personal life.

Some people admire a Christian speaker, teacher, leader, or author so much that it borders on worship, but no one should be given the honor that rightfully belongs to the lamb who was slain for our sins. Whether we're on the earth or in heaven, Jesus deserves all the praise we can give him—and so much more.

> *The lamb who was slain deserves to receive power,*
> *wealth, wisdom, strength, honor, glory, and praise.*
>
> Revelation 5:12

Seven Seals and Seven Trumpets

Revelation 6; 8—9

As John's visions continued, he saw the beginning of God's judgment of sin and rebellion being poured out on the earth. The opening of the first four seals triggered events that caused one-fourth of the earth's inhabitants to be killed by war, famine, plagues, and wild animals. When Jesus opened the fifth seal, the scene shifted to heaven. The souls of those who had been martyred for their faith during this time cried out for justice; Jesus told them to wait a little longer. The sixth seal unleashed a series of disasters as a great earthquake struck, the sun darkened, the moon turned red, and stars fell from the sky. When Jesus opened the seventh seal, heaven fell silent for half an hour.

Seven angels were given trumpets to signal the next series of judgments. The first three trumpets brought fiery destruction that affected one-third of the land, seas, rivers, and fresh water supply. At the fourth trumpet, a third of the sun, moon, and stars darkened. The fifth and sixth trumpets led to increased demonic activity on the earth, resulting in the death of one-third of the remaining population. But there was worse to come—when the seventh trumpet would herald the seven bowl judgments representing God's final judgment of sin (Rev. 16).

Whether we interpret the various events in these chapters literally or symbolically, it's difficult to read about such destruction and loss of life. It's important for us to notice that God will restrain his full wrath up until the very end of the period called the tribulation, hoping that people will have a change of heart. Although the closing verses of chapter 9 indicate that the majority of people will still refuse to turn from sin and acknowledge God, that doesn't stop him from offering mercy and forgiveness. And we should never stop trying to show people that part of his character.

*He doesn't want to destroy anyone but wants
all people to have an opportunity to turn to him
and change the way they think and act.*

2 Peter 3:9

The Woman and the Dragon

Revelation 12

Keeping with the theme of "seven," the visions in chapters 12–15 introduce seven personages who will play key roles during the end times. First, John saw a pregnant woman wearing a crown of twelve stars. A huge red dragon or serpent (later identified as Satan) stood ready to devour the woman's child, but her son was snatched up to God. War broke out in heaven as Michael and his angels fought against the dragon and his followers.

When the dragon was thrown down to the earth, he persecuted the woman who had given birth to the child. He spewed out a torrent of water to sweep her away, but the earth opened up and swallowed the water. Then, since God had hidden the woman away in a protected place, the enraged dragon went off to wage war against her other offspring who believe in Jesus.

Scholars disagree about the timing and interpretation of these events, but most agree that the woman represents the nation of Israel and her son is Jesus. The last verse may refer to Satan's persecution of Jewish believers during the great tribulation or against saints in general. But if we are a follower of Jesus, we can be sure that the "deceiver of the world" has already declared war against us. Satan hates the fact that he can't have our soul because of our faith in Christ, and he will do anything to make us stray from our commitment to God.

First Peter 5:8 warns that our enemy the devil prowls around like a lion looking for someone to devour. Although it's foolish to attribute every negative situation to Satan, it's dangerous to take such a formidable enemy lightly or to underestimate his power. Scripture teaches that we can combat demonic attacks by submitting to God's authority and using God's Word to resist Satan. And we can rejoice in knowing something that Satan is fully aware of: his time is short.

> *So place yourselves under God's authority. Resist*
> *the devil, and he will run away from you.*
>
> James 4:7

An Unholy Trinity

Revelation 13

The description of the beast from the sea has been applied to many historical figures including Nero, who ruled the Roman Empire at the time John wrote Revelation. Most people, however, believe this beast refers to the Antichrist, the future political ruler who will oppose God and his followers. The Antichrist will unite the world under his leadership and gain control of the economy. He will be supported by the beast from the earth, later called the False Prophet. This religious leader will influence people to worship the Antichrist by performing signs and wonders. Both men will be controlled and empowered by Satan.

Satan, the Antichrist, and the False Prophet form an unholy trinity that will deceive the world during the last three and a half years of the great tribulation. As a false messiah, the Antichrist will recover from a fatal wound in imitation of Christ's resurrection. The False Prophet will make fire come down from heaven and appear to give life to a statue, imitating God's fiery judgments and miracles. As the Antichrist and False Prophet try to single out and execute God's people, the mark on those who worship the beast mocks God's earlier sealing of believers (Rev. 7:2–3).

Chapter 13 describes Satan's final attempt to take the place of God and set up a counterfeit religion. But in reality, Satan has been imitating the Creator ever since he rebelled against him. The Bible warns that Satan and his servants often masquerade as something good and moral. Many people are deceived by wholesome-sounding philosophies that appeal to the intellect, meditation techniques that promise enlightenment, or religious practices that give an emotional high. Others are taken in by "miracles" such as a statue that appears to cry or bleed. In order to recognize Satan's counterfeits and displays of supernatural power, we need to be firmly grounded in and guided by God's Word. Then the Deceiver can't fool us, no matter how convincing he is.

Even Satan disguises himself as an angel of light.

2 Corinthians 11:14

Seven Bowls of God's Wrath

Revelation 15–16

Revelation 16 gives us an overview of the final days of the great tribulation culminating in the second coming of Christ. When the seventh trumpet is blown (Rev. 11:15), seven angels are given bowls that represent God's final expression of anger at sin. These events seem to occur in rapid succession and are more severe and global than the previous judgments, which were limited and partial.

When the first angel poured his bowl over the earth, painful sores afflicted all who had worshiped the beast. The second and third bowls turned the seas and the sources of drinking water into blood. The fourth bowl intensified the sun's heat, which severely burned people, and the fifth bowl brought darkness on the earth.

The sixth angel's bowl dried up the Euphrates River, preparing the way for Satan's final battle against Christ. John saw evil spirits coming from the mouths of Satan, the beast, and the False Prophet, representing the propaganda that will entice people to gather and fight. The seventh angel poured his bowl into the air, triggering an earthquake like none the world has ever seen—so powerful that it reduced cities to rubble. Many of the survivors were crushed by huge hailstones.

No one can accuse God of being unjust when he pours out his wrath against sin. The plagues against Egypt (some of which are similar to the judgments in Revelation) were brought on by Pharaoh's cruel treatment of God's people and his repeated refusal to set them free. Revelation 16:9 and 21 show that even in the final days of history, many people will remain hardened against God, choosing to curse him rather than repent. Jesus suffered and died so that we can escape the penalty of our sin. God lets us make the choice: we can either remain an object of his righteous wrath or we can accept his gift of everlasting life.

The reward for sin is death, but the gift that God freely gives is everlasting life found in Christ Jesus our Lord.

Romans 6:23

The Drunken Prostitute

Revelation 17–18

Revelation 17 and 18 zero in on the destruction of Babylon, an event announced by an angel in 14:8 and included in the seventh bowl judgment. The identity of Babylon has sparked countless debates through the centuries. Some believe these chapters refer to the one world religion that will arise during the tribulation, or a political power that will dominate the world during the last three and a half years of that period, or a combination of the two. Babylon has been interpreted as a revived Roman Empire, as the ancient city of Babylon restored, and as the symbol of false religion traced back to the tower of Babel (see Gen. 11). Whether a literal city or not, God portrays Babylon as a prostitute.

John saw a woman dressed in expensive red and purple clothes and covered with gold jewelry, precious gems, and pearls. She sat on a great beast and held a gold cup full of evil things she had done. The woman was drunk on the blood of believers, but a voice from heaven announced that God would make her drink what she had poured out on others. In one day, all of Babylon's glory, riches, and power would pass away.

In 18:4, another voice from heaven called for God's people to come out of Babylon so they would not participate in her sins and suffer from her judgment. Years earlier, John had given believers a similar warning not to love the world and what it offers (see 1 John 2:15). We need to keep our distance from the values of a system driven by lust for pleasure, power, and affluence. God wants to help us resist the seductive pull of worldly attractions and desires that could weaken our commitment to Christ. Remembering that worldly things will pass away someday can help us focus on obedience to God rather than on self-gratification.

> *Not everything that the world offers—physical gratification, greed, and extravagant lifestyles— comes from the Father. It comes from the world, and the world and its evil desires are passing away.*
>
> 1 John 2:16–17

Christ Returns

Revelation 19

As the period of the great tribulation nears its end, all heaven breaks loose in rejoicing and praise to God. On the earth, war has been raging for many weeks, with armies lured to the Holy Land by demonic spirits. Jerusalem has fallen and is suffering at the hands of her enemies. Then it happens—the event for which Satan has gathered all his forces to resist, the moment that represents the culmination of God's plan for the redemption and renewal of the world: Jesus Christ returns to the earth.

This time Jesus doesn't come as a helpless baby or a Lamb to be offered as a sacrifice for the sins of the world. He doesn't ride a donkey to symbolize peace; his white horse represents war and victory. When Jesus came to earth the first time, he submitted to a crown of thorns; now he wears many crowns on his head to show his sovereignty. Just before his crucifixion, Jesus allowed himself to be humiliated, spat upon, and beaten. This time he has come to judge and rule.

The battle turns the moment the King rides out onto the field, with the armies of heaven following behind him. The beast and False Prophet are thrown into the lake of fire. The rest of the opposing forces are killed by the sword that comes from Jesus's mouth. Prophecies are fulfilled and human history is brought to a close by the One named Faithful and True.

As the world moves closer to the final battle between God and the forces of evil, we often feel the effects of that ongoing warfare. During those times when evil seems to triumph, we need to remember the final outcome of history. Jesus came to earth the first time to offer forgiveness for sins; he will return to judge sin and those who have chosen to be his enemies. No matter what happens around us, we can take comfort in knowing that when our King returns, the battle will turn and good will triumph over evil.

> *On his clothes and his thigh he has a name*
> *written: King of Kings and Lord of Lords.*
>
> Revelation 19:16

The Thousand-Year Reign

Revelation 20:1—6

When Jesus returned to the earth in John's vision, it didn't take him long to dispose of the world ruler, his false prophet, and their armies. Then John saw an angel come down from heaven and overpower the one who had manipulated and empowered these enemies of God. The angel locked Satan in the bottomless pit to keep him from deceiving the human race for a thousand years. Those who had become believers and been martyred during the great tribulation were resurrected and given the privilege to rule with Christ during this period.

This period of time is often called the *millennium* (Latin for "a thousand years"); the words "a thousand years" are used six times in Revelation 20. Many scholars interpret this event to be a fulfillment of Old Testament prophecies in which God promised that he would establish his kingdom on the earth. Many passages such as Isaiah 60 describe a time when the Messiah will rule in peace and righteousness.

Many people reject the idea of a literal thousand-year reign. Some see the millennium as a symbolic representation of the time between Christ's ascension and his return. Others interpret it as the period leading up to Christ's second coming, during which the church will preach the gospel and its influence will spread over the earth. Within each major viewpoint, there are countless variations of interpretations, making this passage one of the most controversial in the Bible.

Regardless of how we interpret the passage about the millennium, we need to make sure that Jesus Christ is already reigning in our hearts. God often criticized Israel for going through the motions of worshiping him without being committed to obeying him. "Why do you call me Lord," Jesus asked, "but don't do what I tell you?" (see Luke 6:46). Studying end-time events may be exciting, but our most pressing issue is whether we are letting the Messiah rule our lives at this very moment.

But in your hearts set apart Christ as Lord.

1 Peter 3:15 NIV

Final Judgment

Revelation 20:7–15

Those who survive the tribulation and those born during the thousand years of Christ's reign will enjoy living during a time of great blessing and peace; everyone will know about Jesus Christ. But when Satan is released from his prison, he will be able to deceive the nations into rebelling against Christ. So many people will join Satan in besieging Jerusalem that their numbers will be like "the grains of sand on the seashore" (v. 8). God will send fire from heaven to burn these enemies up, and Satan will finally meet his end when he is thrown into the fiery lake.

The old heaven and earth will pass away as a great white throne is set up and books are opened. Unbelievers will be resurrected and stand before God to be judged. Anyone who died without accepting God's offer of salvation will be thrown into the lake of fire, where they will exist and suffer forever. God will also dispose of death and Hades, the temporary place of punishment for unbelievers.

Throughout history, many people have tried to find a way around the doctrine of eternal punishment. Some try to define hell as symbolic; others claim that the ungodly are simply annihilated. Many people insist that God will give every person a chance to change their mind about him after they die. The Bible teaches in 2 Thessalonians 1:8–9 and other passages that hell is a real place and that the human soul will live forever. Each of us will meet one of two final destinations based on our own choice: we will either be with the Lord forever, or we will be eternally separated from him in a place of torment (see Matt. 25:46).

God doesn't want to see anyone end up in the fiery lake; his desire is for everyone to accept his forgiveness and salvation (see 2 Pet. 3:9). Knowing the terrible truth about hell can be a powerful motivation to urge us to share the gospel every chance we get.

> *Those whose names were not found in the Book*
> *of Life were thrown into the fiery lake.*
>
> Revelation 20:15

Our New Home

Revelation 21:1—22:5

After John saw what would happen to those who rejected Christ, he was allowed to glimpse the final destiny of believers. As the angel showed him things that the human mind is incapable of imagining, John used concepts familiar to his readers to describe what he saw. The New Jerusalem is pictured as a bride beautifully dressed for her husband. The city is constructed of gold as clear as glass, with gates made of huge pearls and walls decorated with a rainbow of precious gems. Whether we see this passage as literal or symbolic, we can't deny that such a description points to the beauty and majesty of God.

John noted that he didn't see a temple in the New Jerusalem. Since God will live there, the entire city will be a place of worship. There will also be no need for the sun or moon; God's glory will pervade and illuminate his city. Since God's righteous judgment will have eliminated the curse that sin brought upon the former world, there will be no more crying, sorrow, pain, suffering, or death. Old Testament and New Testament saints will live together in a perfect environment filled with love, peace, and safety. God will live among his people as he has longed to do since the beginning of time.

This passage in Revelation doesn't answer all our questions about what our heavenly home will be like, or how we'll spend eternity. It does show that the greatest blessing of all will be intimate fellowship with our Father, free from the hindrances caused by our present physical state and sinful nature.

Sometimes people assume that their heavenly home will include things that they especially love or something they were denied in their earthly life. But by the time we arrive in the New Jerusalem, God will have made us new as well. Once we see our Savior, our deepest desire will be fully satisfied, and we will know a joy that we've never dreamed of.

> *The one sitting on the throne said, "I am making everything new."*
>
> Revelation 21:5

An Invitation and a Promise

Revelation 22:6–21

Revelation shares some terrifying realities, but it also contains seven promises of blessing—more than any other book in the Bible. While some people view Revelation as an undecipherable puzzle, Jesus asserts that it was given to teach believers about future events. In the closing of the book, he repeats the special blessing pronounced in the first chapter for those who read and heed its words. Also, a solemn warning is issued to anyone who would distort the words in the book.

The angel instructed John not to seal up the words of prophecy, but to leave the book open for all to read and hear. In the light of Jesus's promise to return and bring his rewards with him, he invites everyone to come and drink of the water of life before it is too late. He is joined by the Holy Spirit and the bride, or church, in extending this offer to anyone willing to admit their need for forgiveness and accept Christ as the way to salvation.

We don't know the day or hour when Jesus is coming, but Revelation says that at the right time it will happen suddenly and quickly. One thing we do know for certain: with each passing day his return draws closer. If we have accepted the free gift of salvation paid for by Jesus's blood, then we can look forward to the future with hope and eagerness.

When we are disturbed by the wrongs and injustices in our present world, we can remember that God will right all wrongs and destroy evil once and for all. During times of suffering, we can be comforted by our future home that will be free from sorrow and pain. Even when our life seems pleasant, we know that there are joys ahead beyond anything that we can now imagine. If we believe the promises in Revelation, then we can agree with John when he says, "Come, Lord Jesus."

> *The one who is testifying to these things*
> *says, "Yes, I'm coming soon!"*
> *Amen! Come, Lord Jesus!*
>
> Revelation 22:20

Dianne Neal Matthews has written numerous devotionals, magazine articles, newspaper features, and stories for compilation books. She is a frequent contributor to websites including CBN.com and FindingGodDaily.com. Dianne is the author of *Drawing Closer to God*, as well as *The One Year On This Day* and *The One Year Women of the Bible* (Tyndale House). Her work will also appear in the 2013 edition of *Mornings with Jesus* (Guideposts).

A mother and grandmother, Dianne teaches at writers' conferences and speaks to women's groups. She is a member of the Christian Authors Network, Advanced Writers & Speakers Association, and Toastmasters International. Dianne and her husband, Richard, live in the Salt Lake City area. For more information, please visit www.DianneNealMatthews.com or follow her on Twitter @DianneNMatthews.